THE ELGAR COMPANION TO INSTITUTIONAL AND EVOLUTIONARY ECONOMICS
L–Z

*In Honour of Thorstein Veblen, John R. Commons
and Gunnar Myrdal*

The Elgar Companion to Institutional and Evolutionary Economics
L–Z

Edited by

Geoffrey M. Hodgson

Judge Institute of Management Studies
University of Cambridge, UK

Warren J. Samuels

Michigan State University, USA

and

Marc R. Tool

California State University, Sacramento, USA

Edward Elgar

© Geoffrey M. Hodgson, Warren J. Samuels, Marc R. Tool, 1994

Published by
Edward Elgar Publishing Limited
Gower House
Croft Road
Aldershot
Hants GU11 3HR
England

Edward Elgar Publishing Company
Old Post Road
Brookfield
Vermont 05036
USA

A CIP catalogue record for this book
is available from the British Library

Library of Congress Cataloguing in Publication Data
The Elgar companion to institutional and evolutionary economics/Geoffrey
    M. Hodgson, Warren J. Samuels, and Marc R. Tool, editors.
        p.   cm.
    1. Institutional economics.   2. Evolutionary economics.
    I. Hodgson, Geoffrey Martin, 1946–   .   II. Samuels, Warren J.,
    1933–   .   III. Tool, Marc R.
    HB99.5.E45   1993
    330—dc20   93–6546
                                                                    CIP

ISBN 1 85278 439 3 (2 volume set)

Printed and Bound in Great Britain by
Hartnolls Limited, Bodmin, Cornwall.

Contents

Contributors to This Volume and Their Entries

Arestis, Philip, Applied Economics, University of East London, Dagenham, Essex, United Kingdom
Macroeconomic Policy (II)

Bartlett, Randall, Economics, Smith College, Northampton, MA, USA
Power (I)

Bausor, Randall, Economics, University of Massachusetts, Amherst, USA
Time

Blaas, Wolfgang, Research Unit for Socio-Economics, Austrian Academy of Sciences, Vienna
Rothschild, Kurt Wilhelm

Boehm, Stephan, Economics, University of Graz, Austria
Spontaneous Order

Brothwell, John F., School of Business and Economic Studies, University of Leeds, United Kingdom
Unemployment

Brown, Doug, Economics, Northern Arizona University, Flagstaff, USA
Worker Participation

Bush, Paul D., Economics, California State University, Fresno, USA
Social Change, Theory of

Cantner, Uwe, Universität Augsburg, Germany
Schumpeter, Joseph Alois

Cypher, James M., Economics, California State University, Fresno, USA
Military Sector

de Bernis, Gerard, Institut de Sciences Mathématiques et Economiques Appliquées, Paris, France
Perroux, François

DeGregori, Thomas R., Economics, University of Houston, TX, USA
Myrdal, Gunnar; Technology, Theory of

Dosi, Giovanni, Economics, University of Rome 'La Sapienza', Italy
Microfoundations of Macroeconomic Competitiveness

Dow, Sheila C., Economics, University of Stirling, Scotland, United Kingdom
Monetary Theory

Dugger, William M., Economics, University of Tulsa, OK, USA
Williamson, Oliver E.

Earl, Peter E., Economics and Marketing, Lincoln University, Canterbury, New Zealand
Simon, Herbert Alexander

Field, Alexander J., Economics, Santa Clara University, CA, USA
North, Douglass C.

Fisher, Peter S., Urban and Regional Planning, University of Iowa, Iowa City, USA
Tax Theory and Policy

Foster, John, Economics, University of Queensland, Brisbane, Australia
Macroeconomic Theory (I); Prigogine, Ilya

Freeman, Christopher, Science Policy Research Unit, University of Sussex, Falmer, Brighton, United Kingdom
Technical Change and Technological Regimes

Gough, Ian, Social Policy and Social Work, University of Manchester, United Kingdom
Need, Concept of

Groenewegen, John, Institutional and Industrial Economics, Erasmus University, Rotterdam, The Netherlands
Planning, National Economic

Hanusch, Horst, Universität Augsburg, Germany
Schumpeter, Joseph Alois

Harcourt, G.C., Faculty of Economics and Politics, University of Cambridge, United Kingdom
Robinson, Joan

Hargreaves Heap, Shaun P., School of Economic and Social Studies, University of East Anglia, Norwich, United Kingdom
Rationality and Maximization

Hindess, Barry, Division of Economics and Politics, Research School of Social Sciences, Australian National University, Canberra, Australia
Rational Actor Models

Hirsch, Abraham, Upper Montclair, NJ, USA
Mitchell, Wesley Clair

Hodgson, Geoffrey M., Judge Institute of Management Studies, University of Cambridge, United Kingdom
Lock-in and Chreodic Development; Marx, Karl; Methodological Individualism; Money, Evolution of; Natural Selection, Economic Evolution and; Nelson, Richard R.; Neoclassical Microeconomic Theory, Critique of; Schotter, Andrew; Selection, Units of Evolutionary; Winter, Sidney G., Jr.

James, Dilmus D., Economics and Finance, University of Texas at El Paso, USA
Technology in Development Policy

Jensen, Hans E., Economics, University of Tennessee, Knoxville, USA
Marshall, Alfred

Jessop, Bob, Sociology, University of Lancaster, United Kingdom
Régulation Theory, French

Khalil, Elias L., Economics, Ohio State University–Mansfield, USA
Rules; Trust

King, J.E., Economics, La Trobe University, Bundoora, Victoria, Australia
Schumacher, E.F.

Klein, Philip A., Economics, Pennsylvania State University, USA
Public Sector, Role of the

Kregel, Jan, Economics, University of Bologna, Italy
Macroeconomic Theory (II)

Lawson, Tony, Faculty of Economics and Politics, University of Cambridge, United Kingdom
Methodology; Realism, Philosophical; Uncertainty

Lee, Frederic S., Economics, De Montfort University, Leicester, United Kingdom
Means, Gardiner C.

Lowry, S. Todd, Economics, Washington and Lee University, Lexington, VA, USA
Market, Institutionalist View of the

Mayhew, Anne, Economics, University of Tennessee, Knoxville, USA
Sahlins, Marshall

Metcalfe, J.S., Economics, University of Manchester, United Kingdom
Richardson, George B.

Miller, Edythe S., Littleton, CO, USA
Regulation, Theory of Economic; Trebing, Harry M.

Mirowski, Philip, Economics, University of Notre Dame, IN, USA
Peirce, Charles Sanders

Mott, Tracy, Economics, University of Denver, CO, USA
Steindl, Josef

Murrell, Peter, Economics, University of Maryland, College Park, USA
Planning, Theory of

Nelson, Richard R., School of International and Public Affairs, Columbia University, USA
Routines

Oakley, Allen, Economics, University of Newcastle, NSW, Australia
Lowe, Adolph

Peterson, Wallace C., Economics, University of Nebraska, Lincoln, USA
Macroeconomic Policy (I)

Pheby, John, Economics, De Montfort University, Leicester, United Kingdom
Shackle, George Lennox Sharman

Ramstad, Yngve, Economics, University of Rhode Island, Kingston, USA
Labour Markets; Transaction; Veblen, Thorstein

Reisman, D.A., Economics, University of Surrey, Guildford, United Kingdom
Olson, Mancur

Rothschild, Kurt W., Wien, Austria
Power (II)

Samuels, Warren J., Economics, Michigan State University, East Lansing, USA
Law and Economics; Marx, Karl; Means, Gardiner C.; Part–Whole Relationships; Property; Smith, Adam; Welfare Economic Theory; Witte, Edwin Emil

Schotter, Andrew R., Economics, New York University, USA
Ullmann-Margalit, Edna

Schmid, A. Allan, Agricultural Economics, Michigan State University, East Lansing, USA
Public Choice

Screpanti, Ernesto, Dipartimento di Scienze Economiche, University of Trieste, Italy
Pasinetti, Luigi L.

Sheehan, Michael F., Fisher, Sheehan & Colton, Scappoose, Oregon, USA
Public Policy: Contributions of American Institutionalism

Shepherd, Deborah A., Political Science, University of Houston, TX, USA
Myrdal, Gunnar; Technology, Theory of

Stanfield, James Ronald, Economics, Colorado State University, Fort Collins, USA
Polanyi, Karl

Tomer, John F., Troy, NY, USA
Leibenstein, Harvey

Trebing, Harry M., Economics, Michigan State University, East Lansing, USA
Public Utility Regulation, Institutionalist Contribution to

Tylecote, Andrew, Sheffield University Management School, United Kingdom
Long Waves

Waller, William, Economics, Hobart and William Smith Colleges, Geneva, NY, USA
Veblenian Dichotomy and Its Critics

Wray, L. Randall, Economics, University of Denver, CO, USA
Monetary Policy

Labour Markets

Economists have long had problems reconciling actual labour market phenomena with the neoclassical theory of the exchange process(es) through which various types of human productive services are priced and allocated. Persistent unemployment, policy-resistant wage inflation, and seemingly inflexible wage relativities are only a few of the phenomena which are inconsistent with the core neoclassical vision of interrelated occupational labour markets in which self-interested, rational individuals and enterprises atomistically compete with one another to buy and sell on the best terms possible. Because of the problems encountered in applying standard microeconomic theory to labour market phenomena, it has long been standard practice to graft assumptions capturing 'peculiarities' associated with the pricing and allocation of labour onto the basic framework, albeit in a manner consistent with the dictates of methodological individualism. Since the influence of 'institutions' is among the 'complications' generally added to the basic neoclassical analysis, it is not always an easy matter to distinguish between 'supplemented' neoclassical analysis (the 'new institutional economics') and a truly alternative approach – that is, a theory of labour market phenomena anchored in an 'institutional' conception of economic processes. Solow (1990) provides an especially instructive example, wherein the 'norm' of fairness is more or less grafted onto general equilibrium analysis in order to account for labour market 'peculiarities'. Of particular significance is Solow's interpretation of the fairness norm through logic consistent with the methodological individualism. Moreover, labour specialists who have attempted to pursue such an alternative approach have to date shown little inclination to agree on an alternative institutional theory of the labour market; indeed, they have yet to evince any agreement at all as to the larger institutional conception of the market system to which labour market analysis must be fitted. As a result, any overview of 'the' institutional approach to labour market analysis will probably prove unsatisfactory to many of those who view their own work as institutional in character. Thus it should be made explicit that the present overview is organized by means of concepts advanced by the American economic theorist and labour economist, John R. Commons. This being the case, an effort has nonetheless been made to provide a synthetic characterization of 'the' institutional standpoint which encompasses the many variants of institutional analysis.

Preliminaries
To assert the existence of 'the' labour market is only to declare that various types of human productive services are priced and allocated through bargaining transactions based on the motive of self-interest. However, it is not

entirely clear what *a* labour market, as an *analytical construct,* connotes within institutional discourse. In mainstream economic theory a market is a notional construct circumscribing mentally the domain within which a notional *equilibrium price* is brought about. But since the concept of equilibrium itself (and hence by implication its companion concept, disequilibrium) is generally considered by institutional writers to be unsound, the term 'a market' clearly must have a different meaning for them. There is thus a need to be precise. In what follows, the term 'labour market' refers to a behavioural domain in which bargaining transactions holistically give effect to a specific matrix of interrelated institutions. Such a matrix potentially consists of institutions that are both internal and external to a given enterprise. Significantly, this conception of a labour market entails no presumption that exchange processes in various labour markets manifest the same, or even a similar, mix of enterprise-specific and external institutions. That is, there is no presumption that various labour markets are governed by the same set of institutions and hence operate according to a common logic or reflect common rules of exchange. Neither does it entail the presumption or implication that wage rates and employment levels obtaining in various labour markets are necessarily interconnected or that a single wage rate, allowing for 'compensating differentials', will obtain within a labour market. It is not even presumed or implied that wage determination and labour allocation (employment decisions) necessarily are directly related. In short, the boundaries of a particular labour market as well as the 'principles' reflected in exchange relationships within its ambit are matters to be discovered through actual observation rather than by abstract logic.

The underlying vision
To the novitiate the institutional literature writ large appears to lack unifying principles. However, submerged beneath the heterogeneous and seemingly incompatible theoretical frameworks put forward by various institutional writers always lies the same premise: *human behaviour is principally an expression of institutions.* By the inclusive concept 'institution' is meant any more or less obligatory rule of action that in one way or another guides conduct – norm, standard practice, customary arrangement, customary standard of judgement, common usage, convention, law, regulation and so on. This conclusion is reached through the following logic and the primacy attributed to institutions emerges from the following conception of economic activity.

Almost all behaviour occurs within 'going concerns,' that is, within families, tribes, manors, business firms, nations and so on. The problem of order requires that the behaviour of individuals within a concern's domain must be controlled by the group so as to ensure that the activities of the various members of the concern are correlated, that is, made mutually consistent. Institutions have the function of effecting such a correlation by spelling out what individuals can, may or must do, or not do, in their transaction with other members of the concern. Since most of the groups into which one gains admission (birth, initiation, enrolment, employment, election, citizenship) over the course of one's life are already in being, it is generally the rule that institutions are something one encounters rather than creates.

In one sense, given this reality, individuals have no choice but to accommodate themselves to the institutions for, if they violate them, sanctions – disapproval, excommunication, poverty, bankruptcy, even imprisonment – will ensue. Viewed this way, it is evident that institutions can be understood as constraints on an individual's self-directing capacity or will. To cast institutions in this mould, however, is to miss their real significance. Human beings seem to desire above all else the acceptance and esteem of, as well as equitable treatment from, the other members of the groups to which they belong. Gaining the acceptance and esteem of others, in turn, almost always requires that one accommodate oneself to the going mode of behaviour (objectified by the concepts of norms, standard practices and so on); that is, to extant institutions. Through repetition and habituation (and, perhaps, because of the psychological need to eliminate cognitive dissonance) behaviour consistent with those institutions sooner or later comes to be understood as natural and right. In other words, preferences gradually fall into line with the governing institutions. That is, far from being constraints on one's will (preferences), institutions are the substance of that will.

Of course, individual will is not only an expression of institutions. An individual often has some degree of choice as to which group (occupation, firm) he will join, even if such choice is normally made in a 'satisficing' manner. In addition, individuals are generally members of more that one going concern (family, school, community, work group, fraternal order, nation) and to some degree there may be conflicts between the concepts of the 'good' and 'right' being engendered in various concerns, again requiring that a choice be made. There will also be instances where new circumstances force individuals to assess not only their instrumental behaviour (means) but the values (ends) toward which it is addressed (instrumental valuing). These realities ensure that, within a chain of circular causation, individuals whose wills are formed under the guidance of governing institutions also act to change governing rules (institutions). But in the main, at a particular moment in historical time, their actions and *values* – that is, their aspirations and criteria of judgement – are but an expression of the institutions under whose guidance their wills have been formed. To repeat, as wills (as purposeful actors utilizing criteria of judgement), individuals tend to *become* the governing institutions. Or put somewhat differently, their preferences are dynamically path-dependent. What all this means, of course, is that in significant respects individual economic actors are shaped via 'socialization' to match the requirements of their niches. To the extent that their wills are formed under the guidance of different sets of institutions, different 'types' of individuals will be encountered, but whatever their type, they are in the main socially conditioned beings who evince habits of mind and patterns of behaviour reflecting the actual web of rules, both formal and informal, correlating group life within the concerns in whose activities they participate. For a very broad range of behaviours, in other words, institutions are the efficient cause.

The foregoing conception of institutionally patterned human behaviour, which in no way conflicts with a belief that individuals are self-interested and acquisitive or that firms in a capitalist economy must sometimes compete vigorously in the rivalry sense, constitutes the heart of 'the' institutional standpoint. As suggested, that standpoint is reflected in John R. Commons's analysis of labour market phenomena, but his work has remained obscure to this day. Though less clearly, it is also manifest in the work of the post-World War II California School of labour economists. Its quintessential expression, however, is the dual labour market theory developed during the 1970s by Michael Piore. This is not to suggest that institutional labour market analysis by other contemporary writers is of lesser merit or to imply that the dual labour market theory is without its problems. Still, Piore's dual labour market theory is not only the best known among contemporary institutional theories but also the most completely articulated alternative to the neoclassical theory. Hence it alone is outlined at some length.

The dual labour market theory
The dual labour market theory categorizes labour markets as being of two fundamentally dissimilar ideal types producing fundamentally dissimilar outcomes. *Primary sector* labour markets produce jobs providing relatively high wages, good working conditions, chances of advancement, equity and due process in the administration of work rules, and perhaps most important, relatively stable employment. *Secondary sector* labour markets, on the other hand, yield jobs providing low wages, poor working conditions, little chance of advancement, a highly personalized relationship between workers and supervisors, harsh and capricious work discipline, unstable employment and a high turnover among the labour force. Primary sector labour markets are further divided into an upper tier and a lower tier, with upper tier markets generally providing professional and managerial workers with substantially higher pay and status, as well as greater promotion opportunities, than are obtained by workers in the lower tier.

The three discrete types of labour markets correspond to a segmentation of jobs in which three fundamentally different modes of thought and understanding underlie three distinct behavioural patterns – instrumental behaviour in the upper tier of the primary labour market, customary behaviour in the lower tier, and commanded (by the supervisor) behaviour in the secondary sector. The threefold division emerges from the attempt to minimize costs and risk in a context in which different jobs call for productive traits acquired through fundamentally different learning processes and two fundamentally different production processes – capital-intensive or labour-intensive – entailing fundamentally different learning curves. Job segmentation, however, is not a phenomenon unto itself. Rather, jobs are seen in their relation to a broader mobility chain. That is, jobs are conceived as stations along more or less regularized channels of socioeconomic movement from family backgrounds and neighbourhoods to schools to a limited set of employment situations. The phenomenon of labour market segmentation, in other words, is maintained by distinct and largely separate mobility chains through which discrete strata of a society or nation are delivered to discrete segments of the labour market. The emergence and perpetuation of separate mobility chains may be traced, first, to factors associated with social class and, second, to the tendency for different environments, such as home, school and work, to evolve in convergent directions. Under the more or less consistent socialization engendered by the various but intertwined environments they participate in, three discrete strata of the population (classes) are gradually shaped so as to have the traits, aspirations, criteria of judgement, and so on, necessary to function appropriately within the three discrete segments of the labour market into which their mobility chains lead them. Particularly troublesome is the actuality that large numbers of people are thus consigned to labour market attainments bearing no necessary relation to qualities they possess independent of their socialization.

Internal labour markets

Jobs in the lower tier of the primary sector require occupants to possess specific traits (job skills) which can only be acquired through lengthy on-the-job training. To facilitate employee acquisition of required traits, job ladders are constructed which allow individuals to move to better jobs as they master new skills. Thus access into all but the entry-level job on the job ladder is restricted to individuals who are already occupying a rung. In short, lower-tier jobs are found principally within internal labour markets sheltering those who are already on the job ladder from the potential competition of workers who are not. Having its roots in the cumulative adaptation of earlier rules relating to specific occupations, sometimes dating back to guild rules, the specific rule structure patterning behaviour within internal labour markets can vary substantially from firm to firm and industry to industry.

Since on-the-job training in these protected enclaves necessarily occurs within social groups, it can only be understood in terms of socialization, that is, as occurring within a coercive structure compelling individual adherence to the standard practices, norms and role patterns of the work group. Indeed, since most jobs involve tasks that cannot be performed in the absence of cooperation by others, many traits cannot even be distinguished independently of the concrete social setting in which they are performed. What this means, once again, is that skill acquisition cannot occur unless an individual conforms to the prevailing customs, norms, roles, and so on, of the workplace – that is, to workplace institutions. And as the patterns associated with conformity to existing institutions are repeated again and again, an individual will gradually become committed to them.

Among the principal customs (institutions) of the workplace are those pertaining to the relationship between wages on different jobs. Thus the development of a commitment to the existing structure of wage differentials is itself inherent in the process through which the internal labour market supply of labour is generated, for both job preferences and the reservation wage are consequences of workplace socialization; that is, of the controlling institutions. In fact, the commitment to existing wage differentials is so strong that workers generally come to view wage relativities as moral or ethical absolutes. Workplace dynamics therefore eviscerate not only the competitive pressures capable of undermining the internal wage structure but also, in large part, those within interfirm orbits of coercive comparisons.

Secondary labour markets
In the primary sector, labour markets are largely internal to the firm. Since jobs in the secondary sector are characterized by high turnover, there is an absence of social cohesion in the workplace and a more individualistic orientation to work. Not surprisingly, therefore, labour markets in the secondary sector are essentially external to the firm. But even here, customary wage relativities (institutions) are the key to understanding wage determination for all but minimum wage jobs, which often provide the foundation for making the relevant comparisons. The relativities which are maintained, however, will vary from market to market and cannot be determined independent of actual investigation. If an insufficient number of workers is forthcoming at the wage obtaining in a specific market, alteration of the recruitment practice, not alteration of the wage offer, is the general rule.

Policy implications

Since wage determination and employment are understood to be largely independent processes, the dual labour market theory suggests that moderate inflation might be brought under control through appropriate incomes policy without the necessity of sharp reductions in employment. Hence, the arguments made by proponents of the 'new classical economics' notwithstanding, the effort to formulate incomes policy programmes appropriate to current circumstances should clearly continue. Also of particular significance is the theory's strong implication that labour market policies designed to raise the attainments of workers in the secondary labour market are unlikely to succeed unless firms are induced to transform secondary sector jobs into primary sector jobs. It is difficult to see how this can occur without a more stable economic environment or direct social intervention into the investment process.

Summary

The foregoing is an extremely sketchy overview of the dual labour market theory, one which has neither done justice to its subtleties nor addressed the reality of its incomplete development. It is important to understand that the basic constructs of the dual labour market theory are *ideal types* summarizing the findings of a large number of actual case studies. Unfortunately, neither friend nor foe has found it possible to formulate the dual labour market theory in such fashion that it can be effectively tested through conventional statistical techniques. The theory is 'confirmed', therefore, only to the degree that a large number of cases can be successfully interpreted through the lens it provides. As with all ideal type constructs, many issues pertaining to the adequacy of the dual labour market theory remain unresolved. For example, in an extensive overview of various stratagems used to deal with labour market 'peculiarities', David Marsden has argued persuasively that there are many cases where the existence of an internal labour market cannot be explained via the 'economistic' reasoning employed by Piore. Indeed, challenging the very notion that competition provides the original groundwork out of which internal labour markets have evolved, Marsden has forwarded a public goods argument to show why primary sector upper tier occupational markets are inherently unstable and hence to explain why it is the usual case that upper tier jobs are brought into internal labour markets, a matter left entirely unexplained by the dual labour market theory. Despite these difficulties, however, the dual labour market theory remains the only theoretical framework currently embraced by a significant number of labour specialists whose character has been shown to be fully consistent with an overarching self-conscious 'institutional' standpoint. See Ramstad (1993) for a lengthy analysis establishing that the dual labour market theory manifests philosophical and methodological precepts associated with the 'old' institutional economics.

YNGVE RAMSTAD

See also:
Commons, John R.; Culture; Distribution Theory; Institutionalism, 'Old' and 'New'; Institutions; Market, Institutionalist View of the; Methodological Individualism; Power; Routines; Rules; Transaction; Unemployment.

Bibliography
Berger, S. and M. Piore (1980), *Dualism and Discontinuity in Industrial Societies*, New York: Cambridge University Press, especially Part I.
Marsden, D. (1986), *The End of Economic Man? Custom and Competition in Labor Markets*, New York: St. Martin's Press.
Piore, M. (1975), 'Notes for a Theory of Labor Market Stratification', in Richard C. Edwards, Michael Reich and David M. Gordon (eds), *Labor Market Segmentation*, Lexington, Mass.: D.C. Heath and Company.
Piore, M. (ed.) (1979), *Unemployment & Inflation: Institutional and Structuralist Views*, White Plains, NY: M.E. Sharpe.
Ramstad, Y. (1993) 'Institutional Economics and the Dual Labor Market Theory', in Marc R. Tool (ed.), *Institutional Economics: Theory, Method, Policy*, Boston/Dordrecht/London: Kluwer Academic Publishers.
Solow, R. (1990), *The Labor Market as a Social Institution*, Cambridge, Mass.: Basil Blackwell.

Law and Economics

The subject of the economic role of government has been a principal concern of the old institutionalism and is likewise of the new institutionalism, although there are significant differences in the treatment accorded the subject. Included within the old institutionalism have been the writings of Henry Carter Adams, Richard T. Ely, Thorstein Veblen, John R. Commons, John Maurice Clark, Edwin E. Witte and numerous others down to the present day, including John Kenneth Galbraith, Randall Bartlett, Philip Klein, Wallace Peterson, Walter Adams, Harry M. Trebing, Daniel Bromley, Allan Schmid and the present author. The new institutionalism incorporates some work from the old but largely represents an amalgam and extension of neoclassical treatments of property rights, transaction costs, rent seeking, economic history, regulation and deregulation, public choice and so on. It encompasses the work of Ronald Coase, James Buchanan, Werner Hirsch, Oliver Williamson, Armen Alchian, Steven Cheung, Carl Dahlman, Harold Demsetz, Douglass North, George Stigler, Gordon Tullock, Richard Posner and many others.

The new institutionalist approach is substantially conducted within the research programme, or paradigm, of neoclassical economics. This means that it embodies such fixtures as stable preferences, the rational choice model, and the search for determinate, optimal, equilibrium solutions. Typically, property rights and organization forms are treated as given; but there is a considerable effort to endogenize and thereby to explain the genesis and development of rights and institutions. However, in order to achieve determinate, optimal, equilibrium solutions, the new institutionalists inevitably must either assume *ex post* some natural selection-like reasoning, such that what developed had to and ought to have developed, or assume *ex ante* that some particular consideration is the touchstone of an efficient solution. There is therefore a fundamental tautology at the core of such reasoning, illustrated by the argument advanced by Posner that courts necessarily do and indeed should promote wealth-maximizing assignments of rights. The problem is that there will be a putative wealth-maximizing assignment specific to any rights assignment determined by the courts. What the courts are deciding is not some unique wealth-maximizing result but whose interests are to count in the allocative results to which their decisions lead. In order to avoid such multiplicity of solutions, new institutionalists invoke the Coase theorem contending allocative neutrality of rights assignments, but the neutrality conclusion is obtained only by ruling out of analytical bounds all the factors which violate neutrality, of which there are over a dozen, including initial income distribution, consequential income distribution and transaction costs.

In contrast, the old institutionalists emphasize the factors and forces at work in the legal–economic arena through which the organization and control of the economic system and its evolution are worked out. In this arena, too, the actually achieved market solutions are prefigured through the determination by the legal system of the rights of economic significance. Rather than seek question-begging and tautologous ostensibly determinate, optimal, equilibrium solutions, the old institutionalists seek to explain what is going on in legal–economic processes, for example, in the determination and assignment of rights, including the exercise of effective choice as to whose interests are to count. The old institutionalists do not focus on reaching presumptuous policy conclusions in search of 'efficient' arrangements. They do not believe that there are unique efficient assignments independent of rights. They believe that rights determine efficiency rather than efficiency determining rights. They also believe that whose interests are to count is a subject that must be left to real-world legal and political processes and cannot be prescribed by economic expertise alone, if at all. The problem here is with the diffidence and restraint advocated by the old institutionalists in their capacity as legal–economic analysts. For those attracted to the new institutionalists' desire to pass judgement and make recommendations about rights and legal institutions in terms of efficiency, the old institutionalists are very unsatisfying: they insist that analysis can properly only identify the choice processes operating in the working out of such policies in real-world institutions, and they deny that their technical economic analysis can itself reach policy conclusions. This latter, however, does not prevent individual old-institutionalist analysts from adding their own normative premises to their otherwise positive analyses in order to generate policy recommendations. However, while they seek to make explicit the normative premises of those policy recommendations, they make no claims of presumptive optimality for them.

One feature of both the old and the new institutionalism, although perhaps only variably present with each, is a cold-bloodedness with regard to rights and other legal institutions. Although there is an obvious conservative tendency in some new institutionalist work to take, albeit selectively, existing rights and structures as given, the more general approach in both old and new institutionalism is to deny these arrangements their conventional presumptively legitimized authoritative status and to treat them objectively like all other socioeconomic variables. These differences apart, a number of conclusions can be stated, propositions which are perhaps more closely consonant with the old institutionalism but which the new institutionalism does not deny – though the latter would prefer to reach the aforementioned conclusions as to specific determinate, optimal, equilibrium solutions to particular problems of policy. These conclusions include the following.

Ideological preconceptions of laissez-faire and non-intervention notwithstanding, law (court decisions and legislation) covers all areas of life. Government is deeply involved in the definition, creation, operation and performance of the economic system, in part through the formation and reformation of the basic economic institutions: property, contract, business organization, negotiable instruments, agency, tort and so on. Law and government are deeply embodied in the status quo.

Both economy and polity are artefacts and thereby matters of social (re)construction. The economy is an object of legal control and law is an instrument of economic gain or advantage. The legal system constitutes and provides social control; legal institutions are power centres and players in economy and society; and law and legal institutions are an object of control.

Given the ubiquity of law, 'interventionism' means, apart from the generation of new law to deal with new technology and other social inventions, legal change of law, or legal change of the interests to which government gives its protection. The disciplines of law and of economics are each part of the social (re)construction of the economy. Legal change is the crux of policy.

Some models treat the economy as a function of law; others treat law as a function of economy; still others interpret the two spheres as largely autonomous and self-subsistent but interacting; another model treats the two as interacting but also and predominantly concurrently emanating from a common legal–economic nexus. The phrase 'economic role of government' used in the first sentence of this entry may be quite misleading, if it is taken to mean that law and government are fundamentally exogenous to the economic system. Twin interactive processes are at work: the reaching through trade of non-unique Pareto optimal resource allocations, given existing rights; and the redefinition, reassignment and creation of new rights. Power and ideology are critical dimensions of the economic role of government. More broadly, policy is a function of power, knowledge and psychology as sets of interacting variables.

Government is an instrument available to whomever can control it. Government is also an arena of power and power play. It is also a process through which values are identified, clarified, juxtaposed to one another and sought. It is also a means of collective action. Government is the premier mode of self-rule in the modern world; and politics is the mode of self-government. The state is an institution within which a ubiquitous array of collective negotiation over policy takes place and is worked out.

Government is both a dependent and an independent variable: government and law are the product of forces that operate on and through it, and at any point in time the existing corpus of law, and its derivative, the existing set of entitlements and powers, must be taken as given. Still, there is a difference between those who, as 'law takers', treat law as something transcendent and given, and those who, as 'law makers', treat law as an object of control and use in promotion of their interests.

Representative of what must be worked out in the legal–economic arena are (a) the values which become the object of policy, (b) the trade-offs which have to be made between those values, (c) the preferences which individuals have for those preferences, and (d) the power structure by which those preferences are weighted to form the actual social welfare function operative in the political economy. Old institutionalists, who may nonetheless have their own private preferences in these matters, tend to insist that policy options and decisions must be worked out by actual economic agents in real-world economic processes and institutions. They argue that new institutionalists, in so far as they attempt to reach conclusions as to efficient policies, inject their own preferences as assumptions in such a manner as to foreclose the operation of process. New institutionalists, because of their neoclassical perspective and its conception of economic science, are preoccupied with reaching determinate, optimal, equilibrium solutions and find incomplete and unsatisfying any analysis which does not do so.

There is a continuing and changing resolution of the three dimensions of the problem of order, achieved in part through law and in part through economic activity: the conflicts between freedom and control, continuity and change, and equality and hierarchy. Courts and legislatures face an inexorable necessity of choice, when economic agents are in conflict, as to whose interests will count – and which resource allocations and income and wealth distributions will ensue as a result of their decisions and policies. Legal determination of whose interests count decides the structure of freedom and exposure to the freedom of others and thereby the structure of mutual coercion in the economy.

Finally, the adoption by government of general functions always requires further determinations of the policy substance of those functions. Macroeconomic supervision of the economy, for example, requires further policy decisions over the trade-off between unemployment and inflation. The protection of property requires policy determinations as to whose interests will be treated and protected as property.

WARREN J. SAMUELS

See also:
Commons, John R.; Institutionalism, 'Old' and 'New'; Methodological Individualism; Power; Property; Transaction.

Bibliography
Hirsch, Werner Z. (1988), *Law and Economics: An Introductory Analysis*, 2nd edn, Boston: Academic Press.
Mercuro, Nicholas (ed.) (1989), *Law and Economics*, Boston: Kluwer Academic Publishers.
Samuels, Warren J. (1989), *Fundamentals of the Economic Role of Government*, Westport, Conn.: Greenwood Press.
Samuels, Warren J. and Allan Schmid (eds) (1981), *Law and Economics: An Institutional Perspective*, Boston, Mass.: Martinus Nijhoff.

Leibenstein, Harvey

Harvey Leibenstein was born in Russia in 1922 and grew to adulthood in Canada. After work at Northwestern University, he received his doctoral degree from Princeton in 1951. For the next 15 years he was on the faculty at the University of California at Berkeley. In 1967, he moved to Harvard as Andelot Professor of Economics and Population. His published work includes nine books and over 70 major papers. His most well known article, 'Allocative Efficiency vs "X-Efficiency"', appeared in the *American Economic Review* in 1966. Tragically, injuries sustained in a motor accident in the summer of 1987 effectively ended his career.

Harvey Leibenstein's published writings include many on economic development, population and welfare, but this summary focuses solely on his pioneering efforts in X-efficiency theory. This theory (also known as micro-micro theory) is concerned with what goes on inside the firm and why firms are ordinarily less than optimally efficient.

In standard neoclassical theory, the firm is a production function run by a profit-maximizing agent. Because of the fixed relationship between input and output, standard theory cannot explain why the outputs of firms with identical inputs might differ. An example of this comes from a *New York Times* story, 13 October 1981, that compared two identically designed Ford plants with the same equipment and production targets, producing the same cars: in 1981, the German plant produced 1200 cars a day with 7762 workers, while the English plant produced 800 cars a day with 10 040 workers. Why do such differences in efficiency exist and persist? X-efficiency theory provides important answers.

First, allocative efficiency, the efficiency concept at the heart of neoclassical economics, cannot answer the question. Allocative inefficiency exists when market prices do not provide the correct signals, thereby leading to an allocation of resources that yields less than the optimal benefits to society. *X-efficiency* (XE), on the other hand, relates to a firm's internal efficiency. XE increases when a firm produces more output with no change in inputs or technology. *X-inefficiency* (XIE), the degree to which actual output is less than maximum output (for given inputs), is the usual state of affairs. Because of XIE, the firm's outputs are below the production possibility frontier, and the firm's costs are higher than minimum costs. The reasons for XIE are many and varied. XIE could result, for example, from inefficiency in labour utilization, capital utilization, extent of employee cooperation, information flow, or the use of traditional and hallowed rules of thumb.

In Leibenstein's analysis, the individual is the basic decision unit. Individuals contract with the firm to supply their labour for a specified time and payment, but these contracts do not specify, at least not clearly, how much effort the worker has to put forth. Therefore the worker has effort discretion. The term 'effort' here refers not just to how hard in a physical sense someone is working but also to the quality and direction of their activities. Because of effort discretion and because workers are agents of the firm's principals, employees may not put forth or choose an amount of effort that is fully in accord with the interests of the principals. According to Leibenstein, in the absence of organizational demands, an individual worker's effort choice is determined by an internal balance of opposing motivating forces. One is the individual's desire to be responsible and conscientious, the other is the urge to avoid responsibility and to be unconstrained. Ordinarily, however, organizational demands which reflect pressures from the firm's external environment will also influence the individual's effort choice. In other words, the resulting effort reflects two compromises, one within the individual and one between the individual and the pressures emanating from authorities and peers in the firm. Because the effort outcome is unlikely to be in the best interests of either the employee or the employer, it can be said to deviate from maximizing behaviour. Individuals thus behave in a *selectively rational* way; they rarely maximize from the standpoint of the employer or firm.

Leibenstein cites the Yerkes-Dodson Law developed by psychologists as a reason why effort, and thus performance, will increase with increasing pressure, up to some point beyond which performance will fall off. Performance declines because too much pressure makes it difficult for the organism to cope effectively. In addition, Leibenstein believes that there is a general tendency to 'effort entropy', a tendency to move to a less organized state of affairs involving lower worker effort unless management actively counters this process. Because of these phenomena, it is expected that firms in sheltered environments (ones affording protection from competitive pressures) will experience a tendency for costs to rise above minimum costs. In Leibenstein's model, maximizing behaviour is only conceivable in a one-man firm in perfect competition.

Leibenstein takes issue with economists who simply assume maximizing behaviour and reject even the possibility of non-maximizing behaviour. He argues that maximizing, for example in decision making, requires the use of optimal procedures and that individuals ordinarily employ many inoptimal procedures because of habit, conventions, emulation of others, responses to ethical or moral imperatives, the use of standard operating rules, and so on. Another reason for non-maximizing behaviour is inertia. To capture this, Leibenstein uses the concept of inert areas. These are areas in which an individual or group is insensitive to external change because they have become habituated to doing things in a certain way. Within these inert areas, individuals will not take advantage of the occurrence of opportunities for utility gain.

George Stigler's 1976 article in the *American Economic Review* was probably the most well known of a number of neoclassical criticisms of X-efficiency theory. Stigler argued that low effort, rather than being an indication of inefficiency, can be understood as a worker/owner's attempt to maximize utility. Thus low effort is simply an individual's substitution of leisure on the job for the goods that would otherwise have been produced. In response, Leibenstein argued:

> People usually want time off *away* from work, not at work. Secondly, X-inefficiency does not mean people necessarily work less hard. It may, in fact, mean that they work just as hard, appear just as busy, but that their effort is less effective. Finally, even where the pace is slower, the work is not necessarily more fun. It may only be more boring. (Leibenstein, 1979, p. 17)

The Prisoner's Dilemma analysis is very useful for showing how there is a latent tendency for cooperation to break down as the result of lack of trust and self-interest. Despite this tendency, Leibenstein points out that the Prisoner's Dilemma solution (the worst case) rarely occurs because people generally behave according to conventions. While these conventions solve coordination problems, they generally do not result in optimal or fully cooperative solutions. Thus they are another source of X-inefficiency.

In most economic theory, man is simply economic man, that is, man the economizer and maximizer of economic outcomes. In contrast, Leibenstein goes beyond economic man, incorporating into his theories social man, a man who is constrained by commitments, social obligations, conventions, identifications and attitudes about cooperation. His theory even incorporates a few elements of psychological man, man with achievement need, with contaminating emotion, and so forth.

X-efficiency theory helps to explain how, from 1980 to 1988, the English Ford plant, which was threatened with extinction, was able to double its labour productivity largely through behavioural changes, thereby reducing the gap between it and its German sister plant (*New York Times*, 28 November 1989). The great value of Leibenstein's writings on X-efficiency theory is that it explains to economists in a familiar language why what they believe about firm behaviour is untrue. In other words, it explains why firms may not be, and usually are not, maximizers.

JOHN F. TOMER

See also:

Firm, Theory of the; Human Nature, Theory of; Neoclassical Microeconomic Theory, Critique of; Rationality and Maximization; Routines; Trust.

Bibliography

Button, Kenneth (1989a), *The Collected Essays of Harvey Leibenstein: Population, Development and Welfare*, Volume 1, New York: New York University Press.

Button, Kenneth (1989b), *The Collected Essays of Harvey Leibenstein: X-Efficiency and Micro-Micro Theory*, Volume 2, New York: New York University Press.

Leibenstein, Harvey (1976), *Beyond Economic Man: A New Foundation for Microeconomics*, Cambridge, Mass.: Harvard University Press.

Leibenstein, Harvey (1979), 'X-Efficiency: From Concept to Theory', *Challenge*, September–October, pp. 13–22.

Leibenstein, Harvey (1987), *Inside the Firm: The Inefficiencies of Hierarchy*, Cambridge, Mass.: Harvard University Press.

Stigler, George J. (1976), 'The Xistence of X efficiency', *American Economic Review*, **66**, pp. 213–16.

Lock-in and Chreodic Development

It has been observed that an economic system can get locked into given paths of development, often excluding a host of other, perhaps more 'efficient' or desirable possibilities. This occurs in natural as well as economic evolution. A natural example is the preponderance of 'left-handed' organic molecules which has evolved from an 'accident' long ago in evolutionary time. Another case is the uniqueness of the genetic code. Still another is the kind of common, basic skeletal design found in humans and other mammals, with backbone, ribs, four limbs, and so on. Most of the past evolution of the skeletal structure was in quadrupeds, yet the basic pattern was passed on to humans, where in several respects it is unsuited to a bipedal stance.

Technological examples of lock-in are plentiful. For instance, we seem to be stuck with the 'QWERTY' typewriter keyboard, which was originally designed to operate with a mechanical rather than an electrical technology (David, 1985). The 4 foot $8^1/2$ inch standard gauge on railways was established in the first half of the nineteenth century. It is highly inappropriate for modern fast trains, but it has nevertheless spread around the world, and it clearly cannot be altered by piecemeal change. A more recent example is the victory of the inferior VHS video system over Betamax. In all these cases technological development has involved the adoption of rigid standards and other attributes, which become 'frozen'.

In other instances, economic and technological development is less rigidly constrained, but strong feedback effects coerce it upon a developmental 'channel' or 'valley'. A relevant example is the development of the system of transport based on the motor car, which, once it had occurred, tended to preclude the gradual development of other alternatives. Once the motor car became well established in use, investment in public transport systems was disadvantaged. In such cases, marginal adjustments towards perhaps more optimal systemic outcomes are often ruled out. While a range of possibilities were available, it became more difficult, for both economic and political reasons, to recast the entire transport system upon different lines.

Another example is the adoption and development of the internal combustion engine, rather than steam or electrical alternatives, at the beginning of the twentieth century. At that time the development of each of all these options seemed viable, yet, once the large corporations adopted the internal combustion engine, and a network of filling stations was established, investment in and development of the alternatives fell well behind. As a result, use of the internal combustion engine became both cheaper and more convenient. However, history could have developed in a different way. It is possible that steam or electrical systems could have been selected in the initial stages, and the internal combustion engine would have become rare.

In general, such developments occur when evolutionary interactions are coupled in a non-linear and dynamic way, involving positive feedback effects. In contrast, conventional economic theory is built on the assumption of diminishing returns, where negative feedback leads to stabilization and equilibrium. Such equilibria are often associated with Pareto optimal outcomes. However, many technological and structural features of a modern economy involve positive feedbacks, which magnify the effects of small changes. Consequently, initial 'accidents' can have a huge effect on the result. Very different evolutionary outcomes can emerge from small variancies in initial conditions, as in the more general case of the 'butterfly effect' in dynamic, non-linear systems. Precise prediction of future development at the crucial formative stages becomes difficult. Without the stabilizing effects of negative feedback there are many alternative paths of development. This suggests that actual developments in economic and technological history can often be far from optimal.

In many cases, such positive feedbacks arise from what are called 'network externalities' (Katz and Shapiro, 1986). All the above examples involve these. Economic and technological developments depend upon the establishment of networks involving multiple users, and no single user is able to have much impact on the conventions and technological standards involved in that network. Another way of describing these phenomena is in terms of the 'coordination game' from game theory. Positive feedbacks are also typically related to parts of the society or economy which are knowledge-based. Language is an old example, involving clear network externalities; we must use the same system of signs and symbols as others, otherwise we would be misunderstood. Similar feedback attributes apply to computer languages, accounting for the survival of relatively outdated languages such as Fortran.

The phenomena considered here have all been described as 'lock-in' (Arthur, 1989, 1990). Given that they relate to positive feedback, they have precedents in the works of institutional economists such as Thorstein Veblen and Gunnar Myrdal, both of whom developed the idea of cumulative causation. In addition, Nicholas Kaldor was much influenced by Myrdal's analysis and in particular stressed the importance of increasing returns. Kaldor argued repeatedly that the adoption of the assumption of increasing returns was damaging for orthodox economic theory. There is thus a common stress in the writings of these three writers on cumulative causation and positive feedback, in contrast to the focus on equilibrium in neoclassical economics.

There are differences between cases where lock-in is very constrained and rigid, and others where a range of outcomes are possible. Examples of very rigid lock-in are the standard gauge on railways, or the VHS video system. More flexibility applies with the development of whole technology systems, such as the motor car driven by the internal combustion engine. Spoken language is perhaps an intermediate case.

In biology, lock-in is sometimes referred to as 'hyperselection', which emerges from strong positive feedback effects that 'freeze' a given attribute or structure. The less rigid cases have been described by the biologist Conrad Waddington as 'chreods', from the Greek 'chre', meaning it is fated or necessary, and 'hodos', a path. A chreod is a relatively stable trajectory of development for a species. The stability is not homeostatic, in that it does not stabilize at one point, on one set of characters. Instead, to use another word coined by Waddington, it is *homeorhetic* (from the Greek 'rheo', to flow), in that it stabilizes on one course of development through time. Waddington argued that external influences may occasionally operate in such a way as to tend to push the system off the trajectory, but the canalization of the chreod or, otherwise expressed, its tendency towards homeorhesis, will tend to bring the system back onto the normal path again.

Norman Clark and Calestous Juma (1987) argue that there are technological trajectories each of which develops a hierarchical control sequence very similar to the chreod. Once a technological 'paradigm' is adopted, this predetermines a general direction or path of development. The concept of chreodic development is more general in scope than hyperselection. The latter idea is generally applicable to the detailed structures of individual components or units where little or no variation can take place once hyperselection occurs. In contrast, the idea of a chreod is most often applied to dominant characteristics and overall structures, where small perturbations can take place, but the system is often pulled back onto a chreodic channel.

Lock-in is an important phenomenon for evolutionary theory, for a number of additional reasons. A system which is locked in has sufficiently stable features for it to be treated as a higher-level unit of evolutionary selection, above individuals, groups or rules. Locked in networks and technological systems are also helpful for understanding the nature of technological 'paradigms' or 'regimes'. Their inertial quality also means that some kind of prediction is possible in evolution, as Waddington has suggested, despite the complexities and non-linearities involved.

As we have seen, in all cases of lock-in the outcomes have an arbitrary quality, depending much on initial conditions. In the economic context the possibility is thus raised of some form of state intervention to set out or change the contours of chreodic development, or to initiate a more desirable hyperselective scenario. This occurs already to a limited extent, when the United States government or the European Community sponsors a given technological system or standard. However, the wider implications that lock-in has for government intervention, as well as its demonstration of the potential sub-optimality of laissez-faire, are not yet widely recognized in policy-making circles.

GEOFFREY M. HODGSON

See also:

Selection, Units of Evolutionary; Technical Change and Technological Regimes; Ullmann-Margalit, Edna; Veblen, Thorstein.

Bibliography

Arthur, W. Brian (1989), 'Competing Technologies, Increasing Returns, and Lock-in by Historical Events', *The Economic Journal*, **99**, (1), March, pp. 116–31; reprinted 1990 in Freeman.

Arthur, W. Brian (1990), 'Positive Feedbacks in the Economy', *Scientific American*, **262**, (2), February, pp. 80–85.

Clark, Norman G. and Calestous Juma (1987), *Long-Run Economics: An Evolutionary Approach to Economic Growth*, London: Pinter.

David, Paul A. (1985), 'Clio and the Economics of QWERTY', *American Economic Review*, **75**, (2), May, pp. 332–7; reprinted 1990 in Freeman.

Freeman, Christopher (ed.) (1990), *The Economics of Innovation*, Aldershot: Edward Elgar.

Katz, M. and Carl Shapiro (1986), 'Technology Adoption in the Presence of Network Externalities', *Journal of Political Economy*, **94**, (4), August, pp. 822–41.

Sahal, Devendra (1985), 'Technological Guideposts and Innovation Avenues', *Research Policy*, **14**, (1), pp. 61–82; reprinted 1990 in Freeman.

Silverberg, Gerald (1988), 'Modelling Economic Dynamics and Technical Change: Mathematical Approaches to Self-Organisation and Evolution', in G. Dosi, C. Freeman, R. Nelson, G. Silverberg and L. Soete (eds), *Technical Change and Economic Theory*, pp. 531–59, London: Pinter.

Waddington, Conrad H. (ed.) (1972), *Towards a Theoretical Biology*, 4 vols, Edinburgh: Edinburgh University Press.

Long Waves

The long wave, or Kondratiev, is a cycle, of some 45–60 years, which is alleged to exist, at the level of individual or world economies, in various aspects of economic growth or prices, since some time in the nineteenth century or before. The idea was first given wide currency by the writings of the Russian economist Nikolai Kondratiev in the 1920s. He saw it as an endogenous, that is, self-replicating, cycle in the world economy, involving both growth and price series and arising during the industrial era – since the late eighteenth century. Among adherents, there are wide divergences as to how to explain long waves, and many economists and economic historians of all persuasions doubt both their empirical existence and their theoretical plausibility.

The idea seems to have been first suggested by the fact that British and French price series showed something of a long wave pattern during the nineteenth century. By 1900, moreover, there was considerable understanding of shorter cycles, which seemed to show some synchronicity in price and volume series. The empirical difficulty was – and remains – to find a long wave in volume series before 1900. Since then, however, there has been an opposite difficulty. Adjusted for World War I, volume series for the world and most countries have followed a pronounced long wave pattern during the twentieth century; price series have 'misbehaved' since the 1970s. However, the econometric debate has remained focused on the volume series. Kondratiev's was the first serious contribution (well reviewed, like other long wave econometrics, in Reijnders, 1990). He recognized that the long wave could only be found if the effects of both the long-term trend and shorter cycles were removed; but he used crude methods to do so. Reijnders uses a 'hidden periodicities' model on a number of long UK series (price and volume) to find a 'full trend' which is then eliminated, and then uses spectral analysis to look simultaneously for Kondratiev, Kuznets and other cycles. Most price and volume series show reasonable evidence of long waves but the volume series have to be adjusted for the world wars first. These findings are quite consistent with the causal empiricism which suggests a long wave in economic growth in the twentieth century but not in the nineteenth. They are thus vulnerable to sceptics like Solomou (1987) who regard fluctuations in growth longer than the Kuznets as episodic, resulting from factors without regular pattern, like the world wars. (He has a similar 'episodic' explanation for the apparent nineteenth-century long wave in prices.)

Van Gelderen, writing in 1913, explained the long wave in terms of the relationship between industrial countries and primary producers. So long as the latter provided ample supplies of gold (which kept interest rates down) and raw materials, expansion proceeded rapidly. Once industrial expansion ran ahead of primary product supplies, prices and interest rates rose, helping to end the upswing. During the downswing, low profits and high unemployment in the industrialized countries drove both capital and labour overseas, helping to provide gold and raw materials for the next upswing. Kondratiev offered a similar explanation, with one important addition, the claim that long waves involve a 'wave' in inventions and innovations: more inventions were made during the downswing, which were then applied as innovations on a large scale only at the beginning of the next long upswing. This suggestion was taken up by Schumpeter (who gave long waves the name Kondratievs) and made the basis of his own theory. Schumpeter stresses the central role of technical progress, in providing opportunities for profits and accumulation. He explains how basic innovations like the steam engine and the railway, and the 'swarming' of smaller, secondary innovations which follow them, can launch a long wave; the initial impulse is gradually dissipated, leading to the downswing. But what explains the arrival of basic innovations, in clusters, every 50 years or so?

Ernest Mandel, who had predicted the 1970s downswing, provided a Marxist explanation consistent with Schumpeter's. Capitalists will not invest heavily until the rate of actual and expected profit is sufficiently high. This is not so during the downswing (see below); investment is therefore low, leading to a depression. This causes a deep social and political crisis, which continues until capitalists win a decisive victory in the world class struggle which opens some new avenue of profitable accumulation. In the late nineteenth century, the victory came through imperialistic expansion abroad; the crisis was resolved at the expense of the conquered peoples, whose territories provided new markets and raw materials. In the next depression crisis this possibility was not available, having already been used. The crisis was accordingly deeper, and led to a bitter internal class struggle. The capitalists emerged victorious in the late 1940s, able to make full use of the technical possibilities of the assembly-line technologies ('Fordism') already developed in the USA. The upswing, once under way, encourages investment and innovation, the two interacting in a virtuous circle. But it is doomed by two developments which reduce the rate of profit. The working class movement takes advantage of favourable labour market conditions to harass capitalism; rising labour costs and the stage of the 'technological cycle' lead to rising capital intensity. Capitalist confidence is shaken and the downswing returns – putting the workers on the defensive, but not of itself providing the victory required.

There are two main objections to this theory: that Mandel's account of the capitalist–working class relationship does not match the historical facts, and that he neglects the role of workers' consumption in demand (see Tylecote, 1991, chs 6 and 11). This cannot be said against the 'régulationist school', led by Aglietta, Boyer, Mistral and Lipietz, who deploy two key concepts: the regime of accumulation and the mode of regulation. The first relates to the capitalist firm, its techniques and methods, the second to the wider society (national and international) and its complex network of relationships, of checks and balances. A radical change of technology, such as we associate with Henry Ford and the assembly line, changes the regime of accumulation, but it does nothing to make the mode of regulation change in harmony. It is likely – one might say inevitable – that the necessary harmony will be lost, and that this will cause a crisis and a depression. Thus the 'Fordist' regime of accumulation involved the growth of large firms, with closer control over their workers and increased market power. This led, among other things, to the redistribution of income away from wages to profits, and a consequent shortfall of consumer demand, which caused the inter-war Depression. The subsequent recovery followed from the gradual growth of a suitable new mode of regulation, which restored harmony; in particular, the operation of the welfare state, and the strength of unions, guaranteed a much more equal distribution of income.

Perez (1983) combined the regulationist and Schumpeterian insights, with her concept of 'technological styles':

A sort of paradigm for the most efficient organisation of production, i.e. the main form and direction along which productivity growth takes place within and across firms, industries and countries. The particular historical form of such a paradigm would evolve out of certain key technological developments, which result in a substantial change in the relative cost structure facing industry and which, at the same time, open a wide range of new opportunities for taking advantage of this particular evolution. (Perez, 1983, p. 361)

Thus the 'Fordist' style had been preceded by innovations which made possible high-performance machine tools, and cheap petroleum products, electricity and electric motors. On this basis Ford and others developed the assembly line and mass production engineering – that was in essence the new paradigm.

A new technological style would cause rapid change in the technoeconomic subsystem. But this subsystem has to coexist with the other main subsystem within capitalism, the social and institutional framework, which has a 'high degree of natural inertia'. The new style is 'mismatched' with the old framework, leading to crisis and depression. 'The crisis forces the restructuring of the socio-institutional framework with innovations along lines that are complementary to the newly attained technological style' (Perez, 1983, p. 361). A new upswing follows, with a 'swarming' of product innovations, which increase demand and employment. This leads to a point 'where the underlying technological style approaches the limits of its potential for increasing productivity'. The new technological style emerges 'to surmount this barrier' (ibid.).

The main objection to Perez's synthesis is that it explains too much. According to Perez there have been four technological styles since the beginning of the Industrial Revolution, at roughly 50-year intervals, and a fifth has just appeared. But this implies four long waves in economic growth, two of which appear to be missing. It seems, then, that a new technological style could appear and diffuse without – in the nineteenth century – provoking a long wave in economic growth; equally, if the 'technological long wave' does exist, it arises and continues without an economic long wave with which to interact.

Tylecote (1991) seeks to resolve this problem in four steps. First, he seeks to establish the 'technological long wave' as a phenomenon which can be empirically accepted back to about 1780, although it has fluctuated considerably in period; and he provides a tentative explanation for it, independent of the Kondratiev. Second, he argues that the social and economic repercussions of the technological long wave are very much dependent on the institutions and structures of the time and place. Perez's model fits the twentieth century much better than the nineteenth, though even in the twentieth it overlooks political 'crises of the upswing', like World War I. Third, there are 'feedback loops', largely independent of technological change, through which demography, money supply and income distribution interact with economic growth: these have evolved in such a way as largely to suppress any long wave in growth during the nineteenth century, but to amplify it in the late twentieth. Finally, it is necessary to take account of a cycle longer than the Kondratiev, the Modelski/Wallerstein long cycle in international relations of 100–120 years, which produces a succession of global wars like the Revolutionary/Napoleonic (1792–1815) and the world wars (one global war with a long interval). The global wars have an impact much like Perez's crises.

Long wave theories have implications for forecasting, depending on the model. They also have implications for policy, with striking differences between Mandel, who in effect prescribes either Thatcherism or revolution, and Perez, Tylecote and the régulationists, who see far-reaching progressive reform as required for a new upswing.

ANDREW TYLECOTE

See also:
Capital Theory; Cumulative Causation; Development Theory; Evolution, Formal Models of; Evolution, Theories of Economic; Fordism and Post-Fordism; Kuznets, Simon Smith; Mitchell, Wesley Clair; Régulation Theory, French; Schumpeter, Joseph Alois.

Bibliography
Perez, Carlota (1983), 'Structural change and assimilation of new technologies in the economic and social systems', *Futures*, October, pp. 357–75.
Reijnders, Jan (1990), *Long Waves in Economic Development*, Aldershot: Edward Elgar.
Solomou, Solomos (1987), *Phases of Economic Growth, 1850–1973: Kondratieff Waves and Kuznets Swings*, Cambridge: Cambridge University Press.
Tylecote, Andrew (1991), *Long Waves in the World Economy: The Present Crisis in Historical Perspective*, London and New York: Routledge.

Lowe, Adolph

Adolph Lowe, born in 1893, is Emeritus Professor of Economics, New School for Social Research and 1979 recipient of the Veblen–Commons Award from the Association for Evolutionary Economics. His writings date back more than 75 years and, as his most recent work, *Has Freedom a Future?* (1988) attests, have the unifying theme of a desire to further the cause of human freedom in a situation of social and economic order and stability. For Lowe, this is by no means an assured outcome of modern capitalism where, to some significant degree, freedom and stable order are potentially in conflict. The price of liberty, then, he argues, becomes individuals' preparedness to conform to the demands of appropriately designed structures, institutions and rules.

In the pursuit of freedom with order, economic analysis, always tempered by social and political exigencies, has a profoundly active role to play. However, Lowe finds orthodox economics, with its 'positive' emphasis on describing and predicting *existential* states of the system, as modified by

standard policy strategies, to be inappropriate to the task. It fails both methodologically and substantively to provide the required intellectual foundations for directing our economic system towards sustainable order and stability. In aspiring to an epistemological status equivalent to that usually
associated with physical natural sciences, received theory does not give due
cognizance to the fact that its object of study lacks the minimum qualities
required for legitimate application of 'scientific' methodology: an autonomous 'natural' existence and an inherent orderliness. Orthodox economics is
forced to *attribute* these necessary qualities to the system by devising ideal-
ized assumptions about its structures and operations that enable them to be
represented as, at least, stochastic generalizations about behaviour, if not as
'laws' *per se*.

Lowe's response to this situation is bold and radical. In his *On Economic
Knowledge* (1977), he proposes an instrumental–deductive methodology in
which the object of theory is provided with the required autonomy and
orderliness by dint of its *ex ante* formal establishment as a given goal-state
of the economic system. Given, that is, by virtue of the democratically based
political process. From the existing state of the system, in combination with
a set of empirical generalizations that flow from the natural, psychological,
social and technological structures and functions through which agents'
decisions are made, it is possible to deduce the behavioural–logical means
by which the goal-state could be reached. In this way, the analysis becomes
instrumental in Lowe's special sense.

More specifically, the unknown means to be specified comprise the following, and while such requirements pose some readily apparent practical
difficulties, their heuristic importance and relevance is clear: (a) the path or
succession of macro-states of the system that would transform the existing
state into the goal-state; (b) patterns of micro-behaviours appropriate to
keeping the system on the stipulated path; (c) the micro-motivations of
agents that would induce the required behaviours; and (d) an 'environmental' state, including appropriate controls, that will elicit these motivations
and the associated goal-adequate behaviours. For Lowe, the required control
design must be such as to ensure, as far as possible, voluntary conformity by
agents to appropriate action directives and motivations in an otherwise free-
market system. The idea, then, is to establish *an ordered freedom through
spontaneous individual conformity.*

In order to give his alternative political economics, or science of controlled economic systems, a substantive context of analysis, Lowe focuses his
theoretical work on the phenomena of growth and technological change. In
particular, as his instrumental analysis is concerned with changing states of
economic systems, he investigates the problem of traverse processes more
fully than most other writers; that is, the problem of understanding the

details of the complex sequential adjustments that must be worked through in various sectors of the economy when the total system changes its state. His objective is to specify the *requirements* for effectuating particular traverse paths in terms of both the physical–structural adjustments involved and the behavioural–institutional means by which they can be facilitated.

It is to be emphasized that Lowe's interest in the theory of growth and technological change is purely instrumental in the sense indicated above. His consequent rejection of the 'positive' explanatory approach of established theories in this field was accompanied in his alternative exposition by corrections to two other aspects that troubled him. First, he noted that the value–price quantification of variables obscures the physical–technical form taken by, and the consequent inflexible and immobile nature of, most produced means of production and many other productive resources. The result is an analytical representation of any dimension of motion that understates the complexity and duration of its constituent adjustments. Second, he found that the degree of aggregation in many of the models used, along with a lack of analytical specification of separate production sectors, often served to obscure details of the particular differential and sequentially specific demands that traverse adjustments place on these various interdependent sectors of the system.

Lowe's response here was to redesign the basic framework in which the analysis of the forces of motion are to be set, by devising a modified and extended version of the reproduction schema developed by Karl Marx. Lowe included an additional sector to make some allowance for the heterogeneity of means of production, along with a vertically expanded and 'linear' treatment of production in each sector to emphasize the role of time and intermediate goods in the process. As he demonstrates with considerable analytical acumen, this framework facilitates some penetrating insights into the problematical nature of the traverse paths required to restore steady-state motion once it is disturbed. The analyses were adumbrated in two papers from the 1950s, included in his *Essays* (1987), and finally worked out in full detail in *The Path of Economic Growth* (1976).

Through these formalized analyses, Lowe emphasizes the high degree of dynamic complexity that change can bring to the motion of an economic system as a matter of abstract principle. The effect is to reinforce the practical need for properly designed controls to complement free-market forces if ever-present disturbances to economic processes are to be absorbed with a minimum of disruption and consequent economic and social losses. Economic control, then, becomes the first step towards realizing and maintaining a stable order in a free society.

ALLEN OAKLEY

See also:

Development Theory; Instrumental Value Theory; Methodology; Technology in Development Policy.

Bibliography

Heilbroner, Robert L. (ed.) (1969), *Economic Means and Social Ends*, Englewood Cliffs, NJ: Prentice-Hall.

Lowe, Adolph (1976), *The Path of Economic Growth*, Cambridge: Cambridge University Press.

Lowe, Adolph (1977), *On Economic Knowledge: Toward a Science of Political Economics*, 2nd enlarged edn, White Plains, NY: M.E. Sharpe; first published 1965.

Lowe, Adolph (1987), *Essays in Political Economics: Public Control in a Democratic Society*, edited with an Introduction by Allen Oakley, Brighton: Wheatsheaf and New York: New York University Press (includes a bibliography of Adolph Lowe's writings).

Lowe, Adolph (1988), *Has Freedom a Future?*, New York: Praeger.

Macroeconomic Policy (I)

Macroeconomic theory is a legacy of the bitter experience of the Great Depression of the 1930s. Intellectually, it is the creation of John Maynard Keynes. His 1936 classic, *The General Theory of Employment, Interest and Money*, set forth the basic principles that undergird contemporary macroeconomic theory.

The key idea in *The General Theory* is that the level of output and employment depends upon the interaction between total spending – which Keynes called aggregate demand – and the economy's capacity to produce, which he designated as aggregate supply. In market capitalism, decisions to produce goods and services are made primarily by private business firms. This is basic. Production, the source of employment, will take place only if producers experience or foresee a market in which the goods and services produced can be sold at prices that cover their production costs and yield a profit. If there is not any demand – actual or potential – productive capacity will stand idle and people will be without jobs. The commonsense notion that spending is the key to output and employment is the bedrock idea in Keynesian economics.

It is in this basic tenet of Keynesian economics that we find the theoretical roots and rationale for macroeconomic policy. In the macroeconomy, as noted, decisions to produce goods and services originate with private business firms. However, the decisions to use the output produced – to spend, in other words – are made by different entities. The latter are consumers, government units and business firms themselves. Herein we find the nub of the policy problem in systems of market capitalism. There is no mechanism within market systems which guarantees that output decisions and spending decisions will always coincide. Most of the time they do not. It is this fact that gives rise to the vicissitudes of the economy we know as the business cycle.

For example, if there is a shortfall of aggregate demand – too little spending, in other words – then there will be unsold goods, cutbacks in production and rising unemployment. An excess of spending, on the other hand, leads to shortages, increasing output and employment (falling unemployment), and rising wages and prices. Imbalances between aggregate demand and aggregate supply open the door for policy actions by a national government. This is what macroeconomic policy is all about. When there is insufficient private spending to maintain a high level of employment, modern governments should take action to offset this. They may either increase their spending, do things that increase private spending, or both. When there is excess private spending relative to capacity, the government should act to reduce spending pressures, either by reducing its own spending or taking actions that dampen down private spending. This is the essence of macroeconomic policy.

What are the means available to modern governments to carry out macroeconomic policy actions? Essentially they are two. First, there is fiscal policy. Fiscal policy involves *deliberate* changes in either government spending or taxes on individuals and business to influence total spending. The target of fiscal policy, in other words, is aggregate demand. By influencing the level of aggregate demand, government can influence the level of output and employment. In the United States, as elsewhere, the budget is the instrument for fiscal actions. The second tool is monetary policy. Monetary policy also involves *deliberate* changes, in the money supply and the rate of interest, the object again being to influence spending levels – aggregate demand, in other words. In modern nations, including the United States, monetary policy works through the nation's central bank, as this is where control of the money supply and the rate of interest is to be found. Both fiscal and monetary policy aim at affecting the level of aggregate demand, which, in accord with the basic tenet of Keynesian theory, is the key to output and employment in the short run.

In sum, the aim of macroeconomic policy is to use the powers of the central government to restore an ailing economy to health. If the problem is recession or depression, the prescription is to cut taxes, increase government spending (fiscal policy) and lower interest rate and increase the money supply (monetary policy). Such measures should nurse the economy back to a full employment state of health. When excess demand (too much spending) leads to the threat of excess inflation, the policy machinery is reversed. This is the basic theory of modern macroeconomic policy.

Institutionalism and macroeconomic policy
How does institutional economics relate to this generally accepted interpretation of macroeconomic policy? That is the question to which we now turn. To understand clearly how institutionalism fits into the picture one must first understand that there is a fundamental, *unresolved* issue confronting contemporary macroeconomic theory and policy. This is the extent to which the modern market economy is a self-regulating system, one that, when left alone, will grow steadily, using all its resources, including labour. This is the same philosophic issue that divided macroeconomics in the 1930s, and it still divides the field today.

From a historical perspective, two broad 'visions', or paradigms, have emerged in response to this basic issue. The oldest vision is that of classical economics, the term used to describe the body of economic thought that developed from Adam Smith's *Wealth of Nations*. The dominant thrust of classical economics is that systems of market capitalism, when unfettered by either state or private monopoly power, will, on their own, seek out and follow an optimum path of economic growth. This path is 'optimum' because it involves the fullest possible use of society's resources, including labour, and the maximum production of the things that people want. Competition is the force that, through the free play of self-interest, brings about these results. The system is self-regulating because, if displaced from the optimum path, forces act to return the system to this path.

The other 'vision' or paradigm flatly rejects the classical view. There is no automatic tendency for systems of market capitalism to reach the optimum growth path. Furthermore, there is no tendency for a market system to remain there if, by chance, it stumbles onto such a path. Further, any departures from an optimum path may be cumulative. Thus, in this vision, the one developed by Keynes in *The General Theory*, there is no inherent equilibrating tendency with systems of market capitalism. Intellectually, this means that there is a need for external intervention if we are to depend upon anything other than chance to put the economy on an optimum, full employment growth path. In contemporary market economies, the central government is the appropriate entity for such intervention.

Institutional economics belongs with the 'heretics', as Keynes called them, who reject the classical view that market economies are inherently self-regulating, and not in need of direction and management by an external force. It rejects, in other words, the basic argument of classical economics that laissez-faire – non-intervention – is the appropriate policy stance today. To put it differently, institutional economists, like Keynesian economists generally, favour activist government, using the tools of modern fiscal and monetary policy for this purpose. This involves more than simply an acceptance by institutional economics of the need for government intervention to correct the flawed workings of systems of market capitalism. The crucial question is how specifically to link institutional thinking to macroeconomic policy decisions. It is to this we now turn.

There are two basic ideas of importance here. The first concerns the evolutionary, continuing nature of the economic process. The economy is not static and mechanical, as depicted in the classical analysis. The second is that a full comprehension of both the possibilities and the limitations of macroeconomic policy is impossible without understanding the key institutions through which *all* policy actions work.

With respect to the first idea it is essential that we not forget that the economy exists in *real,* historic time, not in an abstract, timeless equilibrium world. Economic activity involves a process in which the economy moves continuously from a known past through the present into an unknown and unknowable future. This process is irreversible, which is not the situation in classical equilibrium economics. The economy's existence in real, historic time underscores the critical importance of uncertainty and the impact of uncertainty upon expectations. Capitalistic processes look towards the future. This is especially true of those that involve the creation and acquisition of wealth: that is, investment decisions. Such decisions depend upon future values, but, because uncertainty pervades the real economic world, all expectations rest upon fragile and highly volatile foundations. Real time, uncertainty and the fragility of expectations is the backdrop against which we must view the institutional arrangements through which policy actions are filtered in the market economy.

There are two sets of institutions that are important in this context. First, there are those involving money and finance, including money itself. Second, there are those institutions that reflect power and the drive to get control over one's income. Policy actions that fail to recognize the existence and influence of money, finance and raw economic power will be ineffective.

The driving force of market capitalism is a relentless and restless search for money profits. This is an old idea in institutional economics, which since the time of Veblen has stressed the dichotomy between making goods and making money. This is what gives the institutions of money and finance a dominant role in the way the economy really works. To win profits firms must invest, and to invest they must secure funds, frequently by issuing debt. This entails contractual obligations for future repayment, repayment that can only be met from the income stream created by new investment. The process is volatile, subject to periodic crises and even collapse.

This is why the institutions of market power – the ability to control incomes and prices – are so important. In classical economics market power does not exist, but in a world of uncertainty and fragile expectations it is of crucial importance. Historically, trade unions and the corporation have been the primary instruments for the exercise of market power. Today using the power of government for private ends has become equally important. Economic power, in whatever form it may take, means control over not only the prices of things sold but also the price of inputs, including labour, materials and finance. Power as it is exercised in the economy may be malign or benign in its effects, but the fact that it exists cannot be ignored if policy actions are to succeed.

WALLACE C. PETERSON

See also:

Cumulative Causation; Inflation; Keynes, John Maynard; Macroeconomic Policy (II); Macroeconomic Theory; Monetary Policy; Unemployment.

Bibliography

Bleaney, Michael (1985), *The Rise and Fall of Keynesian Economics*, New York: St. Martin's Press.

Economic Report of the President, Washington, DC: US Government Printing Office, latest edition.

Heller, Walter W. (1966), *New Dimensions of Political Economy*, Cambridge, Mass.: Harvard University Press.
Nourse, Edwin G. (1953), *Economics in the Public Service*, New York: Harcourt, Brace.

Macroeconomic Policy (II)

Especially in macroeconomics, institutionalists derive a great deal of inspiration from Post Keynesian economics. This itself comprises a number of ideas which emerge from different modes of analysis. The assumptions utilized may vary, depending on the problem in hand. Its nature is pluralistic, and the methodology places great emphasis on *realism*, including the core assumptions. A common thread that runs through this economics is that advanced capitalist economies are inherently cyclical and unstable. Left to themselves, they cannot achieve and maintain full employment of resources. These economies are also marred by inequalities in the distribution of market power and, therefore, income and wealth. Unfettered market forces, rather than reducing, tend to exacerbate these instabilities and disparities. Forces of cumulative causation are very much operative in this context. The instabilities of the capitalist system are attributed to the behaviour of private investment as a result of volatile expectations and unpredictable business moods. There is thus enormous potential and need for government involvement in the economic sphere in the form of initiating, pursuing and implementing economic policies. Like Post Keynesian economic analysis, Post Keynesian economic policy is context-specific and generalizations are not always possible. In this sense the analysis provided in what follows is influenced by the UK economy's experience.

Post Keynesians recognize that there are obstacles to an interventionist policy that aims to reach the goals of less instability, full employment and greater income equality. Kalecki (1943) argues that obstacles to the achievement of these economic objectives are deeply rooted in the objections of the industrial leaders to full employment and to a more equitable distribution of income and wealth. An ideological obstacle is found in objections emanating from a dislike amongst the 'captains of industry' of government interference in the private sphere. They believe that such interference entails the danger of workers 'getting out of control', capitalism being replaced by socialism, and profitability and investment being threatened. Another obstacle in open economies is connected with the balance of payments. Expansionary policies that are intended to push the economy to full employment are sometimes associated with severe deterioration (and/or even deficits) in the balance of payments and undesirable movements in the country's exchange rate.

Some economies face other obstacles in reaching these goals: poor research and development leading to an absence of sufficient innovation and investment, lack of a trained skilled labour force, and insufficient and inadequate capacity. In the 1980s at least, those countries that were behind in these respects were those, like the USA and the UK, that relied more on 'unfettered' market forces, whilst others intervened to overcome these difficulties. Post Keynesians therefore believe that government intervention to stimulate aggregate demand is required in principle to help the economy achieve and maintain full employment. This may enhance the power of trade unions and workers during full employment and generate inflationary pressures. These are issues which Post Keynesian macroeconomic policy analysts take very seriously. They argue that the building of a social consensus on incomes shares, and workers' participation, are *sine qua non* for successful 'planning of incomes' policies. Reform of the structure of collective bargaining to make it less inflationary may be required in certain cases. Balance of payments problems can arise at full employment or even well before it is achieved. Such supply-side policies are needed in this context.

Clearly, then, the demand and supply sides of the economy cannot be considered in isolation. On the demand side, the questions of insufficient aggregate demand and the instability of investment are at the forefront of economic policy analysis. Similarly, on the supply side, a number of policies such as planning of incomes, training and active labour market policies and policies that relate to balance of trade difficulties must be considered. Typically, Post Keynesians argue that, even if demand management were able to achieve full employment, it could not alone sustain it. Inadequate or unbalanced supply potential requires that some form of control of investment be introduced to remove these constraints. But even so, control of investment by itself may not be effective if cooperation from the trade union movement and workers in general is not forthcoming. Indeed, trade unions would only be willing to cooperate if they were to be involved in the decision-making process. It follows that the type of investment control envisaged is socialization of investment which would give an active role not just to governments but also to the workforce and trade unions. Consequently, the foregoing does not imply that investment would be massively centrally planned or coordinated.

Socialization of investment in this form should remove the obstacles to achieving full employment mentioned above and about which Kalecki (1943) was so concerned. The dislike of the sociopolitical changes that accompany attempts to achieve and sustain full employment would tend to disappear, because the sociopolitical changes that emerge would be warmly welcomed by the trade unions who, in consequence, become part of the industrial fabric of the economy. These changes strengthen the position of their members and thus enhance their industrial muscle. Most importantly, though, trade unions may be more willing to engage in permanent 'incomes planning' under these conditions than otherwise. It is, in fact, the case that 'incomes planning' is a feature of the Post Keynesian menu of economic policies, given the theoretical position taken on the determination of inflation.

For Post Keynesians, inflation arises from and is firmly embedded in the conflict tradition. Consequently, it is determined by increasing wages, increasing prices of industrial goods, increasing prices of imported raw materials and commodities, and increases in tax and other government charges. Since wage inflation possesses such a central position in the determination of the rate of increase in prices, the need for 'incomes planning' becomes obvious. This planning should not only include representatives of organized labour, but also embrace and constrain the economic power that results from the administration of most industrial prices by the 'megacorps' and incorporate active participation by government agencies. In this way controlling inflation is both possible and important, however secondary to the prevention of unemployment it is. Furthermore, active labour market and manpower policies to encourage labour mobility which would enhance labour market adjustments for the unemployed are another important ingredient of Post Keynesian macroeconomic policies. An important prerequisite here is a firm commitment on the part of the government to tackle any unemployment which may exist. This commitment to full employment would have to be adhered to religiously by the economic policy makers, for otherwise the success of economic policies would be seriously jeopardized by the erosion of labour's support.

Interestingly enough, the socialization of investment element of the economic programme was one important leg of Keynes's (1936) argument on economic policy. His famous passage, so often quoted but worth repeating, is very apt in this context: 'a somewhat comprehensive socialisation of investment will prove the only means of securing an approximation to full employment; though this need not exclude all manner of compromises and of devices by which public authority will co-operate with private initiative' (p. 378). This passage, though, is not very clear as to what precisely Keynes meant by socialization of investment. For example, he did not mean 'State Socialism which would embrace most of the economic life of the community' (ibid.). Elsewhere, Keynes (1980) made the socialization of investment notion more explicit in the following observation:

> If two-thirds or three-quarters of total investment is carried out or can be influenced by public or semi-public bodies, a long-term programme of a stable character should be capable of reducing the potential range of fluctuations to

much narrower limits than formerly, when a smaller volume of investment was under public control and when even this part tended to follow, rather than correct, fluctuations of investment in the strictly private sector. (Keynes, 1980, p. 322).

It surely is true that the post-World War II era provides supportive cases for what Keynes was suggesting. Germany, Japan, Sweden and Austria are vivid examples of what is precisely meant here.

Keynes, therefore, saw socialization of investment as potentially able to fill the gap left by private investment as the result of pervasive uncertainties investors are faced with concerning future economic performance. Socialization of investment is thus seen by Keynes as a means of reducing uncertainty through the creation of a more stable economic environment. He recommends structural changes designed to improve the overall performance of the economy, rather than smoothing out the amplitude of business cycles. The problem with Keynes's proposal is that it does not explicitly include in the process of socialization of investment any trade union involvement. This, we argued above, is absolutely necessary for a successful attempt at socialization of investment.

There are, of course, a number of constraints associated with these economic policy prescriptions. There is the operation of transnational corporations and international financial centres. Left to their own devices they can impose, indeed they have imposed (the UK post-World War II experience is an excellent example in this context), considerable constraints on the implementation of the type of economic policies Post Keynesian analysis alludes to. So much so that it would be difficult, if not impossible, to imagine successful implementation of these types of policies by one country. It is, then, very important for governments to establish control over the operations of transnationals and financial centres. One may suggest at this juncture that policy makers should attempt to affect directly the sphere of regulation of international capital as well as trade flows. Such endeavour not only has the potential to handle these problems, but can also alleviate the balance of payments constraint.

Keynes (1980) proposed permanent capital controls, both inward and outward, to deal with situations when the international financiers become untamable. He also felt that the entire financial system should come under permanent control, and propounded the idea of planning to encapsulate the entire international system (see also, Hicks, 1985). A *transnational regulatory unit* with sufficient muscle should be given the responsibility to monitor and respond to the activities of transnationals. When multinationals become dominant in a particular sector of the economy, positive steps should be taken to discriminate in favour of domestic firms. For example, fiscal measures can be used to promote domestic rather than foreign investment. Concerted action by groups of countries may be another possibility. A very good example in this regard is coordination of economic policies within Europe, a point to which we return shortly.

Another potentially serious constraint to these types of economic policies is their heavy reliance on social cooperation and social consensus between labour, industry and the state. The argument made is that such a consensus is difficult to achieve. There are examples of countries where attempts at consensus have not always been successful (for example, the UK); equally, there are economies that have been conspicuously fortunate with such endeavours (typically Sweden). Furthermore, there is the proposition, and evidence, that increased worker participation in decision making is an important determinant of increases in productivity. So much so, that firms that adopt 'workers' participation' as a conscious policy experience better performances (in terms of sales, growth and profitability, as well as overall effectiveness) than similar firms that do not pursue policies of this type.

Finally, internationalization of both financial and industrial capital has imposed on individual countries further constraints in the implementation of economic policies. Developments of this nature, however, indicate that economic policies should have a better chance of success when they are explicitly and firmly 'internationalist'. A very good example in this regard is the proposed closer collaboration and coordination of macroeconomic policies amongst the member countries of the European Economic Community. This is an area in Post Keynesian economic policy analysis where further research is urgently required.

PHILIP ARESTIS

See also:
Cumulative Causation; Inflation; Kalecki, Michał; Keynes, John Maynard; Macroeconomic Policy (I); Realism, Philosophical; Regulation, Theory of Economic; Unemployment.

Bibliography
Hicks, J.R. (1985), 'Keynes and the World Economy', in F. Vicarelli (ed.), *Keynes's Relevance Today*, London: Macmillan.
Kalecki, M. (1943), 'Political Aspects of Full Employment', *Political Quarterly*, **14**, (4).
Keynes, J.M. (1936), *The General Theory of Employment, Interest and Money*, London: Macmillan.
Keynes, J.M. (1980), *Activities, 1940–46: Shaping the Post-War World: Employment*, Collected Writings, Vol. XXVII, London: Macmillan.

Macroeconomic Theory (I)

The emergence of macroeconomics, as distinctively different from micro-economics, dates from the publication of Keynes's *General Theory* in 1936. The older quantity theory of money is identifiably macroeconomic but it is no more than an aggregation of microeconomic behaviour designed to demonstrate that money is a 'veil' which, if tampered with by governments, will have adverse consequences in the fully informed, competitive market economy that is presumed to exist. At the other end of the political economy spectrum there is the older Marxian economic tradition, which is also identifiably macroeconomic, but part of a wider distributional theory of social dynamics which also contains political and sociological features.

Keynes's *General Theory* remains the initial point of reference in modern macroeconomic theory. This is true of all schools of macroeconomic thought (see Dow, 1985). Keynes created macroeconomics as a specialism dedicated to the formulation of policy. The circular flow model which Keynes developed was cast in historical time, the context within which policy action must take place. The principle of effective demand is a historical principle and, as such, it was possible for it to be applied by schools with a wide range of theoretical preferences. Of course, each interprets the principle from the particular theoretical stance adopted, but there is little doubt that the postwar Keynesian consensus, concerning stabilization policy, which prevailed in the USA and many other countries, centred upon this principle.

Only those determined to exorcize historical time completely from their macroeconomics came to reject the principle and the results of their endeavours are difficult to label as macroeconomics in the sense that we have defined it. New classical 'macroeconomics', like its non-stochastic classical ancestor, is a timeless aggregation of microeconomic theory, usually employing the device of the representative agent. As such, it cannot address actual macroeconomic policy questions in any direct way. Indeed, the weight of new classical policy advice amounts to non-intervention. In effect, an economic policy dimension is absent; a legal or constitutional design dimension is present, but it is unsupported by any scientific evidence.

Keynes helped create the field of macroeconomics by infusing historical time into economic theory to allow questions regarding policy to be dealt with. The theoretical advance which this constituted was not readily appreciated, even by those 'Keynesians' who seemed to support the stabilization policy case. Attempts by, for example, James Duesenberry (1949) to build relativistic and Veblen-inspired microfoundations for the consumption function were to be rejected in favour of a neoclassical alternative in postwar mainstream macroeconomics. There was a 'revolution' in macroeconomics but none in microeconomics. Only institutionalists seemed to appreciate fully Keynes's organic vision of the economy. In particular, W.C. Mitchell, at the US National Bureau of Economic Research, pioneered the classification, collection and analysis of macroeconomic time series data to provide an empirical dimension to Keynesian macroeconomic theory and policy application.

The identification of macroeconomics with policy and microeconomics with theory led to the gradual dismissal of Keynes's theoretical contribution to economics, much to the disgust of Post Keynesians, such as Joan Robinson, and perceptive neo-Austrians, such as George Shackle. However, this may have been partly owing to Keynes's eagerness to persuade. He was advised by, for example, Roy Harrod to allow certain aspects of classical economic theory to enter the *General Theory* to offer a bridge over which wavering classical economists could cross to reach the new field of stabilization policy. This Keynes was happy to do, provided that minimal damage was done to his central thesis. He resisted attempts by, for example, Dennis Robertson to persuade him to revise his fundamental position concerning the logic of operating in historical time. The treatment of uncertainty, the introduction of speculation and animal spirits, the emphasis on money as a pivotal institutional entity in the economic system and the insistence that macroeconomics could only deal with the short period, all followed logically in a historical time context and were non-negotiable.

One by one, the historical time aspects of the *General Theory* were chiselled away through the application of 'rigorous' microfoundations. Much of this chiselling was done by those under the banner of Keynesianism, James Tobin and Franco Modigliani being the most prominent examples. Gradually, the principle of effective demand was deprived of its connection with history and viewed, again by 'Keynesians', such as Don Patinkin, as merely about short-run disequilibrium in a Walrasian long-run general equilibrium context. Stripped of its theoretical novelty by the end of the 1960s, it was only a matter of time before the new classicists pressed their 'expectational' arguments, conducted in abstract time, to their logical conclusion.

By the 1980s, macroeconomic theory was in serious disarray. Battles were lost by Keynesians because they were fought upon the timeless territory of new classical logic. The weapons were increasingly mathematical and distant from the pragmatic arena of policy formulation. Historical time features, such as implicit and explicit contracts, the existence of moral hazard and information asymmetries struggled to have meaning when introduced by 'new' Keynesians in abstract time settings. Only when imperfect competition was assumed did new Keynesian arguments seem to stick. The new classical riposte was to point out that aggregation from imperfectly competitive microfoundations is impossible; therefore no coherent macroeconomic theory could be rigorously derived. Trained in formal reductionism, most new Keynesians found it difficult to rebut this argument. There were exceptions, the most notable being Arthur Okun, an applied macroeconomist with long experience in wrestling with policy in historical time. In Okun (1981) he began to reinstate the non-reductionist view of the macroeconomy as a system, emphasizing the significance of customs, conventions, contracts, legal arrangements, reputation and other features of the macroeconomy largely ignored in mainstream macroeconomics.

The institutionalist flavour of Okun's macroeconomics only began to percolate into macroeconomic theory towards the end of the 1980s, particularly in the work of Joseph Stiglitz and his co-authors. With little or no cross-referencing to previous institutionalist and Post Keynesian writings, the demand/supply dichotomy is questioned as universally applicable in dealing with economic coordination. In particular, money magnitudes are viewed as the outcome of the credit creation process which, in turn, is driven by banks which are seen as screening institutions in the face of uncertainty concerning the credibility of potential borrowers (Stiglitz and Weiss, 1988). Thus the focus is not limited to the analytics of imperfect competition (that is, game theory). The variety of institutional forms, necessitated by the manner in which uncertainty manifests itself in different economic settings, plays a key role in the macroeconomic theory developed.

Keynes was centrally concerned with incorporating historical time into the economics of his day; the new Keynesianism of Stiglitz and his co-authors is less concerned with the question of time, focusing, to a greater degree, upon the impact of specific institutional arrangements in general equilibrium macroeconomics. The question arises, as it does in the case of new institutionalist microeconomics, as to whether institutionalists have been offered a Trojan horse through which they can infiltrate the mainstream to precipitate a fundamental shift of approach.

Institutional economics is holistic in orientation, therefore the macroeconomic level of inquiry is legitimate in its own right. Unlike the reductionist stance of neoclassical economics, there is no necessity to have a strict correspondence between macroeconomic entities and individualistic microfoundations through mathematically tractable aggregation. Cultural norms, conventions, community allegiances, power concentrations and legal arrangements are recognized by institutionalists as holistic features of the economic landscape which yield coherent macroeconomic behaviour. The existence of time irreversibilities and associated deficiencies in knowledge ensure that individuals will subscribe to collective consciousness groupings which yield concrete institutionalized behaviour with macroeconomic coherence.

Unlike the Austrian School, who deny that macroeconomics constitutes a meaningful level of inquiry, institutionalists recognize time irreversibility in the bonds that individuals form when they pursue their best interests in a historical context. Routines, habits and commitments all yield institutional definiteness over time. Furthermore, the institutional economist, accepting this tendency of much of system bonding to be irreversible, takes explicit account of power relations in macroeconomic analysis, recognizing that tensions can be generated which can result in the non-linear disintegration of institutional bonding in particular historical epochs.

In the area of macroeconomics, there is considerable overlap between the institutionalists and the Post Keynesians. Institutionalists accept the principle of effective demand and the case for stabilization. Indeed, the 'New Deal' experiment was the outcome of institutionalist policy prescription even before the *General Theory* had become influential in the United States. The closeness of the two schools on macroeconomic issues in the 1930s is further emphasized in Keynes's admission, in correspondence, that John Commons was the American economist that he admired most. After World War II, this empathy in the area of macroeconomics strengthened, particularly in the prominent contributions of Gunnar Myrdal and John Kenneth Galbraith. Indeed, by the end of the 1960s, the latter was fighting televised debates in the United States with Milton Friedman, not as an institutionalist but as a Keynesian.

The Keynesianism espoused by Galbraith and most other institutionalists is far removed from bowdlerized Keynesianism. For example, there is very little overlap between the Keynesianism of Galbraith and that of James Tobin, despite the superficial resemblance of some of their policy recommendations. In dealing with the interface between the monetary system and the macroeconomy, institutionalists, like the Post Keynesians, have preferred the financial instability model of Hyman Minsky (1986) to the portfolio approach of Tobin. Both institutionalists (Dillard, 1987) and Post Keynesians (Davidson, 1978) view money as a fundamentally important institution, not just another financial asset with special risk characteristics. Both also see money as the 'endogenous' outcome of credit creation, which, in turn, is driven by institutionalized forces (Moore, 1988).

The centrality of the institution of money was emphasized in the early years of institutionalism by Veblen, who insisted that business enterprises are motivated to generate flows of money, not goods. Veblen's distinction of industrial and pecuniary flows is also highlighted by Keynes in his distinction between industry and finance in the *Treatise on Money*. In both, factors determining the volume of money used in financial circulation differ from those determining industrial circulation. Keynes went on, in the *General Theory*, to express this distinction in terms of the transactions/precautionary and speculative demand for money in order to address, directly, the inadequacy of the quantity theory of money as any basis for monetary policy.

With regard to the interest rate, once again, Veblen and Keynes concur. The rate of interest is viewed as a pure monetary phenomenon. Keynes (1937) made this clear when he argued that the rate of interest on money determines the marginal efficiency of capital, not the other way around. Veblen's (1934) similar position is expressed in his criticism of Irvine Fisher for attempting to use marginal utility as a non-monetary explanation of the rate of interest.

Can we say that institutionalism and Post Keynesianism are synonymous in the field of macroeconomics? The review of institutionalist macro-economics, by Peterson (1987), suggests that institutionalism has little to add, theoretically, to Post Keynesianism. Apart from the work of Keynes and institutionalist/Post Keynesians such as Minsky and Galbraith, there are few references to institutionalist macroeconomic theorists. There is a deliberate attempt to argue, more forcibly than Keynes, that macroeconomics is a policy science wherein theory is limited in its applicability. The institution-alist preference for proper treatments of history over the niceties of abstract theory is apparent. It is in this sense that institutionalists sometimes part company with Keynes. Indeed, some institutionalists have argued that Keynes is excessively 'psychologistic' in his approach (see Hodgson, 1988), leading them to accept only a very policy-oriented Keynesian perspective.

Foster (1989) argues that Keynes did espouse, to a considerable degree, the holistic, systemic vision of the macroeconomy favoured by institutional econo-mists. Keynes's advocacy of stabilization policy is itself viewed as an institu-tional adaptation to cope with evolutionary developments in capitalist econo-mies. What Keynes did was to recognize time irreversibility, following Marshall's lead, but not to the extent of institutionalists, whereby only history remains, or to the extent of demolishing all connection between history and theory, as the Austrians did. Instead, Keynes compromises by only theorizing about the historical short period which is rendered theoretically tractable by the existence of time irreversibility. Like Alfred Marshall, he viewed longer periods as evolutionary in character and beyond the compass of economic analysis, thus concurring with both Austrians and institutionalists.

In Foster (1987) an attempt is made to develop an evolutionary approach to macroeconomic theory in a more explicit manner than Keynes, building on insights drawn from institutional economics. Routinized behaviour is analytically separated from creative behaviour in a manner recognizable in institutional economics and macroscopic behaviour receives holistic priority over microscopic motives at the atomic level. Another recent example of evolutionary macroeconomics which extends the macrotheoretical frontiers of institutional economics is that of John Cornwall (1990). He provides theoretical analysis and econometric support for the view that stabilization policy actions not only influence performance but induce lasting institutional changes with macroeconomic repercussions. A clear evolutionary dimension is added to Keynes's short period theory which is analytical in an institutional, rather than a mechanical, sense. Modern time irreversibility concepts such as hysteresis and path dependence are given institutional meaning.

In conclusion, it has been argued that there is considerable overlap between the macroeconomics of Keynes and that of the institutionalists. However, institutionalists have hesitated, to a much greater extent than Post Keynesians, in operating at as high a level of theoretical abstraction, preferring to focus on questions of policy in economic history. Thus the institutionalists may have a much smaller role to play than Post Keynesians in contributing to new Keynesian attempts to embrace institutional diversity in macroeconomic theory. Nevertheless, if we view Keynes as being primarily preoccupied by the development of theoretical constructs in historical time, rather than with the detail of institutional diversity, it may be that institutionalists, with their abstract, but informal, concept of evolutionary processes in historical time, are better equipped to provide a fundamental advance in macroeconomics beyond the *General Theory*. Much depends upon institutionalists abandoning the strict separation of abstraction and history at the macroeconomic level of inquiry and following the lead of, for example, Kurt Dopfer (1986), who urges institutionalists to accept theoretical abstraction if it is 'in' history. In approving of Keynes's principle of effective demand, institutionalists have already taken this step, in an implicit sense, and are now well placed to offer a theoretical alternative to, rather than a critique of, neoclassical macroeconomics.

JOHN FOSTER

See also:

Atomism and Organicism; Consumer Behaviour; Econometrics, The Limits of; Kaldor, Nicholas; Kalecki, Michał; Keynes, John Maynard; Macroeconomic Policy; Macroeconomic Theory (II); Methodological Individualism; Mitchell, Wesley Clair; Monetary Theory; Part–Whole Relationships; Time.

Bibliography

Cornwall, J. (1990), *The Theory of Economic Breakdown*, Oxford: Blackwell.
Davidson, P. (1978), *Money and the Real World*, London: Macmillan.
Dillard, D. (1987), 'Money as an institution of capitalism', *Journal of Economic Issues*, **XXI**, pp. 1623–47.
Dopfer, K. (1986), 'The histonomic approach to economics: beyond pure theory and pure experience', *Journal of Economic Issues*, **XX**, pp. 989–1010.
Dow, S. (1985), *Macroeconomic Thought: A Methodological Approach*, Oxford: Blackwell.
Duesenberry, J.S. (1949), *Income, Saving and the Theory of Consumer Behaviour*, Cambridge, MA: Harvard University Press.
Foster, J. (1987), *Evolutionary Macroeconomics*, London: Allen & Unwin.
Foster, J. (1989), 'The macroeconomics of Keynes: an evolutionary perspective', in J. Pheby (ed.), *New Directions in Post Keynesian Economics*, Aldershot: Edward Elgar.
Hodgson, G. (1988), *Economics and Institutions*, Cambridge: Polity.
Keynes, J.M. (1930), *A Treatise on Money*, London: Macmillan.

Keynes, J.M. (1936), *The General Theory of Employment, Interest and Money*, London: Macmillan.
Keynes, J.M. (1937), 'The general theory of employment', *Quarterly Journal of Economics*, **51**, pp. 209–23.
Minsky, H.P. (1986), *Stabilising an Unstable Economy*, New Haven, Conn.: Yale University Press.
Moore, B. (1988), 'The endogenous money supply', *Journal of Post Keynesian Economics*, **10**, pp. 372–85.
Okun, A. (1981), *Prices and Quantities*, Oxford: Blackwell.
Peterson, W.C. (1987), 'Macroeconomic theory and policy in an institutionalist perspective', *Journal of Economic Issues*, **XXI**, pp. 1587–1620.
Stiglitz, J. and P. Weiss (1988), 'Banks as social accountants and screening devices for the allocation of credit', NBER Working Paper No. 2710.
Veblen, T. (1934), *Essays in Our Changing Order*, New York: Viking Press.

Macroeconomic Theory (II)

With the appearance of Keynes's *General Theory* in 1936, institutional economists found a kindred set of theoretical and policy ideas. However, Keynes's message has since been bowdlerized by orthodoxy, and the label 'Post Keynesian' has been applied to all those economists, including institutionalists, who wish to sustain and develop Keynes's ideas.

Since Keynes's book was presented as revolutionary, economists set about trying to identify the essential differences from received doctrine. John Hicks identified money and uncertainty, rather than the income multiplier, as the distinguishing features of Keynes's *General Theory*. He thus expressed his view of Keynes's contribution via the horizontal stretch of the LM curve, suggesting his own, 'more general', theory through the now familiar IS–LM schema set out in his 'Mr Keynes and the Classics: A Suggested Interpretation', which soon came to represent textbook 'Keynesian' economics.

Although Keynes objected to this rendition, Hicks's presentation had other drawbacks which were not present in Keynes's original approach. Following Keynes's provisional assumption, Hicks assumed rigid wages, thus eliminating the necessity of analysing the labour market. In a 1944 article, Franco Modigliani argued that it was the assumption of rigid wages, not money and uncertainty, that explained unemployment. This shifted attention from money and uncertainty to imperfections in labour markets. When inflation appeared in the 1960s, economists noted the lack of product prices in Hicks's original model. This was due to the use of the price of consumption goods as the *numéraire*; a technical feature of the model was thus remedied by grafting the Phillips curve and a pricing equation onto IS–LM to produce an explanation of prices. When the petroleum crisis dominated attention in the 1970s, IS–LM was criticized by 'supply-side' economists for the absence of any explanation of 'supply shocks'. To meet this criticism, Pigou's 'real balance' effect was resurrected to generate an 'aggregate demand curve' linking output and the price level and an associated supply curve was produced from a transformed Phillips curve relation between prices and output via the addition of a production technology (usually a simple production function). The price level and real aggregate output were now determined by the intersection of both aggregate 'supply' and traditional demand factors, as in simple micro-theory.

Thus the modern 'Keynesian' model which confronted the rational expectations revolution relied on rigid wages, prices set by a mark-up over wage and other costs in non-competitive markets and a fixed money supply to explain unemployment as the result of inappropriate combinations of wages and prices or interest rates. The introduction of market clearing assumptions of the new macroeconomists into this model implied that any equilibrium short of full employment was due to an 'ad hoc' assumption of market failure. A group of 'new Keynesian' economists defended the assumptions of rigid wages, prices and interest rates, deriving them as the result of profit-maximizing behaviour by rational agents. No trace remains of the importance originally attached to money and expectations in Keynes's theory.

A small group of economists, known as 'Post Keynesians' (more extensive discussion may be found in the surveys of Davidson (1980), Eichner (1979), Kregel (1983) and Sawyer (1991)) attempted to preserve Hicks's initial insight, and Keynes's own oft-expressed belief that his theory was unique because it was a theory of a 'monetary production' economy. Their work is divided into those who developed the role of money and expectations, and those who concentrated on production.

One of the first points raised after publication of the *General Theory* was that investment expenditures not only generate current demand, they also produce future productive capacity which requires even greater demand in the future if it is to be operated profitably. This moved discussion from the short-period aspects of demand to the long-period problems of supply and production. Harrod and Domar first worked on this question, and were joined by Joan Robinson, Nicholas Kaldor, Richard Kahn and Luigi Pasinetti in the 1950s and 1960s to produce the first long-period Post Keynesian models of growth and distribution. Pasinetti extended his approach to include Leontief's inter-industry analysis and Sraffa's 'Production of Commodities By Means of Commodities' theory of prices of production, making input–output models, rather than production functions, the core of the Post Keynesian supply–price–production nexus.

Analysis of growth and distribution relied heavily on Kalecki's alternative approach to effective demand in which the ratio of prices to costs as given by imperfect competition determines the distribution of income between wages and profits, and thus effective demand, with the addition of the 'classical' savings assumptions that workers spend all their wages and capitalists spend all their profits on new investment goods. At about the same time, Josef Steindl was extending Kalecki's work to develop a theory of economic stagnation by noting that in the presence of technical progress large monopoly firms would earn profits in excess of their needs to invest to expand capacity, leading to an investment shortfall as all profits were not invested in new plant and equipment.

The relation between distribution, market power and technical progress is also at the centre of Paolo Sylos Labini's work in the 1960s, which starts from Sraffa's early critique of Marshallian price theory. In the United States, Sidney Weintraub was also working on similar aspects, developing Keynes's aggregate supply analysis from an entirely different basis from the aggregate supply curve grafted onto the IS–LM model in modern textbooks, building on Keynes's presumption that prices were primarily determined by production costs, in particular wages, via a mark-up of price over unit costs, and aggregate demand, determined primarily by households' consumption expenditures, also influenced by wages.

Analysis of the industrial structure of the modern economy is the basis of Alfred Eichner's 'megacorp', a 'bell-weather' industrial firm, which is not a short-term profit maximizer, but rather tries to ensure its long-run survival by consolidating and expanding market share through the introduction of new technology via investment. Megacorps set prices as a mark-up over costs to generate a cash flow or 'corporate levy' to finance the new investment required to allow the company to grow at a rate equal to the expansion of its own market. Eichner's approach blends the Sraffa–Sylos Labini–Weintraub concern with pricing and models of technical progress, growth and distribution developed by Pasinetti.

Post Keynesian economics thus developed a varied analysis of the supply, production and price formation process which was discovered to be conspicuously absent from Hicks's IS–LM version when the supply-side shocks and inflation disrupted the industrialized economies in the 1970s. At the same time, the attention of Post Keynesian economists returned to Keynes's original analysis of money and expectations. Paul Davidson has pointed out that the essence of Keynes's theory of effective demand was the use of money as an alternative store of value. Money, with a negligible rate of return, would be used for this purpose only if expectations of future conditions, in particular the prices of alternative stores of value, were uncertain. Since the purchasing power of money does not vary over time, holding it, to satisfy what Keynes called 'liquidity preference', could prevent losses from buying other durable assets whose prices and purchasing power could vary in an unpredictable way. Since the demand for money does not generate demand for output or labour to produce it, investment could be insufficient to achieve full employment if liquidity preference is excessive. It is not the rigidity of wages or prices, but rather the natural preference of households, firms and even banks, for liquidity in conditions of uncertainty over future conditions which explains unemployment. Davidson subsequently formalized this concept of uncertainty as that present in a 'non-ergodic' system where future values of variables cannot be predicted from a knowledge of past conditions. Increasing competition or price flexibility does nothing to diminish the impact of uncertainty on economic behaviour in non-ergodic conditions. On the other hand, most traditional Keynesian economists and new macroeconomists assuming rational expectations limit the scope of economic analysis exclusively to ergodic conditions where the factors necessary to explain the crucial importance of monetary factors are absent by definition.

Money's role in producing inherent instability is emphasized in Hyman Minsky's 'Financial Fragility Hypothesis'. The creation of money occurs when banks 'accept' debt issued by firms in exchange for deposit liabilities. In tranquil conditions, borrowers meet interest and principal payments without difficulty, encouraging banks to be more optimistic about firms' prospects and to increase lending. As confidence increases, balance sheets of both the non-financial firms and the banks become more highly leveraged, or 'fragile', for interest payments account for a higher proportion of their gross cash flows and any chance movement in demand or interest rates may exceed firms' margins of safety to produce a liquidity crisis or even insolvency. Banks adjust their liquidity premium on lending by charging higher interest rates and strengthening their balance sheets for future defaults by reducing lending. This leads to a collapse of asset prices, or 'debt deflation' in which the value of bank assets falls and firms try to increase sales of output and sell assets to meet financial commitments, all of which drives prices lower. For Minsky, a monetary economy is inherently cyclical. A reason why a Great Depression has not recurred is the rising proportion of government spending in GNP, setting an ever-increasing floor under aggregate demand. Stephen Rousseas, starting from the concept of velocity, provides a similar explanation in terms of a variable velocity of circulation model, and Fausto Vicarelli has noted that the analysis of economic instability is a constant throughout Keynes's published work.

Although capital and distribution theory did not deal with monetary factors directly, it did show the concept of a 'real rate of interest' determined by the marginal physical productivity of capital which lies at the heart of modern post-Wicksellian monetary theory to be without theoretical foundation. Keynes had already reached this conclusion when he indicated liquidity preference as the prime determinant of the money rate of interest. Indeed, Keynes suggested that his theory reversed the traditional concept of equilibrium in which money rates are driven to equality with the real rate; instead, it is the money rate that 'rules the roost'. Since money rates of interest are ratios of present and future prices, if liquidity preference determines interest rates it also determines intertemporal prices. Kenneth Boulding was among the first to suggest that liquidity preference was the basis of a theory of asset prices. Keynes discusses this in Chapter 17 of the *General Theory*, building on his previously enunciated interest rate parity theorem and Sraffa's concept of commodity rates of interest. His approach to prices thus links up with Sraffa's. Since changes in interest rates must reflect changes in asset prices relative to changes in expected returns to investing in capital goods, any increase in investment and related multiplier expansion in output due to lower interest rates must also represent a process of price adjustment. The present writer thus concludes that, alongside any income multiplier adjustment process, there must be a simultaneous price adjustment process in the Post Keynesian analysis of the process of economic expansion. Hicks's IS–LM model assumed a given money supply to generate the upward-sloping LM curve, and the exogeneity of money is one of the tenets of modern monetarism. This position was first criticized by Nicholas Kaldor, and Basil Moore argued that money was endogenous and could best be represented by a horizontal supply curve, rather than the usual vertical line of LM analysis. This means that the central bank sets the interest rate, which appears to contradict the determination of the interest rate by liquidity preference. Others such as Alain Parguez and Augusto Graziani have instead argued that it is the financing of all economic activity (and not only investment expenditures) via credit creation of the banking system which is the crucial aspect of monetary economy. Randall Wray has shown how this analysis of finance based on the circular flow of credit may be integrated with the endogenous money approach and the theory of liquidity preference. Current Post Keynesian theory recognizes the integrated nature of production and financing activities in determining supply and price relations within the theory of effective demand. Post Keynesian theory has thus expanded Keynes's original concerns to explain the possibility of sustained unemployment to deal with a wide range of economic problems. Since the behaviour of money and production, the main elements of Keynes's approach, cannot be analysed independently of specific social institutions and their process of change, much recent work has concentrated on topics which traditionally have been of concern to institutional and evolutionary economics.

JAN KREGEL

See also:

Boulding, Kenneth Ewart; Kaldor, Nicholas; Kalecki, Michał; Keynes, John Maynard; Macroeconomic Policy; Macroeconomic Theory (I); Monetary Theory; Pasinetti, Luigi L.; Robinson, Joan; Uncertainty.

Bibliography
Davidson, P. (1980), 'Post Keynesian Economics', *The Public Interest*, special issue.
Eichner, A. (ed.) (1979), *A Guide to Post Keynesian Economics*, Armonk, NY: M.E. Sharpe.
Kregel, J.A. (1983), 'Post-Keynesian Theory: An Overview', *The Journal of Economic Education*, **14**.
Sawyer, M. (1991), 'Post Keynesian Economics: The State of the Art', in W.L.M. Adriaansen and J.T.J.M. van der Linden (eds), *Post-Keynesian Thought in Perspective*, Gröningen: Wolters-Noordhoff.

Market, Institutionalist View of the

The traditional institutionalist view of the market process is characterized by the questioning of mainstream market theory along with some or all of its fundamental assumptions. Institutionalists seek to build a more realistic analysis of economic interactions based on empirical observation, historical or evolutionary understanding and anthropological and sociological insights. This is not to say that they have always avoided a tendency to drift back into equilibrium formulations. Reciprocally, the economists who call themselves the 'New Institutionalists' respond to real-world criticisms of neoclassical theory by amending and qualifying the traditional analyses instead of questioning the core of the theory. Lazonick's more radical work may not be so easily characterized (Lazonick, 1991).

The anthropological interest of the traditional institutionalists in ancient and primitive markets is encapsulated in the work produced under the leadership of Karl Polanyi. Institutions such as palace trade and silent trade were studied. In the great empires of antiquity, such as Egypt and Babylonia, goods were aggregated through tribute or taxation and then redistributed by administrative fiat. These systems of allocation were social or institutional structures, frequently with the formal purpose of the redistribution embedded in the institutional fabric of the society. There are even institutions, not discussed by Polanyi, where the apparently rational competitive forces of the market process are specifically circumvented by institutionalizing two-party exchange with the traders making hand signs under a cloth to protect the secrecy of their transaction. They thereby guarantee 'isolated exchange', even though it occurs in a market setting where each transaction could be influenced by a background of accessible information. This custom has been observed from East Africa to China (Lowry, 1987, p. 188). At the same time, many of the administrative structures that have accompanied exchange have contributed to the apparent integrity of the market process as a natural phenomenon.

In agrarian societies, variations in yield from region to region and from year to year are combined with variations in products based on cultural and regional variations in soil and climate. These characteristics of ethnic and physical regions lead to an unevenness in supply so that neighbours and neighbouring groups have had more of one thing and less of another than they wanted. Such surpluses have been either wasted, extorted or taxed and redistributed, or brought to religious festivals for sacrifice and/or consumption.

Some petty trade obviously occurred in the early Near Eastern empires with barter or weighed precious metals; however, ratios (such as three sheep equal one cow) appearing in early law codes were most likely equivalencies for purposes of paying taxes or settling fines. Where goods were brought into administrative centres by independent traders, they were commonly unpacked at a specific place, a central square or at the city gate, where they were examined, evaluated, weighed and tithed (10 per cent, sometimes only 5 per cent, and only 2 per cent at the port of Athens in its heyday: Andreades, 1933). Obviously, private buying and selling evolved at these market places with tax values and public weights and measures influential in shaping private exchanges, particularly when the tribute or taxing system supporting massive redistribution for military and palace projects was the dominant economic activity. The image of a semi-divine ruler–administrator redistributing goods as rations to soldiers, scribes, artisan slaves and other dependants on an orderly and measured basis contributes to an image of a rational system implicit in a redistributive process.

The Egyptian pharaohs even institutionalized the tradition of an annual accounting for officials, originally the stewards in charge of royal granaries. The formal inventory, made precise by the use of a great balance or scales, set the imagery for divine judgement and for judicial fairness (Brandon, 1969). It should be kept in mind that the equilibrium concept grew out of an administrative practice that was borrowed as a legal and commercial symbol of consistency and rationality.

From an analytical perspective, however, the concept of justice in exchange appears to have roots in a simple distributive technique that was institutionalized throughout the Near East and the Mediterranean Basin from very early times. The mythic form of this system is presented in Hesiod's account of Prometheus's division of a slaughtered ox with Zeus (Lowry, 1987, pp. 126 ff.; Lowry, 1991). Prometheus divided the meat and bones into two piles. Zeus then had the freedom to choose either pile. Both parties exercised a free choice in establishing the equality of the division, one as divider and one as chooser. Both endorsed the fairness of the division. One cannot claim injustice resulting from a voluntary act with accessible information. The logic of this institutionalized technique was transferred to the freely arranged exchange and supported the tradition of the natural or implicit justice of the market process. Nevertheless, even at the most primitive level, we find in Aesop's Fables wry commentaries on the role of power in the distribution of the game after the hunt. Using this very technique to divide the meat, a lion proceeded to claim all of it and dared the other participants to do anything about it. This gave rise to the expression, 'the lion's share'. Other exchange and redistribution systems such as 'guest-friendship', gift exchange and the potlatch ceremony illustrate systems of structured exchange and/or redistribution.

Throughout the ancient Greek and Roman world, the frequent regulation of prices on staples, such as subsistence goods for the poor, and the designation of market-places characterized the municipal system. This institutional heritage continued in the medieval Muslim and north European commercial cities. A good example of the administered market was the cattle market, instituted by statute in England during the Middle Ages. Cattle had to be sold at specified market towns on specified days. This created an information source for the peasants who were frequently selling to foreign buyers from across the Channel. It also served to control cattle theft since stolen cattle could be recognized by their owner at the market. Forestalling, that is, buying from peasants on the way to the market, was illegal (Holdsworth, 1924, vol.4, pp. 375–9). Such markets were administrative structures implemented with the purpose of rationalizing exchange. A legally framed *market arena* remained where informed individual choice was freely exercised. Modern graded feeder cattle markets organized by the US Department of Agriculture are in the same tradition. On the other hand, during the commercial and industrial upsurge of the Elizabethan and early Stewart reigns, patents and monopolies on trade innovations, organizations and technical improvements were granted for the good of the commonwealth, codified in 21 James I (1624) and persisting until the nineteenth century (Holdsworth, 1924, vol.4, pp. 300–3. A sixteenth-century illustration of a structured market process is the custom of auctions called 'sale by the candle'. Goods were presented for sale and a stub of a candle was lighted. The last bid that was called out before the candle flickered out took the goods at that price. The institution survives in the common saying, 'not worth the candle'.

Another more modern expression of a synthesized market is the primary legal status given to publicly recorded land titles, dating from the seventeenth and eighteenth centuries in the Anglo-American tradition. This legal intervention was necessary in order to create a definite legally ascertainable title that could be bought and sold. This was a precondition for the reallocations of land resources as feudal tenures gave way to alienable freehold estates at the dawn of capitalism. One now buys or sells 'record title' – a publicly defended right – rather than formally transferring physical possession of the land. The final step was the relatively modern requirement in the United States that tax stamps proportional to the price paid for land be affixed to the recorded deed, thus forcing price information into the public domain and providing the information base requisite for rational individual choice in the context of a more broadly accepted value system. (The significance of recorded titles was raised in a class lecture in 1944 by C.E. Ayres at the University of Texas.)

Wendell Gordon's analysis of the frustration of the market ideal in less developed economies deserves more attention than it has received. As Gordon points out, in the absence of political stability and legal security, short-run profit will be maximized. The short-run rationality in such a market setting leads to the exploitation of current supply, 'low volume', at a 'high unit price'. Such opportunism dampens any long-run productive or allocative response to market demand (Gordon, 1965).

Empirical evidence of enduring customary prices such as $1.00 per day for labour or 25 cents a dozen for eggs has led institutionalists to question the continuing rationality of the market process. In addition, the emergence of the corporate entity, a pseudo-person created by the law, gave rise to a power imbalance in negotiations in the market-place that belied the assumptions of equilibrating free choice supported by natural law. American economists such as Richard T. Ely, trained in the German Historical School, presumed that industry required restraining and shaping by law and custom to achieve publicly desired ends. John R. Commons, Ely's colleague at the University of Wisconsin in the 1920s and 1930s, formulated a general analytic structure to guide policy making, replacing formal neoclassical analysis. He generalized the market and the exchange process as *transactions* that took place in a setting circumscribed by sovereign authority, future considerations, material scarcity, considerations of efficiency, and working rules (laws and customs: Commons, 1934). These five elements offered no rigorous format for quantitatively specifying the character of any given transaction, so they could not compete with the pseudo-scientific rigour of equilibrium price theory. They did, however, provide a frame of reference for policy making and legislation.

By contrast, Thorstein Veblen formulated an image of the market process as a primitive world of predatory capitalists with power as the criterion of success. He developed an explanatory tension between the efficiency of technology and engineering, on the one hand, and the destructive power of monopoly and market manipulation, on the other. This latter element was derived from institutionalized power and anachronistic customs, tending to sabotage the potential efficiency of the production and distribution system. This friction between constructive scientific forces and destructive or capricious institutions has a rough parallelism to Karl Marx's formulation of the friction between the 'forces of production' (the material elements including labour power and technology) and the 'relations of production' (the legal and institutional structures that control and organize production). Both these formulations revive an age-old tradition in European thought of posing sets of paired opposites as polarized or equilibrating elements, but, in the case of Veblen and Marx, there is an implicit presumption that these oppositions are elements in a dynamic process of change and evolution towards 'a more technologically or materially efficient system.

Historically, the Egyptian tradition of a God–King–Administrator who could resurvey the fields after the Nile flood became Plato's 'Great Geometer' (the land measurer). This tradition of a controlling mathematically coherent super-entity was reinforced by the Stoics and, later, the Renaissance image of the state as a body politic with blood or the humours of the body symbolizing money circulating in an equilibrating homeostatic system. The culmination of these lines of thought in the eighteenth century developed a picture of a *natural market process*, *natural justice*, and *natural man* asserting *natural rights* that served rhetorically to neutralize the royal divine right that reinforced the administrative authority of the mercantilist system. The wedding of the exploding commercial and industrial activity of the eighteenth and nineteenth centuries with popular democratic upheavals underwrote a spurious parallelism between the free legislative body and the unregulated market process. This ideologically convenient parallelism ignored the pressure of subsistence in the labour and consumption choices of those living in the fabric of a modern society. Political rights are more volitional and comparable with the freedom of the self-sufficient peasant to buy or not buy luxury goods in a village market. This parallelism has even been extended in recent years to political arguments that the unregulated market process is the true repository of the democratic process and that it should replace decision making by democratically elected legislative bodies and public administrative agencies wherever possible.

At the same time, institutional economists, dating from the founding of the American Economic Association in 1885, have revived and reinstated many of the ancient caveats about the imbalance of power in transactions. The emergence of the legally created institution called the corporation has led to the questioning of the implicit justice and allocative rationality of bargains and choices among entities with disparate power. The nature of the corporate entity has been further investigated by institutionalists such as Gardiner Means, who found that corporate decision-making power had gravitated into the hands of management with interests that diverge from those of the profit-oriented stockholders (Samuels, 1990). The development of executive cliques with personal empire-building agendas alters the neoclassical premise of owner-managers seeking conventional profit maximization. When this is combined with the economic power to set prices – 'administered pricing' – and with other adjustments such as advertising and product differentiation, the corporation becomes the effective force in the economy, not an individual participant in a self-equilibrating market process.

Another facet of institutionalist market theory is John Kenneth Galbraith's theory of countervailing power in which the natural forces of political and economic evolution are pictured as evolving reciprocally so that, as the concentration of economic power grew in the corporate–industrial structure, government power over the economy and industrial labour unions evolved in response. This created a new institutional structure, an economy regulated by a self-equilibrating set of countervailing mega-forces that grew in response to one another. There is, however, an interventionist overtone to this picture, making adjustments in order to achieve 'workable competition' and a balance of forces in this mega-market of political economy.

The approach of institutionalist thinkers to the market is, in its broadest terms, twofold. First, there is a recognition that economic and political power are ultimately the true components of economic relationships. Second, institutionalists have a profound respect for human rationality when formally exercised through appropriate institutions which leads them to reject the mysticism of an alleged 'revealed rationality' ostensibly welling up from an economic anarchy of isolated transactions.

There is an extensive literature documenting the evolution of market-places and market structure in the municipal and national economies of Europe and the rest of the world. The legal and theoretical support for the market has roots in the 'divide and choose' structure that rationalized justice in distribution on the basis of voluntary choice. Combined with the symbolism of the balance or scales, appropriated from ancient traditions of justice and accountability, volition and equilibrium have provided the theoretical basis for mainstream market theory. Institutionalists find empirical evidence in modern economic life that brings this ideologically influenced theory of a just and rational market process into question. They reinforce this criticism with historical evidence that explains the evolution of contemporary ideas and practices.

S. TODD LOWRY

See also:

Administered Prices; Ayres, Clarence E.; Commons, John R.; Corporate Hegemony; Full Cost Pricing; Galbraith, John Kenneth; Hale, Robert Lee; Institutions; Law and Economics; Natural Selection, Economic Evolution and; Polanyi, Karl; Power; Property; Smith, Adam; Transaction; Veblen, Thorstein.

Bibliography

Andreades, A.M. (1933), *History of Greek Public Finance*, 2 vols, rev. edn, Cambridge, Mass.: Harvard University Press.

Brandon, S.G.F. (1969), 'The Weighing of the Soul', in J.M. Kitagawa and C.H. Long (eds), *Myths and Symbols: Studies in Honor of Mirced Eliade*, pp. 91–110, Chicago: University of Chicago Press.

Commons, J.R. (1934), *Institutional Economics*, London: Macmillan.

Galbraith, John Kenneth (1980), *American Capitalism: the concept of countervailing power*, White Plains, NY: M.E. Sharpe, first published 1956.

Gordon, W.C. (1965), *The Political Economy of Latin America*, New York: Columbia University Press.

Holdsworth, W.S. (1924), *A History of English Law*, vol. 4, Boston: Little Brown and Company.

Lazonick, W. (1991), *Business Organization and the Myth of the Market Economy*, Cambridge: Cambridge University Press.

Lowry, S.T. (1987), *The Archaeology of Economic Ideas: The Classical Greek Tradition*, Durham: Duke University Press.

Lowry, S.T. (1991), 'Distributive Economics and the Promethean Meat Division: Myth, Folklore and Legal Precedent', in Morris Silver (ed.), *Ancient Economy in Mythology: East & West*, pp. 45–55, Totowa, NJ: Rowman and Littlefield.

Polanyi, K., C.M. Arensberg and H.W. Pearson (eds) (1957), *Trade and Market in the Early Empires: Economies in History and Theory*, New York: Free Press.

Samuels, W.J. and S.G. Medema (1990), *Gardiner C. Means's Institutional and Post Keynesian Economics: An Interpretation and Assessment*, Armonk, NY: M.E. Sharpe.

Marshall, Alfred

Alfred Marshall was born in 1842 and died in 1924. He held the position of Professor of Political Economy in the University of Cambridge from 1885 to 1908. In 1890, he published his famous *Principles of Economics* that established him as a principal architect of neoclassical economics. He did not, however, forge his tools of analysis for the sole purpose of demonstrating how equilibrium prices are determined. His aims were broader. In the first place, Marshall strove to locate the causes of poverty. Secondly, he wished to prepare the requisite armament for attack on this scourge. He pursued the former goal by means of an inquiry into the nature and evolution of key institutions. The latter objective he sought to achieve through his construction of a box of analytical tools. Hence this box is perched, as it were, on top of a foundation composed of evolutionary and institutional ingredients.

Marshall's evolutionary point of view is based on a particular theory of human nature that supplied the conceptual framework within which he interpreted history and read institutional facts into current data. He constructed his theory of human nature through a synthesis of Benthamite psychology and Darwinian–Spencerian evolutionism. Marshall argued, therefore, that human nature is dichotomous in that it consists of a constant kernel that is surrounded by changing elements. The kernel, which Marshall conceptualized in Benthamite terms, constitutes the unchanging part of human nature because it contains man's instincts and innate propensities, such as intelligence, reasoning power, intellectual curiosity, a capacity to learn and to form habits, and a desire to acquire pleasure and avoid pain. The elements, on the other hand, Marshall cast in the mould of evolutionism. Hence he viewed these as generators of change in the *manner* in which the kernel's instincts manifest themselves. The elements effect such change in consequence of their absorption of experientally formed impressions of socioeconomic phenomena. Hence human nature is pliable.

The pliability of human nature constitutes the premier variable in Marshall's analysis of institutions. That is so for two reasons. In the first place, he argued that it is only through the invocation of behaviour-changing social forces that poverty can be ameliorated. Secondly, his empirical observations and his adopted behaviourism convinced him that institutions are social bodies of organized behaviour that are potentially mutable by virtue of the underlying pliability of human nature. Whether or not behaviour will change, however, depends upon the relative strength of two sets of customs with opposite signs, as it were.

One class of customs is static, whereas the other is dynamic. As static phenomena, customs have their origin in myths and legends of the past. Consequently, this type of customs and habits discourages any breach with institutionalized tradition. The dynamic customs are different. They are moulded in, and by, what Marshall called new activities: activities that have their origins in the intertwined processes of scientific discoveries and technological inventions. Scientific and technological advancement tends to reduce the impact of static customs and to foster the growth and influence of dynamic customs. That is to say, under the right circumstances, a progressive and dynamic behavioural element may be injected into the relevant institutions by technological progress. The circumstances may not always be right, however. Consequently, Marshall found that it might be necessary to subdue static customs and kindle dynamic customs by means of social engineering.

Upon a detailed survey of the institutional landscape, Marshall concluded that poverty was attributable to the interaction of four classes of perversely operating institutions: the institution of the state, educational institutions, monopoloid business institutions and the institution of the working-class family. Marshall located the root cause of poverty in the institution of the state which had been cajoled by politically powerful groups into coupling a policy of laissez-faire in business with a malignant neglect of public education.

Because of the inability of existing educational institutions to reach their youthful members, the working-class family has become *the* agency for the creation and perpetuation of poverty. Because of their own slender means and lack of education, working-class parents are unable to invest capital in the education and training of their children. Hence the education of each cohort of school-age children is broken off early in order to enable them to go to work and toil for meagre wages. The toil produces those stunted minds and coarse characters that Marshall viewed as the hallmarks of the working classes. He concluded, therefore, that, given the fact that the working men's habits are cast in a mould of grinding poverty and educational starvation, it is no wonder that their customs and world outlook are so rigidly static that they habitually accept their station in life as a preordained state.

What is the solution? Twofold, said Marshall: government control of private price administration and acceleration of the rate of public investment in human capital. Both proposals were linked to Marshall's evolutionism. Government control of business was necessary because, once initiated, growth of firms is organic and cannot be reversed. It is caused by dynamic advances in the knowledge of how to do things. The increasing returns that result from this process may, however, become the basis of those monopoloid powers that the managers' static habits induce them to pursue, powers that must be checked. Public investment in human capital must entail free access to education from elementary school to college and university. As a result, the working classes will be improved away, in the sense that their old, static customs and habits will be replaced by dynamic habits. They will therefore improve their productive efficiencies, enlarge their incomes, become wise consumers and knowledgeable of things beautiful and full of care for such things. In short, Marshall had a strong faith in the improvability of the institution of the working-class family because he believed that human beings are improvable. But social engineering had to be employed if the promised land were to be reached. Being an advocate of such an employment, Marshall labelled himself a socialist.

HANS E. JENSEN

See also:

Ayres, Clarence E.; Biology and Economics; Clark, John Maurice; Evolution, Theories of Economic; Neoclassical Microeconomic Theory, Critique of; Technical Change and Technological Regimes.

Bibliography
Economie Appliquée (1990), **43**, (1), a special issue devoted to a rediscovery of Alfred Marshall; nine of the 12 articles are in English.

Jensen, Hans E. (1991), 'Alfred Marshall on the Structural and Behavioral Properties of Social Institutions', *International Journal of Social Economics*, Winter.

Keynes, John Maynard (1925), 'Alfred Marshall, 1842–1924', in A.C. Pigou (ed.), *Memorials of Alfred Marshall*, London: Macmillan.

Reisman, David (1990), *Alfred Marshall's Mission*, London: Macmillan.

Review of Social Economy (1990), **48**, (4), December, a special issue, 'The Social Economics of Alfred Marshall'.

Thomas, Brinley (1991), 'Alfred Marshall on economic biology', *Review of Political Economy*, **3**, (1).

Marx, Karl

Marx was born in Trier in the Rhineland in 1818 and died in London in 1883. He is famous for his contribution to social science and for his revolutionary politics. Marx aimed to show that capitalism had inner contradictions, leading to its breakdown and supersession by another type of socio-economic system. In this sense Marx was a scientist, rather than a mere propagandist.

However, Marx argued that the task was not simply to study society but to change it. The change he had in mind would involve the emancipation of the working class and the creation of what he considered a classless society. In support of this view, Marx developed an economic theory, a philosophy of history and a theory of the state which constituted both an explication and diagnosis of capitalism and a prediction of the coming proletarian society as inevitable. In developing these ideas Marx treated society as progressing through a sequence of modes of production, from tribalism through antiquity and feudalism to the capitalism of the present and the communism of the future. However, contrary to popular myth, there is negligible detailed discussion of socialism or communism in Marx's work.

Instead, Marx devoted much of his life to the study of the workings of the capitalist economic system. His *Contribution to the Critique of Political Economy* and the first volume of *Capital* – his most important work – were first published in 1859 and 1867, respectively. At his death he left many manuscripts concerned with what today we would loosely call 'economics'. They include the *Economic and Philosophic Manuscripts of 1844*, the weighty *Grundrisse*, and the even longer *Theories of Surplus Value*. Whatever his faults and merits, Marx was a prolific economic theorist.

Marx's economic theory
Unlike many orthodox textbooks, Marx's work does not start with the illustrative example of Robinson Crusoe alone on his island, as a means of illuminating a general and ahistorical 'economic problem'. This procedure would ignore the social culture and institutions which mould the individual. Instead, Marx's economic analysis starts from the characteristic social relations of the capitalist mode of production. This is clear from the key words in the titles of the opening chapters of *Capital*: commodities, exchange, money, capital and labour power. Marx did not aim to write a text on economics which would be applicable to all economic systems. No such work, in his view, is possible. Instead, it is necessary to focus on a particular economic system and the particular relations and laws which governed its operation and evolution.

Marx uses the labour theory of value to generate a paradigmatic picture of capitalism as an exploitative system. Capital is regarded not simply as a thing, that is capital goods whose value is transferred to final products, but also a social relation. Under this social relation, workers are required to work hours longer than is necessary to repay the employer the value of their labour power. All non-labour income derives from the surplus value thus acquired by capital but produced by labour.

In addition to portraying capitalism as an exploitative system, Marx indicates that several inherent contradictions characterize the dynamics of capitalism, and these augur the demise of this epoch of world history. They principally concern the concentration of capital and the centralization of production, by which the capitalist system ironically socializes itself, and economic crises and cycles. Marx argued that one source of crisis is the falling rate of profit. The quest for super-profits leads to the substitution of capital for labour in production. But this in turn undermines the presumed source of profit in surplus value extracted from labour.

Parallel to the idea of exploitation is the concept of alienation. According to Marx's theory of alienation, under capitalism the individual is not permitted to realize his or her potential as a human being. One is alienated from society, from the commodities through which one lives, and even from oneself. Only in a classless society, it is argued, can the authentic human potential be realized.

Marx and evolution

It is well known that Karl Marx was impressed by Darwin's *Origin of Species*, although the idea that he went so far as to ask permission from Darwin to dedicate a volume of *Capital* to him turns out to be a myth. Marx mentions Darwin in a few places in *Capital*, but on close examination there is much in the Marxian theoretical system that is antagonistic to Darwinian evolutionary ideas. Marx did not assimilate Darwinian theory in his social science because there it was incompatible with the mechanistic *zeitgeist* and classical Newtonian world-view within which he was still entrapped. For instance, for Marx, the socioeconomic system moves from revolution towards the equilibrium of a classless society, in which the sources of fluctuations and struggle are eliminated. In contrast, when historical movement is made to proceed in terms of Darwin's biological principles it is impossible to predict the character and form of social change. On the basis of Darwinism, change would occur as chance variations; it would be unpredictable and lead to no predetermined goal. The idea of change resulting from a process of natural selection amongst a population of individual entities exhibiting great diversity and variety is markedly different from the conception of history as the clash of collectives engaged in class struggle.

In fact, the Marxian conception of history has more in common with evolution's Latin etymology as *evolvere*, or unrolling, than with Darwinian natural selection. With the supposed development from 'primitive' to 'full' communism there is precisely a suggestion of a revolving movement, returning to the original position but at a 'higher' level. Even more importantly, communism refers to a unified social order in a state of harmony. Not only is the basis and actuality of social struggle presumed to have disappeared, but also there is no variety in the forms of ownership and of productive institutions. It is assumed that under communism there is neither conflict between classes nor a diversity of material interests and socioeconomic forms. Arguably, a uniform, integrated and supposedly harmonious society would be very vulnerable to external shocks, such as natural disasters, or to major internal changes, such as those resulting from important developments in technology.

Another reflection of Marx's nineteenth-century and mechanistic outlook is his belief that post-capitalist economies could be administered and planned on a complete and comprehensive scale. According to this naive and rationalistic outlook, all the information necessary for such a task can in principle be gathered together and processed as if in a single human head. Marx's economics thus lacks sufficient regard to problems of decentralized information and tacit knowledge. There is a significant contrast here with the emphasis on uncertainty in the economics of John Maynard Keynes and the emphasis on habit and routine in the economics of Thorstein Veblen.

Socio-economic development

Resident in Marx's analyses are several fundamental tensions: for example, between his historical determinism, by which the revolution is inexorable, and his emphasis on revolutionary practice, by which the revolution must be motivated; between institutions comprehended as subsidiary to the mode of production and resistant to change, and institutions as the arena in which are developed the details of social life; and, more important theoretically, between deterministic and conditionistic interpretations of his philosophy and theory of history.

Marx's philosophy of history represents a combination of Hegelian dialectics, by which change takes place through the conflict of opposites, and materialism, by which is understood an emphasis on the forces of production as the driving force in the process of development. The mode of production is seen as the foundation of institutions (legal, political, religious, aesthetic, philosophical, ideological) and social life in general. Each mode of production gives rise to its particular institutional superstructure. As the forces of production develop, superstructural change lags, because parts of the old superstructure resist the forces of change. These conflicts are expressed in terms of class struggles: between the established and rising or progressive classes. Thus, to Marx, history is the history of class struggle.

Marx wrote in his Preface to *A Contribution to the Critique of Political Economy* that 'The mode of production in material life determines the general character of the social, political and spiritual processes of life. It is not the consciousness of men that determines their existence, but, on the contrary, their social existence determines their consciousness.' This wording needs to be read carefully: the mode of production is said to determine 'the general character' of the superstructure, which presumably leaves room for other factors and forces to determine institutional particulars. The important point, of course, is that human society with its institutions and structures is an artefact, subject to change, and the object of efforts at social reconstruction. This argument thus leads us to question all pretensions of the sanctity of existing institutions. It combines the transcendental force of the mode of production with the exercise of individual choice in the production and reproduction of individual and social life; and it thereby leads to considerations of both structure and agency in social change.

However, Thorstein Veblen (1919, p. 441) suggested that, whilst Marx saw the importance of human action, his assumed basis of its motivation reduced to the problematic notion of 'class interest'. This ignores the processes in which perceptions of circumstances are *interpreted* through 'habits of thought' into human purposes. Thus for Veblen, in contrast, motivation is more 'an outcome of habit and native propensity' than 'of calculated material interest'. Consequently, there is no reason 'for asserting *a priori* that the class interest of the working class will bring them to take a stand against the propertied class'.

State and revolution
Although Lenin was to elaborate and refine some particular clues left by Marx, Marx himself left no single or straightforward theory of the state. For instance, in some passages the state is seen as an instrument of class domination and exploitation, in others it is seen as a bearer or representation of general social relations. Both Marx and Lenin envisaged the 'withering away' of the state under communism. In a classless society, by definition, there would be no apparatus of class oppression, only the administrative machinery.

The theory of the state is, however, but one part of Marx's political theory. If 'political' refers to 'power', then for Marx the economy is a system of nominally private power under capitalism. Capitalism is a system in which is unleashed the will to power through money (capital accumulation), a system of economic rulership. The prime field of power relations is, accordingly, the production process. The activity of the state is only part of this; the

entire capitalist superstructure is a political, that is, power-ridden, phenomenon.

Marx predicted that the revolution could or would come about only when
the productive forces in advanced capitalist societies were propitious. The
irony is that not only have the advanced capitalist societies as yet failed to
undergo revolution but that Marxism has been a principal vehicle for the
export of Western, post-Enlightenment, even capitalist values – for example,
that more goods are better than less – to second and third world countries.
Hegel's cunning of history, or Smith and Ferguson's doctrine of unintended
and unforeseen consequences have thus entered Marx's dialectical, historical materialism.

Conclusion

Whilst Marx's economics has many limitations, these should not allow some
of the important insights to remain ignored. As long as Marx is regarded at
best as an irrelevance and at worst as a demon then there is no hope of
progress in economic science. It is necessary that Marx be discussed and
understood, before, it is hoped, he is transcended.

GEOFFREY M. HODGSON AND WARREN J. SAMUELS

See also:

Class, Social, in Institutional Economics; Cognition, Cultural and Institutional Influences on;
Corporate Concentration and Interdependence in Europe; Corporate Interdependence in the
United States; Culture; Determinism and Free Will; Evolution, Theories of Economic; Institu-
tional Economic Thought in Europe; Kalecki, Michał; Law and Economics; Part–Whole
Relationships; Power; Property; Régulation Theory, French; Schumpeter, Joseph Alois; So-
cial Change, Theory of; Spontaneous Order; Technical Change and Technological Regimes;
Technology, Theory of; Unemployment; Worker Participation.

Bibliography

Howard, M.C. and J.E. King (1985), *The Political Economy of Karl Marx*, 2nd edn, Harlow:
Longmans.
Jessop, R. (1982), *The Capitalist State*, Oxford: Martin Robertson.
Moore, S. (1980), *Marx on the Choice Between Socialism and Communism*, Cambridge,
Mass.: Harvard University Press.
Veblen, T.B. (1919), *The Place of Science in Modern Civilisation and Other Essays*, New
York: Huebsch; reprinted 1990 with a new introduction by W. J. Samuels, New Brunswick:
Transaction Publishers.

Means, Gardiner C.

Gardiner Coit Means (1896–1988) received his doctorate in economics from
Harvard in 1933 but never held a tenured academic position. Instead, from
1934 to 1941 he held government positions as economic advisor to the
secretary of agriculture; member of the Consumer Advisory Board of the

National Recovery Administration; director of the Industrial Section of the National Resources Committee; and fiscal analyst at the Bureau of the Budget. He was subsequently associated with the Committee for Economic Development and the Fund for the Republic. Means was by both temperament and treatment by others the consummate outsider. He developed ideas which were adversely received by mainstream economists because either they were incongruent with economic orthodoxy (for example, separation of ownership and control, and administered prices and inflexibility) or he drew more radical conclusions from ideas also developed, albeit with less radical implications or usages, by others (for example, the theory of the firm in relation to the market, and inflation control).

Means was the co-author, with Adolf A. Berle, Jr, of *The Modern Corporation and Private Property* (1932), one of the most seminal and widely cited books of the twentieth century. Berle and Means developed several themes which for them, and for many others, especially institutionalists and Post Keynesians, but not for the neoclassical mainstream of economic writers, defined a revolution in the organization and control, and thereby the fundamental nature, of the American economy in the twentieth century. They argued that the corporation, especially the giant national corporation, had become the principal institutional device by which economic life was organized and controlled. They documented the growth both of size and of market concentration of a relative handful of industrial corporations. Within the modern corporation they documented the dispersion of stock ownership and the separation of ownership and control, such that corporate management was a largely self-perpetuating group substantially independent of historic control by equity owners.

Berle and Means concluded that the economy of the United States was not the historic system of small individual enterprise but a corporate system; it was a system of power in which the modern corporation was for practical purposes an institution of private government. For Means especially, the economic system had been fundamentally transformed in its structure, its microeconomic and macroeconomic operation and performance, and its processes of economic adjustment, but, for both authors, the most fundamental transformation resided in the economy's most fundamental institution: private property. For them, the rise of the corporation, the diffusion of stock ownership and the separation of ownership and control meant that a most important species of property had become diametrically changed. Ownership is mainly passive; control of property is exercised by others: the market at times, often by law, and usually by corporate management – who in theory but not in practice are nominal agents. Berle and Means did not hesitate to point out that the imagery and theory of traditional property and of economic individualism were being used to define – really to obfuscate – and legitimize the new corporate system with its passive property and managerialism.

On the basis of these early insights, Means developed his doctrine of administered prices which explained the microeconomic and macroeconomic functioning of a corporate economy. He argued that prices were not a simple function of market demand and supply relationships but were administered by corporate management. This theme constituted a major starting-point for Means's proposed revisions to both microeconomics and macroeconomics. In microeconomics, recognition of administered prices would change the predominance given to both markets and the price mechanism in orthodox theory, including economists' conception of the price adjustment process. It would also emphasize that the administration of prices is part of a larger matrix of decisions governing when market allocation is to be replaced by corporate administrative decisions, that is by private governance rather than by market forces.

In macroeconomics, recognition of the importance of administered prices would alter the theory of the business cycle and the theory of inflation and account for stagflation. Means argued that in the modern corporate economy both the market price and the administered price sectors exist and are inter-dependent, thus preventing the coordination of economic activity solely through price adjustments. That is, if a balanced economy with a balanced structure of market and administered prices suffered a decline in aggregate demand, the immediate result would be an unbalancing of both the economy and the price structure. On the one hand, prices in the market sector would decline, thus maintaining its production and employment while production and employment in the administered price sector would decline in the face of relatively stable administered prices. Because of this asymmetrical response, the level of economic activity for the economy would decline further owing to the decline in demand caused by the existence of unemployed workers combined with relatively stable administered prices. An increase in aggregate demand at this point would, conversely, raise market prices, thus bringing the price structure back into balance and increasing production in the administered price sector. Means's disagreement with John Maynard Keynes, some of whose other ideas were congruent with his, for example the problematic *ex ante* equality of saving and investment, centred on the latter's apparent unwillingness to accept price inflexibility as a key factor in the generation of 'equilibria' at less than full employment.

Inflation, for Means, was neither a monetary nor an effective demand phenomenon solely, but was increasingly a result of administrative decisions which had an inflationary bias, a source largely beyond the effective control of conventional monetary and fiscal policy. Stagflation was due to a perverse managerial response to declining demand: an increase in prices, in search of

maintaining cash flow, coupled with a reduction in output, the former constituting inflation and the latter associated with increasing unemployment, the
two constituting the essence of stagflation.

Because of the fundamental threat they posed, Means's leading ideas were
rejected by most orthodox economists. His attractiveness to institutionalists
and Post Keynesians, however, was due precisely to these ideas.

FREDERIC S. LEE AND WARREN J. SAMUELS

See also:

Administered Prices; Corporate Concentration and Interdependence in Europe; Corporate
Hegemony; Corporate Performance; Firm, Theory of the; Full Cost Pricing; Inflation; Keynes,
John Maynard.

Bibliography

Bonbright, James and Gardiner C. Means (1932), *The Holding Company*, New York: McGraw-
Hill.
Lee, Frederic S. (1990), '*The Modern Corporation* and Gardiner Means's Critique of Neo-
classical Economics', *Journal of Economic Issues*, **XXIV**, September, pp. 673–93.
Lee, Frederic S. and Warren J. Samuels (eds) (1991), *The Heterodox Economics of Gardiner
C. Means: A Collection*, Armonk, NY: M.E. Sharpe.
Means, Gardiner C. (1962), *The Corporate Revolution in America*, New York: The Crowell-
Collier Press.
Samuels, Warren J. and Steven G. Medema (1990), *Gardiner C. Means: Institutionalist and
Post Keynesian*, Armonk, NY: M.E. Sharpe.

Methodological Individualism

'Methodological individualism' is a phrase used much more often than it is
clearly defined. Frequently it is confused with political individualism or
ontological individualism. Political individualism involves statements about
individual rights, about respecting individual liberty, and so on. Ontological
individualism involves propositions like 'society is composed of (nothing
but) individuals'. Neither of these statements is equivalent to methodological individualism, which above all must be about *explanations* of socioeconomic phenomena.

Joseph Schumpeter is alleged to have been the first to coin the term
'methodological individualism', in *Das Wesen und der Hauptinhalt der
theoretischen Nationalökonomie*, published in 1908. The economists that
have given it the most explicit methodological prominence are the Austrian
School, particularly Ludwig von Mises (1949). Orthodox economists have
often proclaimed adherence to the term, along with a so-called 'rational
choice Marxism' which employs neoclassical theoretical tools. A clear definition of methodological individualism is provided by the 'rational choice
Marxist' Jon Elster, who defines it as 'the doctrine that all social phenomena

(their structure and their change) are in principle explicable only in terms of individuals – their properties, goals, and beliefs' (Elster, 1982, p. 453). This clear definition is quite adequate for our purposes, and is consistent with the classic statement and discussion of methodological individualism by von Mises (1949). Note the unqualified key words 'all' and 'only', and the appropriate focus on explanation in the cited definition.

The obverse methodological position could be described as 'methodological holism' and it would amount to the proposition that all social phenomena are explicable only in terms of social structures, social institutions or social culture. In the case of methodological individualism, explanation reduces to the exclusive matter of the individual parts; in the case of methodological holism, explanation reduces to the exclusive matter of the social whole. Both of these are thereby *reductionist* positions. It will be suggested below, however, that there are non-reductionist alternatives to both methodological individualism and methodological holism.

Hence methodological individualists in a sense take the individual 'for granted'. The individual, along with his or her assumed behavioural characteristics, is taken as the elemental building block in the theory of the social or economic system. As Steven Lukes (1973, p. 73) puts it, 'individuals are pictured abstractly as given, with given interests, wants, purposes, needs, etc.'. Clearly, assumptions of this type are typical of neoclassical economics, as well as of the 'new institutionalism'.

Individuals and explanation

The obvious question to be raised is the legitimacy of stopping short at the individual in the process of explanation. If individuals are affected by their circumstances, then why not in turn attempt to explain the very causes of individual 'goals and beliefs'? Why should the process of scientific enquiry be arrested as soon as the individual is reached? Several methodological individualists, particularly from the Austrian School, have devised arguments to suggest why explanation can or should stop with the individual. Friedrich Hayek (1948, p. 67), for instance, has argued that if 'conscious action can be "explained", this is a task for psychology but not for economics ... or any other social science'. This argument rests on a dogmatic statement that economists and other social scientists should not concern themselves with 'psychology' and explanations of purpose and preference. There are a number of points to be raised here, some relating to the question of psychology. The idea that such explanations, if pursued, have to be couched in purely psychological terms is called 'psychologism' and is rebutted by Sir Karl Popper and others. Second, it is impossible to exclude psychology – especially social psychology – from the domain of social science. In fact, Hayek suggests a questionable division between social sciences and sciences which are more immediately related to natural phenomena: a dubiously hermetic division between the natural and social world.

However, the most important objection to Hayek's statement is that it involves a dogmatic and over-restrictive conception of the domain of the social sciences. It amounts to saying that we should not try to explain individual preferences and purposes simply because such explanations are deemed to be outside social science. All alternative conceptions of the disciplinary domain are thus dismissed. Similar dogmatism is expressed in the oft-repeated statement by orthodox economists that tastes and preferences are not the *explananda* of economics. This is equally intolerant of alternative perspectives of the nature and boundaries of this discipline.

A more sophisticated defence of the view that explanations have to stop at the level of the individual is supplied by Ludwig Lachmann and the Austrian-inspired Post Keynesian theorist G.L.S. Shackle. In a series of works they stress the uncaused nature of imagination and expectation and the indeterminacy of the economic process. They proclaim the essential indeterminacy of human decision making: of individual decision and action as a first or uncaused cause. In arguing that the forces moulding expectation and decision cannot be explained at all, the Lachmann–Shackle position is different from that of Hayek, who suggests that they could possibly be explained by psychology but it would not be legitimate to do so, and from that of neoclassical theorists, who give a limited 'explanation' of behaviour by reference to all-determining and exogenous preference functions.

The assertion of the possibility of an uncaused cause is no more dogmatic than the suggestion that an event is caused. Neither the existence nor the absence of a cause can be proved. Indeed, the idea of an uncaused cause at the level of the individual may be necessary to sustain a notion of free will. The possibility of such uncaused causes can be admitted. However, the full defence of methodological individualism has to go further than this. It has to be proposed that *all* human preferences or purposes are entirely uncaused and unmoulded. If, on the contrary, it is admitted that some human goals and desires can be caused or moulded by circumstances, then the attempt to explain *those* preferences or purposes cannot be excluded by the Lachmann–Shackle argument.

In sum, the methodological individualists have provided us with no good reason why explanations of social phenomena should stop short with the individual. There is no good reason to exclude the idea that at least some human intentions have causes which are worthy of investigation. It will now be explained why the above conclusion is fatal for methodological individualism, at least as the term is defined above.

Influences on individuals

If there are determinate influences on individuals and goals then these are worthy of explanation. In turn, the explanation of them may be in terms of other purposeful individuals. But where should the analysis stop? The purposes of an individual could be partly explained by relevant institutions, culture and so on. The latter, in their turn, would be partly explained in terms of other individuals. But these individual purposes and actions could then be partly explained by cultural and institutional factors, and so on, indefinitely.

We are involved in an apparently infinite regress, similar to the puzzle, 'which came first, the chicken or the egg?' Such an analysis never reaches an end point. It is simply arbitrary to stop at one particular stage in the explanation and say 'it is all reducible to individuals' just as much as to say 'it is all social and institutional'. As Robert Nozick (1977) remarks in a critique of methodological individualism: 'In this apparent chicken and egg situation, why aren't we equally methodological institutionalists?' The key point is that, in this infinite regress, neither individual nor social factors have legitimate explanatory primacy. The idea that all explanations have to be in terms of individuals is thus unfounded.

Conclusion

Methodological individualism implies a rigid and dogmatic compartmentalization of study. It may be legitimate in some limited types of analysis to take individuals as given and examine the consequences of the interactions of their activities. This type of analysis, whether it be called 'situational logic' or something else, has a place in social science. But it does not legitimate methodological individualism because this involves the further statement that *all* social explanations should be of this type. If methodological individualism is redefined to be 'the doctrine that it is legitimate to explain *some* social phenomena only in terms of individuals' then it is relatively harmless, if used with due modesty and care. But if so proposed then it must be carefully demarcated from the standard definitions of Elster, von Mises and others.

Despite the impression given by many adherents of methodological individualism, it is quite legitimate to deny that only purposes or actions of individuals are explanatory, whilst at the same time holding to individual rights and 'valuing their autonomy, their privacy and their self-development' (Lukes, 1973, p. 148). Hence critics of methodological individualism do not necessarily dismiss individualism of a political or ethical kind. Furthermore, methodological individualists, who inflate the causal role of the individual while pushing into the background the extent to which he or she is socially formed, have no exclusive claim to political virtue, or to theoretical integrity.

In theoretical terms, the rejection of methodological individualism opens up space for a non-atomistic and social conception of the individual. It may be argued that there are external influences moulding the purposes and actions of individuals, but that action is not entirely determined by them. The environment is influential but it does not completely determine either what the individual aims to do or what he or she may achieve. Versions of such a non-reductionist standpoint in which individuals both form and are formed by their social environment are developed elsewhere (Giddens, 1984; Hodgson, 1988; Lawson, 1985).

GEOFFREY M. HODGSON

See also:

Atomism and Organicism; Determinism and Free Will; Hayek, Friedrich A.; Institutionalism, 'Old' and 'New'; Part–Whole Relationships; Rational Actor Models; Schumpeter, Joseph Alois; Shackle, George Lennox Sharman.

Bibliography

Elster, J. (1982), 'Marxism, Functionalism and Game Theory', *Theory and Society*, **11**, (4), pp. 453–82.
Giddens, A. (1984), *The Constitution of Society: Outline of the Theory of Structuration*, Cambridge: Polity.
Hayek, F.A. (1948), *Individualism and Economic Order*, Chicago: University of Chicago Press.
Hodgson, G.M. (1988), *Economics and Institutions: A Manifesto for a Modern Institutional Economics*, Cambridge: Polity.
Lawson, A. (1985), 'Uncertainty and Economic Analysis', *The Economic Journal*, **95**, (4), December, pp. 909–27.
Lukes, S. (1973), *Individualism*, Oxford: Basil Blackwell.
Mises, L. von (1949), *Human Action: A Treatise on Economics*, London: William Hodge.
Nozick, R. (1977) 'On Austrian Methodology', *Synthese*, **36**, pp. 353–92.

Methodology

In philosophical discourses methodology is usually taken to denote the study of method, an activity concerned with the procedures and aims of a particular discipline, along with an enquiry into the manner in which the discipline is organized. In economics, especially in recent years, the term 'methodology' has been employed both in a narrower and in a broader sense than this. The narrow usage, prevalent especially amongst econometricians and other 'modellers', but which will not be considered further here, is merely a heading given to a brief statement of techniques applied in specific analyses. The second, broader, interpretation, adopted by most contributors to explicitly methodological texts, is essentially *philosophy of science* as applied, or as of concern, to economic issues (see, for example, Blaug, 1980; Caldwell, 1982, 1987, 1989, 1990; Hands, 1990; Hausman, 1989; Lawson and Pesaran,

1985; Mäki, 1990; Pheby, 1988; Tool and Samuels, 1989). This interpretation is wider than the study of method *per se* in that, among other things, it entails, or at least allows, an explicit attention to and elaboration of ontological issues – a questioning of the nature of being, of the object of analysis – an activity that is presupposed by, but which cannot be reduced to, the study of methods and procedures. Given the prevalence in economics of this broader interpretation, the terms 'methodology' and 'philosophy' will be used interchangeably below.

Why should economists bother with methodology so conceived? This is the question that is often asked (Caldwell, 1990; Hands, 1990; Mäki, 1990; Salanti, 1989). Essentially the task of methodology or philosophy is, in the manner of Locke, to act as an under-labourer for science. It cannot license any particular substantive theory. Instead, it serves as a ground-sweeping device, concerned, for example, with assessing claims to scientificity made by economists of whatever hue. The aim is to provide a set of perspectives on the nature of the economy and society and how to understand them. However, although it cannot support any particular substantive claim, and always remembering that methodological analysis is as corrigible as any other, the current state of malaise in economics is such that extensive ground clearing through explicit, sustained and informed methodological analysis and debate may be just what the subject most needs.

What, then, are the main perspectives so far provided or supported via methodological reasoning in economics, and their strengths and limitations? And what, currently, is the orientation that is most sustainable? More specifically, what are the traditionally prominent conceptions of social science found within economics and how, if at all, can recent methodological insights improve upon the perspectives they entail? With some stretching, the history of economic methodology so conceived, that is of philosophical discussions over all issues bearing upon the actual or ideal nature of economic analysis, has been dominated, at least until recently, by two broad traditions. The first, a naturalistic tradition, has viewed science as, actually or ideally, an activity grounded in positivist principles based ultimately on the Humean notion of laws and causality. This tradition within economics is typified by the project of econometrics (see Lawson, 1989b) but can be seen to underpin most orthodox substantive positions (amongst others). Even orthodox 'pure theorizing', to the extent that it constitutes substantive economics at all, is rooted in this tradition. Although the emphasis here is not always on the empirical, the deductivism on which it rests in turn presupposes a closure while any lack of immediate empirical content is sustained, when it is, only on a promissory note. Ultimately, the form of empirical assessment it does, and must, subscribe to places it firmly within the positivist camp. The second, a broadly anti-naturalist tradition, which can be referred to as subjectivist or hermeneutic, has by contrast asserted a radical distinction between the natural and social sciences stemming from presuppositions concerning corresponding differences in the nature of their subject matters. The lineage of this tradition is traceable back through Hayek, Weber and Dithey to the transcendental idealism of Kant, and is currently most prominent among modern Austrians and Shakelians (see, for example, Hayek, 1942).

The dominant naturalist tradition sees science as concerned to identify, or to test or to refute claims about, empirical invariances between discrete events or states of affairs and so on. This tradition is rooted in an essentially Humean dismissal of the possibility of any ontology of deeper structures, or account of being, and specifically in a denial that it is possible, rationally, to hold to an account of the independent existence of things or the operation of natural necessity. Instead, at least according to Hume as usually interpreted, all we have are impressions. Experiences of atomistic events and their conjunctions are consequently seen as exhausting our knowledge of nature.

From Hume onwards, then, natural science has been identified with the search for constant conjunctions of events – a conception which the dominant, positivist, tradition in economics (even where it accepts, unlike Hume, the reality of deeper structures and mechanisms that govern empirical phenomena) has taken over as the basis for social science (Bhaskar, 1978). In consequence, epistemological problems in positivist economics take such forms as the problem of induction, of how to reason from one experience to another, procedures for predictive testing and so on. In the econometrics realm, specifically, any methodological focus is almost exclusively upon the comparison of competing procedures for estimating the parameters of empirical regularities, or methods of comparing two or more such empirical relations (such as methods of nested and non-nested testing) and so on.

The contrasting hermeneutic tradition accepts much of the positivist account of natural science but, while noting the complete absence of universal empirical regularities of a significant kind in the social sphere, contends that social science is, or ought to be, concerned instead with such matters as the elucidation of meaning, the tracing of conceptual connections and constructing social wholes or collective entities out of individual opinions, beliefs and actions – matters which have no counterpart in the natural realm. The starting-point of the hermeneutic or subjectivist tradition is an emphasis upon the conceptual nature of social phenomena coupled with an insistence upon taking seriously the fact of human agency including choice. Its aim, as noted, has been a distinct anti-naturalistic science of economics. However, its presupposition that the natural sphere is subject to laws conforming to the Humean specification – its acceptance of the Humean conception of science – coupled with a recognition that such laws, if operative in the social sphere, would leave no space for human agency, have in consequence often encouraged a total voluntarism along with an impoverished role for social science.

Much of the history of the philosophy of economics, then, can be viewed as a kind of toing and froing between these basic conceptions, though with the positivist tradition usually the more dominant. However, recent developments in the philosophy of social science systematized under the heading of *realism* or, more accurately, *critical realism* (see Bhaskar, 1978, 1979, 1987; Lawson, 1989a, 1989b) and more consistent with the institutionalist writings of, say, Veblen, provide an alternative conception of economics as science – identifying problems with *both* the positivist and hermeneutic positions and providing a means for their transcendence. According to critical realism, the positivist tradition is correct to view all science (including economics) as unified in its essential method, and the hermeneutic tradition is correct to view science as differentiated in ways governed by, or specific to, its object. But just as critical realist and positivist conceptions of the shared essential method of science are drastically opposed, so significant differences between critical realist and hermeneutic conceptions are evident.

In viewing science as unified in its essential method, critical realism rejects the Humean view (shared by the positivist and hermeneutic traditions alike) that natural science is concerned with seeking out, or with testing claims formulated as, empirical regularities. According to critical realism the world, both natural and social, is, among other things, structured and open. It is structured in the sense that underlying manifest phenomena at any one level are deeper structures, powers, mechanisms and necessary relations and so on which govern them. It is open in the sense that manifest phenomena are typically governed by various countervailing mechanisms simultaneously, so that the deeper structures can rarely be directly 'read off'. According to critical realist analysis, then, science is unified in its essential movement from manifest phenomena, at any one level, to the deeper structures and relations that govern them, that is with retroductive (Hanson, 1958) or abductive (Peirce, 1867) reasoning (under the control of methods of analogy and metaphor, among others) and not merely with inductive and/or deductive inference. On this conception science is primarily concerned not with the flux of events at all but with identifying and understanding the necessary relations, mechanisms and so on that govern or condition it.

Now this particular realist perspective positivism can be seen to rest upon the illegitimate generalization and inadequate analysis of a special case – the closed system. This is a situation in which a non-empirical mechanism is physically isolated or insulated and thereby empirically identified. Typically, this case only arises in situations of experimental control. Critical realism of course can accommodate and, unlike positivism itself, explain this case too. But it is a case that is far from being essential to science or even generally available within the natural realm. And it is without any clear application whatsoever in the social sphere. Consequently, the whole positive project is found through realist argument to be largely beside the point for economic analysis.

If critical realism, as against hermeneuticism, conceives of science as unified in its essential method it shares with the hermeneutic tradition the understanding that economics, unlike natural science, deals with a pre-interpreted reality, a world already conceptualized by lay agents in their activities, and like that tradition it acknowledges the epistemological consequences of this. But, while accepting that social material is concept-dependent, critical realism parts company with the hermeneuticist/subjectivist tradition in insisting that social material is not exhausted by its conceptual component. Critical realism also recognizes that social reality exists intransitively, being both social and yet inadequately conceptualized by lay agents, and thus prone to rational conceptual critique. Critical realism, then, views economics as potentially revealing just like any other science, being concerned to identify the unacknowledged (in part material) conditions, tacit skills and unconscious motivations that are necessary for some activity to take place, as well as the unintended consequences of such activity. And, being potentially revelatory, it also lays the basis for emancipatory development, rather than the mere amelioration of states of affairs.

In sum, methodology is essentially an under-labourer for economic science, being concerned to sweep away existing debris through elucidating a set of perspectives on the nature of the social world and on how to understand it. In this sense methodology, or philosophy, or meta-theory – wherein critical realism appears currently to be the most sustainable position – can certainly make a difference to the conduct of economic science, always remembering, of course, that it constitutes at most a necessary (and never a sufficient) condition for enlightened change and development.

TONY LAWSON

See also:
Econometrics, The Limits of; Methodological Individualism; Peirce, Charles Sanders; Realism, Philosophical; Veblen, Thorstein.

Bibliography
Bhaskar, R. (1978), *A Realist Theory of Science*, Brighton: Harvester.
Bhaskar, R. (1979), *The Possibility of Naturalism: A Philosophical Critique of the Contemporary Human Sciences*, Brighton: Harvester.
Bhaskar, R. (1987), *Scientific Realism and Human Emancipation*, London: Verso.
Blaug, M. (1980), *The Methodology of Economics*, Cambridge; Cambridge University Press.
Caldwell, B. (1982), *Beyond Positivism. Economic Methodology in the 20th Century*, London: Allen & Unwin.
Caldwell, B. (1987), 'Methodological diversity in economics', *Research in the History of Economic Thought and Methodology*, **5**, pp. 207–39.

Caldwell, B. (1989), 'The trend of methodological thinking', *Ricerche Economiche*, **43**, pp. 8–20.

Caldwell, B. (1990), 'Does methodology matter? How should it be practised?', *Finnish Economic Papers*, **3**, (1), Spring, pp. 64–71.

Hands, D.W. (1990), 'Thirteen theses on progress in economic methodology', *Finnish Economic Papers*, **3**, (1), Spring, pp. 72–6.

Hanson, N.R. (1958), *Patterns of Discovery: An Inquiry into the Conceptual Foundations of Science*, Cambridge: Cambridge University Press.

Hausman, D. (1989), 'Economic methodology in a nutshell', *Journal of Economic Perspectives*, **3**, pp. 115–27.

Hayek, F.A. (1942), 'Scientism and the Study of Society', *Economica*, August; reprinted 1952 (slightly revised) in *The Counter Revolution of Science: Studies in the abuse of reason*, Glencoe, Ill.: The Free Press.

Lawson, T. (1989a), 'Abstraction, Tendencies and Stylised Facts: a realist approach to economic analysis', *Cambridge Journal of Economics*, **13**, (1) March, pp. 59–78; reprinted 1989 in T. Lawson, G. Palma and J. Sender (eds), *Kaldor's Political Economy*, London and San Diego: Academic Press.

Lawson, T. (1989b), 'Realism and Instrumentalism in the Development of Econometrics', *Oxford Economic Papers*, **41**, (1), pp. 236–58; reprinted 1990 in N. De Marchi and C. Gilbert (eds), *The History and Methodology of Econometrics*, Oxford: Oxford University Press.

Lawson, T. and M.H. Pesaran (1985), *Keynes Economics: Methodological Issues*, London and Sydney: Croom Helm.

Mäki, U. (1990), 'Methodology of Economics: Complaints and Guidelines', *Finnish Economic Papers*, **3**, (1), Spring, pp. 77–84.

Peirce, C.S. (1867), in C. Hartshorne and P. Weiss (eds), *Collected Papers of Charles Sanders Peirce*, Cambridge Mass.: Harvard University Press.

Pheby, J. (1988), *Methodology and Economics: A Critical Introduction*, London: Macmillan.

Salanti, A. (1989), 'Recent work in economic methodology: Much ado about what?' *Ricerche Economiche*, **43**, pp. 21–39.

Tool, M.R. and W. Samuels (eds) (1989), *The Methodology of Economic Thought*, New Brunswick: Transaction Publishers.

Microfoundations of Macroeconomic Competitiveness

The intuitive notion of 'competition' held by most historians and business-men alike refers to an uncertainty-ridden process which mobilizes individual or organizational problem-solving capabilities, checked by some interaction that establishes rewards and penalties on individual behaviours. The idea of competition as a process full of discoveries, mistakes and differential rewards closely relates to an equally intuitive notion of *competitiveness* ('firm A is more competitive than firm B'). In turn, both of these concepts of 'competition' and 'competitiveness' imply microeconomic *heterogeneity*. The latter might concern (a) some organizational traits of firms; (b) behaviours and strategies; (c) production technologies and efficiencies; (d) product characteristics; and (e) realized economic results, such as profitability or market shares.

Evidence on all these indicators of microeconomic diversity is extremely abundant, albeit often messy and theoretically unstructured. In fact, a good deal of business economics rests on taxonomical interpretations of corporate diversities, the derived normative implications and also the private appro- priation of the related inferential procedures (otherwise little money would be available there for consultants!). Moreover, applied industrial economics highlights plenty of examples of heterogeneous behaviours and perform- ances which often appear to be quite persistent over time (on these points, see, for example, Porter, 1990; Rumelt, 1974; Mueller, 1990). Finally, at least equally striking inter-firm diversities concern corporate attitudes to- wards innovation/imitation, the degrees of success in doing so, and the correlated economic payoffs (Freeman 1982).

Do these micro diversities carry aggregate implications, in the sense that they influence the dynamics of aggregate variables such as GDP and average productivity? Moreover, even if they do, can one extend the notion of 'com- petitiveness' to composite aggregates such as countries? In the economic literature there are at least three broad analytical perspectives for which the answer to both questions is negative. First, one could consider the observa- tions on micro diversity as mere epiphenomena: in short, ephemeral 'disequilibrium' manifestations of an underlying process of convergence to some equilibrium defined by the 'fundamentals' of the economy (that is, given technologies, preferences and endowments). In one tradition of eco- nomic thought, such process – which, notably, is generally *postulated* al- though rarely studied explicitly – is assumed to be an unspecified selection dynamics acting upon heterogeneous micro traits and leading to equilibria which are, by assumption, independent from the distributions of the traits themselves. It is the so-called 'as if' view, put forward in the 1950s by Alchian and M. Friedman, among others, and more recently reappraised as a possible justification of equilibrium dynamics models.

Second, one can maintain a similar epiphenomenological view of micro diversity but place much more emphasis upon the powers of calculation and forecasting of individual agents in the interpretation of both the presence of heterogeneity and its purported aggregate irrelevance. For example, one can assume that the diversities that one observes in behaviours or profitabilities stem from errors of estimation – with the familiar statistical properties of independence and zero-mean of error distributions and so on – which do not carry aggregate implications since 'fundamentalist' equilibria are supported by some underlying learning process, again, mostly taken by assumption. The spirit of many rational expectation models-cum-representative agents comes within this perspective.

Third, one can attempt to rule out at least part of the evidence on micro heterogeneity by claiming that what one observes is in fact equilibrium realizations of strategic interactions (which would explain, for example, apparent diversities in innovativeness, non-instantaneous adoption of innovations and equilibrium diffusion paths, although it would not in general explain persistent asymmetries in productivities and profitabilities without further and rather ad hoc modelling assumptions on such matters as asymmetric information games). This is the thrust of a good number of efforts within 'new industrial organization' theories.

In fact, one need not subscribe to the whole evolutionary view of the economy to show that micro diversity does entail aggregate effects. In the last resort, it is enough to show that, even in otherwise quite orthodox models, micro diversity is not 'sterilized' or 'averaged out', either by market selection or by learning dynamics (say, via Bayesian learning or OLS estimations). Indeed, Winter's pathbreaking critique of 'as if' equilibrium models can be interpreted as a general argument on the possibility of multiple selection dynamics – holding the 'fundamentals' constant – dependent on the distributions of micro characters and behaviours (Winter, 1964). Suppose, for example, that we consider a world where both 'production possibility sets' and preferences do not change. One also has some invariant mechanism of market selection among heterogeneous firms (for example, based on differential profitabilities). Will that mechanism lead *in general* to equilibria independent from initial distributions of micro characteristics? Winter's compelling answer is that it does not: that is, specific micro distributions entail permanent aggregate effects. (Incidentally, note that the properties of selection processes in economic evolution still remain largely under-investigated topics.)

Much later, roughly from the 1980s, a similar story has become increasingly accepted in the economic profession, based on multiple equilibria stemming from either (or combinations) of (a) systematically different micro beliefs; (b) imperfect and asymmetric information; and (c) technological, informational or demand externalities. This broadly includes 'sunspots' equilibria, 'new Keynesian economics' and 'hysteresis' macro models: that is, by the time of the writing of this entry (1991), a good deal of macroeconomic literature except the most stubborn believers in the rationality-cum-equilibrium orthodoxy. (Relatedly, these perspectives of analysis have also become growing and respectable industries for articles and PhDs.) In brief, most learning dynamics, it is increasingly acknowledged, do not wither away micro diversities in initial beliefs and information partitions. Hence the nature and distributions of micro heterogeneity ought to become, in principle, integral parts of the interpretation of aggregate phenomena, including macro dynamics.

An 'evolutionary' perspective, of course, subscribes to this view and adds two further properties. First, it claims that micro diversities do not only entail permanent aggregate consequences, but also are a *necessary condition* for the innovative exploration of a rich and largely unknown set of innovative opportunities. Second, it has started analysing the processes through which diversity continuously emerges via innovative activities and at the same time it is permanently checked and selected by competitive interactions. In fact, one of the most general characteristics of evolutionary models is a diversity-driven dynamics (see Nelson and Winter, 1982; Eliasson, 1986; Chiaromonte and Dosi, 1992; Metcalfe, 1992; Silverberg, Dosi and Orsenigo, 1988; Allen's chapter in Dosi *et al.*, 1988). So, for example, Silverberg, Dosi and Orsenigo (1988) show that the paths and sometimes the very possibility of diffusion of innovation crucially depend on heterogeneous expectations, including some that turn out to be systematically 'wrong'. More generally, Chiaromonte and Dosi (1992) present a model whereby it is the heterogeneity in micro behaviours which sustains macro dynamics. Conversely, various processes of selection – which, *ceteris paribus*, tend to reduce micro diversity – have been studied. In particular, generalized Polya urns seem to provide quite robust representation of increasing-return processes whereby initially small advantages of, for example, particular technologies or behaviours or firms become self-reinforcing; extensions of the Fisher-Pry selection equation have been used to represent the dynamics of frequencies (for example, of market shares) driven by the dynamics of 'competitiveness' of heterogeneous interacting agents (see Arthur's and Silverberg's chapters in Dosi *et al.*, 1988). Clearly, both processes reduce diversity because they alter frequencies (or probabilities) of appearance of whatever micro trait as a function of their differential competitiveness. Needless to repeat, in an evolutionary perspective diversity is continuously recreated by innovative activities.

What has been said so far applies to the relationships between micro characteristics and some aggregate entities, say individual industries or whole economies. Can the arguments be extended to interacting economies? After all, statements like 'Britain has been steadily losing competitiveness'; 'Japan is showing a superior competitiveness' pertain to this level of analysis. Unfortunately, microfounded open-economy evolutionary models are still in their infancy and one can mainly suggest only conjectures and elements of a largely unexplored research agenda. Let us start from the following, rather impressionistic, definitions of national competitiveness:

> competitiveness is the expression of a global property (both micro and macroeconomic) specific to each national economy – the efficiency with which each country mobilizes its factorial resources and, in doing so, modifies the technical and social characteristics of industrial activity. At the same time, competition on the world market as a whole ... reveals the success of those national performances relative to each other. (Mistral, 1983, p. 2)

> The competitiveness of a national economy is more than the simple outcome of the collective 'average' competitiveness of its firms; there are many ways in

which the features and performance of a domestic economy, viewed as an entity with characteristics of its own, will in turn affect the competitiveness of the firms. (OECD, 1985, p. 6)

There are two parts to these statements. First the distribution of heterogeneous micro characteristics is not uniform across countries. Putting it the other way round, there is a *country specificity* in the form and the means of the distribution across national firms of features like technological capabilities of innovating and imitating. In Dosi, Pavitt and Soete (1990) it is argued that in fact such international asymmetries represent a fundamental source of *absolute advantages/disadvantages* of each country in each particular sector and of countries as a whole: that is, unequivocal technological gaps and leads. These advantages are 'absolute' in the sense that they do not involve any inter-sectoral intra-national comparison akin to those involved in more familiar comparative advantage measures (Germany has a comparative advantage in producing machine tools and a comparative disadvantage in producing bananas): rather, they simply involve comparisons across countries within particular lines of business (Germany is 'better' than England in machine tools) or for tradeables, in general. In turn, these absolute advantages/disadvantages – it is argued – determine, jointly with input prices, the average competitiveness of each national economy. Finally, the relative levels of nations competitiveness determine national market shares on domestic and foreign markets and their changes over time. (From a modelling point of view, it is straightforward to apply, for example, also at a country level, some variant of the Fisher-Pry selection dynamics mentioned earlier.) Indeed, econometric evidence of the link between technology-based competitiveness and export market shares appears to be quite robust (see Dosi, Pavitt and Soete, 1990, ch.6).

Second, the foregoing definitions of 'national competitiveness' entail some notion of country-specific externality: the levels and changes in the competitiveness of individual national firms are also influenced by the performances of all other firms in the system and their linkages with each other, in addition, of course, to extra-economic institutions, such as those shaping the educational system, the labour market, and so on. These country-specific externalities plausibly concern phenomena such as technological spillovers, non-traded information flows and idiosyncratic user–producer relationships (see Lundvall's chapter in Dosi *et al.*, 1988).

The microfoundations of national competitiveness also entail an organizational dimension. At the microeconomic level, this implies that, given any set of technological competences which a firm can master, particular organizational structures and strategies affect the actual efficiency that a firm displays, the rates and direction of accumulation of innovative knowledge and its competitiveness. At an aggregate level, the general conjecture is that the international distribution of such organizational structures and strategies is not random but reflects, too, some country-specific characteristics displaying persistence over time. Size distributions, degrees of diversification and vertical integration, propensity to invest abroad, and so on are obvious indicators, but at least equally important are the attitudes towards growth, profitability, the willingness to take risks, the nature of internal hierarchies, the relationship between industry and finance and the ways conflict is managed. The fundamental evolutionary point here is that country-specific organizational characteristics may reproduce over time despite the selective pressures of international competition (Cantwell, 1989). Indeed, economic history provides a rich set of examples of this phenomenon. For example, M-form types of corporate organization had only a limited diffusion outside the Anglo-Saxon world despite – so Alfred Chandler argues – their superior ability to manage complex multi-product activities at least in some industrial sectors (Chandler, 1990). More recently, Masahiko Aoki has analysed the organizational differences between an archetypical American firm and an equally archetypical Japanese firm, showing under a broad set of circumstances the higher learning efficiency of the latter (Aoki, 1988). Yet that type of organization remains largely confined to a single country. Moreover, in each country the organization of each industry maintains recognizable specificities: for example, even within the same sectors, Italy seems to rely more on relatively decentralized networks of firms than does, say, Germany or the United States, and this in turn affects the levels of Italian competitiveness and its sectoral distribution.

An evolutionary interpretation of these phenomena of persistence of country-specific microeconomic traits is the following. Environmental selection – in the form of differential economic performances – together with technological and organizational imitation tends to reduce the variety of both technological and organizational innovation that continuously emerge. However, the 'locality' of learning, the 'opaqueness' of the environment and the embeddedness of organizations within particular institutional contexts all contribute to the persistence of different forms of corporate and industrial organizations, even when *ex post* they lead to different competitive performances. Putting it another way: as one can easily generate multiple equilibria stemming from non-convexities and increasing returns, so one can easily conjecture multiple 'organizational trajectories' stemming from path dependencies in organizational learning about norms, competences and corporate structures.

In fact, one of the major tasks ahead for evolutionary analysis is a sort of taxonomical mapping between the nature of learning processes, the forms of market selection and the patterns of change in microeconomic organization.

It is also a major point of contact between evolutionary theories and theories of organization.

GIOVANNI DOSI

See also:
Corporate Interdependence in the United States; Evolution and Optimality; Evolution, Formal Models of Economic; Evolution, Theories of Economic; Firm, Boundaries of the; Firm, Theory of the; Industrial Policy; Industrial Structure and Power; Innovation, National Systems of; Lock-in and Chreodic Development; Natural Selection, Economic Evolution and; Nelson, Richard R.; Neoclassical Microeconomic Theory, Critique of; Rationality and Maximization; Routines; Selection, Units of Evolutionary; Technical Change and Technological Regimes; Technology, Theory of; Winter, Sidney G., Jr.

Bibliography
Aoki, M. (1988), *Information and Incentives in the Japanese Economy*, Cambridge: Cambridge University Press.
Cantwell, J.A. (1989), *Technological Innovation and Multinational Corporations*, Oxford: Basil Blackwell.
Chandler, A. (1990), *Scale and Scope*, Cambridge, Mass.: Harvard University Press.
Chiaromonte, F. and G. Dosi (1992), 'The microfoundations of competitiveness and their macroeconomic implications', in Foray and Freeman (1992).
Day, R. and G. Eliasson (eds) (1986), *The Dynamics of Market Economies*, Amsterdam: North Holland.
Dosi, G., K. Pavitt and L. Soete (1990), *The Economics of Technical Change and International Trade*, Hemel Hempstead: Harvester Wheatsheaf.
Dosi, G., C. Freeman, R. Nelson, G. Silverberg and L. Soete (eds) (1988), *Technical Change and Economic Theory*, London: Pinter and New York: Columbia University Press.
Eliasson, G. (1986), 'Microheterogeneity of firms and the stability of industrial growth', in Day and Eliasson (1986).
Foray, D. and C. Freeman (eds) (1992), *Technology and the Wealth of Nations*, London: Pinter.
Freeman, C. (1982), *The Economics of Industrial Innovation*, 2nd edn, London: Pinter.
Metcalfe, J.S. (1992), 'Variety, Structure and Change: An Evolutionary Perspective on the Competitive Process', *Revue d'économie industrielle*, **59**, (1), pp. 46–61.
Mistral, J. (1983), *Competitiveness of the productive system and international specialization*, Paris: OECD, DSTI 83.31.
Mueller, D. (ed.) (1990), *The Dynamics of Company Profits*, Cambridge: Cambridge University Press.
Nelson, R. and S. Winter (1982), *An Evolutionary Theory of Economic Change*, Cambridge, Mass.: Harvard University Press.
OECD (1985), 'Trade in high technology products. An initial contribution to the statistical analysis of trade patterns in high technology products', Paris: OECD, mimeo.
Porter, M. (1990), *The Competitive Advantage of Nations*, London: Macmillan.
Rumelt, R.P. (1974), *Strategy, Structure and Economic Performance*, Cambridge, Mass.: Harvard University Press.
Silverberg, G., G. Dosi and L. Orsenigo (1988), 'Innovation, Diversity and Diffusion: A Self-Organisation Model', *Economic Journal*, **98**, (4), December, pp. 1032–54.
Winter, S. (1964), 'Economic "Natural Selection" and the Theory of the Firm', *Yale Economic Essays*, **4**, (1), pp. 225–72.

Military Sector

After World War II, as military expenditures regularly absorbed in excess of 10 per cent of US GNP and provided in excess of 10 per cent of employment, social scientists were challenged to analyse a constellation of emerging institutional arrangements and ideological constructs encompassing new domestic and international political economic relationships. Commonly referred to as 'the military–industrial complex', this portmanteau term suggested little beyond the idea that (a) a new and semi-autonomous crystallization of large corporations and state managers had been forged, and (b) these corporations and state managers possessed a 'vested interest' in perpetuating the Cold War and other policies designed to enhance US military capabilities.

While orthodox neoclassical economists were extremely reluctant to explore this complex nexus between economics and politics, other schools of economic analysis intermittently took up the challenge. However, critical analysis of the causes and consequences of high levels of military spending was forestalled and diverted by the virulence of McCarthyism (1947–55).

Veblen and the institutionalist analysis
Through Thorstein Veblen's work, institutionalists offered the first serious and sustained attempt to analyse the political economy of military spending. Veblen's analysis hinged upon the dichotomous tensions of 'monopoly capitalism'. A major contradiction existed between the systemic force of technological dynamism (a prime manifestation of instrumental or functional human activity) and the entrenched predatory animus (a residual of the precapitalist era). Given that dysfunctional tendencies dominated under monopoly capitalism, and given that this system was marked by a 'progressively widening margin of deficiency', the majority had little reason to form an allegiance to such a system (Veblen, 1923). Consequently, it was necessary for the state to 'rest its case on a nerve-shattering popular fear of aggression from without' (Veblen, 1945b). There was no other way to contain the aspirations of the underlying population than through the state's inculcation of 'patriotic fervour' via 'warlike preparation' (Veblen, 1945a).

The state, as 'a predatory institution', assured the *legitimation* of the status quo (for example, monopoly capitalism) in the short term, while functioning to undermine it in the long term. Rather than promoting reason and science, the state was structurally situated in a role which demanded that it perpetuate the predatory militaristic culture. The military 'virtues' of ritual, ceremonialism, rank, allegiance, passivity, fealty and patriotism had to be upheld at the expense of denying the corrosive 'vices' of scientific inquiry, rationalism, efficiency and critical analysis.

Veblen established two important points regarding the political economy of military spending: (a) perpetuating the military animus served to create bonds of commonality between the underlying population and the captains of industry and finance; (b) under the guise of 'national security', the state could reserve to itself a degree of 'autonomy', operability and flexibility that it could not otherwise attain. (Under the guise of serving the national interest it could serve the 'vested interests' without fear of a critical scrutiny.)

Veblen's ruminations on the social and economic effects of military spending and the central cultural role played by the military ethos received renewed attention in the early 1950s from the sociologist C. Wright Mills, a careful student of Veblen's writing and a former student of Clarence Ayres. In *The Power Elite*, Mills believed he had found evidence of a 'military ascendancy' and a situation wherein the USA was dominated and controlled by a power elite trinity comprised equally of the 'corporate rich', the 'political directorate' and the 'warlords' (Mills, 1956). Subsequent research has rather conclusively demonstrated that Mills overestimated the autonomous power and reach of the 'warlords' (Domhoff, 1967). More focused on economic matters was the writing of the institutionalist J.K. Galbraith, who adopted the stagnationist interpretation of Alvin Hansen, while arguing that well-placed and well-timed military spending could serve to stave off secular stagnation (Galbraith, 1952).

During the 1960s, largely because of the Vietnam war, an outpouring of heterodox research on the political economy of arms spending ensued. This body of work has been relatively unencumbered by an invidious compulsion to demonstrate doctrinal purity. A productive, tolerant and dynamic fusion of heterodox intellectual paradigms has ensued. Institutionalist analyses have intermingled with insights drawn from the Post Keynesian, Cambridge, neo-Marxist and Marxist traditions. This developing body of literature has been demarcated by certain issues, among which three have drawn considerable commentary: the 'depletion hypothesis', 'stagnation and stabilization', and 'arms and accumulation'.

The depletion hypothesis
Much of the discourse affirming the dysfunctional aspects of US military spending has been dominated or at least influenced by the writing of Seymour Melman – of particular note in this regard is the work of Mary Kaldor (Kaldor, 1981). An early work, *Our Depleted Society*, advanced the 'depletion hypothesis' and struck a resonant chord (Melman, 1965).

To an important degree, much of Melman's analysis lies outside the institutionalist school of thought. Methodologically, Melman relied upon a neoclassical device, trade-off of 'guns v. butter'. For example, as the 'depletion school' emphasized, the military sector in the postwar period has employed between 20 and 30 per cent of all research scientists and engineers while absorbing as much as two-thirds of all US R&D outlays. Melman's argument is straightforward: *if* less was spent on the military, *more* would be available for the civilian sector of the economy. It is assumed that these 'released resources' would, through either automatic market forces or the actions of the state, find their way into optimal usage. If so, the US industrial base could be revitalized and the competitiveness problem could be conjured away as civilian technological dynamism accelerated (Melman, 1988).

Although Melman has not attempted to draw any connections between his research and that of the institutional economists, his view of military spending as essentially 'predatory' and his stress on military contracting corporations as 'cost-maximizing' entities certainly fit well into a broad Veblenian framework. Further, his emphasis on the centrality of science and engineering as the chief element underpinning industrial advance loosely accords with the institutionalists' tendency to prioritize technology in the context of analyses of economic growth.

Three major recent works suggest that closure on the depletion hypothesis may be near. David Gold recently deepened observations presented in a 1987 study with Gordon Adams (Adams and Gold, 1987). Gold demonstrated that (a) defence spending is not an important determinant of investment levels; (b) there is no long-term trade-off between defence and civilian R&D; (c) the diversion of scientists and engineers to the defence sector has been exaggerated: since the 1950s, the supply of scientific workers has been adequate; (d) Pentagon–defence sector 'cost-maximizing' production practices have not spread to the civilian economy; and (e) no evidence demonstrates that relatively high US arms outlays explain the fact that other nations have economically outperformed the USA since the late 1960s (Gold, 1990).

Richard DuBoff demonstrated that, while arms outlays have not depleted the civilian sector of the economy (on the contrary, they have bolstered the private sector via the expansion of aggregate demand and corporate profits), they *have* deprived the public sector of adequate levels of social welfare spending. Furthermore, this outcome has been the conscious work of ideological conservatives (DuBoff, 1989).

Stagnation and stabilization: military Keynesianism
Prominent in the early formulation of the concept of 'military Keynesianism' was Joan Robinson, who shared many perspectives with the institutionalist school, and who, of course, deplored the inability of the powers-that-be to find a humanistic form of state spending sufficiently large to ensure full employment.

Heavily in debt to the tradition of Joseph Schumpeter and Keynes, the 'neo-Marxists' Paul Baran and Paul Sweezy vigorously advanced the hypothesis that military spending was *the* antidote to embedded stagnationist tendencies: 'If military spending were reduced to pre-Second World War proportions, the nation's economy would return to a state of profound depression' (Baran and Sweezy, 1966).

Drawing on the Keynesian premise that the expansion and stabilization of aggregate demand and the avoidance of civilian excess industrial capacity comprised the dilemma of postwar US capitalism, James Cypher demonstrated that military expenditures had been the foremost countercyclical device utilized by policy makers in the 1947–70 period (Cypher, 1974). This research also maintained that the composition of arms outlays had shifted dramatically during this period, having the effect of sustaining a relatively higher level of capital formation with a given amount of military spending. High, sustained, expanding and relatively stable levels of aggregate demand were demonstrated to be associated with the postwar arms spending programme.

In the 1970s and 1980s, as US economic policy making became relatively less concerned with sustaining high levels of employment and strong increases in real wages for unionized workers, emphasis on 'military Keynesianism' as a means of offsetting cyclical turns declined, as did research on the topic. Nonetheless, among a wide circle of social scientists the concept of military Keynesianism became accepted as one of the defining characteristics of the postwar US economy during its 'golden age' (1945–70), although some dismissed it as mere underconsumptionism (Ron Smith, 1977).

Arms and accumulation
Heavily influenced by Baran and Sweezy, James O'Connor (1973) offered an analysis of state expenditures which was broadly utilized in subsequent analyses of arms spending – these expenditures served either a *legitimation* function or an *accumulation* function. In concentrating on the accumulation function of military spending, O'Connor reopened one of the oldest debates in economics. Spending on legitimation was 'unproductive'; but was military spending also 'unproductive', as the depletion hypothesis maintained?

Exploring the research on technical change and arms spending, James Cypher maintained that arms programmes had underwritten the development of key product and process technologies in the golden age period (Cypher, 1987). Arms outlays, then, could be viewed as 'indirectly productive' to the extent that they underwrote the application of technologies which reduced production costs in broad areas of the economy.

The work of Tom Riddell and Ron Smith explored relationships between military spending and capital accumulation that are too often neglected in other works – the functional relationship between military power projection and the maintenance or reestablishment of US (and British) hegemony in sectors of the global economy. Arms spending may foster capital accumulation in the USA, or capital accumulation by US-based transnational corporations, to the degree that it helps ensure stable access to crucial resources located abroad, or cheap labour located abroad, or production sites free of regulatory restraint, or entry into otherwise closed or limited foreign markets, or access to foreign arms sales, or improved terms of trade. Deeper and broader access to foreign nations can improve capacity utilization, raise labour productivity and increase profit margins (Riddell, 1988; Smith and Smith, 1983).

Beyond the USA
A recent issue of the *Cambridge Journal of Economics* (1990, **14**) dedicated to the political economy of military spending demonstrates the considerable breadth and depth of research in Europe on military–economic linkages. Of particular interest to institutional analysis is the work of John Lovering and David Edgerton. Lovering's work emphasizes the pivotal role of military-sponsored science and engineering in the evolution of British industry. His research suggests that the defence industry sector 'became relatively sophisticated in terms of the research intensity of its products' – in contrast to the civilian economy which has been characterized by low innovation, low investment in labour force skills and anaemic marketing strategies (Lovering, 1990, p. 456). Furthermore, the arms industry is at present seen as a major means to achieve British industrial competitiveness through weapons exports. Edgerton's equally innovative research focuses on similar themes, with somewhat greater emphasis on historical dynamics, while emphasizing that theoretical work on military spending cannot be taken beyond the context of particular social formations and historical settings (Edgerton, 1991).

Historical specificity
Many researchers, in the USA and abroad, have sought to locate 'regularities' and relationships between macroeconomic variables and arms spending without adequate attention to such a historical context, yet it is often maintained that the economy moves through 'epochs', 'periods', or long waves: historical phases when particular institutional structures of accumulation define the underlying features of capitalism. Institutional economists agree that capitalism is evolutionary. As such, one should expect evolutionary relationships between the economic system and arms spending. Contingent

relationships, perhaps lasting 20 to 30 years, are likely to be encountered. Constant (ahistorical) relationships are not to be anticipated.

Cross-national attempts at analysis have yielded meagre results in this field of research. The most ambitious attempt to produce such broad generalizations was conducted by Robert DeGrasse, who drew heavily on earlier work by Ron Smith (DeGrasse, 1983). Critical empirical and analytical discussion of this research suggested that many of DeGrasse's cross-national results were not compelling (Cypher, 1985). This outcome would surprise few institutionalists, since such studies usually implicitly assume historical homogeneity even though different nations are likely to occupy distinct evolutionary phases and, in any case, exhibit their own defining idiosyncrasies.

JAMES M. CYPHER

See also:
Galbraith, John Kenneth; Industrial Policy; Interest Groups; International Economic Policy; International Economic Relations; Macroeconomic Policy; Macroeconomic Theory; Power; Public Sector, Role of the; Veblen, Thorstein; Veblenian Dichotomy and Its Critics.

Bibliography
Adams, Gordon and David Gold (1987), *Defense Spending and the Economy*, Washington, DC: Defense Budget Project.
Baran, Paul and Paul Sweezy (1966), *Monopoly Capitalism*, New York: Monthly Review.
Cypher, James (1974), 'Capitalist Planning and Military Expenditures', *Review of Radical Political Economics*, **6**, (3), pp. 1–21.
Cypher, James (1985), 'Review of DeGrasse, *Military Expansion, Economic Decline*', *Journal of Economic Issues*, **XIX**, (1), pp. 227–32.
Cypher, James (1987), 'Military Spending, Technical Change and Economic Growth', *Journal of Economic Issues*, **XXI**, (4), pp. 33–60.
DeGrasse, Robert (1983), *Military Expansion, Economic Decline*, Armonk, NY: M.E. Sharpe.
Domhoff, G. William (1967), *Who Rules America?*, Englewood Cliffs, NJ: Prentice-Hall.
DuBoff, Richard (1989), 'What Military Spending Really Costs', *Challenge*, **32**, (5), pp. 4–10.
Edgerton, David (1991), 'Liberal Militarism and the British State', *New Left Review*, **185**, January–February, pp. 138–69.
Galbraith, J.K. (1952), *American Capitalism*, Boston: Houghton Mifflin.
Gold, David (1990), *The Impact of Defense Spending on Investment, Productivity and Economic Growth*, Washington, DC: Defense Budget Project.
Kaldor, Mary (1981), *The Baroque Arsenal*, London: Hill & Wang.
Lovering, John (1990), 'Military Expenditure and the Restructuring of British Capitalism', *Cambridge Journal of Economics*, **14**, pp. 453–67.
Melman, Seymour (1965), *Our Depleted Society*, New York: Dell Publishing.
Melman, Seymour (1988), 'Economic Consequences of the Arms Race', *American Economic Review*, **78**, (2), pp. 55–9.
Mills, C. Wright (1956), *The Power Elite*, New York: Oxford University Press.
O'Connor, James (1973), *The Fiscal Crisis of the State*, New York: St Martin's Press.
Riddell, Tom (1988), 'U.S. Military Power, the Terms of Trade, and the Profit Rate', *American Economic Review*, **78**, (2), pp. 60–65.
Smith, D. and Ron Smith (1983), *The Economics of Militarism*, London: Pluto.
Smith, Ron (1977), 'Military Expenditure and Capitalism', *Cambridge Journal of Economics*, **1**, (3), pp. 61–76.

Veblen, Thorstein (1923), *Absentee Ownership*, New York: Viking.
Veblen, Thorstein (1934a), 'Dementia Praecox', in Leon Androoni (ed.), *Essays in Our Changing Order*, pp. 423–36, New York: Viking.
Veblen, Thorstein (1934b), 'Between Bolshevism and War', in Leon Androoni (ed.), *Essays in Our Changing Order*, pp. 437–49, New York: Viking.

Mitchell, Wesley Clair

Wesley Clair Mitchell (1874–1948) came to the University of Chicago as an undergraduate when it first opened its doors in the autumn of 1892. Among the distinguished faculty recruited by President Harper were Thorstein Veblen and John Dewey, both of whom left their mark on the young man, but their influence is not apparent for some years in Mitchell's writings, which began when he was still an undergraduate. In the period between his first published piece, 'The Quantity Theory and the Value of Money' (1896), and his first contribution to institutional economics, 'The Rationality of Economic Activity' (1910), what we see is that Mitchell was one of the bright young students of J. Laurence Laughlin, head of the department of economics at Chicago, the type of thinker against whom Veblen and Dewey, each in their own way, were directing their devastating criticism.

After recruiting Mitchell to the anti-quantity theory crusade, Laughlin assigned to him the task of writing a dissertation whose purpose it was to show the silliness of issuing the inconvertible 'greenbacks'. Mitchell used all of the data he could find that had a bearing on this question, and after discovering in the process of doing this work that there were data bearing on the consequences of instability, he proceeded to explore this related subject as well after he had acquired his degree. Since he found that there were data too, for the greenback period after the war, he went on to study that period also, but before he had quite completed this latter work he began to develop broader notions of 'what economics ought to be' (L.S. Mitchell, 1953, p. 186). It was 'the ferment of philosophy and ethnology', studies he had first begun as a student of Veblen and Dewey, as well as reflection on his own work as it progressed, that brought this about. He turned to broader questions than 'this detailed work with a passing episode in monetary history' (ibid., p. 168).

The philosophy of economics that Mitchell derived rested on three general beliefs. The first, worked out in the course of arguing against the quantity theory, was that the quantity theory, like other theories which were part of the orthodox tradition, could not be said to be right or wrong. There might be some truth in them, as there was in the quantity theory; their serious shortcoming was that they did not help much to explain what happens in the real world. Mitchell's second belief was that orthodox economists were not doing very much to improve this situation: they devoted a great deal of attention to formulating abstract models that often had only the most tenuous relationship to what goes on in the real world. He was not so much concerned with the shortcomings of prevailing economic theory *per se* as he was with the fact, as he saw it, that the main work that orthodox economists were doing was not likely to improve matters. In his work on the greenbacks he felt he had discovered a way to generate knowledge that would in time help to better understand what went on in economic affairs. Both these beliefs of Mitchell's raise the question: why was it that economists were doing less than they could to further our understanding of what goes on in the economy? Mitchell's answer, inspired by Veblen, was that to truly understand what happens in the modern economy one had to be aware of the nature of the culture of the money economy, which in a very fundamental way leaves its mark on the way economic processes work out their effects. Orthodox economists did not generally see this, Mitchell felt, with the result that, though they might have reservations about the adequacy of their theories, they were unable to make major improvements. The last conception led Mitchell to formulate his Veblen-based critique of orthodox economic theory; the first two led him to devote his life to doing the kind of quantitative work for which he is best known.

Veblen believed that cyclical fluctuations in economic activity were an inherent feature of the money (or market) economy: Mitchell found traces of such a phenomenon in his work on the consequences of the greenback issue. But Veblen's type of theory, as insightful as it might be, Mitchell felt, like the orthodox variety was to a large extent based on speculation and not on detailed observation. It was clear to Mitchell that what was needed was to conduct the kind of inquiry he had carried out on the greenback era, only with more extensive data and in a broader context. He established his context by identifying what he took to be the main pertinent features of the money economy, to a large extent derived from Veblen. Since he had come to believe that there was some truth in prevailing theories in economics, he also undertook a survey of theories of business cycles as part of his research. He did not look for logical flaws, rank theories on what he considered to be their validity, or try to 'verify' them. His purpose in considering them was to make certain that insights others had derived from observing and thinking about cyclical phenomena were not overlooked.

Mitchell's early work did not result in an overall theory of business cycles of the conventional sort. Instead he came up with what he called an 'analytic description', which consisted of a detailed account of what he had found in the data, including explanations of those parts of the process which could be understood on the basis of the evidence. For example, the lagging of wages behind selling prices is part of the explanation for the economy expanding briskly in the early stages of the expansion phase of the cycle. There is a wealth of material in Mitchell's analytic description, including accounts of processes others have theorized about, including, for example, a 'Keynesian' type of process (Friedman, 1950). To Mitchell the great detail was a virtue because in his view relatively simple theories, like the quantity theory which he had grappled with as a student, did not tell us all that we needed to know to deal adequately with pressing social problems. The question this raises, of course, is whether in economics one can expect to find relatively simple theories which would adequately explain very complex phenomena, as do gravitation and relativity theories in physics. Though Mitchell often sounds as though he believed that the methodology of economics was essentially the same as that of physics, judging by what he did, he in effect favoured the opposite view that simple economic theories do not adequately explain complex cyclical phenomena.

At about the time that he started to work on the problem of business cycles, Mitchell 'began to look back on economic theory from the viewpoint of [his] particular problem', his particular problem being to try to show why economic theory did not explain the workings of the money economy better than it did. The first result of this probing was the article (1910) previously referred to, which is Veblenian in nature, where Mitchell tries to show that the premises or preconceptions of prevailing economic theory are inadequate, if not wrong, when read within the context of the latest findings in psychology and anthropology. Mitchell further developed these ideas in a series of articles, the most important of which, except for 'The Role of Money in Economic History' (1944), are reprinted in *The Backward Art of Spending Money and Other Essays* (1950). Also in this period he did work on the history of economics, very little of which was published, which is part of Mitchell's institutionalist critique of the orthodox approach to the money economy. Yet the output which deals primarily with the more common and obvious institutional themes is relatively small, even if we include in this category his lecture notes on the history of economics not published during his lifetime. Perhaps this is not surprising since, except for the early period at the University at California, where Mitchell taught after leaving Chicago, he devoted relatively little time to it. He was quite explicit about the reason: 'My criticisms of economic theory as commonly practiced were valid, but when it came to accomplishing something constructive I had to come down to more concrete and definite issues' (L.S. Mitchell, 1953, p. 563). His work more easily identified as institutional economics was primarily critical and incidental to what was for Mitchell the main task, which was to derive knowledge, supported by evidence, preferably in quantitative form, about the workings of the money economy. On the face of it this work does not look particularly institutional or evolutionary in character, especially so the later work.

In the light of this it is hard to avoid the question whether Mitchell deserves the important place he is generally accorded as an institutional economist. This question seems pertinent today because Mitchell's great involvement with quantitative data, now that this has become common in mainstream economics, looks far more mainstream than institutional, as does his strong desire to help develop a *science* of economics which is like the most advanced physical sciences. After all, few if any researchers at the National Bureau of Economic Research, said to be Mitchell's lengthened shadow, have identified themselves as institutionalists, and few if any present-day leaders of institutional economics do or recommend the kind of work which Mitchell favoured. Would it be right, then, to say that Mitchell fits better into the mainstream than the institutionalist camp?

Such a conclusion is even more questionable. Mitchell was very much concerned that his explanations account for what actually happens in the real world. That is why detailed observation of what John Stuart Mill called 'specific experience' played such an overwhelmingly important role in his work. Mill had argued that specific experience should play no other role in economic inquiry than that of 'verification' of theories derived by *a priori* means; mainstream economists today by and large are still Millian in this regard. This difference between Mitchell and the orthodox became ever greater in his later work.

After World War I and the establishment of the National Bureau of Economic Research, Mitchell returned to the problem of business cycles. Instead of concentrating on improving some aspects of the 'analytic description', Mitchell tried to thoroughly revise every aspect of the earlier work. Five years after the beginning of this effort, a revised version of Part I of the 1913 work, called *Business Cycles: The Problem and Its Setting* (1927) was published, which had a wide circulation even among mainstream economists. At the end of this volume we are told of a new (descriptive) statistical technique that Mitchell was experimenting with, to be used in further work. It was almost two decades before a volume (Burns and Mitchell, 1946) appeared which outlined the new method in great detail and described the extensive tests it had been subjected to. Mitchell had almost completed a revision of Part II of the earlier work (on the contribution of statistics) when he died; the manuscript was edited and revised by Arthur F. Burns and published as *What Happens During Business Cycles* (1951). The revised 'analytic description' which, according to his plan, was to pull together the extensive findings into a meaningful whole was never done.

Mitchell had always had critics but in later years the criticism intensified. He was, ironically, chided for not deriving results which were practically useful (Robbins, 1931, pp. 114–15; Hansen, 1949) and because his work was not truly 'scientific'. The charge made by Koopmans (1947) that Mitchell stood for 'facts without theory' is widely held by mainstream economists and one still not infrequently sees this phrase used, with Mitchell or The National Bureau pointed to as exemplars. To these charges a supporter of Mitchell can respond in at least two ways. Firstly, one can argue that the work is useful but in a different way from the more orthodox formulations; the work of Arthur Burns in his policy-advising role illustrates this. And as far as 'science' is concerned, one can argue, as did Vining (1949), that to come to grips with the complexity of business cycles one needs to know a great deal of what actually happens. One must observe before one can derive an adequate abstract model. Mitchell did not have time to get to the theory stage. Had he lived longer he might eventually have succeeded in formulating a theory which was acceptable to mainstream thinkers. Secondly, it can be argued that, since Mitchell's methodology was different from the mainstream one, his results take on a different form. From the first Mitchell had concentrated on forecasting as both a scientific and a practical problem; he believed that both our understanding of the phenomenon and our ability to deal with it practically depend on a thorough knowledge of the normal timing sequences of the different endogenous variables involved and on the way exogenous variables, which make one cycle different from another, can influence the results. Mitchell himself had begun the study of 'statistical indicators', which has since been updated and published by the Department of Commerce and researched further by Geoffrey Moore (1983). These two possible answers to critics, of course, are not necessarily competitors; the 'statistical indicators' can be viewed as the short-term product and a full-fledged theory of business cycles as a possible long-term objective.

While there may be disagreement about Mitchell's later work in business cycles, other aspects of his contribution are less controversial. Mitchell was an inspiring teacher and his *Lecture Notes* (1967, 1969), which reveal a pragmatic approach to the history of economics and the view that economic theory represents the attempts of people to understand the particular problems of their societies, is a leading work in its field. Mitchell's notion that self-generating cycles are an inherent part of the capitalist economy and that they are diffused throughout the system is now taken for granted by economists and laymen alike. Further, few would deny that Mitchell made an immense contribution in helping to make available a vast amount of quantitative data, in developing descriptive statistical methods when little work of this kind was done, and in helping economists to become aware of the importance of reliable data. That theories should ultimately be 'verified' or 'falsified' is now generally taken for granted, and even those who hold *a priori* views tend to agree that, for practical purposes, if not for 'science', a huge amount of data is needed to be able to make good decisions. For these reasons as well as others there is general agreement, both among mainstream and institutional economists, that Wesley Mitchell is a leading figure in modern economics.

ABRAHAM HIRSCH

See also:
Keynes, John Maynard; Macroeconomic Policy; Macroeconomic Theory; Monetary Policy; Monetary Theory; Money, Evolution of; Realism, Philosophical; Veblen, Thorstein.

Bibliography
Burns, Arthur F. and Wesley C. Mitchell (1946), *Measuring Business Cycles*, New York: National Bureau of Economic Research.
Friedman, Milton (1950), 'Wesley Clair Mitchell as an Economic Theorist', *Journal of Political Economy*, December, reprinted in A.F. Burns (ed.) (1952), *Wesley Clair Mitchell: The Economic Scientist*, New York: National Bureau of Economic Research.
Hansen, Alvin H. (1949), 'Wesley Mitchell, Social Scientist and Social Counselor', *Review of Economics and Statistics*, **31**, November, pp. 245–55.
Koopmans, Tjalling C. (1947), 'Measurement without Theory', *Review of Economic Statistics*, **29**, August, pp. 161–72.
Mitchell, L.S. (1953), *Two Lives: The Story of Wesley Clair Mitchell and Myself*, New York: Simon & Schuster.
Mitchell, Wesley C. (1896), 'The Quantity Theory and the Value of Money', *Journal of Political Economy*, **4**, March, pp. 139–65.
Mitchell, Wesley C. (1910), 'The Rationality of Economic Activity', *Journal of Political Economy*, **18**, February and March, pp. 97–113 and pp. 197–216.
Mitchell, Wesley C. (1913), *Business Cycles*, Berkeley: University of California Press.
Mitchell, Wesley C. (1927), *Business Cycles: The Problem and Its Setting*, New York: The National Bureau of Economic Research.
Mitchell, Wesley C. (1944), 'The Role of Money in Economic History', *Journal of Economic History*, **4**, December Supplement IV, pp. 61–7.
Mitchell, Wesley C. (1950), *The Backward Art of Spending Money and Other Essays*, New York: Augustus M. Kelley.
Mitchell, Wesley C. (1951), *What Happens During Business Cycles: A Progress Report*, New York: National Bureau of Economic Research.
Mitchell, Wesley C. (1967, 1969), *Lecture Notes on Types of Economic Theory, Volumes I and II*, New York: Augustus M. Kelley.
Moore, Geoffrey H. (1983), *Business Cycles, Inflation and Forecasting*, Cambridge, Mass.: Ballinger.
Robbins, Lionel (1949), *An Essay on the Nature and Significance of Economic Science*, 2nd edn., London: Macmillan; first published 1931.
Vining, Rutledge (1949), 'Koopmans on the Choice of Variables to Be Studied and of Methods of Measurement', *Review of Economics and Statistics*, **31**, May, pp. 77–94.

Monetary Policy

Orthodox theory and policy
In order to understand orthodox approaches to monetary policy, it is first necessary to understand orthodox theory. Briefly, in orthodox theory, money

was invented to eliminate the necessity of a double coincidence of wants required for barter to take place. Money, then, facilitates exchange by reducing transactions costs. Once money has been created, it can also act as a store of value and as a unit of account. In orthodox theory, the economy may be dichotomized into a *real* sector and a *monetary* sector. In the long run, the dichotomy between the two sectors is complete and money is neutral: real values are determined without reference to nominal values, and nominal values are strictly determined by the supply of money. However, money may not be neutral in the short run if there is 'money illusion' (agents mistake nominal values for real values), if there are wealth effects (the 'Pigou effect', which arises when an increase in the nominal price level reduces the real value of money balances), or if there are wage and price rigidities.

The three main orthodox approaches have relatively minor disagreements concerning the importance of each of these factors. Old-style monetarists believe that this short-run period during which money has real effects is on average relatively short, but emphasize that the length of the period is unpredictable. Textbook Keynesians (also called 'bastard Keynesians' because the mother of the approach is clearly neoclassical theory, but the father is unknown – Keynes was most certainly *not* the father) emphasize wage and price rigidities which render money non-neutral over fairly long periods. Finally, new-style monetarists (who accept rational expectations) argue that money is neutral even in the short run, except where random supply shocks make it impossible to predict the quantity of money. Thus orthodox economists generally agree that money is neutral in the long run, although transitory non-neutrality provides a role for monetary effects on the real sector in the short run.

In orthodox theory, the central bank ultimately determines the quantity of money supplied through its control over bank reserves. Reserves are primarily the liabilities of the central bank, which are expanded when the central bank buys government bonds in open market operations, or when it makes loans to banks at the discount window. All modern, developed capitalist economies operate with a *fractional* reserve system, in which banks hold a small quantity of reserves against the deposits they issue. For example, a bank might hold one dollar in reserve for every ten dollars of demand deposits issued, in which case the 'reserve ratio' is 10 per cent. In the USA, the Federal Reserve Bank (Fed) sets the legally required reserve ratio, while in the UK this ratio is established individually by banks. Whether the reserve ratio is established by law or by custom, if this ratio is constant then there will be a stable relationship between reserves and bank deposits. The Fed is believed to directly control reserves, while the money supply is established through the 'money multiplier' (reserves multiplied by the inverse of the reserve ratio). Thus, if the central bank can control reserves, if there is a constant ratio between reserves and bank deposits, and if bank deposits comprise most of the money supply, the central bank can control the money supply.

Orthodox policy, then, focuses on the supposed ability of the central bank to control the money supply. Those who emphasize the neutrality of money would like to have the central bank expand the money supply at a rate equal to the growth rate of real output. For example, monetarists have argued that the central bank should be constrained by such a policy rule, which would, according to them, generate a stable price level and stable growth of real output along a full employment path. Textbook Keynesians would allow the central bank to use discretionary policy: increase the rate of growth of the money supply in a recession, but decrease the rate of growth when there is inflation. In this way, the central bank would take advantage of the short-run non-neutrality of money to fine-tune the economy. Monetarists reject discretionary policy because they believe a 'free market' economy will naturally tend towards a stable, full employment growth path (so that discretionary policy is not needed) and because they believe that the non-neutral effects of money on the economy are unpredictable (so that the short-run effects of discretionary policy would be unpredictable). Rational expectations monetarism goes even further – predictable policy would not affect the real sector, so that only random policy would have real effects. In this case, all non-random policies have the same effect, so a constant growth rate rule is preferable to discretionary policy (which would merely increase or decrease the aggregate price level).

Post Keynesian and institutionalist theory and policy

According to Post Keynesians and institutionalists, orthodoxy misrepresents the historical origins of money, misunderstands the role played by money in a capitalist economy, ignores the institutional roles played by banks and by the central bank, and advocates impossible policy prescriptions.

First, money was not created to facilitate exchange, but evolved with the development of private property. The creation of the institution of private property gave rise to the possibility of loans of private property, to the responsibility of each individual for his or her own welfare, and to the existence of propertyless individuals. Money was first created as a unit of account to standardize the terms on which loans were to be repaid. For example, the earliest form of money was apparently wheat – the loan of a cow would be recorded in terms of its wheat equivalent and could be repaid in terms of wheat. Each such contract involved interest: a loan of two bushels of wheat today would require repayment of three bushels (or its equivalent) next year. Private property would not be loaned without interest because the lender faced uncertainty concerning eventual repayment and might need the loaned property at some time before repayment. Thus interest compensated the lender for the insecurity he or she faced when surrendering use of loaned property.

The existence of propertyless individuals led to the creation of wage labour (those who work for property owners), to the development of markets and to the use of money as a medium of exchange. Payment of money wages rather than goods reduced uncertainty for both workers and employers: money contracts would allow flexibility in consumption by workers and in payment of the wage bill. The development of a working class led to the creation of market demand, while the development of money contracts led to the creation of market supply as employers produced for market to obtain the money required to fulfil money contracts. At this point, money as a medium of exchange evolved from the original money of account. Money was also used as the means of payment (to retire debts) as contracts came to be written in money terms.

Given that each individual became responsible for his or her security, money hoards were desirable because they would reduce the possibility that one might have to borrow from others. Furthermore, since money became the universal unit of account, one could always meet contractual obligations by delivering money. Finally, money hoards could also be used to purchase the necessities of life once a market had developed. For this reason, possession of money hoards increased individual security and reduced uncertainty.

With the evolution of capitalism and the development of large-scale production, monetary relations gained prominence. The capitalist required credit (money functioning as a unit of account) to obtain labour and raw materials in order to produce goods to be sold in markets. The primary purpose of money in a capitalist system is to transfer purchasing power across time from the future to the present: the capitalist may 'buy now, pay later' by using credit to purchase inputs for the production process, and can retire debt upon the sale of the finished goods. In the early stages of development, a wide variety of credit arrangements were available; thus various types of 'money' were used. However, specialized institutions gradually evolved whose liabilities became widely accepted as money. Most importantly, banks developed which would issue their own notes (and, later, deposits) as they made loans. These notes would circulate as media of exchange. Banks developed clearing houses so that the notes of one bank could be converted into the notes of another. They frequently found it convenient to hold a common reserve asset for such purposes – the reserve asset could be government-issued coin, notes of a respected bank, the debt of prominent manufacturers and, later, the liabilities of the central bank.

Through a combination of private and government initiative, most capitalist countries developed a monoreserve system, in which the liabilities of the central bank became the sole reserve asset. At first, governments merely saw this as a means of providing government finance: if the liabilities of the central bank were the primary reserve asset, these would be in high demand; this would enable the government to obtain finance merely by selling its bonds to the central bank. However, governments gradually realized that the monoreserve system gave the central bank some control over private banks.

The most pressing problem facing the financial system was that of periodic crises during which the public would lose faith in banks. Since no bank held more than a small fraction of reserves against its liabilities, if the public tried to exchange bank liabilities for the reserve asset, each bank would fail. When faced with a run, an individual bank would first use reserves to meet the demand of noteholders or depositors; it would then try to discount its most liquid assets (that is, use these as collateral in order to borrow reserves); as a last resort, it would try to sell assets. The problem is that most bank assets are not marketable: each bank establishes close relations with its borrowers; since other banks will not know these borrowers, they will not be willing to buy these loans. Furthermore, even if most bank assets were marketable, when there was a generalized run on banks, all banks would be trying to sell assets, which would drive down the value of assets below outstanding bank liabilities. Thus it is impossible to 'liquidate' bank assets to stop a run, as this leads to a generalized 'debt deflation' in which assets lose value.

However, if the central bank were willing to loan reserves to private banks, it could supply sufficient reserves to stop any run. Thus, by acting as a 'lender of last resort', the central bank could prevent financial crises and help to stabilize the financial system. The Bank of England (the central bank) gradually recognized in the nineteenth century that it should act as a lender of last resort to stabilize the financial system. The Fed was created in the USA in 1913 precisely to act as a lender of last resort. When the Fed failed to do so in the Great Depression (resulting in wide-scale bank failures), Congress created the Federal Deposit Insurance Corporation (FDIC) which was designed to guarantee that depositors would always be able to substitute Fed liabilities for those of a failing bank.

Central banks also typically regulate and supervise banks in order to encourage certain activities and prohibit others. Historically, banks have been reluctant to make loans to small firms, small farmers and consumers. Thus, in almost every country, the government and central bank have intervened to increase the supply of credit to these groups. Often the government guarantees loans to these groups to reduce the risk faced by banks. On the other hand, banks have historically displayed a tendency towards euphoric speculation as they buy very risky assets in the hope of large returns. If their expectations are not met, however, they are forced to default on liabilities –

which means that bank depositors and other creditors (or the government insurer) lose their funds. Thus banks and other financial institutions are normally closely regulated regarding the permissible activities they may finance.

As the monosupplier of reserves, the central bank gains control over the price of reserves: by setting the interest rate at which it discounts eligible paper (the discount rate) and through its open market operations, the central bank can determine the marginal price of reserves. This will then influence the whole spectrum of interest rates as it affects bank costs. This does not mean that the central bank is unconstrained in its ability to set the discount rate. First and foremost, the central bank must be concerned with the stability of the private financial system. High and rising interest rates tend to reduce bank profitability as banks find it more expensive to issue short-term liabilities to finance their longer-term positions in assets. Thus the central bank is forced to take bank profitability into account when determining the price at which it will supply reserves.

The central bank is not able to control either the supply of reserves or the supply of money. The central bank cannot refuse to lend reserves to a bank which needs them, for the reasons discussed above: a bank which needs reserves would have to sell assets, which are, for the most part, unmarketable. Even if the central bank could control reserves, this would not lead to control of the money supply, even where reserves are legally required. Banks and other financial institutions innovate and engage in reserve-economizing behaviour to subvert reserve constraint. For example, if the legal reserve ratio is only against demand deposits, banks can encourage the public to hold time deposits, jumbo CDs and repurchase agreements and thereby avoid reserve requirements. Even if the central bank could control demand deposits, this will not give it control over the money supply, broadly defined. A wide range of bank and non-bank liabilities have always been used as the money of account, as the medium of exchange and as the means of payment. Central bank constraint of reserves and demand deposits will merely lead to greater use of other forms of money.

This is not desirable. The current institutional arrangements whereby the central bank agrees to provide reserves through lender of last resort operations, and through which deposits are government insured, were created to prevent bank runs and financial crises. To the extent that the central bank forces banks and the public to use other forms of money, runs and crises again become possible. During the 1980s, the Fed tried to constrain the growth of bank reserves and demand deposits in the USA, even as it reduced regulation of the financial system. The results were high and variable interest rates, greater use of non-bank (riskier) liabilities, runs on various types of financial liabilities and financial crises. The Fed was forced to intervene repeatedly as a lender of last resort to prevent total collapse, taxpayers were forced to bear the burden of the crisis in the saving and loan industry, and financial institutions became increasingly involved in destabilizing speculative behaviour.

In conclusion, the central bank cannot control the money supply. Money is created as agents transfer purchasing power from the future to the present. Ideally, the function of financial institutions is to provide credit to those who wish to increase production and productive capacity now in return for a promise to pay later. However, as there is no guarantee that 'free' markets will place credit in the correct hands, some government supervision is required to ensure that the allocation of credit fulfils key social functions. Furthermore, the central bank must stand ready to provide reserves and maintain financial stability. Low and stable interest rates should be one of the targets of monetary policy, although the central bank can directly control only the discount rate. Other goals, such as a stable foreign exchange rate, low unemployment and low inflation, are of secondary importance, primarily because the central bank may have very little direct impact on these variables. However, well designed and coordinated monetary and fiscal policy can certainly do much better than have the misguided policies which have been pursued since the mid-1970s in most capitalist countries.

Clearly, in an uncertain world in which production takes time, money can never be neutral – whether in the short run or in the long run – and policies which might be appropriate when money is neutral cannot be appropriate for a capitalist economy. Money contracts allow flexibility in an uncertain world in which money is created as agents 'buy now, pay later', which always has real effects. Money hoards offer security even as they break the link between spending and income, invalidating Say's Law and negating any tendency toward full employment equilibrium. While the money supply expands to finance growing spending, attempts to decrease spending and hoard money can cause a crisis when produced goods cannot be sold. Finally, in the absence of a lender of last resort, privately issued money can lose its value during a run to liquidity, which causes a debt deflation as bank assets lose value. Monetary relations are not neutral. For this reason, monetary policy must be carefully designed to allocate credit in a socially desirable manner and to prevent financial crises and debt deflation.

L. RANDALL WRAY

See also:
Inflation; Keynes, John Maynard; Macroeconomic Policy; Macroeconomic Theory; Monetary Theory; Unemployment.

Bibliography
Davidson, P. (1978), *Money and the Real World*, Second Edition, London and New York: Macmillan.
Greider, William (1987), *Secrets of the Temple*, New York: Simon and Schuster.
Moore, Basil J. (1988), *Horizontalists and Verticalists: The Macroeconomics of Credit Money*, Cambridge: Cambridge University Press.
Wray, L.R. (1990), *Money and Credit in Capitalist Economies: The Endogenous Money Approach*, Aldershot: Edward Elgar.

Monetary Theory

Introduction

Institutionalist monetary theory has its origins in the writing of several key 'old' institutionalists, Veblen, Mitchell and Copeland, who regarded money as an important institution in capitalist economics. Since this view held much in common with that of Keynes, it is not surprising that subsequent developments in institutionalist monetary theory should have occurred within the substantial common ground between institutionalism and Post Keynesianism in the work of Hyman Minsky, Victoria Chick, Alfred Eichner and Philip Arestis. In what follows, much of what is described as institutionalist could also be described as Post Keynesian.

The institutionalist analysis of money can be understood at different levels. The old institutionalist analysis is the most fundamental, focusing on the enduring role of money in capitalist economics. Subsequent developments have focused more on the way in which money and financial institutions have evolved over time. A particular emphasis now is placed on money as credit, and the endogenous process by which it is supplied; this emphasis has had a particular impact during the recent period of experimentation with monetarism. In what follows, we will elaborate on each of these aspects of institutionalist monetary theory: the role of money in capitalism, the evolution of money and finance, and the endogenous money argument. Given the strong Post Keynesian element in this account, it is then specified where institutionalism and Post Keynesianism part company on monetary theory. Finally, new institutionalism within monetary theory has focused on the role of the state in financial systems. In the last section we consider the foundation and content of the resulting arguments for deregulation and free banking.

The role of money in capitalism

The institutionalist view on the fundamental role of money in capitalism (see further Dillard, 1987) has much in common with Marx (although developed independently). Marx defined the transition from feudalism to capitalism in terms of the transition from money as a medium of exchange to money as the object of production. In place of the feudal circuit C-M-C′, where money is used as a means of acquiring commodity C′ with commodity C, capitalism involves a circuit M-C-M′ whereby commodities are the means of converting one money value, M into a higher money value M′. Advanced capitalism can be represented by the circuit M-M-C...P...C′-M′-M″: money is lent by finance capitalists to industrial capitalists (M–M) to acquire commodities, C, to be employed in production P, to produce commodities C′, to make money profits M″, of which M′ is repaid to the finance capitalists.

Veblen developed the implications of the distinctions on the one hand between industry and finance, and on the other between the consumption motive of workers and the monetary accumulation motive of both industrial and finance capitalists. His analysis found a strong echo in Keynes's monetary theory of production, although the second distinction was emphasized less in Keynes's published work. Both Veblen and Keynes used these distinctions to explain unemployment as the norm in capitalist economies, and the customary fluctuations in economic activity; Veblen's theory of the business cycle found an empirical counterpart in the work of Mitchell.

According to this approach, unemployment is the norm because neither full employment nor production as such feature in the goals of capitalists; the levels of employment and output are those which are expected to generate the highest money profits. Veblen reinforced this argument with the argument that individual capitalists see profits as being promoted by industrial concentration, with the attendant significance of advertising and of technological change in the direction of mass production. As with Marx, Veblen saw these forces at the aggregate level as in fact eroding profits, eventually culminating in periodic crises, associated with falling output and employment. Employment and output increase again as further industrial concentration increases the expected rate of money profit, but these expectations are again vulnerable to disappointment and the emergence of another crisis. Macroeconomic analysis along these lines has been carried forward most notably by Minsky. Minsky's (1982) financial instability hypothesis shows how financial behaviour (of borrowers and lenders) exacerbates the instability arising from changes in long-term expectations of returns on capital investment. Minsky thus shows the business cycle to have an intrinsic monetary character as a result of the manifestation of the monetary motivation of capitalists in financial markets, as well as product markets. More explicit use of the monetary circuit concept has been developed by the French Circuitiste School.

Subsequent developments within old institutionalist monetary theory have concentrated on different aspects of the monetary circuit: study of the evolution of financial systems has concentrated on the M-terms at either end of the circuit, while the endogenous money approach has focused more on the relationship between the M-terms and production. We now consider these two types of institutionalist monetary theory in turn.

The evolution of financial systems

Money has institutional significance, not only in the macroeconomic sense outlined above, but also in the sense that money can itself be regarded as an institution. Media of payment are conventional in nature, confidence in them being built on long experience. The evolution of modern financial systems, dominated as they are by inside money, can best be understood, then, in institutional terms. Such an approach, too, allows for the possibility that the way in which money has played its role in capitalist economies (in particular, the terms on which credit has been available) may have changed over time.

There is a large body of literature which has focused on the institutions which generate or influence credit, and on the institutional relationship with the state. Such an approach is epitomized by the Radcliffe Report. The study of the evolution of banking has been most successfully systematized by Chick (1986). This study sets out a framework of banking development which considers each stage in terms of scope for, and nature of, credit creation. The first stage, in which bank liabilities are not used significantly as money, is the only stage at which credit availability is constrained by bank reserves (usually in the form of specie). Investment by industry is then dependent on prior saving; finance capital has no distinguishing role, other than as an intermediary between savers and borrowers. But, once bank liabilities become used widely as a means of payment, a fractional reserve banking system can emerge. Investment can then anticipate saving; finance capital exerts a more significant role as arbiter of credit creation, although reserves still constitute a constraint. In subsequent stages of development, finance capital's role expands further. An inter-bank market eases the reserves constraint on individual banks. But the emergence of a central bank has a more powerful impact; customarily this involves a lender of last resort facility, to promote the public good of confidence in the banking system. But at the same time the direct reserves constraint is removed. In the most recent stages of development, liability management has involved struggle over market share within the financial sector. This has driven up interest rates, which has increased profitability in the financial sector relative to the industrial sector. In terms of the circuit framework, the number of M-terms has been proliferating. Indeed, industrial companies themselves have found it profitable to engage increasingly in financial intermediation, rather than production, breaking down the conflict of interest between finance capital and industrial capital.

Chick's analysis refers to banks, over which the state has at times exerted some control. Others have focused on the financial system as a whole, demonstrating the capacity, even at early stages of financial development, for credit to be created. The causal priority is given to credit rather than money as such by the strand of institutionalist monetary theory associated with the endogenous money approach.

The endogenous money approach

The endogenous money approach (as set out in Arestis and Eichner, 1988) sees money creation as the by-product of credit creation. The volume of credit is determined by the demand for credit, which arises from firms' production and investment plans. Banks create deposits, that is, money, as the vehicle for extending credit; deposits are destroyed when loans are repaid. The money supply is thus determined by the demand for credit. Banks are unconstrained in meeting demand because of the lender of last resort facility provided by the central bank, a facility which is regarded as necessary for maintaining confidence in the banking system.

This feature of institutionalist monetary theory has profound implications for monetary policy; indeed, the recent experience of experiments in monetarist policy have fuelled a general interest in the capacity of financial systems to evade control. The possibility of irreversible institutional change in response to high interest rates now features in some mainstream macroeconomic models. But mainstream models in general assume that the money supply is exogenous, in the sense of being under the control of the monetary authorities, either directly through supply of reserves, or indirectly through the price, and thus demand for, reserves.

Institutionalists do allow that the authorities have considerable influence over interest rates, but argue that this influence has other consequences than discouraging demand for reserves. These consequences follow from a mark-up model of bank interest charges combined with a mark-up model of firms' pricing behaviour. Higher interest rates may then cause inflation and/or increased borrowing as a means of covering higher interest costs. They may also encourage industrial concentration as firms unable to pursue either of these possibilities are taken over or go bankrupt. The implications for policy are that demand for credit should be the focus of attempts to control aggregate expenditure, not the money supply, and that interest rate policy should focus on interest rate stability, rather than activism.

Differences between institutionalist and Post Keynesian monetary theory

The key figures picked out so far in the account of recent developments in institutionalist monetary theory (Minsky, Chick, Arestis and Eichner) are all closely identified with Post Keynesianism. But there are differences: not that these differences are necessary or, indeed, that they apply to all institutionalists and Post Keynesians. They are differences between fictional representative institutionalists and Post Keynesians. These differences arise from differences in epistemology: institutionalism is more concerned with historical regularities and the continuities of evolution. Institutional change is central, but as part of a long-term continuous process. Post Keynesians (particularly those involved in the analysis of the *Treatise on Probability*), focus on the uncertainty with which most knowledge is held. This has implications for the conventional nature of decisions to buy capital goods and/or to manage financial portfolios; these conventions allow for stability while the conventions persist, but instability when they are subject to discrete shocks.

Post Keynesian monetary theory, therefore, puts liquidity preference alongside endogenous credit. Liquidity preference has consequences for the capacity for financial institutions to extend credit: the higher is liquidity preference, the more constrained are financial institutions in their credit creation, and the higher the interest they must charge; but in addition, high liquidity preference among banks itself discourages extension of credit. Credit is still endogenous, but does not fully accommodate demand.

While uncertainty and liquidity preference have their most manifest impact in the short period, they do in addition have profound effects on the long period, and on the pattern of institutional evolution. Indeed, money itself can be seen as an institution for dealing with uncertainty and liquidity preference. There is every reason, therefore, for institutionalist monetary theory to incorporate these factors; they are present in the writing of some, notably Minsky, whom Dillard (1987) treats as an institutionalist.

New institutionalist monetary theory

Finally, there has been a recent burgeoning of literature which could be classified as new institutionalist, although it does not adopt that nomenclature. This approach has in common with old institutionalism a concern with the historical evolution of financial systems, and the institutional aspects of monetary policy. The view is also shared that the money supply is primarily endogenously determined inside money. But, while Minsky, for example, warns of the danger of endogenous finance, the new institutionalists argue for regulatory change to allow for a greater degree of endogeneity. As elsewhere in new institutionalism, the basic building-blocks of the underlying analysis are neoclassical; in particular, a perfectly competitive industrial structure and the possibility of a perfectly competitive banking system are assumed.

This new institutionalist literature thus focuses on the role of the state in the provision of money and the regulation of financial markets. Although all advocate a laissez-faire approach to policy in these two areas, different groups adopt different views on money. These views arise from different interpretations of monetary history. Both the new monetary economics and legal restrictions theory suggest that financial development has been such that money is no longer distinctive as a financial instrument; indeed, there is no need for outside money regardless of whether it is a liability of the state or some commodity. Competition within unregulated financial markets would enforce prudent and profit-maximizing behaviour, which would increase efficiency within financial markets. The new free banking school (drawing on the 'old' free banking theory of Vera Smith and of Hayek, 1976) argues that competition would in fact force banks to offer convertibility into an outside money. This group therefore devotes attention to the nature and role of the outside money the market would opt for and, in some cases, allows for some limited role for the state in influencing the choice of outside money. The provision of inside money would result purely from market forces. This, it is argued, would eliminate the inflation and instability which have arisen from the public sector monopoly on money.

The new institutionalist monetary theorists thus share with old institutionalist theorists a focus on the historical evolution of banking systems, but totally absent is the central theme of the old institutionalist literature that money is integral to the capitalist economic process and that this monetary process is inherently unstable.

SHEILA C. DOW

See also:

Hayek, Friedrich A.; Inflation; Keynes, John Maynard; Macroeconomic Policy; Macroeconomic Theory; Mitchell, Wesley Clair; Monetary Policy; Money, Evolution of; Veblen, Thorstein.

Bibliography

Arestis, P. and A.S. Eichner (1988), 'The Post Keynesian and Institutionalist Theory of Money and Credit', *Journal of Economic Issues*, **XXII**, (4), pp. 1003–21.

Chick, V. (1986), 'The Evolution of the Banking System and the Theory of Saving, Investment and Interest', *Economies et Sociétés, Monnaie et Production*, **20**, (8–9), pp. 111–26.

Dillard, D. (1987), 'Money as an Institution of Capitalism', *Journal of Economic Issues*, **XXI**, (4), pp. 1623–47.

Hayek, F.A. (1976), *Denationalisation of Money*, London:IEA.

Minsky, H.P. (1982), *Can 'It' Happen Again?*, New York: M.E. Sharpe, published in the UK as *Inflation, Recession and Economic Policy*, Brighton: Wheatsheaf.

Money, Evolution of

The Austrian economist Carl Menger viewed money as a paradigmatic 'organic' social institution, alongside language or common law. By 'organic' he did not mean natural or biological, but a social institution which, although the product of human action, is not the product of human design. In particular, money is seen to arise out of the combination and interaction of individual decisions, although no one may have intended the outcome. Accordingly, this view differs from the 'state theory of money' or 'monetary nominalism' of the institutionalist Georg Knapp (1924) and others. In opposition to the latter viewpoint, for Menger and the Austrian School the emergence and continuance of a monetary system of exchange does not necessarily require the legislation and backing of the state.

Menger (1963, p. 153) accepts that 'history actually offers us examples that certain wares have been declared money by law'. But these declarations are often seen to be 'the acknowledgement of an item which had already become money'. Although cases of the emergence of money by agreement or legislation are important, Menger argues:

> the origin of money can truly be brought to our full understanding only by our learning to understand the *social* institution discussed here as the unintended result, as the unplanned outcome of specifically *individual* efforts of members of society. (Menger, 1963, p. 155)

An account of the supposed evolutionary process through which money could emerge is found in his *Principles*:

> As *each* economizing individual becomes increasingly more aware of his economic interest, he is led by this *interest, without any agreement, without legislative compulsion*, and *even without regard to the public interest*, to give his commodities in exchange for other, more saleable, commodities, even if he does not need them for any immediate consumption purpose. With economic progress, therefore, we can everywhere observe the phenomenon of a certain number of goods, especially those that are most easily saleable at a given time and place, becoming, under the influence of *custom*, acceptable to everyone in trade, and thus capable of being given in exchange for any other commodity. (Menger, 1981, p. 260)

Clearly, a trader may hold a stock of a commodity for reasons other than the purpose of direct personal consumption. In this case the commodity will be held with a view to immediate or future trade. However, commodities will differ in their saleability and acceptability. Some commodities will be widely accepted in exchange, others less so. A commodity that is seen to be accepted in exchange will have its saleability enhanced as individuals act on the basis of such a perception. Hence money is seen to emerge through subjective evaluations, and become progressively reinforced through action and the perception of this action by other individuals. This could be described as some kind of evolutionary process. Apart from the attribute of being 'most marketable', which is a culmination and consequence of individual perceptions and choices, Menger (1963, p. 154) suggests that the good that emerges as money may be 'the most easily transported, the most durable, the most easily divisible'. Consequently, over time, a single commodity or group of commodities will emerge as money.

Smithian reasoning

Menger's theory of money is reminiscent of Adam Smith's 'invisible hand' reasoning. Indeed, there is a direct lineage in the approach to evolutionary theory from Smith through to the Austrian School. Smithian evolutionary theory has a number of features, including, first, an emphasis on the spontaneous and unintended emergence of a social order via the 'invisible hand'; second, a process of evolution which normally reaches a harmonious steady state, rather than being continuously disrupted and undermined; and third, a disposition towards a non-interventionist policy based on the belief that such complex evolutionary processes cannot be readily out-designed, nor easily improved upon.

Menger goes further than Smith, however, in examining this process in more detail. For example, he shows how the initial emergence of a convention, or social institution such as money, may be largely accidental. Subsequent to its tentative emergence in a given locality, it becomes better established through a process of continuous feedback. The initial and local emergence of a convention is thus progressively reinforced by the positive feedback of perceptions and actions in accord with the convention. With this kind of evolutionary selection process, the unit of selection is the convention, or potential monetary unit, itself. Although the convention or monetary unit has durable qualities, it is not at all like the gene in modern biology. Such a unit does not survive because its genetically programmed qualities are well adapted in a given environmental context. The monetary unit is wanted because it is wanted; the convention is followed because it is followed. Such reciprocating causation means that cause becomes effect, just as effect becomes cause.

The Mengerian evolutionary process is Smithian in character, in that it posits the end state at which money (Menger) or the social order (Smith) has become widely accepted, established and thereby stabilized. For both Darwin and Lamarck there was no such end point to an evolutionary process. Clearly, the object of evolutionary analysis is an emerging monetary unit and the focus is on the cumulative reinforcement of a given unit. The 'genetic material' is the individuals with their given preferences and goals. Importantly, this 'genetic material' does not change during the emergence of money. There is not necessarily even a process of evolutionary selection between rival units, nor is there a consideration of the changes in individual goals or preferences.

The role of government

Subsequent theoretical work on the evolution of money has shown that the emergence of the monetary unit is a case of path dependency. The selection process may also depend on a combination of accidents or initial perceptions. As long as the commodity is reasonably durable and not too cumbersome, it can serve as a medium of exchange. In this case the initial 'accidents' leading to the emergence of one rather than another commodity determine whether money is to be coins, cows or cowrie shells. This path dependency undermines the sanctity of any *de facto* evolutionary outcome. To some extent, therefore, Menger's market liberalism is compromised. With strong path dependency, the initial salience of an inferior outcome may lead to a sub-optimal result. In sum, the Mengerian process of the evolution of money is one of the many, even typical, cases where evolutionary outcomes are not the most efficient. Consequently, there may be some justification for state regulation of the monetary system.

A debate over whether it is possible to remove the state entirely from involvement in the monetary system has simmered on in recent years, with many contributions favouring the 'denationalization' of money (Hayek, 1976). However, attempts to point to historical precedents for such a dubious system of 'free banking' in modern times are not convincing. The cited historical forerunners of Scotland up to 1848 and New York State from 1836 to 1863 still involved substantial state intervention and regulation. The failure of the 'free banking' theorists to point to a convincing precedent raises serious questions about the viability of their proposal.

Furthermore, it should not be assumed that the modern monetary system in advanced capitalist economies is primarily a matter of the government 'printing' money. Most of the money supply emanates from credit from private banks, and the state itself is involved in much more than the issue of note and coin. Even if the Menger-type arguments support the proposition that state intervention is not necessary for emergence of money, we are entitled to draw the conclusion that the legal establishment of money by the state may often be necessary for a more efficient outcome, or to maintain a given outcome in the face of disturbance or threat.

Quality variation

According to Philip Mirowski's 'social theory of value', money is as 'a socially constructed institution'. However, 'precisely because it is socially instituted, its invariance cannot be predicated on any "natural" ground, and must continually be shored up and reconstituted by further social institutions, such as accountants and banks and governments' (Mirowski, 1990, p. 712). In other words, the 'value' of money is continually under threat from many devices and strategems, from coin clipping to the modern expansion of debt.

Menger ignores this possibility by treating the evolving monetary unit as invariant, but even gold can be melted down and alloyed with inferior metals. As in modern biology, there is no single, pure, typological item. In contrast, Menger's analysis is a case of 'typological thinking', with a population of identical and invariant proto-monetary units. As Mirowski points out, the relaxation of this assumption of invariance undermines the case for the emergence of money in disembodied market competition and without the assistance of a strong institution such as the state.

Menger and his followers assume that the supposedly spontaneous emergence of money is similar to the evolution of language and law. However, there are important differences. With money, and with potential quality variation, individual agents have an obvious incentive to use a less costly or poor-quality version of the medium of exchange in preference to the good. Similar incentives to debase social norms exist in the case of many laws. Consequently, state intervention may be necessary to validate the acceptability of the monetary unit, just as state intervention is often required, albeit sometimes as a last resort, to enforce law. However, language is different because individuals have an incentive to make their meaning clear. In communication we are impelled to use words and sounds in a way that conforms as closely as possible to the perceived norm. Our inbuilt drives to imitate are used to the full, and we have no incentive to bar their operation. Although languages do change through time, there are incentives to conform to and thus reinforce the linguistic norms in the given region or context. Linguistic norms are thus almost wholly self-policing, unlike currency values and most laws. The argument for the intervention of the state is thus much stronger in the case of law and money than in the case of language. Legal designation of what is money is important, just as the state is important in the process of originating and sanctioning law.

Concluding remarks

Notably, the 'old' institutionalist account of the emergence of money, particularly as developed by Wesley Clair Mitchell (1937), suggests that this event cannot be explained simply because it reduced costs or made life easier for traders. The penetration of money exchange into social life altered the very configurations of rationality, involving the particular conceptions of abstraction, measurement, quantification and calculative intent. It was thus a transformation of individuals rather than simply the emergence of institutions and rules.

Menger sees social evolution as starting from an institution-free 'state of nature' and reaching an end state with the established monetary unit. However, we can never reach a primary, institution-free state from which explanation in the Mengerian or 'new institutionalist' vein can begin. In contrast, the 'old' institutionalists such as Thorstein Veblen see evolution as an unending process of cumulative causation, in which habits and institutions are both causes and effects.

GEOFFREY M. HODGSON

See also:
Evolution, Theories of Economic; Institutionalism, 'Old' and 'New'; Lock-in and Chreodic Development; Methodological Individualism; Mitchell, Wesley Clair; Monetary Theory; Natural Selection, Economic Evolution and; Smith, Adam; Spontaneous Order; Veblen, Thorstein.

Bibliography
Hayek, F.A. (1976), *The Denationalisation of Money*, London: Institute of Economic Affairs.
Knapp, G.F. (1924), *The State Theory of Money*, London: Macmillan.
Menger, C. (1963), *Problems of Economics and Sociology*, translated by F.J. Nock from the German edition of 1883, with an introduction by Louis Schneider, Urbana, Ill.: University of Illinois Press.
Menger, C. (1981), *Principles of Economics*, edited by J. Dingwall and translated by B.F. Hoselitz from the German edition of 1871, New York: New York University Press.
Mirowski, P. (1990), 'Learning the Meaning of the Dollar: Conservation Principles and the Social Theory of Value in Economic Theory', *Social Research*, **57**, (3), Fall, pp. 689–717.
Mitchell, W.C. (1937), *The Backward Art of Spending Money and Other Essays*, New York: McGraw-Hill.

Myrdal, Gunnar

The ideas and life work of the Swedish economist Gunnar Myrdal (1898–1987) exemplify the institutionalist perspective in economics. His contributions to dynamic analysis of social systems, of valuations in economic research and his work in international development establish him as one of the most significant economists of the twentieth century. Myrdal received his education at Stockholm University, attaining a law degree in 1923 and PhD in economics in 1927. He began his career as a neoclassical macroeconomist interested in price and monetary theory and was in fact hostile to the institutionalism he encountered in the United States when he and his wife, Alva Reimer Myrdal, visited that country as Rockefeller fellows in 1929–30.

At that time he saw the work of Mitchell and other American institutionalists as naive, denouncing 'theory' while retaining implicit biases. Even in these early years, however, Myrdal's writing reflects a questioning and critical spirit which recognized and began to analyse some of the limitations of conventional neoclassical analysis.

Myrdal may be recognized most for his two major research endeavours. The first, *An American Dilemma: The Negro Problem and Modern Democracy*, was funded by the Carnegie Corporation. Begun in 1937, this project was to examine exhaustively and objectively the problem of race relations in the United States. The research culminated in 1943 and was published in 1944. The second major study is *Asian Drama: An Inquiry into the Poverty of Nations*, published in 1968. Both of these multi-volume studies develop the methods and theory of economics in a social context which typifies the institutionalist approach. The Myrdals were also active in Swedish politics; their work on population and social policy in Sweden in the 1930s significantly influenced the development of the welfare state in the Scandinavian countries. In 1974, Gunnar Myrdal was awarded the Nobel Prize in Economics along with Friedrich von Hayek. Hayek and Myrdal represented opposing views on the role of policy in economic affairs. The prize underscores Myrdal's and institutionalism's contribution to economics.

Two areas of concern mark the early years of Myrdal's career. The first, a product of both his academic training and the political scene in Sweden in the early 1930s, was monetary theory and government policy. The Swedish economist Knut Wicksell (1851–1926) provided a model of the role of the monetary sector based on the inadequacy of traditional quantity theories and the importance of the difference between the real and the money rates of interest in contributing to a cumulative process moving away from equilibrium. Myrdal developed and critically examined Wicksell's work and moved the discussion forward by introducing the concepts of risk and uncertainty (in investment) and of anticipations (of prices) into Wicksell's framework of cumulative processes in the monetary sector. Later writers, including G.L.S. Shackle, in his *Years of High Theory*, recognized in Myrdal's early work the development of a theoretical framework comparable to later Keynesian analysis of unemployment and investment/savings behaviour. Shackle concluded: 'had the *General Theory* never been written, Myrdal's work would eventually have supplied almost the same theory'. Myrdal's work in monetary theory influenced later economists including Nicholas Kaldor.

The economic crises of the period drew Myrdal and his colleagues into the political process. Myrdal contributed the theoretical underpinnings for the ensuing fiscal and monetary policies and served on many committees and commissions. He collaborated with Alva Myrdal in writing *Crisis in the Population Question*, which addressed the issues of housing and social policy.

This book became a major influence in the evolving social welfare policies of the countries of Scandinavia. An advisor for the Labour Party in 1933, Myrdal became a senator for the Social Democrats in 1934, and later, in 1945, Commerce Minister.

Myrdal studied the political and value-based biases, including his own, inherent in the formulation of economic policy on the part of supposedly unbiased economic scientists. The problem of values, of the influence of the world-views and historical traditions from which the social scientist does not, and indeed, cannot totally extract himself, forms the second theme of Myrdal's early writing. This concern for the place of valuation in the social sciences, particularly its corrupting influence when not explicitly recognized and delineated, was developed throughout his career, and constitutes one of Myrdal's major contributions to economics.

In *The Political Element In The Development of Economic Theory*, a revision of lectures given in 1931, Myrdal traces the evolution of economic thought and theory and shows that the purported scientific, positive economic theory of the neoclassicalists is actually influenced by subjective valuations and developed directly out of utilitarianism, hedonistic associational psychology and natural law philosophy. Myrdal particularly took issue with value and welfare theory, citing marginal utility theory as based on metaphysical and teleological premises rather then empirically verifiable assertions. Economics, and the social sciences in general, had to be cleansed of these illogical underpinnings in order that a truly scientific theory could be developed. Then policy could be formulated with ends in mind which explicitly reflected chosen social values. Later, Myrdal criticized the naivety of his younger days, recognizing that the social sciences, as the study of human institutions and behaviour, could not purge itself of valuations. Data do not organize themselves into a theoretical framework, rather researchers formulate theories from their own anticipations. The questions the scientist asks, the way one defines and collects data and the structures postulated are all influenced by valuations. Myrdal found the only solution was to clarify the chosen value premises and state them rather than allow them to remain implicit. The remaining work of Myrdal's intellectual life reflects this commitment to developing the methods necessary to objectify, as much as possible, scientific research in the social sciences by recognizing and stating the chosen value premises. This insight into the problem of valuations, and particularly the development of techniques to address it, represents a vital addition to economics as institutionalism approaches it.

Myrdal cites the influence of various Swedish intellectuals of his day in the development of his own ideas. Perhaps most important among them was the Swedish philosopher Axel Hagerstrom. A philosophical sceptic, Hagerstrom emphasized the difference between beliefs about reality and valuations of it. He insisted on making concepts explicit in the social sciences. Other influences included Wicksell, who prepared the way for Keynes in the minds of Swedish economists, and Gustav Cassel, who was criticized by Myrdal for his laissez-faire doctrine, but who also insisted on the necessity to quantify empirically theoretical assertions.

In 1937, Myrdal began work on *An American Dilemma*. Richard Sterner and Arnold Rose assisted in this ambitious effort to examine race relations in America. It quickly became one of the most important contributions to the subject and to the study of American culture in the twentieth century. *Brown* v. *Topeka* (Board of Education), the landmark Supreme Court decision finding segregation unconstitutional, cited Myrdal's study in its ruling. *An American Dilemma* was an exhaustive study, encompassing every aspect of life in America: political, social, economic and historical. It examines all the social institutions affecting blacks and analyses the norms, mores and belief systems, in short, the American culture which supported racism. Myrdal set out to understand and state explicitly the concepts and value premises inherent in the research endeavour and in American culture. He thus demonstrated a systematic method for addressing the value problem. He also offered an example of significant magnitude of the institutional approach to social research. *An American Dilemma* examines all relevant variables and seeks to analyse the dynamic interplay which results in the social situation. The economic status, opportunities and context of black life in America is a result of, and results in, the whole complex of social factors. This holistic perspective, above all others, embodies the essence of institutionalism. Myrdal himself reminisced that it was his work on *An American Dilemma* that led to his mature identification as an institutionalist.

In his early discussion of Wicksell's monetary theory, Myrdal had criticized the dependence on the concept of stable equilibrium in classical economic theory, a model borrowed from physics which, according to Myrdal, provides simplicity, but does not accurately describe economic processes. Instead he posited a dynamic process which involves cumulation. Each factor or variable in the social system responds to or affects another variable and so on in a dynamic interaction where primary changes cause the whole system to move. Assuming an initial static balance of forces, though not necessarily a stable one, changes moving through the system will accumulate, causing changes in one or another direction through the whole system. Thus the idea of the 'vicious circle', where the dynamic process is moving in a deleterious direction is only one possible outcome: a 'virtuous circle', where forces are moving in a positive direction is also possible. Understanding which social and economic factors cause changes in other variables, and what is the direction and magnitude of that change, could, theoretically at least, be quantified. This pursuit, according to Myrdal, should be the goal of the social scientist. Economic and social policy would then be motivated from a realistic understanding of social processes.

Myrdal became Secretary General of the Economic Commission for Europe in 1947, directing research there for a decade. He embraced the opportunity to apply the model of cumulative dynamic processes to international economic issues, particularly to the study of international cooperation, economic integration and development. In his *Rich Lands and Poor*, Myrdal outlined the processes and factors which impeded this economic development. His analysis of cumulative dynamics reaches maturation in this work, where he presents the principle of circular and cumulative causation. As described above, circular and cumulative causation involves a dynamic model of social processes where primary or initial changes start an interactive process among all variables. Rather than moving back to a 'stable equilibrium' after some factor changes, the system moves in the same direction as the primary change. In other words, the secondary reactions are not necessarily counteractive. Not only 'economic' factors are affected, but 'noneconomic' variables as well. The latter, in fact, are usually more important in determining the outcome. Application of the model of circular and cumulative causation enables the economist better to analyse the problem of underdevelopment where conventional economics with its laissez-faire bias has been unable or unwilling to formulate effective theory and policy. Institutionalism therefore provides the insight crucial to alleviating the large and growing disparity between the rich and poor nations.

Myrdal describes the cumulative processes which hinder development in poor regions as the 'backwash effects' felt by regions peripheral to an area of economic expansion. Three factors, trade, capital movement and migration, work to worsen conditions of the 'hinterland' as the expanding region attracts resources, investment and labour. This effect is now well documented for the sub-Saharan region of Africa. Expanding development of a region can also 'spread' to the adjacent regions, improving conditions cumulatively in an ever-wider area. Roads, communications, general literacy and a healthy population support and enhance new economic opportunity. Myrdal observed that the spread effects dominate in the developed countries, mitigating the backwash effects, while poorer regions experienced inhibition of the spread effects and the backwash effects dominated.

In the 1950s, Myrdal recognized that, because of this structural resistance to growth characteristic of underdeveloped regions, aid from the Western countries, though essential, would not be adequate to achieve development. He recommended an emphasis on technology, on the transfer of ideas and skills as necessary to achieving success. The tremendous gains resulting from the Green Revolution in Asia since the time of his recommendation and the growing recognition of the role of technology in the development process serve to validate his theories and the wisdom of his perspective.

THOMAS R. DEGREGORI AND DEBORAH A. SHEPHERD

See also:
Cognition, Cultural and Institutional Influences on; Cumulative Causation; Development Policy; Development Theory; Discrimination, Economic Policies to Counter; Institutional Economic Thought in Europe; International Economic Policy; International Economic Relations; Kaldor, Nicholas; Keynes, John Maynard; Neoclassical Microeconomic Theory, Critique of; Time; Welfare Economic Theory.

Bibliography
Myrdal, Alva and Gunnar Myrdal (1934), *Crisis in the Population Question*, Stockholm: Bonnier.
Myrdal, Gunnar (1944), *An American Dilemma: The Negro Problem and American Democracy*, 2 vols, New York and London: Harper & Row.
Myrdal, Gunnar (1953), *The Political Element in the Development of Economic Theory*, London: Kegan Paul.
Myrdal, Gunnar (1958a), *Rich Lands and Poor: The Road to World Prosperity*, New York: Harper; first published 1957 as *Economic Theory and Underdeveloped Regions*, London: Duckworth.
Myrdal, Gunnar (1958b), *Value in Social Theory*, ed. P. Streeten, London: Routledge and New York: Harper.
Myrdal, Gunnar (1962), *Monetary Equilibrium*, New York: Kelley; first published 1939, London: Hodge.
Myrdal, Gunnar (1968), *Asian Drama: An Inquiry into the Poverty of Nations*, 3 vols, London: Penguin; New York: Pantheon Books
Myrdal, Gunnar (1972), *Against the Stream: Critical Essays on Economics*, New York: Pantheon Books.
Myrdal, Gunnar (1978), 'Institutional Economics', *Journal of Economic Issues*, **XII**, (4), pp. 771–83, December.
Shackle, G.L.S. (1967), *The Years of High Theory: Invention and Tradition in Economic Thought, 1926–1939*, Cambridge: Cambridge University Press.

Natural Selection, Economic Evolution and

The term 'evolution' has a number of definitions and meanings in the social sciences. Here we shall consider its application to economics in a relatively narrow sense, analogous to the process of natural selection in modern biology. Natural selection involves several component principles. First, there must be sustained variation among the members of a species or population. Variations may be blind, random, or purposive in character but, without them, as Darwin insisted, natural selection cannot operate. Second, there must be some principle of heredity or continuity, through which offspring have to resemble their parents more than they resemble other members of their species. In other words, there has to be some mechanism through which individual characteristics are 'passed on' through the generations. Third, natural selection itself operates either because better adapted organisms leave increased numbers of offspring, or because the variations or gene combinations that are preserved are those bestowing advantage in struggling to survive. The latter is the principle of the struggle for existence. It is important to note that evolutionary selection in biology occurs both by differential rates of death and differential rates of birth; it is a matter of procreation as well as destruction.

The application of the metaphor of natural selection to economics must be on the basis of analogous principles. Arguably, the units of selection in economic evolution can be individuals, routines, institutions or systems. A methodological individualist, however, would insist that the only appropriate unit of selection is the individual. The possibility of other units of selection is raised elsewhere. We now consider each of these principles in turn, with an eye to the economic analogue.

The principle of variation
The principle of variation emphasizes the essential, developmental role of variety and diversity. The biologist Ernst Mayr establishes the importance of 'population thinking' in which variety and diversity are all-important. Such 'population thinking' contrasts with the Platonic notion of 'typological essentialism' in which entities are regarded as identifiable in terms of a few distinct characteristics which represent their essential qualities. In typological thinking, species are regarded as identifiable in terms of a few distinct characteristics which represent their essence. Accordingly, all variations around the ideal type are regarded as accidental aberrations. By contrast, in population thinking, species are described in terms of a distribution of characteristics. Whereas in typological thinking variation is a classificatory nuisance, in population thinking it is of paramount interest because it is precisely the variety of the system that fuels the evolutionary process.

The relevance of 'population thinking' to economics has been stressed by Stanley Metcalfe (1988) and others. It suggests the importance of the examination of frequencies and their distribution, rather than ideal cases. Hence, instead of the Marshallian 'representative firm', the evolutionary economist should address the population of firms and the distribution and variation of key characteristics. How does variation arise and how is it retained? In biological evolution the principal mechanisms here are, first, mutation and, second, sexual recombination along Mendelian lines. In the theory of the firm developed by Richard Nelson and Sidney Winter (1982), there is an analogue to mutation. When a firm's profit levels become intolerably low, it is forced to search for a new technology. Arguably, mutation, in an economic context, can include both the planned reorganization of, and unintended changes within, institutions and it is thus much more frequent and pervasive than mutation in biology. Other than the direct merger of institutions and firms, however, there is no obvious analogue to sexual recombination or Mendelian genetics in the socioeconomic sphere.

Importantly, the maintenance of variety involves constant error making, as well as continuous selection of the more adapted forms. For selection to work there must be rejection, and the process must thus involve ceaseless mistakes as well as refinements.

The principle of heredity
The principle of heredity suggests that the units of selection in economic evolution must have some durability and resilience, even if they are not as permanent as the DNA. Furthermore, there must be some mechanism through which characteristics are 'passed on' to other units.

Thorstein Veblen observed that habits and routines have a stable and inert quality, and often sustain their important characteristics through time. Whilst these are more malleable and do not mutate in the same way as their analogue in biology, habits and routines do have a sufficient degree of durability for them to be regarded as having quasi-genetic qualities. The idea that routines within the firm act as 'genes' to pass on skills and information is also adopted by Nelson and Winter (1982) and forms a crucial part of their theoretical model of the modern corporation.

Institutions are the outcome of sustained habit and routine. In turn, they feed back and reinforce habits and routines in a number of ways. For instance, anthropologists and psychologists have argued that institutions play an essential role in providing a cognitive framework for interpreting sense data, and in sustaining intellectual habits and routines for transforming information into useful knowledge. There is thus a possibility that habits and routines can become reinforced by cumulative feedback. The process of feedback generates conformity to their norms, and in turn reinforces them.

Consequently, habits and routines can acquire a quality of durability that makes them a surrogate for the gene in socioeconomic evolution.

Habits and routines may also be passed from one institution to another. For example, the skills learned by a worker in a given firm become partially embedded in his or her habits, and may endure to some extent through changes in employment. In addition, skills may be transferred from institution to institution, from group to group and from individual to individual, through conscious or unconscious propensities to imitate. However, as Nelson and Winter (1982) make clear, routines do not act as genes in the modern Darwinian sense because the inheritance of acquired characteristics is possible. Thus the evolutionary process in society is in this respect Lamarckian. Nevertheless, habits and routines are both durable and present in a variety of forms in any complex economy. As in the case of Darwin's theory, this combination of variety with durability provides the raw material for evolutionary selection.

Selection and survival

The principles of natural selection and struggle for existence posit some selection mechanism in which better adapted types of unit can increase their numbers, either relatively or absolutely. Veblen (1899, p. 188) saw clearly that the units of selection in socioeconomic evolution were institutions: 'The life of man in society, just as the life of other species, is a struggle for existence, and therefore it is a process of selective adaptation. The evolution of social structure has been a process of natural selection of institutions.' Veblen's suggestion is that some institutions become extinct because they are not well adapted to their general socioeconomic environment. We must also consider the possibility that some institutions are less likely than others to pass on their characteristics and thus 'procreate' through imitation. The natural selection of institutions is not simply a matter of relative death rates of different types of institution but also the probability that institutions of different types will be established in the first place.

As in the case of biological evolution, the selection of some entities and the extinction of others does not necessarily imply that the favoured entities are morally just, or even superior in an absolute sense. One reason for this is that selection always operates relative to a given environment. The dinosaurs prospered for millions of years. Relative to the environment of that period they were highly successful. They were probably wiped out because of a sudden and cataclysmic environmental change, such as that caused by a large meteorite.

In biology the concepts of adaptation, fitness and evolutionary success have been controversial and problematic, and only recently have adequate definitions emerged (Arnold and Fristrup, 1982). Evolutionary *success* is a retrospective measure of the relative increase or decrease in the descendants of a lineage, as a fraction of a specified population over a specified time interval. In contrast, *fitness* refers to the propensity of a unit to be successful in those terms. *Adaptation* refers to any heritable character that increases the fitness of an entity within a given set of environments, or the evolutionary process resulting in the establishment of such a character in the population of entities. Notably, with the appropriate terms defined in this way, the idea of 'the survival of the fittest' is not a tautology. Fitness is not the same as survival. It is possible for units with greater fitness to be unsuccessful.

If the general unit of selection in economic evolution is the institution, it is not appropriate to consider evolutionary success simply in terms of the number of such institutions. Addressing economic evolution in the context of a capitalist economy, a better measure of the success of an institution within that system would be the growth rate of its assets, valued through the market in money terms. On this basis, Stanley Metcalfe's (1988) definition of the 'fitness' of an economic institution – as the 'propensity to accumulate' – can be adopted. Usefully, this connects some notion of economic efficiency with that of economic growth. An adaptable institution is one which possesses characteristics which give it a greater propensity to invest or accumulate, such as higher profits and a tendency to plough back much of that profit into investment.

The neoclassical economist Jack Hirshleifer (1978, p. 322) has adopted a conception of economic evolution in which 'Competition is the all-pervasive law of natural-economy interactions.' This is misleading, however. In both biological and socioeconomic evolution, natural selection does not necessarily imply competition over scarce resources nor even that one species must prosper to the detriment of another. As the philosopher of biology Elliott Sober (1984, p. 191) argues: 'Competition is a special case, not a defining characteristic, of natural selection.' Accordingly, natural selection in the economic sphere need not necessarily imply ruthless struggle and destructive competition. Furthermore, it is possible for cooperation to emerge through natural selection.

Concluding remarks
The standard conception of 'natural selection', whether in the biological or the socioeconomic sphere, implies a relatively stable environment. This is necessary so that the process of selection in relation to that environment is sustained long enough for the particular characteristics of the more adapted entities to demonstrate their relative superiority. Arguably, however, socioeconomic environments change much more rapidly than in the normal biological context. This creates a problem for the application of the theory of natural selection to the socioeconomic sphere. Either the changes in the

environment and the interactions between it and the constituent institutions have to be incorporated in some way into the theoretical model, or a partial and short-run evolutionary analysis must be performed in which the environment is assumed constant for some time.

Nevertheless, certain features of socioeconomic systems are stable for decades, even in systems that are changing and experiencing rapid growth. Social culture has enduring features, along with many encompassing social and political institutions. Accordingly, one approach would be to consider the processes of 'natural selection' in these periods of relative continuity alongside the episodes of disruption and upheaval when the general structures of society themselves endure substantial change.

This conception of socioeconomic evolution is more like the idea of 'punctuated equilibria' advanced by biologists Niles Eldredge and Stephen Jay Gould (1977) than orthodox Darwinian gradualism. The theory of punctuated equilibria suggests that biological evolution is not as continuous and gradual as is often supposed: nature can indeed make jumps. These jumps occur at particular times of rapid environmental change and stress. An analogous conception, involving steady growth interspersed with dramatic bifurcations, is found in modern systems theory (Laszlo, 1987). It is also suggestive of the idea of institutional development involving periods of relative stability interspersed with rapid and dramatic structural change and 'creative destruction'.

As in biology, economic natural selection does not give rise to predictable outcomes. Perhaps the most that can be done is to use extrapolation or parametric modelling in the cases of relative socioeconomic stability, combined with a very cautious assessment of the likely effects of disruptions of a certain degree or type (Hodgson and Screpanti, 1991, ch.10).

GEOFFREY M. HODGSON

See also:
Biology and Economics; Cooperation, The Evolution of; Darwinism, Influence of Economics on; Evolution and Optimality; Evolution, Theories of Economic; Habits; Lock-in and Chreodic Development; Marshall, Alfred; Methodological Individualism; Microfoundations of Macroeconomic Competitiveness; Nelson, Richard R.; Routines; Schumpeter, Joseph Alois; Selection, Units of Evolutionary; Veblen, Thorstein; Winter, Sidney G., Jr.

Bibliography
Arnold, A.J. and K. Fristrup (1982), 'The Theory of Evolution by Natural Selection: A Hierarchical Expansion', *Paleobiology*, **8**, pp. 113–29; reprinted 1984 in R.N. Brandon and R.M. Burian (eds), *Genes, Organisms, Populations: Controversies Over the Units of Selection*, Cambridge, Mass.: MIT.
Eldredge, N. and S.J. Gould (1977), 'Punctuated Equilibria: The Tempo and Mode of Evolution Reconsidered', *Paleobiology*, **3**, pp. 115–51.
Hirshleifer, J. (1978), 'Natural Economy versus Political Economy', *Journal of Social and Biological Structures*, **1**, pp. 319–37.

Hodgson, G.M. (1993), *Economics and Evolution: Bringing Life Back Into Economics*, Cambridge: Polity.
Hodgson, G.M. and E. Screpanti (eds) (1991), *Rethinking Economics: Markets Technology and Economic Evolution*, Aldershot: Edward Elgar.
Laszlo, E. (1987), *Evolution: The Grand Synthesis*, Boston, Mass.: New Science Library – Shambhala.
Metcalfe, J.S. (1988), 'Evolution and Economic Change', in A. Silberston (ed.), *Technology and Economic Progress*, London: Macmillan.
Nelson, R.R. and S.G. Winter (1982), *An Evolutionary Theory of Economic Change*, Cambridge Mass.: Harvard University Press.
Sober, E. (1984), 'Holism, Individualism, and the Units of Selection', in E. Sober (ed.), *Conceptual Issues in Evolutionary Biology: An Anthology*, Cambridge, Mass.: MIT.
Veblen, T.B. (1899), *The Theory of the Leisure Class: An Economic Study of Institutions*, New York: Macmillan.

Need, Concept of

The idea of need is usually ignored in modern economics. For example, it does not rate a mention in the otherwise comprehensive *New Palgrave Dictionary of Economics* (1987). Orthodox economics, it would seem, has no need for need. In part this reflects the undoubted difficulties associated with any notion of need. The topic touches on almost all disciplines within and around the social sciences: anthropology, sociology, psychology, political economy, political theory and moral and analytical philosophy. It is a slippery 'bridge concept' linking subjective and objective conceptions of welfare, individual and collective prerequisites for social action and 'positive' and 'normative' concerns. There are also linguistic traps associated with the very word. In some other languages the distinction which has accrued in English between 'need and 'want' is not found, and even in English the words have been used interchangeably in much of the economics and political economy literature. Yet despite all these pitfalls the concept will not go away and continues to be used in a variety of discourses.

This survey begins by surveying definitions of need. It then briefly summarizes the status of need and associated concepts in classical political economy, neoclassical economics, radical political economy and the human development literature. Finally a theory of universal human needs developed elsewhere (Doyal and Gough, 1991) is summarized. The theory of need proposed here has strong parallels with the theoretical tradition of instrumental value theory as developed by some American institutionalists. For instance, Tool's search for a 'social value principle' which 'provides for the continuity of human life and the noninvidious recreation of community through the instrumental use of knowledge' is also essentially an attempt to construct a theory of human need (Tool, 1979, p. 291).

Definitions

Let us distinguish three common usages of the noun and verb 'need' (Doyal and Gough, 1991, ch.3). First, it can refer to a 'drive' or motivational force, such as the need to sleep or eat. Maslow (1954) interprets the term thus in his famous hierarchy of needs. This meaning draws our attention to the biological aspects of human behaviour over which we have no choice. But over a far broader spectrum of behaviour biology constrains rather than determines human choice; hence we shall say no more here about this meaning of need.

Second, 'need' is universally used to refer to any necessary *means* to a given end. For example, to say 'I need a new hi-fi' implies that I have the goal of a better quality of reproduced music. It is this protean use of the word that in part explains the widespread view that needs are essentially relative, and which elides needs with wants. The truth behind this is that all needs statements conform to the relational structure 'A needs X in order to Y'. We shall wish to refer at times to the means necessary to attain specific ends, but when doing so shall qualify the word 'need' in some way, or use the term 'need satisfier'.

Third, 'need' can be used to refer to some Y which it is thought to be in the interest of everyone to achieve, whatever their culture. Generally speaking, a need in this sense (often with the prefix 'basic') refers to the essential and universal prerequisites for any and all persons to pursue their vision of the good, whatever their normative environment. Others have argued that this entails an ability to participate in the form of life in which they find themselves. If there are preconditions for social participation which apply to everyone in the same way then universal needs can be said to exist.

It is in this way that needs can be distinguished from wants. To repeat a hackneyed example, a diabetic may want sugar, but she needs insulin. She even needs insulin if she does not know of its existence – indeed, if she lived at a time before its discovery. She needs it ultimately because without it her social participation will become more and more impaired. It is this strong link between need and harm so defined that provides the possibility of identifying common human needs in a cross-cultural way. We wish to hold on to the distinction between needs and wants, and will therefore use the term 'need' only in this third sense, unless otherwise stated. This definition also establishes that human need is of fundamental importance in conceptualizing and evaluating human welfare.

Wants, needs and classical political economy

Classical political economists including Adam Smith operated with some notion of objective, if socially relative, need. Smith's distinction between 'value in use' and 'value in exchange' draws attention to the famous paradox that things which have the greatest value in use, like water, frequently have little of no value in exchange, whilst commodities like diamonds have 'scarce any value in use' but have high exchange value. This implies a non-subjective notion of usefulness, since diamonds undoubtedly have great subjective value to those willing and able to purchase them (Hodgson, 1988, p. 303).

In his separate discussion of 'necessaries', Smith goes on to argue that these consist of 'not only the commodities which are indispensably necessary for the support of life, but whatever the custom of the country renders it indecent for creditable people, even of the lowest order, to be without'. Putting the two concepts together, we may conclude that, for Smith, necessities are socially relative, but objectively knowable at any moment in time. They are neither subjective preferences nor universalizable needs as defined above. It is clearer and more accurate to regard this as a theory of *wants*.

Marx took over this position and developed a richer analysis of the determination of wants in capitalist society, though this was never systematized in a single place. Unfortunately, these wants are usually translated as 'needs'. Hence Elster (1985, ch.2) distinguishes in Marx's writings between physical needs, necessary needs, luxury needs and a variety of social needs. Marx clearly believed that capitalism develops the system of wants, although it cannot satisfy those wants. He endorses and elaborates a dynamic and socially relative theory of the determination of wants.

It is elsewhere, in his writings on human nature, that Marx utilizes a notion of need in the sense identified above. On numerous occasions he castigates the capitalist system of his time because it subjects workers and their families to physical and mental degradation and other evils. Here he is clearly using an *external yardstick*, a viewpoint from outside capitalism, with which to condemn it. This implies that there are standards of human welfare and need which are not simply shaped by the relations of capitalist society. It is unclear whether there is an ambiguity at the heart of Marx or whether the inconsistency is simply a result of the elision of want and need in the discourse of the time.

Neoclassical economics and demand theory
From the 1870s onwards, these theories of want were overshadowed by the marginal revolution of Jevons, Menger and Walras and the foundations of the modern theory of *demand*. Jevons derived from the notion of total utility or use value the concept of marginal utility. (Though, interestingly, Menger derives his marginal analysis via a hierarchy of needs. This ambivalence with older notions is also found in Marshall's writings (Hodgson, 1988, p. 247).)

However, the problems associated with the notion of utility led in the twentieth century to its replacement by desire fulfilment as indicated by choice in market situations as a criterion of welfare. From here it was but a short step to the direct equation of well-being with opulence, or the real income of people as measured by the vector of commodities which they consume. Eventually, welfare economics and the principle of private sovereignty emerged. Considering only the latter here, this stated that what is to be produced, how it is to be produced and how it is to be distributed should be determined by the private consumption and work preferences of individuals (Penz, 1986, pp. 55, 40). Yet there are so many inconsistencies within the principles of want satisfaction and consumer sovereignty, and so many problems in measuring want satisfaction, that welfare economics cannot do without some other criterion of welfare external to the subjective preferences of individuals. These problems include: limits to people's knowledge and rationality; the 'circularity of evaluation' entailed if wants are shaped by the institutions and processes of production and distribution which meet those wants; problems in making interpersonal comparisons of utility and in ranking levels of want satisfaction as higher or lower; and the plethora of well-known critiques levelled at markets as arrangements for meeting individual wants.

Two conclusions may be drawn from this catalogue of problems and inconsistencies. First, 'want satisfaction is a principle that cannot be made measurable without additional normative judgements that are neither contained in nor entailed by the preference principle'. Second, were such external normative judgements to be drawn up:

> their insertion into the want satisfaction principle subverts the principle's fundamentally open-ended and subjective character. Yet not to insert them leaves it open to the problems of ignorance and irrationality, of the evaluation circularity, and of non-comparability. This dilemma quintessentially reflects the shortcomings of the want satisfaction principle and of the sovereignty conceptions that are based on it. (Penz, 1986, pp. 132, 136)

Penz argues that the best candidate for these 'additional normative judgements' is some conception of human need.

Alternative approaches

Whilst neoclassical and welfare economics were ignoring need, radical and Marxist political economy were turning to other systems of thought to try to buttress the idea. At least three were of importance here. First, there was Marxism itself which, as we have seen, maintained alongside a historicist view of wants an ahistorical conception of human need. Second was the anthropological perspective of Malinowski and others, for whom basic needs were the environmental and biological conditions which must be fulfilled for the survival of the individual and the group. Third, there was psychology and Maslow's famous hierarchy of needs as motivations (Maslow, 1954; cf. Lutz and Lux, 1979).

All of these systems of thought constituted a powerful antidote to the individualism and subjectivism of orthodox economics, but unfortunately they all suffer from grave defects. Humanist Marxism, and the resulting distinction between 'true and false needs', entail the profound danger of imposing the will of the party or of experts over the wishes and wants of the people. Malinowski's anthropology of need runs the risk of a functionalism in which individual needs simply mirror the 'demands' of their social environment. Maslow's hierarchy of needs interprets biological constraints as determining human actions. In other words, radical and alternative approaches all run the opposite risk to that faced by orthodox economics – of substituting a radical structural functionalism for a radical individualism.

The 'basic needs' approach

A more sustained attempt to conceptualize and operationalize human need within the economics literature emerged after World War II in the guise of 'the social indicators movement' and 'the basic needs approach', which reflected dissatisfaction with GDP per head as a measure of welfare in the first world and of development in the third world. Drewnowski and others associated with the UN Research Institute of Social Development pioneered the concept of 'level of living', direct measures of need satisfaction in various areas of life. This was subsequently theorized by other social scientists, mainly in the Nordic countries (Erikson and Uusitalo, 1987). However, the movement for social indicators and human development focused on human need appears to have run into the sand in the 1980s. This reflected changes in dominant economic opinion, but also the weakness of the conceptual basis. The basic needs approach, it was argued by some, incorporated arbitrary postulates about human nature (in particular Western cultural values) and about social change (in particular a uniform, linear model of development). Either the very idea of a universal approach was rejected, or the theoretical possibility of universal needs was granted, but their concrete assessment was perceived as beyond reach owing to the cultural and political bias of concepts and evidence (for example, Rist, 1980; Galtung, 1980). The basic needs approach ignored these conceptual questions and was thus vulnerable to these and other wide-ranging relativist critiques (Sen, 1987, pp. 24–5; cf. Doyal and Gough, 1991, ch.1).

A theory of objective and universal human need

The most important attempt to formulate a rigorous framework with which to reconstitute the idea of universal welfare is that by Sen (1984, 1985, 1987). Interestingly, this has emerged from his work at the meeting point of welfare economics, development economics and philosophy. Between a commodity and its characteristics, and the final mental state induced by consuming the commodity, he posits a third conceptual domain of 'capabilities' and 'functionings'. Functionings refer to what the person can achieve with the commodity (or rather, following Lancaster, 1966, its characteristics). Capabilities refer to the freedom of choice a person has over his or her functionings.

Sen shows how functionings/capabilities offer the prospect of a direct and objective measure of the standard of living, notwithstanding the social variability of commodities. In a related discussion of poverty he expresses this as follows: 'Poverty is an absolute notion in the space of capabilities but very often it will take a relative form in the space of commodities or characteristics' (Sen, 1984, p. 335). However, though he has applied this concept in numerous papers, he nowhere provides us with a list or taxonomy of capabilities. As a theory of need is still required, we conclude with a summary of our recent attempt to provide this theory (Doyal and Gough, 1991, Parts 2 and 3) which draws upon a wide range of recent philosophical writing.

We begin by positing a universal goal for minimally disabled participation in one's social form of life. Basic human needs are then the universal prerequisites for such successful participation. We identify these universal prerequisites as *physical health* and *autonomy of agency*. Both can be assessed negatively by their absence. Physical health can be assessed via measures of mortality and cross-cultural measures of disability. Autonomy of agency consists of a deficit of mental health, cognitive skills and opportunities to engage in social participation. We argue against the relativist view that such ideas are intrinsically internal to particular cultures. In a separate argument an 'optimum' standard of physical health and autonomy is advocated, with which to evaluate present achievements and alternative policies.

However, basic needs can be met in a number of different ways. Common needs do not imply uniform *satisfiers*. There is an almost infinite variety of goods, services, activities and relationships which, to greater or lesser extent, meet basic needs. To deal with this problem we may, following Sen and Lancaster, define all characteristics which have the property of contributing to the satisfaction of basic needs in one or more cultural settings as 'satisfier characteristics'. Then we can identify a subset of *universal satisfier characteristics* referring to all those properties of goods, services, activities and relationships which enhance physical health and autonomy in all societies and cultures. For example, provision of energy and/or protein is (or should be) a common property of foodstuffs, protection from the elements is (or should be) a common property of dwellings, and so on. Such characteristics are from now on referred to as *intermediate needs*.

We distinguish eleven categories of intermediate need: adequate nutritional food and water, protective housing, a non-hazardous working environment, a non-hazardous physical environment, appropriate health care, security in childhood, significant primary relationships, physical security, economic security, safe birth control and child-bearing and basic education. Like all taxonomies these groupings are in one sense arbitrary. The crucial thing is that all the characteristics gathered under these headings are universally and positively associated with one or more of the components of physical health and autonomy, according to the best available natural and social scientific knowledge. Nine of these categories apply to all people, and one refers to the specific needs of children. The other refers to the specific needs of women for safe birth control and child-bearing, reflecting the one salient biological difference *within* the human species. Again, for each of these categories, components can be identified which suggest appropriate indicators of their satisfaction. The appropriate evaluative standard here is the minimum level of intermediate need satisfaction necessary to achieve optimum levels of basic need satisfaction.

We still face the problem of subjective disagreements over the best satisfiers and economic/social programmes for improving need satisfaction, and over priorities to be accorded different groups or different needs in a situation of scarcity. This last set of problems raised by relativist critics requires that the *substantive* theory of need outlined above be complemented by a *procedural* theory which sets out the framework wherein such disputes can be resolved in the most rational way possible. Taking issue with Arrow's impossibility theorem, we draw upon the works of Habermas and Rawls to sketch certain communicational and constitutional preconditions for optimizing need satisfaction in practice. These too can be objectively assessed using indicators of civil and political rights and social rights to welfare.

In making this assessment a theory of need must move beyond its starting-point – those preconditions required for successful participation in any social form of life – and posit further preconditions for *critical* autonomy. Successful participation in a cruel or exploitative system is hardly a recipe for objective welfare. Hence, beyond the goal of successful participation, there lies the goal of critical participation in a social life form which is, as far as possible, of one's own choosing. Critical autonomy – the ability to situate, criticize and if necessary challenge the rules and practices of the culture one grows up in – is a necessary precondition for the informed and democratic process of debating and thus improving social arrangements for meeting needs.

Finally, the huge variations today in the material capacity of the first and third worlds to meet needs raises one last issue which any theory of human need must tackle. Are rights to need satisfaction to be limited to members of specific nation states, or should they be cast more broadly? We develop a moral argument that the right to need satisfaction cannot be limited to members of the same culture or political system. Strangers in other cultural and political systems have an equal right to need satisfaction, and to need satisfaction at optimal, not just basic, levels. A theory of human need cannot stop at national boundaries and national welfare states; it must, with Myrdal, go 'beyond the welfare state' to consider human welfare on a world scale. The concept of human need must extend forwards through time to embrace the needs of future generations, however difficult this is to conceive of and operationalize. However, once individual preferences are rejected as a unique yardstick of human welfare, these difficult issues cannot be avoided. The concept of need extends our auditing of human welfare across both space and time.

In short, universal and objective human needs exist and are knowable. At any point in time there is a body of best knowledge about what they are and how best to meet them. Such knowledge is dynamic and open-ended and specific social arrangements are required to enable such continual exploration of their nature to continue. Needs are not reducible to subjective wants or preferences best understood by sovereign individuals (though they will on many occasions overlap). Nor are they reducible to static essences best understood by planners, professionals or party officials (though some of these will also have much to contribute). A theory of need can contribute to a third model of economics and economic systems which reject both untrammelled consumer sovereignty and top-down statist planning.

IAN GOUGH

See also:

Atomism and Organicism; Cognition, Cultural and Institutional Influences on; Consumer Behaviour; Culture; Development Policy; Development Theory; Discrimination, Economic Policies to Counter; Habits; Human Nature, Theory of; Instrumental Value Theory; Kapp, K. William; Marshall, Alfred; Methodological Individualism; Myrdal, Gunnar; Rationality and Maximization.

Bibliography

Doyal, L. and I. Gough (1991), *A Theory of Human Need*, London: Macmillan; New York: Guildford Publications.
Elster, J. (1985), *Making Sense of Marx*, Cambridge: Cambridge University Press.
Erikson, R. and H. Uusitalo (1987), 'The Scandinavian approach to welfare research', in R. Erikson *et al.* (eds), *The Scandinavian Model*, Armonk, NY.: M.E. Sharpe.
Galtung, J. (1980), 'The basic needs approach', in K. Lederer (ed.), *Human Needs*, Cambridge, Mass.: Oelgeschlager, Gunn and Hain.
Hodgson, G.M. (1988), *Economics and Institutions*, Cambridge: Polity.
Lancaster, K. (1966), 'A new approach to consumer theory', *Journal of Political Economy*, **74**, April, pp. 132–57.
Lutz, M. and K. Lux (1979), *The Challenge of Humanistic Economics*, Menlo Park, CA: Benjamin/Cummings.
Maslow, A. (1954), *Motivation and Personality*, 2nd edn, New York: Harper & Row.

Penz, P. (1986), *Consumer Sovereignty and Human Interests*, Cambridge: Cambridge University Press.

Rist, G. (1980), 'Basic questions about basic human needs', in K. Lederer (ed.), *Human Needs*, Cambridge, Mass.: Oelgeschlager, Gunn and Hain.

Sen, A. (1984), *Resources, Values and Development*, Oxford: Blackwell.

Sen, A. (1985), *Commodities and Capabilities*, Amsterdam: Elsevier.

Sen, A. (1987), *The Standard of Living: the Tanner Lectures*, ed. G. Hawthorn, Cambridge: Cambridge University Press.

Tool, M.R. (1979), *The Discretionary Economy*, Santa Monica, CA: Goodyear.

Nelson, Richard R.

Richard Nelson was born in 1930 in New York City. Being one of the leading figures in the revival of evolutionary economics in the 1980s, he is known both for his numerous writings on industry and technical change, and for his book on economic evolution written jointly with Sidney G. Winter.

In several respects, Nelson's work offers a challenge to mainstream economic theory. For instance, in an important article he criticizes the orthodox treatment of information and knowledge, including technological knowledge, as codifiable and cumulative. He rejects the common idea that 'technological knowledge is in the form of codified how-to-do-it knowledge which provides sufficient guidance so that if one had access to the book one would be able to do it' (Nelson, 1980, p. 63). Also discarded is the notion that such knowledge is easily or directly expanded by expenditure on research and development: 'If the salient elements of techniques involve special personal skills, or a personalized pattern of interaction and cooperation among a group of individuals in an important way, then one cannot easily infer how it would work from an experiment conducted elsewhere' (ibid., p. 67).

This conceptualization of human knowledge involves, so to speak, a unity of knowing and doing. Furthermore, knowledge may relate to the shared practices of the group, and not simply individuals. Notably, these ideas have strong and earlier precedents in the writings of the American pragmatists who influenced early American institutional economists such as Thorstein Veblen and John Commons. Nelson's argument also has precedents in the economic writings of Edith Penrose and the philosophy of Michael Polanyi. Contrary to the treatment of 'information problems' by neoclassical theorists, 'tacit' or 'unteachable' knowledge cannot be reduced simply to 'information' because it is partly embodied in habits and routines, and it cannot be reduced to, or transmitted in, a codified form.

In other articles, Nelson draws out a number of the implications of this view. Because knowledge relates to the structures and routines of the firm, and is often in a non-codifiable form, 'management cannot effectively "choose" what is to be done in any detailed way, and has only broad control over what is done, and how well. Only a small portion of what people actually do on a job can be monitored in detail' (Nelson, 1981b, p. 1038). This important view of the role and distribution of knowledge in corporate organizations is a clear rival both to Frederick Winslow Taylor's *Scientific Management* (1911) and to Harry Braverman's Marxist analysis in *Labor and Monopoly Capital* (1974). Both involve the untenable idea that the worker has become 'an appendage to the machine'. The supposed 'separation of conception and execution' which is stressed by these theorists, where managers conceive and give orders, and workers carry them out, is implicitly denied by Nelson. He argues that the firm is a 'social system' and not 'a machine'.

In another paper, Nelson (1981a, p. 109) aims to hammer 'on the point that the analysis contained in contemporary welfare economics provides an extremely shaky intellectual basis for the favorable views that most West-ern-trained economists apparently have for private enterprise'. It is not that private enterprise is without its virtues, but Nelson shows that the evaluation of the merits of private enterprise is far more complex than the mask of orthodox theorizing would suggest. Typically, the aim here is both to avoid all simplistic policy conclusions and to suggest a programme for major renovation or even replacement of orthodox theory.

In their joint book, Richard Nelson and Sidney Winter (1982) develop an alternative theoretical framework to profit maximization for the analysis of the firm. Instead of such an optimizing procedure, they propose an evolu-tionary model in which selection operates on the firm's internal routines. Nelson and Winter argue that such an evolutionary process does not always result in a preponderance of profit-maximizing firms. Being concerned to show how technological skills are acquired and passed on within the economy, they argue that habits and routines act as repositories of knowledge and skills. In their words, routines are the 'organizational memory' (ibid., p. 99) of the firm. Nelson and Winter do not simply argue that habits and routines are widespread, but in addition that they have functional characteristics.

Because of their relatively durable character, routines act as the economic analogue of the gene in biology. Routines may help to retain skills and other forms of knowledge, and to some extent they have the capacity to replicate through imitation, personal mobility and so on. Nelson and Winter also propose a 'mutation' mechanism through which routines can be changed through managerial action when the firm's profits are below a satisfactory level. In developing their ideas, Nelson and Winter acknowledge the influ-ences of Joseph Schumpeter and Herbert Simon. In addition, their idea of the quasi-genetic quality of routines also has a strong resonance in the earlier evolutionary economic theory of Veblen.

More recently, Nelson (1991) has extended his evolutionary approach to the analysis of the firm, arguing that the differences between real-world firms must be recognized by economic theory. Orthodox theory often ignores intra-industry firm differences, or denies that they are of any economic significance. In contrast, within an evolutionary approach, both the generation and function of corporate diversity is explicable. Nelson has also developed a pioneering analysis of 'national systems of innovation'. The argument here is that innovation and technical change are not simply matters for individual entrepreneurs, but also involve cultural and institutional features at the national level. As in all his studies, the aim is to help develop economics as an operational and empirically enriched science, which can engage with real-world problems and avoid the dogmatic and simplistic policy pronouncements with which we are unfortunately all too familiar.

GEOFFREY M. HODGSON

See also:
Commons, John R.; Evolution and Optimality; Evolution, Theories of Economic; Firm, Theory of the; Innovation, National Systems of; Institutions; Microfoundations of Macroeconomic Competitiveness; Natural Selection, Economic Evolution and; Rationality and Maximization; Routines; Rules; Schumpeter, Joseph Alois; Simon, Herbert Alexander; Technical Change and Technological Regimes; Technology, Theory of; Veblen, Thorstein; Winter, Sidney G., Jr.

Bibliography
Dosi, Giovanni (1988), 'The Sources, Procedures, and Microeconomic Effects of Innovation;, *Journal of Economic Literature*, **26**, (3), September, pp. 1120–71; reprinted 1990 in Christopher Freeman (ed.), *The Economics of Innovation*, Aldershot: Edward Elgar.
Nelson, Richard, R. (1980), 'Production Sets, Technological Knowledge and R&D: Fragile and Overworked Constructs for Analysis of Productivity Growth?', *American Economic Review (Papers and Proceedings)*, **70**, (2), May, pp. 62–7.
Nelson, Richard R. (1981a), 'Assessing Private Enterprise: An Exegesis of Tangled Doctrine', *Bell Journal of Economics*, **12**, (1), pp. 93–111.
Nelson, Richard R. (1981b), 'Research on Productivity Growth and Productivity Differences: Dead Ends and New Departures', *Journal of Economic Literature*, **29**, September, pp. 1029–64.
Nelson, Richard R. (1987), *Understanding Technical Change as an Evolutionary Process*, Amsterdam: North-Holland.
Nelson, Richard R. (1991), *Why Do Firms Differ, and How Does it Matter?*, Working Paper No. 91–7, Berkeley, CA: Consortium of Competitiveness and Cooperation.
Nelson, Richard R. (ed.) (forthcoming), *National Innovation Systems: A Comparative Study*.
Nelson, Richard R. and S.G. Winter (1982), *An Evolutionary Theory of Economic Change*, Cambridge Mass.: Harvard University Press.
Penrose, Edith T. (1959), *The Theory of the Growth of the Firm*, Oxford: Basil Blackwell.

Neoclassical Microeconomic Theory, Critique of

There have been abundant critiques by heterodox economists of the methodological, conceptual and behavioural foundations of neoclassical microeconomics. However, whatever their intrinsic value, their combined effect so far has been marginal. Nevertheless, there are increasing tensions within the neoclassical camp, and an unprecedented degree of critical reflection even over core concepts such as 'rationality' in recent years.

Several quotations from leading neoclassical economists are given here, so that the degree of internal dissent may be gauged. It is suggested that these internal developments give increasing encouragement for the future transition to an evolutionary and institutional approach, even if social structures and inertia in academic institutions may currently militate against the reform of economic science. Neoclassical economics may be defined as an approach which has the following attributes:

1. the assumption of rational, maximizing behaviour by agents with given preference functions;
2. a focus on attained, or movements towards, equilibrium states;
3. the absence of chronic information problems (there is, at most, a focus on probabilistic risk: excluding radical uncertainty or divergent perceptions).

Notably, these three attributes are interconnected. For instance, the attainment of stable optima under (1) suggests an equilibrium (2); and rationality under (1) connotes the absence of severe information problems outlined in (3).

It is also important to recognize that these core assumptions reflect the adoption of a mechanistic metaphor in economic theory (Mirowski, 1989). In a mechanistic world there are no information problems. Economic agents are seen as akin to particles subject to forces, interacting and often attaining an equilibrium outcome. This particular definition of neoclassical economics clearly excludes members of the Austrian School, particularly because of their explicit critique of attributes (2) and (3). There is also the question as to whether some recent developments in game theory can also be described as 'neoclassical economics'. This question can only be answered by close inspection and refinement of the boundary conditions in the above definition.

Critical developments

We now briefly examine some of the recent critical developments in economic theory which have opened up some possibilities for change. First, the core concept of rational maximizing behaviour was subjected to a powerful critique by Herbert Simon several decades ago. This critique has been largely ignored until recently, when developments in game theory gave the concept of 'bounded rationality' a new boost. Game theory has legitimized discussion of both bounded rationality, 'near rationality' and 'irrationality', as well as breaking from the previously held strict assumption of perfect knowledge.

Hence, the door having been bolted for decades, neoclassical theorists now, albeit in a limited fashion, admit discussion of problems of imperfect or asymmetric information. Whilst these are welcome developments they have created havoc with orthodox presuppositions. For instance, as Joseph Stiglitz (1987) has elaborated, even standard demand analysis is now called into question.

Second, theoretical work in game theory and elsewhere has raised questions about the very meaning of core notions such as rationality. As Robert Sugden (1990, p. 89) argues, 'game theory may rest on a concept of rationality that is ultimately little more than a convention'. Consequently, the assumption of 'rational economic man' now looks much more problematic to the informed neoclassical theorist than it did even a decade or so ago. Surveying recent developments which have given rise to this shift, Sugden (1991, p. 783) writes:

> There was a time, not long ago, when the foundations of rational-choice theory appeared firm, and when the job of the economic theorist seemed to be one of drawing out the often complex implications of a fairly simple and uncontroversial system of axioms. But it is increasingly becoming clear that these foundations are less secure than we thought, and that they need to be examined and perhaps rebuilt. Economic theorists may have to become as much philosophers as mathematicians.

Third, the intrusion of chaos theory into economics has put paid to the general idea that economics can proceed simply on the criterion of 'correct predictions'. With non-linear models, outcomes are over-sensitive to initial conditions and thereby reliable predictions are impossible to make in regard to any extended time period. In particular, chaos theory has confounded the rational expectations theorists by showing that, even if most agents knew the basic structure of the economic model, in general they cannot derive reliable predictions of outcomes and thereby form any meaningful 'rational expectations' of the future.

Fourth, Nicholas Kaldor argued repeatedly that a key problem with neoclassical economic theory was its neglect of the phenomenon of positive feedback based on increasing returns. He also pointed to the related problem of path dependency in economic models. Recently, Brian Arthur (1990) has shown that many technological and structural features of a modern economy involve positive feedbacks, which magnify the effects of small changes. Consequently, initial 'accidents' can have a huge effect on the result. There can be technological 'lock-in' and, instead of gravitating towards preordained equilibria, outcomes can be path-dependent. Consequently, there may be several possible – and sub-optimal – equilibrium outcomes. The work of Arthur and others has now put Kaldor's ideas back on the agenda.

Fifth, the development of general equilibrium theory – neoclassical microeconomics at its theoretical apogee – has now reached a serious impasse. Quite early on it was realized that the potential diversity amongst individuals threatened the feasibility of the project. Consequently, many types of interaction between the individuals have to be ignored. Even with the restrictive psychological assumptions of rational behaviour, severe difficulties are faced when the behaviours of a number of actors are brought together. As the leading neoclassical general equilibrium theorist and Nobel Laureate Kenneth Arrow (1986, p. S388) has been led to declare: 'In the aggregate, the hypothesis of rational behavior has in general no implications.' Consequently, it is widely assumed that all individuals have the same utility function. Amongst other things this denies the possibility of 'gains from trade arising from individual differences' (Arrow, 1986, p. S390). Thus, despite the traditional celebrations of individualism and competition, and despite decades of formal development, the hard core theory of neoclassical economics can handle no more than a grey uniformity amongst actors.

Sixth, recent research into the problems of the uniqueness and stability of a general equilibrium have shown that it may be indeterminate and unstable unless very strong assumptions are made, such as that society as a whole behaves as if it was a single individual. Addressing such problems, Alan Kirman (1989, p. 138) writes: 'If we are to progress further we may well be forced to theorise in terms of groups who have collectively coherent behaviour. ... The idea that we should start at the level of the isolated individual is one which we may well have to abandon.' The theoretical implications of the uniqueness and stability results discussed by Kirman are profound. A fundamental consequence is the breakdown of the type of economic analysis typically associated with these assertions: that the rationality of self-interested and autonomous individuals is sufficient to produce and maintain equilibrium and social order; that such an equilibrium is efficient; and that social institutions like the state can interfere only to disrupt the equilibrium conditions.

Clearly, this type of reasoning has had a long string of followers since it was promoted by Bernard Mandeville in the *Fable of the Bees* (1714). The general presumption is that, from private vices, public virtues spring. The indeterminacy and instability results produced by contemporary theory lead to the conclusion that an economy made up of atomistic agents has not structure enough to survive. As Fabrizio Coricelli and Giovanni Dosi (1988, p. 136) argue:

> Most contemporary accounts of ... aggregate economic 'order' lead to a curious paradox. They generally start with an act of faith in both the 'invisible hand' and the substantive capabilities of individual agents to process information and

'choose' correctly and freely – constrained only by their endowments – and end up with results that show a very crippled hand, incapable of orderly coordination even in extremely simple environments.

Perhaps in the light of these developments, even Arrow (1987, p. 233) has commented: 'People just do not maximize on a selfish basis every minute. In fact, the system would not work if they did. A consequence of that hypothesis would be the end of organized society as we know it.'

The remarks above are confined to some special cases at the 'hard core' of the subject. There are many other problems, from capital theory to monetary analysis, from the theory of the firm to the economics of welfare. Frank Hahn (1981) notes, for instance, the absence of power and the neglect of real time in general equilibrium analysis and the failure equally to incorporate money.

Formalism and inertia
In the main, the internal shifts in neoclassical economic theory outlined above occurred in the 1980s. They suggest a deep internal crisis in the subject, the effects of which have not yet fully reverberated through the profession. It may be that the internal challenges to the core assumptions (1), (2) and (3) of neoclassical theory give a substantial opening for the development of economic theory along institutional and evolutionary lines. There are reasons to be cautious about the possibilities, however. First, there is a tremendous inertia in any institutionalized profession. The microeconomic textbooks – with partial exceptions such as Kreps (1990) – are largely oblivious to the aforementioned developments. Although heretical ideas have now been promoted by leading neoclassical theorists and have appeared in prestigious economic journals, the majority of the profession still continue in their theoretical and applied work much as before. Many thousands of students are still taught less to think, more to assimilate dogma and to perform tricks of technique.

Second, economic theory still remains highly formalistic. Despite the power and utility of mathematical analysis, it can often prevent discussion of the underlying conceptual and methodological issues, by focusing attention exclusively on formalities. It will be some time until the damaging effects of 'formalistic revolution' in economics can be undone. The situation bemoaned by Nobel Laureate Wassily Leontief (1982, pp. 104–7) still unfortunately pertains:

Page after page of professional economic journals are filled with mathematical formulas leading the reader from sets of more or less plausible but entirely arbitrary assumptions to precisely stated but irrelevant theoretical conclusions. ... Year after year economic theorists continue to produce scores of mathematical models and to explore in great detail their formal properties; and the econometricians fit algebraic functions of all possible shapes to essentially the same sets of data without being able to advance, in any perceptible way, a systematic understanding of the structure and the operations of a real economic system.

Third, although the aforementioned theoretical developments challenge some core presuppositions of neoclassical economic theory, there are other, absolutely fundamental, philosophical assumptions which emerge unscathed. These include both ontological atomism and methodological individualism, closely related to the hedonistic and utilitarian philosophical assumptions of neoclassical economics about which institutional economists have long complained. They are furthermore associated with the Cartesian–Newtonian paradigm which still dominates economics and several other sciences. In contrast, institutionalists, as well as some philosophers of biology, have challenged the Cartesian–Newtonian world-view, and promoted an organicist alternative. This reflects the foundations of institutional economics in the anti-Cartesian, anti-mechanistic and anti-reductionist philosophical writings of Charles Sanders Peirce and John Dewey.

Nevertheless, the situation of crisis at the core of economic theory is without precedent. Note the words of neoclassical general equilibrium theorist Frank Hahn; some time ago he noted the absence of power in neoclassical economics:

> those who regard power as central to economic understanding must look beyond classical general equilibrium theory. I rather count myself among those, and my early strictures were directed at the unfortunate fact that no serious work in new directions is available. (Hahn, 1981, p. 132)

Ten years later he has gone so far as to write:

> I am pretty certain that the following prediction will prove to be correct: theorising of the 'pure' sort will become ... less and less possible ... rather radical changes in questions and methods are required ... the signs are that the subject will return to its Marshallian affinities to biology. ... Not only will our successors have to be far less concerned with ... grand unifying theory ... [but also] less frequently for them the pleasures of theorems and proof. Instead the uncertain embrace of history and sociology and biology. (Hahn, 1991, pp. 47–50)

If such words can be written by a leading neoclassical theorist then there must be some hope in economics for the institutionalist and evolutionary alternative.

GEOFFREY M. HODGSON

See also:

Atomism and Organicism; Capital Theory; Cartesianism in Economics; Chaos Theory and Economics; Consumer Behaviour; Cost–Benefit Analysis; Culture; Cumulative Causation; Determinism and Free Will; Dewey, John; Distribution Theory; Econometrics, The Limits of; Firm, Theory of the; Formalism in Economics; Game Theory and Institutions; Habits; Hayek, Friedrich A.; Household, Economics of the; Human Nature, Theory of; Information Theory in Economics; Institutionalism, 'Old' and 'New'; Institutions; Instrumental Value Theory; Kaldor, Nicholas; Labour Markets; Lock-in and Chreodic Development; Macroeconomic Theory; Market, Institutionalist View of the; Methodological Individualism; Methodology; Microfoundations of Macroeconomic Competitiveness; Monetary Theory; Money, Evolution of; Need, Concept of; Part–Whole Relationships; Peirce, Charles Sanders; Power; Public Choice; Rational Actor Models; Rationality and Maximization; Realism, Philosophical; Routines; Rules; Simon, Herbert Alexander; Time; Trust; Uncertainty; Veblen, Thorstein; Welfare Economic Theory.

Bibliography

Arrow, Kenneth J. (1986), 'Rationality of self and others in an economic system', *Journal of Business*, **59**, (4.2), October, pp. S385–99; reprinted 1987 in Robin M. Hogarth and Melvin W. Reder (eds), *Rational Choice: The Contrast Between Economics and Psychology*, Chicago: University of Chicago Press.

Arrow, Kenneth, J. (1987), 'Oral History I: An Interview', in G.R. Feiwel (ed.), *Arrow and the Ascent of Modern Economic Theory*, pp. 191–242, London: Macmillan.

Arthur, W.B. (1990), 'Positive Feedbacks in the Economy', *Scientific American*, **262**, (2), February, pp. 80–85.

Coricelli, Fabrizio and Giovanni Dosi (1988), 'Coordination and Order in Economic Change and the Interpretative Power of Economic Theory', in G. Dosi, C. Freeman, R. Nelson, G. Silverberg and L. Soete (eds), *Technical Change and Economic Theory*, pp. 124–47, London: Pinter.

Hahn, Frank H. (1981), 'General Equilibrium Theory', in D. Bell and I. Kristol (eds), *The Crisis in Economic Theory*, New York: Basic Books.

Hahn, Frank H. (1991), 'The Next Hundred Years', *The Economic Journal*, **101**, (1), January, pp. 47–50.

Kirman, Alan P. (1989), 'The Intrinsic Limits of Modern Economic Theory: The Emperor Has No Clothes', *The Economic Journal (Conference Papers)*, **99**, pp. 126–39.

Kreps, David M. (1990), *A Course in Microeconomic Theory*, Hemel Hempstead: Harvester Wheatsheaf.

Leontief, W. (1982), Letter in *Science*, (217), 9 July, pp. 104, 107.

Mirowski, Philip (1989), *More Heat Than Light: Economics as Social Physics, Physics as Nature's Economics*, Cambridge: Cambridge University Press.

Stiglitz, Joseph E. (1987), 'The Causes and Consequences of the Dependence of Quality on Price', *Journal of Economic Literature*, **25**, (1), March, pp. 1–48.

Sugden, Robert (1990), 'Convention, creativity and conflict', in Yanis Varoufakis and David Young (eds), *Conflict in Economics*, pp. 68–90, Hemel Hempstead: Harvester Wheatsheaf.

Sugden, Robert (1991), 'Rational Choice: A Survey of Contributions from Economics and Philosophy', *The Economic Journal*, **101**, (4), July, pp. 751–85.

Ward, Benjamin (1972), *What's Wrong With Economics?*, London: Macmillan.

North, Douglass C.

Douglass C. North received his undergraduate and graduate training in economics (BA, 1942; PhD, 1952) from the University of California at Berkeley.

His early research in economic history focused on the balance of payments, and led to his notable elaboration of an export-led model of US antebellum growth (North, 1961). His 1966 textbook helped popularize a new approach to economic history: quantitatively oriented and explicitly informed by theory. This work is remarkable for its brevity (under 200 pages) and lack of attention to details of institutional or legal change that had been a feature of earlier (and bulkier) surveys. Paradoxically, while North stressed the dependence of economic growth on free market institutions, readers received little exposure to the details of the changing legal and regulatory environment that delineated such an evolving economy. His approach to institutions here can be usefully contrasted with the opening chapters of Hughes (1990), which recalls earlier traditions in its treatment of the American legal heritage from Europe, and its consequences.

North's interest in institutions ultimately consumed the bulk of his scholarly attentions over the next quarter-century. His 1968 article on productivity growth in ocean shipping concluded that declines in piracy and improvements in organization (rather than technological change) had been the main engine of growth in that sector, sharpening his interest in transactions costs as a potential brake on the growth of output and on the role of political and economic organization in potentially overcoming them. A growing explanatory ambition, however, now moved his work beyond sectorally focused empirical studies. Beginning in 1971, a series of articles and books explored at national and international levels the causes and consequences of institutional variation.

Davis and North (1971) drew inspiration from the public choice literature to try and account for when and why interest groups organized to change rules which otherwise constrained them, in the process altering the incidence of transactions costs and prospects for growth. North and Thomas (1973) was even more ambitious, claiming in 158 pages to account for eight centuries of European development. Particularly with respect to the pre-1500 period, North and Thomas attempted to use what they viewed as purely 'economic' variables (technology and demographic changes) to explain the decline of feudalism and the rise of institutions of market economy. Their attempt was notable for its apparent avoidance of 'ad hoc' appeals to institutions, culture or legal persistence as forces in their own right.

North and Thomas's work was criticized by Fenoaltea (1975) for its superficial treatment of the historical record, and by Field (1981) for its failure to meet an unattainable methodological promise. Why, if population growth led to the breakdown of feudalism in the eleventh to the thirteenth centuries, did not population decline after the Black Death reverse the process? North and Thomas's answer was that the rise in the land–labour ratio increased the bargaining power of those cultivators who survived. But this argument runs contrary to that put forward by Evsey Domar (1970) to explain the emergence of serfdom in Eastern Europe, as well as the American slave system. High (or rising) land–labour ratios cannot simultaneously be the explanation of freedom in Western Europe and of serfdom/slavery in Eastern Europe and the American South.

To make sense of these histories one must, either explicitly or implicitly, recognize an independent role for institutional regimes themselves, and the cultural forces that may reinforce them. To understand why such regimes sometimes do and sometimes do not change, one needs, moreover, an historical, case-specific methodology. In contrast, North and Thomas were driven by a powerful imperative to view rules as ultimately derivative of more 'fundamental' givens, such as technologies and endowments. From such a perspective, institutional details are developed primarily to illustrate the power of the model, rather than because such details may be causative in their own right. Ultimately, institutional variation becomes epiphenomenal, and cannot itself help explain why regions with access to similar endowments and technology experience different growth paths.

North's subsequent publications reflect an ultimately unsuccessful struggle to reconcile two imperatives: first, to account for institutional variation as the outcome of maximizing behaviour constrained only by technology and endowments, and, second, to use institutional variation to account for differences in economic performance. His third book on institutions (1981) responded, at least in part, to criticisms of earlier work. In Chapter 5, North explicitly acknowledged ideology as an independent influence binding individuals together and overcoming free-rider problems. In other words, ideology could have bound together Eastern lords, or American slaveholders, making it possible for them to impose their coercive labour regimes in regions with high land–labour ratios, in spite of the otherwise favourable bargaining conditions for cultivators. Much of the rest of the book, however, carried over the language and objectives of earlier work. The implications of criticisms responded to in one part of the book were not systematically acknowledged in its remainder. North's 1990 book is similar in this respect. As its title would suggest, sections, particularly Part III, place even more explicit emphasis on the consequences of institutional variation, but elsewhere the public choice analysis of why and when institutions change persists, albeit with more qualifications.

North's major achievement is related to the indefatigable manner in which he has forced large segments of the economic profession to acknowledge at some level the 'importance' of institutions. While he has never entirely abandoned the attempt to develop an endogenous theory of institutional change, which does not itself make reference to institutions or norm-like phenomena, his writings have evolved and now include more statements and sections with which a critic of his earlier work can agree. As a result, it is possible, by searching, for almost anyone to find something appealing here. But the converse also remains true. As North has responded to critics, he has built a larger and larger tent and invited in people of different persuasions to celebrate. Many leave with a good feeling, and positive sentiments towards what he has accomplished. But it is important that critical sensibilities not be dulled. North's work has not, by its example, encouraged economists and economic historians to emulate the attention to detail common in legal scholar-ship and work in comparative law. His writing on institutions has been broad-brush, based largely on secondary sources. His attention to institutional detail has been further limited by the space devoted to exposing (or, at times, criticizing) the theoretical literature from which he has drawn inspiration.

Secondly, his tolerance of ambiguity and his willingness to bring to bear ideas from differing theoretical traditions generate frustration in those trying systematically to make sense of his work. The key to resolving this frustration may lie in distinguishing between research concerned with the origins of institutional variation and that addressed to consequences. Questions related to causes are of undoubted importance, but economists as economists have relatively little comparative advantage in addressing them. In contrast, economists have a great deal to say about consequences, which is why our counsel can be valuable in making public policy. By focusing on consequences, and recognizing that research addressing origins requires historical and case-specific sensitivities not necessarily fostered by the study of economic theory *per se*, we may be able to make more progress in understanding how and why institutions do indeed matter. Through his writings and persistence, Douglass North has forced us to clarify intellectual objectives, and for that we owe him an important debt. He was awarded the Nobel Prize for Economics in 1993.

ALEXANDER J. FIELD

See also:
Cumulative Causation; Evolution and Optimality; Game Theory and Institutions; Institutionalism, 'Old' and 'New'; Institutions; Methodological Individualism; Methodology; Property; Public Choice; Rules; Social Change, Theory of; Transaction; Williamson, Oliver E.

Bibliography
Davis, Lance and Douglass C. North (1971), *Institutional Change and American Economic Growth*, Cambridge: Cambridge University Press.

Domar, Evsey (1970), 'The Causes of Slavery and Serfdom: A Hypothesis', *Journal of Economic History*, **30**, pp. 18–32.

Fenoaltea, Stefano (1975), 'The Rise and Fall of a Theoretical Model: The Manorial System', *Journal of Economic History*, **35**, pp. 386–409.

Field, Alexander J. (1981), 'The Problem with Neoclassical Institutional Economics: A Critique with Special Reference to the North/Thomas Model of Pre-1500 Europe', *Explorations in Economic History*, **18**, pp. 174–98.

Field, Alexander J. (1991), 'Do Legal Systems Matter?', *Explorations in Economic History*, **28**, pp. 1–35.

Hughes, Jonathan (1990), *American Economic History*, 3rd edn, New York: Scott Foresman.

North, Douglass C. (1961), *The Economic Growth of the United States, 1790–1860* , Englewood Cliffs, NJ: Prentice-Hall.

North, Douglass C. (1966), *Growth and Welfare in the American Past: A New Economic History*, Englewood Cliffs, NJ: Prentice-Hall.

North, Douglass C. (1968), 'Sources of Productivity Change in Ocean Shipping, 1600–1850', *Journal of Political Economy*, **76**, pp. 953–67.

North, Douglass C. (1981), *Structure and Change in Economic History*, New York: Norton.

North, Douglass C. (1990), *Institutions, Institutional Change and Economic Performance,* Cambridge: Cambridge University Press.

North, Douglass C. and Robert Paul Thomas (1973), *The Rise of the Western World: A New Economic History*, Cambridge: Cambridge University Press.

Sutch, Richard (1982), 'Douglass North and the New Economic History', in Roger L. Ransom, Richard Sutch and Gary M. Walton (eds), *Explorations in the New Economic History*, pp. 13–38, New York: Academic Press.

Olson, Mancur

Mancur Olson was born in 1932 in Grand Forks, North Dakota. He obtained his BS degree from North Dakota State University in 1954 and later a BA and an MA from Oxford University, which he attended as a Rhodes Scholar from 1954 to 1956. His distinguished PhD thesis, submitted at Harvard in 1963 and published two years later as *The Logic of Collective Action*, established his name as an important contributor to the multidisciplinary conceptualization of pure public goods. It paved the way for an academic career (first at Harvard, then at Princeton, subsequently at Maryland, where he holds the personal title of Distinguished Professor of Economics), albeit with a brief period from 1967 to 1969 spent in the civil service as Deputy Assistant Secretary in the Department of Health, Education and Welfare. His brief was to develop social indicators of welfare capable of complementing the narrowly economic national income statistics. The product of his team's efforts was *Towards a Social Report* (1969). Olson's interests in public sector involvement in the modern mixed economy have led him to examine externalities, indivisibilities, health, defence and the environment; while his *The Rise and Decline of Nations* (1982) has sought to make a political economist's contribution, building on the *Logic,* to the debate on why it is that growth rates differ.

Olson's starting-point is the neoclassical orthodoxy's abstract logic that makes his own *Logic* in some ways a less than fully satisfying account of the non-market social experience. Olson in his *Logic* relies heavily on the maximizing economist's standard methodology of deductions made from the twin axioms of self-interest (narrowly defined to avoid tautology) and calculative rationality (presumed *as if*). Olson's concern is to derive a theory of group formation applicable to the non-trading relationships that obtain in social units with a common interest; and to do so without reference to any constructs (intuition and emotion, social conventions and societal pressures, moral obligation and childhood socialization) other than those that are employed by the non-institutional textbook when it accounts for oligopoly and perfect competition. In the small-group case (the minority alliance or exclusive lobby serving as the non-market counterpart of the oligopolistic cartel), Olson makes a distinction between the 'privileged' group (the unequal collectivity in which one member has an interest in the public good so much in excess of the others that he will contribute towards its provision even if his confederates do nothing) and the 'intermediate' group (the club in which relative equals seek to take as much and give as little as possible in total ignorance of the strategic moves that their friendly enemies are simultaneously plotting in a bid to saddle the losers with the costs while retaining for themselves the benefits). In the large-group case (the union with many members resembling the industry with many firms), Olson makes much of the temptation faced by each insignificant atom to act the free-rider on the efforts of the others. One piece of litter dropped is hardly a littered common. One shareholder absent from the annual general meeting is hardly a threat to the control over management that is exercised by capital. What one can do, however, all cannot; and thus is Olson led by his economist's logic to the conclusion that, while affluent societies will increasingly stand in need of shared non-excludabilities, they will be less and less likely, *ceteris paribus*, to enjoy them: *ceteris paribus* since there are two techniques that the large group can employ to protect its common purpose against the uncoordinated tyranny of the small decision. The first is coercion, as where a democratic polity makes taxation compulsory even for the sincerest of patriots. The second is the provision of selective incentives, as where a political party offers both a public good in the form of attractive policies and a private good in the form of entertainments and socials accessible only to its canvassers. Olson takes a one-dimensional and perhaps even a rather cynical view of human nature, but no more so than any other maximizing theorist. What he does not do is to take the next step by testing his assertions against a representative cross-section of external reality: as it stands, the evidence presented in his *Logic* is both anecdotal and selective.

The *Rise and Decline* strives to be more rigorously inductive, more concerned with *ex post* outcomes and less with *a priori* expectations. Inevitably, however, and perhaps because of the inherent complexity of the hypotheses themselves, Olson's account of the impact of corporate bodies on growth rates tends to lapse into story-telling. Britain has experienced relatively slow growth because of 'institutional sclerosis', an accretion of special-interest groups lobbying for redistribution by statute in a nation not shaken up by invasion since 1066. The Germans and the Japanese have grown rapidly in the post-1945 period at least in part because the pulverizations of totalitarianism, war and occupation freed their economies from selfish collectivities and rent-seeking collusions determined to twist the state to the advantage not of the nation but of the segment. France benefited thoroughly from the bracing cold shower of 1789, followed less than two centuries later by the threat to cosy stability from German invasion in two world wars and the Treaty of Rome in the peace. Olson is curiously unable to identify any positive impact that might have been made by the corporatized groupings on the growth effort (the impact of unions, say, on *morale)* and he leaves the reader with the impression, presumably unintended, that the free-rider cannot be such a bad fellow if by sabotaging group formation he so effectively stimulates the rate of advance. Again, and while acknowledging Olson's interesting incorporation of legal and other institutional constraints, he fails to situate his non-orthodox social and behavioural explanations within the framework of a broader growth model that also accounts for the contribution to differing growth rates of the land, the labour and the capital that are the maximizing economist's stock in trade. Olson's greatest contribution is not, however, to be sought in his evidence but rather in his insights. Olson demonstrates the role and excitement of abstract ideas in an academic discipline increasingly starved of philosophical perspectives and imaginative speculations. For that all economists of ideas must owe him a great debt of gratitude.

D.A. REISMAN

See also:

Institutionalism, 'Old' and 'New'; Institutions; Methodological Individualism; Property; Public Choice; Social Change, Theory of.

Bibliography

Barry, B. (1978), *Sociologists, Economists and Democracy*, Chicago: University of Chicago Press.

Mueller, D.C. (ed.) (1983), *The Political Economy of Growth*, New Haven, Conn.: Yale University Press.

Olson, M. (1965), *The Logic of Collective Action*, Cambridge, Mass.: Harvard University Press.

Olson, M. (1982), *The Rise and Decline of Nations,* New Haven, Conn.: Yale University Press.

Reisman, D. (1990), *Theories of Collective Action*, London: Macmillan.

Part–Whole Relationships

The study of human beings and their society, polity and economy, perhaps especially their economy, is complicated by diverse relationships and diverse ways of representing those relationships, between individuals and between the individual (or other units) and larger social processes or 'wholes'. In both positive and normative respects (though only the former is of present concern) the relationship of the individual to society is a ubiquitous question and subsumes numerous other questions, such as, can the individual be contemplated as existing self-subsistent and separate from society, and is society different from, perhaps more than, the sum of the individuals which comprise it?

Methodological individualism (distinct from varieties of normative individualism) affirms that the most productive way of pursuing knowledge of human beings and society is to study individuals *qua* individuals; most strictly, all explanations of social phenomena have to be reduced to and expressed in terms of individuals and not, for instance, institutions, collectives or wholes. Methodological collectivism (distinct from varieties of normative collectivism) affirms that the most productive way of pursuing knowledge of human beings and society is to study group processes and activities, that explanation can be reduced to and expressed in terms of institutions, collectives or wholes. Stated so categorically, it is easy to overlook the putative facts that studies ostensibly methodologically individualist tend to encompass methodologically collectivist processes, such as the market, and that studies nominally of the other type tend also to focus on, and certainly do not include, individuals and/or other units. As with so many other matters, it seems that it is not so easy to practise one without also engaging in the other. As a result, the concept of institutional individualism has been generated to enable more or less simultaneous attention to be given to individual choice and behaviour and to the socialization of the individual as well as the location of individuals within specific sets of institutions or organizations; that is, that social institutions and the social environment, as well as individuals *qua* individuals, are part of the explanation of human action. One result of the use of institutional individualism is a lesser tendency to conflate ideologically methodological and normative individualism.

Two fallacies especially pertain to the study of part–whole relationships: the fallacy of composition and the reductionist fallacy. It will be remembered that the idea of a 'fallacy' is not unequivocal or absolute error but potential error in reasoning. The statement of a fallacy points to a problematic situation: the point at issue may be the case but it also may not be the case and is certainly not necessarily the case.

The fallacy of composition occurs when one states that what explains or is true of each part or some parts of a whole necessarily explains or is true of the whole; and vice versa, that what explains or is true of a whole necessarily explains or is true of one or more of its parts. The reductionist, or reductive, fallacy occurs when one states that the meaning of a whole is neither other nor more than the sum of its parts, such that description and/or explanation of the parts is sufficient to describe and/or explain the whole. The part may or may not encompass all of the referent elements of the whole, and therefore may or may not be considered representative of the whole.

Examples of the fallacy of composition abound in economics, not surprisingly principally in macroeconomics: the lowering of factor prices deemed at the microeconomic level to increase employment (the part) but which at the macroeconomic level may contribute to a lessening of effective demand and thereby decrease employment (the whole); increases in individual saving which, by reducing aggregate expenditure, lead to declines in income and thereby in saving itself, as saving adjusts to the level of investment through changes in income (the paradox of thrift); and, *inter alia*, the (neo-)mercantilist belief that a favourable balance of payments will promote economic growth, whereas it may only increase the general price level.

The reductionist fallacy is evident in any use of strict methodological individualism that postulates autonomous self-subsistent individuals and thereby neglects considerations of, first, socialization or acculturation, and, second, the power structure governing the determination of which individuals count. In both respects (socialization and power structure) methodologically individualist analyses readily take as given either the status quo or some presumed set of processes and situations; indeed, they typically make assumptions which implicitly include methodologically collectivist considerations.

Acting somewhat as a bridge between methodological individualism and methodological collectivism is structuralism. Structuralism points to the set(s) of relationships which connect parts to each other and which in the aggregate may be seen as constituting the whole. Thus social and power structure may be understood to determine which individuals or whose interests count and thereby to enter analysis as an explanatory variable. Alternatively, structural factors, such as language, may be understood to comprise the larger system of meaning which in one way or another attaches to parts.

Mechanistic causation constituting explanation is not the only context in which parts may be related to wholes. Organicism characterizes any theory which explains parts of wholes in terms of some analogy with living organisms, for example, the function which a part may perform for the whole within a given social system. In such a case, the whole may be understood as both more than the sum of its functioning organs and the coordinating system in terms of which the organic parts themselves have meaning. Atomism, which may or may not strictly conflict with organicism (the individual units may or may not be themselves understood organically), focuses on discrete, indivisible and self-subsistent units which are only contingently related to each other and only contingently interrelated to form the relevant whole(s). Clearly, consideration of atomism raises both the conflict between methodological individualism and methodological collectivism and the possibility of the fallacies of composition and reduction.

A further matter has to do with the identification of parts and of wholes. With regard to the question of parts, it is not clear that for all social science purposes the fundamental unit is the individual, which is often taken to be the representative adult individual. Doing so already presumes, as above, socialization and acculturation. For many purposes the definition of the unit constitutive of the part may be the family, which itself is also a social construct. But there are also larger units less encompassing than whole societies or states. The corporation is a case in point. But it too is a social construct. One problem is that the imagery of human individual beings is often transferred to the corporation (or other organization), though it is not clear that such is conclusively and unequivocally justifiable for all analytical and interpretative, as well as ideological, problems. Another case in point is the market. The market may itself be a metaphor for the institutions which form and operate through it and for the resulting interrelationships, and it is also a social creation. One problem here is that there is no one market but a system of interacting markets. Another is that the identification of particular markets depends on definitional considerations, for example, whether an industry (and its market) is defined to encompass the producers and so on of a relatively homogeneous good or all producers of products with a high cross-elasticity of demand.

Finally, there is the society or state itself. For some problems the society–state is the largest unit, though it too can be juxtaposed to a more encompassing larger civilization, for example, France as a part of Western civilization; for others, it is a part, such as the world nation state system or international world economy. The question of unit determination is frequently begged, the matter left to rest on conventional practice; but, among other things, this can render conclusions tautologous and ethnocentric. Of particular importance is the relevance of mid-level institutions, such as corporations and occupational associations, which both mediate between individual units and social wholes and serve as transmission mechanisms for forces at both levels.

A related question has to do with the formation of parts and wholes. The matter, as has already been stressed, is of particular significance for creation of individuals in society, but it also applies to the processes, both internal and external to a society–state, by which societies (and even civilizations) are formed and reformed in a continuous evolutionary process. And it has to do with the formation and reformation of particular institutions. The study of these processes can, of course, be conducted in nominally methodological individualist or methodological collectivist terms, with the important qualifications already noted, or with an institutional individualism which embodies the heuristic power of both.

Throughout the history of modern economic thought from the middle of the eighteenth century to the present, economists have emphasized the interconnectedness of economic (and perhaps other) variables. The most abstract form in which this insight is given effect is general equilibrium theory, which, while typically expressed in methodological individualist terms, has evident methodological collectivist aspects to it. Among other things, the general equilibrium perspective challenges the simple juxtaposition of parts and wholes, in effect affirming that what is important is the interactive interrelationships between units (however those parts may be defined and identified) and not solely the units themselves. This position resides part way between those who believe that social science study can focus solely on individuals and that society, in so far as the term is analytically meaningful, is merely the sum of the individuals who comprise it and has no independent explanatory role; and those who believe the opposite, at least that the study of group processes, institutions and forces needs to and can be meaningfully undertaken and enter into explanation.

Going beyond simple interaction between given individuals or units is the concept of emergent evolution, or overdetermination. This concept embodies the perception that parts or units are not individually self-subsistent and given fully formed once and for all time, but are themselves the changing product of internal and external processes, including those of interaction. In this respect, if in no other, then, individual units or parts relate to each other as both cause and consequence in a process in which the units are themselves both transformed and transforming and in which the whole is itself also both transformed and transforming. The different evolutionary approaches of Karl Marx, Thorstein Veblen and even John Maynard Keynes involve, among others things, simultaneous development of both parts and wholes.

Something similar may be said of particular social sub-processes. For example, economy and polity can be comprehended either as interacting but otherwise independent and self-subsistent subprocesses or as not independently given, self-subsistent and then interactive processes but as products of a common legal–economic nexus. Such considerations emphasize both the importance of mid-level social formations in between atomistic parts and social wholes, and the different ways in which subprocesses (as well as the relationships between parts and wholes) can be modelled or otherwise understood.

The part–whole distinction, which is sometimes also a dichotomy, gives rise to two modes of analysis, modes that are different from methodological individualism and methodological collectivism: on the one hand, incremental analysis focuses, as a general rule, on mutual adjustment between actors or agents; on the other, holistic systems analysis analyses the system in which individual actors or agents operate. One subject on which part–whole relationships frequently focus is the relationship between private and social interests. Serious questions inevitably arise: How are private interests formed and identified? Whose private interests are to count? Is there a social interest different from the sum of individual interests? What precisely is the meaning of the 'sum of individual interests'? How is the social interest, however defined, to be determined? What are the relationships between market, legal social control and non-legal social control as mechanisms for the integration or composition of conflicts between private interests and between private and social interests? And so on.

Finally, considerations also arise concerning the relationships between parts in their individual and/or collective relations with the relevant whole. One has to do with freedom and control: freedom, the capacity to choose, always exists in the context of particular patterns or structures of freedom *and* control; freedom always depends upon, and gives effect to, the correlative system of control. One example is the Alpha–Beta dualism with regard to rights. First, in zero-sum cases for Alpha to have a right is for Beta to have a non-right and thereby to be exposed to the exercise by Alpha of Alpha's right. Second, systems of rights are methodological collectivist in nature, in both their origin and their operation; in both respects they are technical public goods. Just as the social nature of the individual is worked out through complex socialization and acculturation processes, so too is the individual as an entity possessed of rights (protected interests) of economic and other significance whose genesis and meaning derives from the larger system of which they are a part.

WARREN J. SAMUELS

See also:

Atomism and Organicism; Market, Institutionalist View of the; Methodological Individualism; Microfoundations of Macroeconomic Competitiveness; Neoclassical Microeconomic Theory, Critique of.

Bibliography

Agassi, Joseph (1975), 'Institutional Individualism', *British Journal of Sociology*, **26**, pp. 144–55.
Hodgson, Geoffrey (1988), *Economics and Institutions*, Cambridge: Polity Press and Philadelphia: University of Pennsylvania Press.

Lange, Oskar (1965), *Wholes and Parts: A General Theory of System Behaviour*, London: Pergamon.
Little, Daniel (1991), *Varieties of Social Explanation*, Boulder, Colo.: Westview Press.

Pasinetti, Luigi L.

Luigi Lodovico Pasinetti was born in 1930 at Zanica (Bergamo), Italy. After receiving his first degree at the Catholic University of Milan in 1954, he went on to do graduate work at Cambridge, England (1956–7), Harvard, Massachusetts (1957–8), Cambridge again (1958–9) and Oxford (1959–60). He received his PhD in economics in 1962, at Cambridge, and became a teaching Fellow of King's College. In 1976, he went back to Italy, to the Catholic University, where he is full professor of economic analysis and has continued teaching economics to the present. (For more biographical information see Blaug, 1988, and Baranzini, 1991.)

Pasinetti's theoretical views were formed in the climate of the Keynesian and Sraffian enthusiasms that dominated Cambridge in the late 1950s and early 1960s. By that time he had got in touch with and become a close friend of some of the members of the famous Keynes Circus: Sraffa, Kaldor, Robinson and Kahn. These are the economists from whom he received the greatest influence, and of whom he is considered one of the most important intellectual heirs. His first well-known theoretical contribution is an article (Pasinetti, 1959–60) in which one can find a rigorous treatment of the Ricardian system based on the notion of 'natural equilibrium' and focused on the analysis of the growth process in a multi-commodity production system under Say's Law and perfect competition. This article contains the seeds of much of the future work of Pasinetti, especially in his attempt to combine the classical approach with the Keynesian theory; an attempt further pursued in Pasinetti (1974b), where the non-neoclassical orientation of Keynes's economics is brought to light.

The same Keynesian vein is to be found in a fundamental essay (Pasinetti, 1962), which is actually the most original contribution made by Pasinetti to Post Keynesian economics. It contains the famous and much debated 'Pasinetti theorem', according to which the rate of profit in a capitalist economy with different saving propensities of workers and capitalists depends only on the capitalists' expenditure. Workers are treated as owners of a part of the stock of capital. Therefore a part of the profits is distributed to them, whilst the profits paid to pure capitalists are reduced accordingly. Then capitalists' savings are lower than they would have been if workers did not save. But workers' savings precisely match the amount by which the capitalists save less income. In the Post Keynesian approach it is the equilibrium savings ratio that adjusts to the investment ratio. As the economy grows with full employment, the adjustment of the savings ratio occurs through the changes in income distribution. Therefore the rate of profit is determined as the one that guarantees the equilibrium savings ratio. As the investment ratio depends only on the capitalists' decisions, the rate of profit also depends on them. In particular, it is determined by the rate of accumulation and the capitalists' propensity to consume. Wages are determined residually.

The controversy with Samuelson, Modigliani and other neoclassical economists triggered off by this article was continued in the harsh capital debate. To this Pasinetti contributed several articles, the most important being Pasinetti (1966) which was the first article (presented at the 1st World Congress of the Econometric Society, Rome, 1965) to challenge the Levhari–Samuelson non-switching theorem. Subsequently, he developed his Sraffian heritage in a number of contributions on the theory of production, joint production, value and prices.

The notion of 'vertical integration' developed in Pasinetti (1973) is another of Pasinetti's innovative contributions. A vertically integrated sector is a subsystem whose labour and capital coefficients express, respectively, the quantity of labour directly and indirectly used in the whole economy to produce one unit of a particular final good and the physical quantities of all commodities directly and indirectly used in the whole economy to produce that same unit of final good. This notion was fruitfully used in Pasinetti (1981), an ambitious work in which is tackled the problem of singling out the conditions of full employment growth in a multi-sector economy subject to structural change. In such an economy productivity grows at constant but differential rates in different sectors, while the pattern of final demand changes over time, obeying a special kind of Engel's law, one modified in such a way as to account for the emergence of new goods. The economy is capable of growing with full employment and full capacity utilization only if two conditions are realized: at the sectoral level, productive capacity must grow in any industry at the same rate as demand; at the macroeconomic level the rate of investment must be such as to absorb all the potential output exceeding the production of consumption goods. In this economy the 'natural' rates of profit would be different in different industries and would depend on the growth rate of population and the growth rate of per capita demands. In a competitive capitalist economy, however, the rate of profit must be uniform. It is proved, in a sort of expanded Pasinetti theorem, that it depends on the capitalists' propensity to save, on the growth rate of population and the average growth rate of per capita demands.

More recently, Pasinetti has developed the notion of 'vertically hyper-integrated sectors', especially in connection with some problems posed by the labour theory of value (Pasinetti, 1988). His continuing interest in the labour theory of value seems to be justified by the conviction that labour is the ultimate source of wealth, in a vision much reminiscent of Smith's.

Pasinetti's contribution to modern economic thought is remarkable but quite at odds with mainstream economics. His main efforts have been invested in the difficult enterprise of integrating the Sraffian and the Post Keynesian wings of Cambridge contemporary economics. The enterprise is in progress and as yet unfinished, but it is too great to be the work of only one man. At the same time one could say that Pasinetti has contributed to the fulfilment of this project, not only with his own scientific work, but also with the stimulus he gave to the formation of a vast gathering of pupils and followers who are now working in his wake.

ERNESTO SCREPANTI

See also:

Capital Theory; Kaldor, Nicholas; Keynes, John Maynard; Macroeconomic Policy; Macroeconomic Theory; Marx, Karl; Robinson, Joan.

Bibliography

Baranzini, M. (1991), 'Luigi Lodovico Pasinetti', in P. Arestis and M. Sawyer (eds), *A Biographical Dictionary of Dissenting Economists*, Aldershot: Edward Elgar.

Blaug, M. (1988), 'Pasinetti, Luigi L.', in *Great Economists since Keynes*, Brighton: Harvester Wheatsheaf.

Pasinetti, L.L. (1960), 'A Mathematical Formulation of the Ricardian System', *The Review of Economic Studies*, **XXVII**, February, pp. 78–98.

Pasinetti, L.L. (1962), 'Rate of Profit and Income Distribution in Relation to the Rate of Economic Growth', *The Review of Economic Studies*, **XXIX**, October, pp. 267–79.

Pasinetti, L.L. (1966), 'Changes in the Rate of Profit and Switches of Techniques', *Quarterly Journal of Economics*, **LXXX**, November, pp. 503–17

Pasinetti, L.L. (1973), 'The Notion of Vertical Integration in Economic Analysis', *Metroeconomica*, **XXV**.

Pasinetti, L.L. (1974a), *Growth and Income Distribution: Essays in Economic Theory*, Cambridge: Cambridge University Press.

Pasinetti, L.L. (1974b), 'The Economics of Effective Demand', in Pasinetti, 1974.

Pasinetti, L.L. (1981), *Structural Change and Economic Growth: A Theoretical Essay on the Dynamics of the Wealth of Nations*, Cambridge: Cambridge University Press.

Pasinetti, L.L. (1988), 'Growing Subsystems, Vertically Hyper-Integrated Sectors and the Labour Theory of Value', *Cambridge Journal of Economics*, **XXII**, (1), pp. 125–34.

Peirce, Charles Sanders

C. S. Peirce (1839–1914), founder of the American school of philosophy called 'pragmatism', is important for the tradition of institutionalist economics for three reasons: one, most of the first generation of institutionalist writers were influenced by pragmatism, either directly through Peirce or else through William James (1842–1910) or John Dewey (1859–1952); second, various aspects of pragmatic doctrines are at present experiencing a revival coincident with the spreading disaffection with twentieth-century analytical philosophy; and third, Peirce was one of the first to bring what might be called an 'economistic approach' to analysing science.

Peirce never published a synoptic account of his philosophy, which was largely left as voluminous unpublished manuscripts after his death. Even his core doctrine of 'pragmatism' was repeatedly redefined and revised over the course of his lifetime, particularly in response to what he felt were unwarranted uses by such writers as James and Dewey. The doctrine began as a revision of common conceptions of truth based upon Kantian and Hegelian sources. Peirce sought to define truth as the ultimate limit to which the opinions of the relevant scientific community would converge, given their adherence to appropriate methods. The novelty of this doctrine was that it tended to contextualize truth with regard to the relevant community of inquiry or, as the pragmatic maxim of 1878 put it, 'Consider what effects, that might conceivably have practical bearings, we conceive the object of our conception to have. Then, our conception of these effects is the whole of our conception of the object.' (*CP*, vol. 5, p. 1). For Peirce, 'the essence of belief is the establishment of a habit', a doctrine which found its way into the work of Veblen, Commons and other early institutionalists. This was often misconstrued as a simple instrumentalism or a crude version of utilitarianism, but Peirce had at least read the political economists, and was sceptical of any 'exaggeration of the beneficial aspects of greed' (*CP*, vol. 6, p. 193) and Benthamism (*CP*, vol. 5, p. 98). Rather, Peirce proposed the striking doctrine that natural laws themselves evolve (*CP*, vol. 4, p. 84) and therefore scientific hypotheses had to be tethered to the continuity of purposes of the community of inquiry in order to define success in the quest for truth.

In the period of the resurgence of empiricist philosophies in the first half of the twentieth century, pragmatism was treated (if at all) as a pale precursor of such doctrines as operationalism and logical positivism; and a few authors have claimed that it was the major inspiration for Milton Friedman's essay on economic method. Since most of these movements sought to banish all metaphysical considerations from science, they clearly tended to misrepresent the spirit and substance of Peirce's ideas. With the revival of pragmatic philosophy in the last quarter of this century, and particularly through the efforts of Richard Rorty, it has only recently become possible to reevaluate the heritage of pragmatism in a more favourable light.

The classes of methods which would serve to bring about the eventual convergence of scientific opinion in Peirce's view were deduction, induction and (this Peirce's own neologism) abduction. The first was the province of logic (to which Peirce also made substantial contributions), but by its very character could not be a source of any novelty, and thus could not explain the success of science. Induction plays a very substantial role in Peirce's writings, particularly as he was one of the first to explore the philosophical implications of statistical inference (Hacking, 1990). But the centrepiece of his doctrine of the progress of science was abduction, from which all creativity and explanatory advance sprang. For Peirce, 'the question of pragmatism ... is nothing else than the question of the logic of abduction' (*CP*, vol. 5, p. 121). Abduction was the sum total of methods used to generate hypotheses in a scientific community which then subsequently provided the grist for the mills of induction and deduction. When discussing abduction, Peirce had recourse to two sorts of language: that of 'instincts' (which found its way into the work of Veblen) and that of economics. The former mixed an evolutionary outlook with an individualist approach to describing the metaphysics of the scientist, while the latter tended to dominate when the scientific community was the unit of analysis (Stewart,1992).

No summary of Peirce's philosophy would be complete without some acknowledgement of his role as a founder of semiotics, the theory of signs and their interpretation. Peirce regarded the sign relation as fundamentally triadic, a relation between the denotation of a word, the designated object and the observer. This was again used to assert the primacy of the communitarian nature of science, anticipating in many respects the mature Wittgenstein's critique of rules and language games.

The literature on Peirce has grown exponentially in recent times, but it is fair to say there is no solid consensus that his thought has been fully comprehended, categorized or described. He stands as an unscalable peak amidst the foothills of American philosophy, cantankerous, elusive and irreducibly original. Some of this originality rubbed off on the first generation of institutionalist economics, but his influence has waned in subsequent generations of institutionalists.

PHILIP MIROWSKI

See also:

Cartesianism in Economics; Cumulative Causation; Dewey, John; Formalism in Economics; Habits; Instrumental Value Theory; Methodological Individualism; Methodology; Rational Actor Models; Realism, Philosophical; Veblen, Thorstein; Veblenian Dichotomy and Its Critics.

Bibliography

Apel, Karl (1981), *Charles S. Peirce: From Pragmatism to Pragmaticism*, Amherst: University of Massachusetts Press.
Hacking, Ian (1990), *The Taming of Chance*, Cambridge: Cambridge University Press.
James, William (1943), *Pragmatism*, New York: Longmans, Green.
Murphy, John (1990), *Pragmatism from Peirce to Davidson*, Boulder, Colo.: Westview Press.
Peirce, C.S. (1931–58), *Collected Papers of Charles Sanders Peirce* (*CP*), 8 vols, edited by Charles Hartshorne, Paul Weiss and Arthur Burks, Cambridge, Mass.: Harvard University Press.

Peirce, C.S. (1982–6), *Writings of Charles S. Peirce, A Chronological Edition*, 4 vols, Bloomington: Indiana University Press.
Stewart, William (1992), 'Social and Economic Aspects of Peirce's Conception of Science', *Transactions of the Charles Sanders Peirce Society.*

Perroux, François

François Perroux (1903–87) was born in Lyon and taught successively at the Universities of Lyon (1928) and Paris (1937) before being elected professor at the Collège de France in 1953. Until 1982 he directed the Institut des Sciences Mathématiques et Economiques Appliquées which he had founded in 1944.

While Perroux felt himself intellectually indebted to Barone, Morgenstern, Pantaleoni, Spann and von Mises, and although he read, annotated and commented on Marx and Keynes, it was Schumpeter from whom he said, 'I learned everything'.

Perroux carefully studied the general equilibrium theories of Walras and the marginalists, Wicksell and Debreu. He then decided not to make it his key concept in economic theory. His mode of criticism was quite personal. He kept out of the debate between the two rival Cambridge schools. Instead of discussing the concept of capital, he preferred to comment on the model's explanatory power, to inquire whether, rather than being the best possible representation of reality, it was not intended to state those conditions with which reality was to comply in order to give a unique and stable equilibrium. Nor did he participate in the debates over the work of Sraffa, quite probably because he had not dwelt upon the equilibrium model in Marx which underlies the transformation of values into prices, but had turned his attention to the formation and evolution of the phenomenon of power and to the construction of a multidisciplinary, long-term dynamics. His rejection of general equilibrium theory is based on two equally decisive sets of arguments, the first negative, the second positive.

The *axiomatic* character of general equilibrium theory raises three problems that Perroux reveals in decomposing the model. Its language is abusive: its hypotheses – the neoclassical theory affirms the freedom of choice – are simply constraints under which an ensemble defined as economic can be equilibrated. These hypotheses, which are defined *ex post* by the functioning of the model (they are the conditions under which the model can be closed), do not necessarily coincide with the actual characteristics of reality. Further, this model, which is incapable of analysing situations other than at equilibrium, omits from its field of application the great majority of concrete situations (inflation, unemployment, disequilibrium of balances). It thus disregards the essential question of knowing what procedures make it possible to contain these disequilibria within tolerable limits (hence, in Perroux's writing, the theme of 'equilibration' or 'regulation', in the French sense). Moreover, if equilibrium is said to be an optimum, then the axiomatic theory is transformed into a normative one, whereby the hypotheses' constraints become recommendations for economic policy for those who do not respect the model's limits of applicability.

Perroux's personal experience protected him from such a vision of the world. He was akin to Balzac or Zola. Thanks to his father, a shoemaker, he learned the reality of labour: his dynamics is rooted in the standpoint of production and not that of exchange. Moreover, from the same familial experience, he learned that competition between unequal agents ruins the weaker. E.H. Chamberlin and J. Robinson were to confirm his view in 1933. His dynamics accepts asymmetrical relations among agents, and emerges through a multitude of disequilibria.

Perroux's analytical behaviour can be compared to the theorists of classical economics or to Marx: he was obsessed by knowing reality. Only then could he try to understand it, thanks to concepts which it is only useful to create if they represent reality in a satisfactory manner, simplifying without destroying it. In order to deepen his theoretical work, he devoted himself to vast studies of facts that appeared to him to throw light on his dynamics. As far back as the 1930s, he inquired into many different themes, such as the formation of profit, public health programmes and the 'Nazi myths'; after World War II, he collected important files on national accounting, the Marshall Plan, the reconstruction of Europe, oil companies, underdevelopment, pacific coexistence, the conquest of space, the sectorial nature of inflation, the strategies of enterprise and so on. The foregoing are in fact the titles of books or special issues of the review *Economie appliquée*, which he directed.

Perroux's long-term economic dynamics results from the way in which the relations among agents are articulated. His agents are active, endowed with unequal powers, inspired by a project. They act within structures whose limits they are subjected to, and within groups that are capable of a collective project. Through his activity, each agent transforms himself within the framework of a process of collective creation. These agents live in society, and living in society does not mean being in a market; no human society resembles a perfect market in which price, offer and demand reduce the agent to a simple point in the intersection of a pair of curves. The most frequent relations between agents are non-market relations: gift or pseudo-gift, constraints, asymmetry, domination, conflicts, competition–contest, active dialogues and participation. The units, simple or complex, public or private, unequal in power, make wagers, engage in anticipations, know and use their relative powers, give themselves rules of the game and also act to modify them, associate with one another and also in nations that may enjoy some degree of relative independence.

The agents' inequality lends their relations a dissymmetric character: action and reaction are unequal, reciprocity and interdependence are imperfect. Perroux sees in this the essence of *power*. The equilibrium model tried to banish its very idea, but this 'refractory outlaw' is nonetheless omnipresent. Power is 'the capacity of exerting constraints on things and people'. As such, it is one of the attributes of that specific economic agent which is the state, 'monopolist of public constraint'. However, Perroux did not write at length on the theory of the state. He said, 'Every State is a structure of domination. Governing elites depend on dominant groups who impose their decisions on dominated groups, by means of menace or the exercise of supreme violence which is superficially and imperfectly legitimated.' However, if it is true that everywhere the state has a supporting class, it is at the same time more than and something other than the 'representative' of this class. As such, it 'cannot dispense with arbitrating the conflicts of interest within the latter and to reconcile them with the complaints of the rising social classes'.

But the power phenomenon by far transcends the state: 'every system of agents contains an element of power'. We find it at all organizational levels in the form of 'subordination and influence'. Perroux wrote, 'The enterprise is defined by the power exercised by a decision-maker, who is either individual or collective. Since it is social, economic activity contains and combines the search for power, the power relationship and rationality in the use of power as an objective and as an economic means.' Hence, 'power is an inalienable component of economic activity'. Finally, 'its nature is economic, it costs and it pays'. In a word, if dynamics makes progress possible, the appraisal of the latter may differ according to whether one is oneself subject to power or whether one exercises it. What is 'progress' for some can be a loss for others. From the existence of progress for the dominators it cannot be inferred that it is a reality for the community.

The social dialogue can only be clear when there are 'exact social accounts'. Because 'progress' must be defined, Perroux indicates his criterion, 'scientific humanism' or 'fundamental economics', the advance towards the accomplishment of the 'project of the species'. He defined its three requirements: 'feed the living, take care of them, free the slaves', or 'the development of all human beings and of the whole person in each'. Perroux consequently devoted a large part of his work to the questions of underdevelopment, which he precisely interpreted as one of the most brutal consequences of domination, and of development which he considered to be the fulfilment of this human project.

La Fondation François Perroux has the objective of publishing a complete edition of his work.

GERARD DE BERNIS

See also:
Development Theory; Formalism in Economics; Institutional Economic Thought in Europe; Keynes, John Maynard; Marx, Karl; Neoclassical Microeconomic Theory, Critique of; Power; Régulation Theory, French; Robinson, Joan; Schumpeter, Joseph Alois.

Bibliography
Perroux, François (1948), *Le Plan Marshall ou l'Europe nécessaire au monde*, Paris: Librairie de Médicis.
Perroux, François (1954), *L'Europe sans rivages*, Paris: PUF; reprinted 1990 by Fondation François Perroux at Presses Universitaires de Grenoble.
Perroux, François (1956, 1957), *Théorie générale du Progrès économique*, Paris: Cahiers de l'ISMEA, Serie I, 3 vols.
Perroux, François (1964, 1970), *Industrie et creation collective*, 2 vols, Paris: PUF.
Perroux, François (1969), *L'Economie due XXème siècle*, 3rd edn, Paris: PUF.
Perroux, François (1970), *Aliénation et Société industrielle*, préface à l'édition complète des oeuvres de Karl Marx par Maximilien Rubel, coll. La Pléïade, Paris: Gallimard.
Perroux, François (1973), *Pouvoir et Economie*, coll. Etudes. Paris: Bordas.
Perroux, François (1975), *Unités Actives et Mathématiques Nouvelles: révision de la théorie de l'équilibre économique général*, Paris: Dunod.
Perroux, François (1980), *Economie et Société. Contrainte, Echange, Dons*, Paris: PUF.
Perroux, François (1983), *A New Concept of Development*, London: Croom/UNESCO.

Planning, National Economic

Planning has to do with the formulation of goals and means. What does society consider a desirable outcome of the economic process and how should the objectives be realized? In economic planning a distinction is made between directive and indicative planning; the former refers to a centrally planned command economy in which individual firms have no autonomy, the latter to a market economy in which autonomous firms are guided by the indications in the plan. Because of the recent developments in centrally planned economies attention is focused on systems of indicative planning.

Theoretical underpinnings
The central idea of indicative planning is to provide information about future developments in order to reduce uncertainties for the economic actors. In orthodox theory there is no strong reason for planning to be put on the agenda. In orthodox general equilibrium theory all trades are once-and-for-all; there is thus no real future, no historical time, no radical uncertainty. If plans concerning the future are introduced in orthodoxy then the problem

of uncertainty is 'solved' by introducing a full set of futures markets. It is useful in this respect to make a distinction between market uncertainty and environmental uncertainty. The former concerns the uncertainty about the behaviour of the participants in markets, the latter is about developments in the environment of the actors. Market uncertainty is endogenous and can be reduced or eliminated by letting buyers and suppliers reveal what their future actions will be. Environmental uncertainty is exogenous and no one in the system has conclusive information about it – sometimes no one has any information about it. Examples are technological development, the weather, wars and the like. Economists often refer in this context to the 'state of nature'. In the general equilibrium analysis of Kenneth Arrow and Gerard Debreu the uncertainty problem was tackled by introducing futures markets, where future equilibrium prices are settled for every possible state of nature.

James Meade developed a theory of indicative planning based on the general equilibrium analysis. His indicative plan is formally equivalent to the list of equilibrium prices that emerge from the operation of a full set of future markets. In his theoretical model, Meade gathers all buyers and suppliers into the 'Albert Hall' and a Walrasian auctioneer finds out what the future equilibrium prices and quantities will be at different states of nature. For every possible state, that is to say for every possible development in the environment, the auctioneer finds an equilibrium price. When these prices are published in a national plan and known to all the agents, no one is willing to buy above or to sell below the published price.

A second theory of indicative planning is based on Keynesian growth models. Roy F. Harrod considers indicative planning to be an instrument for macroeconomic policy with which the rate of growth can be raised or stabilized. In his view the demand side of the economy can be influenced by government through Keynesian fiscal and monetary policies. Such a policy will only be effective when the supply side is in line with the developments on the demand side. Harrod discusses the disaggregation of the macro-projections into sectoral projections and would let industry in sectoral committees comment on their feasibility. According to Harrod, after some iterations, an internally consistent projection for each sector will result in which business has confidence. Based on such an exchange of information the expectations of business are influenced in the direction of the macro-projections.

Both the approaches of Meade and Harrod are problematic, among other things because the questions of information costs, bounded rationality and opportunism are not taken into consideration. It is simply assumed that, after a few rounds of consultation, internally coherent plans will result and that actors will adjust their strategies in line with the objectives in the plans. Saul Estrin and Peter Holmes follow another approach by introducing concepts from new institutional economics. In an uncertain world with information costs, transaction costs and opportunism, they ask themselves what kind of information actors need, what kind of information is available in the market and what kind of information should be produced in an indicative plan by a public agent. In market economies actors receive information from many sources, such as prices, through norms and values and via relations in networks with other firms. Actors can also produce information themselves or buy information in the market from specialized firms which can realize economies of scale and scope. Because information is often costly and the 'market for information' fails, there is reason for a public agent to fill the gap and to produce information in an indicative plan as a public good. Estrin and Holmes conclude that a public agent should produce a national plan with information on leading indicators: 'These [indicators] would be largely macroeconomic variables, but governments' and firms' imprecise information about the future would also be pooled over particular markets to highlight expectational inconsistencies and broaden opportunity sets' (Estrin and Holmes, 1983, p. 54).

According to institutionalist writers in the Veblen–Commons tradition, an important theoretical ground for indicative planning is to be found not only in the increase of efficiency due to the supply of additional information, but also in the contribution of indicative planning to a more democratic society. Their social and political arguments for planning refer to the increasing asymmetry of power between corporations and governments. Because the strategies of corporations are not necessarily the ones which are best from the point of view of local, regional and (supra) national governments, planning by governments is considered vital in the interest of communities. Democratically chosen governments should act as countervailing powers and set clear guidelines for corporations concerning entry in national markets, the conditions for investments, cooperation with local small and medium-sized firms and the like. If they do not do so, then the process of concentrating economic power in fewer and fewer hands will continue and the tendencies towards more transnational corporations guided by short termism will progressively undermine the possibilities for people to determine their own future.

Policy implications
The policy implications of the theoretical views are not all of the same tenor. What governments want and can do depends on specific historical situations and social and political conditions. Government in Japan, for instance, has other possibilities and constraints from the one in France or the USA. The two ideal types of the developmental state and the regulatory state are considered useful in discussing the policy implications of indicative planning.

In a so-called 'developmental state' explicit goals with respect to the structural development of the economy are formulated and published in a national indicative plan. At the macro level the goals concern the growth of GNP, the deficit on the balance of payments, the rate of inflation and so on. These objectives are translated into mesoeconomic objectives, that is to say into the consequences and implications for sectors and regions. What does a 5 per cent growth of GNP mean for the developments in the steel or the electronic sector? What does a restructuring of a specific sector imply for the development in a specific region? In the indicative plan such questions at the meso level can also be translated into the micro level: what does a meso-development mean for a specific private or public firm?

Plans concerning the structure of the economy are based on expected developments in the environment and an assessment of their implications for the comparative advantages of the country. If, for instance, in a sector the technology changes and cheap labour is not needed any more, that comparative advantage will disappear. In market economies it is first of all a task of entrepreneurs to anticipate such changes and to invest in new directions. If at the micro level the right decisions are taken in time then the structure of the economy adapts more or less smoothly to changes in the environment. However, if uncertainties are too large, entrepreneurs can easily become too prudent and also short-sighted; long-term projects with relatively uncertain outcomes are not undertaken and the adaptation of the economic structure stagnates. The idea in the developmental state of setting long-term structural objectives is to reduce uncertainties for management through the creation of a relatively stable environment. Information about possible and desirable structural changes can help management in formulating their own strategies. Information about macro- and meso-developments concerning technologies, market structures, government policies and the like is often difficult or expensive to produce for individual firms. This is precisely the information published in the indicative plans of the Japanese Ministry of International Trade and Industry.

For the elaboration of the plan, consultation of all interest groups is essential, not only with respect to the exchange and production of information, but also for the legitimation of the plan. The idea is that interest groups involved in the production of the plan are more willing to participate also in the implementation of the plan objectives. After the consultation the ideas of the different groups have to be formulated in a coherent view (the so-called concertation) after which the planning agent will try to bind the parties involved to behave in conformity with the plan. In a market economy the firms and interest groups are autonomous and cannot be forced through directives to act in line with the plan objectives. However, it is possible to bind parties by means of contracts in which the rights and obligations of the parties involved are formulated. The three elements of consultation, concertation and contracting constitute the core of indicative planning. In a developmental state the existence of a powerful planning agency is essential. Both the strategies of the large enterprises and the policies of the different ministries have to be coordinated in line with the plan objectives. An effective consultation, concertation and coordination demands a well-respected, well-informed and well-equipped planning agency responsible for the long-term structural developments.

In a regulatory state no explicit objectives concerning the structural development are formulated. Government is only responsible for the market process and it is hoped, believed or known that structural adaptations will automatically result. In a regulatory state conjunctural and competition policies are the main activities of government. It is clear that the central agency will be the Ministry of Finance, together with the commission responsible for competition policies. The planning activities of the Ministry of Finance concern the internal and external equilibria; central are stabilization plans in order to control inflation, plans to reduce deficits on the balance of payment, plans concerning the budget of the government and the like. Such conjunctural planning is of a completely different nature from the structural planning: in the former, Keynesian demand policy, policies concerning the control of costs for the firms (wages, taxes, premiums) and competition policies are central and so is the Ministry of Finance, whereas, in the latter, industrial and technology policies and the Ministry of Industry and the Central Planning Agency play a major role. It is possible that in a regulatory state questions about industrial policy may be on the agenda, but that policy will then be of a generic nature, not aiming at the realization of specific objectives concerning the industrial structure. In a regulatory state industrial policy consists of, for instance, a general tax reduction in order to improve profits of the firms, leading to an increase in investments and an improvement in the firms' competitiveness. In a developmental state also conjunctural policies are on the agenda, but these policies are complementary to the structural ones; for instance, when demand is stimulated it should be a specific stimulation in line with the objectives in the plan.

JOHN GROENEWEGEN

See also:

Development Policy; Development Theory; Galbraith, John Kenneth; Gruchy, Allan Garfield; Macroeconomic Policy; Planning, Theory of; Regulation, Theory of Economic; Uncertainty.

Bibliography

Borstein, M. (ed.) (1975), *Economic Planning, East and West*, Cambridge, Mass.: Ballinger.
Cave, M. and P. Hare (1981), *Alternative Approaches to Economic Planning*, London: Macmillan.

Estrin, S. and P. Holmes (1983), *French Planning in Theory and Practice*, London: Allen & Unwin.
Hare, P. (1985), *Planning the British Economy*, New York: St Martin's Press.
Harrod, R.F. (1973), *Economic Dynamics*, London: Macmillan.
Meade, J.E. (1971), *The Controlled Economy*, London: Allen & Urwin.

Planning, Theory of

Planning, in a majority of theoretical works, as well as in the vernacular, has usually been taken to imply an attempt to improve future outcomes through deliberation in the present. The call for planning, whether emanating from the viscera or derived from some theoretical argument, has usually been based on the thesis that unfettered markets follow a blind course that can be improved by collective deliberation over the choice of future outcomes. Whether the failures of markets are couched in terms of Marxian forces of history or neoclassical incomplete futures markets, the conclusion is that society would gain by using institutions that directly force it to confront the future. Thus Marxist and neoclassical views are similar in the sense that they identify failures of the market and suggest an expanded role for government.

A thoroughly distinct, although not inconsistent, approach has arisen within the institutionalist camp (Gruchy, 1984, 1987). Planning in this conception is prompted not only by dissatisfaction with unfettered markets, but also by the perceived failures of existing policy mechanisms, particularly when these mechanisms are viewed within the larger democratic context. Hence planning involves a change in the techniques of governmental decision making and in the processes of democracy, as well as an increase in the scope of government activity. Planning ensures that the policy process is neither fixated on the short term, nor controlled by powerful, and narrow, economic interests. In this view, planning is seen as a future-oriented instrument of the democratic process.

We adumbrate below the theory underlying three distinct conceptions of planning, which represent pure types among a host of alternatives. We also reflect upon the interactions of theory and practice, commenting on the practical planning experiences that seem to conform most closely to each of the theoretical models.

Indicative planning
In the 1950s, planning rose to a position of popularity and prominence in France, under the tutelage of Jean Monnet. Whether as a result or not – and opinions greatly vary – the French economy was very successful at that time. Hence there was much interest in the conceptual basis for French planning. The planning process was a consultative and forecasting exercise

that had seemed to evolve quite independently of any existing underpinning in economic theory. For economists, then, there arose the challenge of searching for an abstract justification for this exercise, one that was rooted in economic theory. Pierre Masse, an economist and planning commissioner, gave this search its strongest impetus. His theoretical line has been followed by legions of neoclassical theoreticians in the ensuing years.

The basic notion underlying the theory of indicative planning is that economic agents are uncertain about the future actions of other agents, that this uncertainty can be reduced, and that the market does not reduce uncertainty to an optimal degree. Since the reduction of uncertainty – or, equivalently, information creation – is a public good, there exists a market failure argument for planning. Some type of public forecasting procedure might improve economic efficiency. If this procedure is combined with consultation between the main actors in the economy, one can view the process as a substitute for the non-existent futures markets beloved by general equilibrium theorists.

This line of argument has been pursued with much eagerness by neoclassical economists. Indeed, the informational problems of markets are now at the centre of neoclassical inquiry and it seems that an informational market failure argument for planning is at least as sound as the rather comparable public goods justification for government provision of national defence.

In a clear example of the gulf between the development of theory and the world of practice, the French were becoming disenchanted with planning while indicative planning theory was reaching new heights. Planning in France is now relatively neglected and seems unlikely to rise again to its former position of prominence. Similar sorts of planning exercises have been carried out in other countries, for example, Japan, the UK and the former Yugoslavia. However, little new theory was used to justify the exercises and little was developed in parallel with them. (See Brada and Estrin, 1990, for a review of the theory and practice of indicative planning from a neoclassical perspective.)

Democratic–coordinative planning

For the conception of planning most closely associated with the institutionalist view, one begins with the premise that the market does not conform to the self-regulating ideal popular in textbook economic models. Government intervention already occurs in capitalist economies for myriad reasons. Moreover, the sheer size of modern businesses ensures that they can have undue influence on government policy. From the viewpoint of institutionalists, then, the power held by modern corporations provides as much reason to engage in planning as does the uncertainty emphasized by advocates of the indicative approach.

Planning, then, has several goals. First, there is a need to keep policy makers focused on the long term in the face of the pressure to concentrate on short-term stability. Thus, according to Allan Gruchy (1987), the policy process should become anticipatory, not purely reactive. Second, government decisions must be rescued from the baneful influence of large interest groups and must reflect in a more egalitarian way the needs of the whole society. By placing policy decisions within the democratic process, planning procedures will ensure that those decisions reflect a broad conception of society's welfare. It is argued that in an open, deliberative process the making of government policy can come much closer to a democratic ideal than seems to be the case at present.

This conception of planning, which I will call democratic–coordinative, has been an object of economists' attention since the days of the Great Depression. Indeed, it was during the Depression and under the important influence of institutionalists, particularly Wesley Mitchell and Rexford Tugwell, that economic planning first became an accepted idea in the United States. (Since those times, the degree of public acceptance has waxed and waned with the fortunes of the economy itself.) In postwar years in the United States, institutionalists such as J.K. Galbraith (1973) and Allan Gruchy have served to develop the idea of planning and keep it on the economists' agenda.

Within the democratic–coordinative conception of planning, there have always been two distinct approaches. The first, emphasizing the consultative and democratic aspects, has focused upon the processes of planning. It has therefore been more closely aligned with the institutionalist school. However, according to Gruchy (1984, p. 184), institutionalist proposals for national economic planning have not been elaborated in great detail. The second has focused more on the technocratic aspects of the exercise and has been more closely associated with neoclassical economists. In the second approach, there has been concern with the development of macro-models of the economy, the use of these models in policy choices, and the optimal choice of policy instruments. The names particularly associated with such techniques are Jan Tinbergen, Henri Theil and Leif Johansen.

The Dutch planning exercises in the immediate postwar years are perhaps the best known implementation of democratic–coordinative planning. These exercises achieved renown among economists because of the extent to which sophisticated theory was developed within the context of the planning process. In the 1950s, the results produced by technicians probably had considerable influence on Dutch policy choices. The technical approach facilitated the removal of the policy process from parliamentary supervision, something that was helpful to government officials because of the extreme divisiveness of Dutch politics. Therefore, in the instance in which theory was most influential, the planning exercises had, at best, an uneasy relationship with democratic process.

Command planning

A thoroughly distinct set of planning episodes has been associated with the implementation of command planning in the Soviet Union, China, Eastern Europe and many allied third world countries. If there was a theoretical force behind the advocacy of such planning, it was primarily antipathy towards the market, rather than any concrete conception of the nature of planning. Hence, given the need to create an economic mechanism that supplanted the market, the creation of the structures of the command economy relied little on theory. (The experience of wartime planning in imperial Germany may have been the most important influence.) The theory of command planning was created *ex post*, essentially as a description of existing procedure.

In practice, the planning that was pursued by such entities as Gosplan in the USSR focused on the short run. The name attached to its theoretical representation – material balance planning – indicated its limited goals. Material balance planning focused on the construction of inter-industry input balances for the short run. Orientation towards the future was only embodied in this methodology through the imposition of some growth priorities, decided within an unarticulated political mechanism. The tenor of the material balance approach is aptly summarized by the term commonly used by Soviet planners – 'from the achieved level' – implying that plan calculations are always based on small adjustments to existing outcomes. The term summarizes a whole methodology that is the best theoretical statement of the nature of planning as implemented in the post war years in the countries formerly in the Soviet bloc. For a description of this approach and an evolutionary perspective on its effects, see Murrell (1990), where it is argued that the central-planning agencies did a passable job on short-run resource allocation, but that the real failure of command planning was in the absence of attention to the long run.

In its realization, command planning bore little relation to the type of process envisioned in the theories constructed by planning's strongest advocates. Socialist theorists saw planning as an attempt to rescue society from the blind forces of history, from a perceived directionless market. For such theorists, the purpose of planning was not to control day-to-day economic decisions, but rather to ensure that those decisions were consistent with a development path reflecting the needs of society. (The writings of Michał Kalecki are most instructive here.) But command bureaucracies seemed less able than the market to address long-term needs.

There is a curious relation between command planning and neoclassical theory. The creation of a static central plan and the design of incentives for socialist managers are neoclassical problems par excellence. All the usual optimization techniques, with their rationality assumptions, become useful for such problems. Thus there is an enormous literature in the West relevant to central planning, and, indeed, Soviet mathematical economists published much material in this vein. Hence there are myriad articles in both Soviet and Western journals on iterative schemes for constructing optimal plans, on managerial incentive structures, on optimal long-run plans and on a host of other technical aspects of planning. This has led some to suggest that neo-classical economics is really the economics of socialism, while institutional and evolutionary theories in their many forms provide the economics of capitalism.

This last point is exhibited by the socialist controversy, the debate in the 1930s and 1940s between neoclassicals and Austrians, particularly von Mises and Hayek, on the workability of socialism. In this debate, it was neoclassicals who argued for the viability of a (market) socialist economy. The Austrians persistently raised the problems of information processing that would confront a socialist regime and the informational benefits of capitalist markets (Murrell, 1983). In a slightly updated form, the same approach has been used to criticize those types of national economic planning that are applicable in a capitalist economy (Lavoie, 1985). However, in that context, the Austrian arguments are less than convincing, since they hardly touch upon the issues raised by the proponents of indicative and democratic–coordinative planning: the informational problems of markets and the behaviour of the state in a modern economy.

Hybrids

The three modes of planning identified above are pure types. In practice, planning schemes have combined elements of two or more of these modes. For reasons of space, there is no possibility of describing these hybrids here. Particularly prominent is development planning, which can be loosely viewed as a form of democratic–coordinative planning (focusing perhaps more on the coordinative aspect) implemented when the state undertakes a large amount of industrial investment. Also Hungary's reforms prompted inquiry into the types of planning that would be suitable for a market–socialist society, without any insightful conclusions.

The missing element: a theory of planning institutions

The theory of command planning has not risen above narrow technical questions concerning the calculation of a central plan that replaces the market in its capacity as the allocator of resources, but, in this narrowness, theory tracked the reality of planning in the Soviet bloc reasonably well. The theory of command planning provided no suggestion on how to design planning institutions that would implement the long-term goals of the advocates of planning.

In the theories of indicative and democratic–coordinative planning, the planning process itself was viewed as a neutral element that provided far-sighted analyses reflecting the democratic process. In these conceptions, planners were removed from power. This too mirrored reality. Unfortunately, the consequence was that, apart from some prominent, but brief, interludes, planning had a fairly limited significance in market economies.

The progress of planning in the last four decades mirrors a problem at the heart of planning theory. Planning, as viewed by its strongest advocates, would be most consistently brought to fruition by an institution that is removed from daily concerns and whose power is not rooted in narrow economic interests. However, when that institution has real power over the allocation of resources, as in the former USSR, it seems to have been forced by exigencies to focus on the short term and its decisions have been dominated by narrow economic interests. When that institution is removed from daily economic concerns, it has been largely ignored, as has been the case in most implementations of planning in developed capitalist economies.

Planning theory has almost completely ignored the design of the institutional base of planning itself. There has been little theoretical deliberation on how to construct a truly democratic, future-oriented institution, a planning body, that can produce and implement economic policy, even by institutionalists (Gruchy, 1984, p. 184). If theory is ever going to be a force in the implementation of planning in a manner envisaged by the visionaries of planning, theorists need to reflect on matters of institutional creation and design. Theorists will have to show how to construct a body that is neutral in economic policy matters in the same way that Western courts are neutral in the production and implementation of commercial law. Given the rudimentary state of our knowledge on the way the legal system of capitalist economies developed and how the legal structure came to exercise power in a neutral manner, one cannot hold out great hopes for swift theoretical advances in the design of planning institutions. As for so many of society's mechanisms, chance events, which mutate existing institutions, will be more likely to show us the way to a workable set of planning arrangements than will the deliberations of theorists.

PETER MURRELL

See also:

Galbraith, John Kenneth; Gruchy, Allan Garfield; Hayek, Friedrich A.; Information Theory in Economics; Kalecki, Michał; Market, Institutionalist View of the; Planning, National Economic; Spontaneous Order; Uncertainty.

Bibliography
Brada, J. and S. Estrin (eds) (1990), 'Special Issue on Indicative Planning', *Journal of Comparative Economics*, December.
Galbraith, J.K. (1973), *Economics and the Public Purpose*, Boston, Mass.: Houghton Mifflin.
Gruchy, A. (1984), 'Uncertainty, Indicative Planning, and Industrial Policy', in Marc Tool (ed.), *An Institutionalist Guide to Economics and Public Policy*, Armonk, NY: M.E. Sharpe.
Gruchy, A. (1987), *The Reconstruction of Economics: An Analysis of the Fundamentals of Institutional Economics*, Westport Conn.: Greenwood Press.
Johansen, L. (1977), *Lectures on Macro-Economic Planning*, Amsterdam: North-Holland.
Lavoie, D. (1985), *National Economic Planning: What is Left?*, Cambridge, Mass.: Ballinger.
Murrell, P. (1983), 'Did the Theory of Market Socialism Answer the Challenge of Ludwig von Mises? A Reinterpretation of the Socialist Controversy', *History of Political Economy*, **15**, (1), Spring, pp. 92–105.
Murrell, P. (1990), *The Nature of Socialist Economies: Lessons from Eastern European Foreign Trade*, Princeton, NJ: Princeton, University Press.

Polanyi, Karl

Karl Polanyi was born in Hungary in 1886 and died in North America in 1964. He was one of many emigrants from Central European fascism who enriched British and American intellectual development in the mid-twentieth century. Polanyi observed in the uprooting of his personal life the cataclysm that a poorly instituted economy can provoke (Stanfield, 1986, ch.1). His central interest became the problem of lives and livelihood: the relation of community life to the way in which the community makes its living, the place of economy in society. He studied early economic systems to provide perspective and depth for his analysis of market capitalism and his dissent from its characteristic economic thought. Though considerations of space restrict what follows to a review of this analysis and dissent, the reader is encouraged not to neglect the important work on early economic systems (Dalton, 1968; and Polanyi, 1977; Stanfield, 1986, ch.3).

On market capitalism
The nature and evolution of market capitalism is the focal point for placing the modern economy in society (Polanyi, 1944). Polanyi's analysis is based on the distinction between embedded and disembedded economies. He argued, generally speaking, that pre-capitalist societies had no separate economic sphere with a distinct and explicit set of motives and functions. Instead, economic activity was motivated by the individual's general social location and interest, and acquisitive self-interest was negatively sanctioned by the fabric of religious, familial and political life.

In sharp contrast, economic interests in modern society appear distinct and predominant in the determination of an individual's social location and interest. The motive of gain operating through the institutional complex of the market mechanism has been promoted to a pillar institution, and this, for Polanyi, constituted the peculiar nature of nineteenth-century market capitalism. This is the disembedded economy: an autonomous sphere of human activity, motivated by greed or the threat of hunger and self-governed through a system of price-making markets. For Polanyi, this concept of a self-regulating market economy is dangerously utopian because it neglects the primacy of society and leaves social life open to disruption by the disturbances of an uncontrolled market process. Economic or material provisioning is an integral part of social reproduction. The inherent instability and insecurity of the self-regulating market threatens that reproduction. The market mentality also generates character traits which undermine social cohesion. The bargaining mentality of securing maximum advantage for oneself is fundamental to the operation of a market economy and must be inculcated by socialization and acculturation if the market economy is to operate upon a set of rational relative prices. Yet this mentality cannot fail to erode social bonds and generate pessimism, distrust and cynicism.

The impossibility of a self-regulating market economy is shown in the inconsistency of such an arrangement with the continuation of a functioning social order. The market process enforces continuous economic adjustment to reallocate resources to better uses. This incessant economic change necessarily disrupts and displaces existing political, social and cultural patterns. The friendships, family ties and civic roots of the working class are no match for the necessity of relocation to secure employment or career advance. Naturally or historically significant sites or human emotional attachments cannot stand in the way of pecuniary success and progress. The incessant change in the means of earning a livelihood uproots and degrades the lives to be lived.

But this is only one side of the story. Polanyi pointed to the other side with his concept of the *double movement*: the effort to establish a self-regulating market economy was necessarily accompanied by a contrary effort to protect society from the disruption which otherwise would have occurred. The protective response is very diverse. Governments have intervened to protect labour with legislation regulating child and women labour, working conditions, workday lengths and subsequent income maintenance programmes. Legislation was enacted on land use planning, resource conservation, pollution control and modern comprehensive environmental protection. Central banking, capital market regulations and aggregate demand management have been introduced in an effort to stabilize the macroeconomy. Regulatory agencies exist to ensure consumer product safety and service standards for those providing care for the young and old. Trade unions and other voluntary associations, such as civic, historical preservation, or naturalist societies, play a major role. Even the modern corporation can be viewed as part of the protective response, since its principal animus is the urge to stabilize and control the uncertain exigencies of the market mechanism.

On contemporary economic thought

The relationship between this disembedded economy and mainstream, formal economics is one of mutual reinforcement. Mainstream economics is the theoretical expression and ideological justification of the self-regulating market economy (Stanfield, 1979, chs 2–5; 1986, ch.2). Without this expression, indeed, this seventeenth-century cultural revolution (Appleby, 1978), it is inconceivable that the body politic would have turned over to competitive markets the vital task of material provisioning.

Orthodox economic analysis obscures the reality of society by taking the individual's preferences and capacities as given. This abstract individual of liberal thought is antecedent to the social process. Hence issues related to the formation of the individual's character *within* society cannot arise. Inevitably, questions of social control and social reform are thereby reduced to political intervention in the affairs of already extant individuals. This distortion of the social existence of human life virtually ensures a suspect attitude towards social policy. By taking society as their methodological point of departure, Polanyi and other social or institutional economists emphasize the ever-present reality of social control and social reform, including the vital issue of the formative socialization of the individual (Stanfield, 1979, ch.7).

The lesson of Polanyi's protective response concept is that the developmental tendency is towards an *administered economy* in which economic decisions are made and implemented through organizations of various kinds. This collective action involves replacing the forces of the impersonal market with political and bargaining modes of decision making. Such decisions may be implemented via market prices, but that does not make the market the integrative mechanism. The market economy is an integrative mechanism in which the supply and demand groups establish the relative prices. To the extent that organized groups negotiate the prices, the market ceases to be the integrative mechanism and the market mentality becomes obsolete (Dalton, 1968, ch.4).

In a very real sense, the formalist view is unable to conceive the major political economic tendencies of the twentieth century. Socialism and the welfare state have arisen largely to counter the threat to society posed by the unregulated market economy. The leading issues of this trend are those of the place of the economy in society. A methodology that treats the economy as an isolable social system with its own terrain cannot conceive the issues that occur in the effects on society of a particular institutional configuration of economic activity. The problem of lives and livelihood confronts us anew every day and, for its continuous resolution, we must look not to formalist, mainstream economics but to the social, institutional economics of scholars such as Karl Polanyi.

JAMES RONALD STANFIELD

See also:

Comparative Economic Systems; Development Theory; Institutions; Kapp, K. William; Market, Institutionalist View of the; Marx, Karl; Sahlins, Marshall; Spontaneous Order; Veblen, Thorstein.

Bibliography

Appleby, J.O. (1978), *Economic Thought and Ideology in Seventeenth-Century England*, Princeton, NJ: Princeton University Press.
Dalton, G. (ed.) (1968), *Primitive, Archaic, and Modern Economies: Essays of Karl Polanyi*, Garden City, NJ: Doubleday.
Polanyi, K. (1944), *The Great Transformation*, New York: Rinehart.
Polanyi, K. (1977), *The Livelihood of Man*, ed. H.W. Pearson, New York and London: Academic Press.
Stanfield, J.R. (1979), *Economic Thought and Social Change*, Carbondale: Southern Illinois University Press: London: Feffer and Simons.
Stanfield, J.R. (1986), *The Economic Thought of Karl Polanyi*, London: Macmillan; New York: St Martin's Press.

Power (I)

A concern for issues of power is one of the distinguishing marks of institutional economists. Among institutionalists, however, there is no single shared definition or concept of power. Each analyst must specify his or her own definition which may be more or less consistent with that offered by others. Most often, power is restricted to social interactions where some persons have an ability to affect other persons. Occasionally, the concept is broadened to include simple physical capabilities of persons (my 'power' to move a chair) or the outcomes of inanimate natural phenomena (the 'power' of the wind to cause erosion).

Even when limited to social interactions among persons, the term 'power' is used to cover a wide variety of relationships in a broad range of contexts. The three most often explored in institutional thought are power exercised by market actors, power over non-market social choices, and power over the content of human values.

Power and markets

One focus of power analysis is the ability of some market traders to do more than merely respond to impersonal prices. In the imperfect markets of the real world many actors are seen by institutionalists as having significant 'discretionary power'. The concept of administered prices is the classic example (Means, 1935). Given sufficient size and scope, large corporate institutions are seen as having a significant range within which they can and do set prices. Prices in concentrated markets are measurably more stable than either market conditions *per se* or the behaviour of prices in less concentrated markets would seem to predict. This is taken as evidence of power to control market interactions. Thus significant increases in concentration in global markets, made possible by the development of large-scale corporate institutions, are also an expansion of discretionary market power.

Discretionary power may extend beyond pricing decisions. It may also refer to latitude in investment choice, rates of technology adoption, or product mix. It may involve an ability to dictate the terms and conditions of trade. It defines who must come to whom. Such power is seen as rooted in control of scarce but essential inputs. Technological and social evolution can thus shift the locus of this power. Galbraith describes the evolution from agriculture-based society to large-scale manufacturing as a shift in market power from the owners of land to the owners of capital. Capital was the foundation of production; its owners had power to dictate market, and perhaps even social, conditions. He then sees a subsequent transfer of discretionary market power to those who control scarce but essential technical knowledge, that is, to his 'technostructure' (Galbraith, 1967).

Discretionary market power is usually seen as dynamic. It can be eroded by changes in technology, as above, or it can be countered by modification in key institutions. Some see a tendency towards the neutralization of discretionary power via the organization of 'countervailing power'. For example, growth of employers' power over terms of employment caused by expansion of the corporate control of capital inevitably calls forth labour organization on the other side of the market to contain and counter its effects (Galbraith, 1952).

Finally, power in market transactions may go beyond an ability to define the terms or conditions of trade. It may even be seen as an ability of sellers in some markets to shape the preferences of their customers. Rather than consumer sovereignty with business responding to the needs of consumers, some see a 'revised sequence' in which the preferences of consumers are shaped via advertising to 'demand' the products which powerful producers need to sell (Galbraith, 1967). Institutionally rich markets are neither powerless nor impersonal. They are arenas for the exercise of power.

Business firms and other formal organizations large enough to possess and exercise discretionary power are misperceived when viewed as if a 'single entrepreneur' or simply a 'production function'. They are formal aggregations of persons and are defined by explicit authority relationships. They are administrative structures defining who may make group decisions and who will guide the activities of others – in short, who will exercise power. They are mechanisms to collect, aggregate and interpret information. They are channels of authority defining who must 'report' to whom. Therefore power refers not only to the outward-directed 'behaviour' of large organizations: it is an element of internal institutional physiology. It is also a source of study in that context.

One approach focuses on institutional authority as an item to be traded for in markets. Independent contracting for complex and varying tasks is inevitably incomplete and expensive. Thus the employment relation replaces task contracting and labour contracts become a willing sale of control over future activity, that is, a submission for power in exchange for wages. The 'new institutional economics' extends this approach to all interactions characterized by opportunistic exploitation of imperfect information. It examines the use of authority as a substitute for markets, and the way in which dynamic technology redefines the boundaries of organizational power (Williamson, 1985).

Power is thus an important element in modern economies with large-scale organizations at two levels. The perceptions, decisions and actions of corporate 'persons' are the outcomes of internal authority-based interactions. The boundaries on the external influence of those actors on all aspects of market interactions are not limited by traditional market forces. They have discretion. At both levels, there is power.

Power over social choices

Property rights are themselves a form of power. They define who may do what to whom, with what, when, how and under what conditions. What is traded in markets is not really goods themselves but socially defined and defended rights – power socially granted. They are the *sine qua non* of markets and are themselves clearly *social* institutions. Thus institutionalists emphasize the role played by property rights as a fundamental form of social power (Schmid, 1987).

They also see the essential prior question. The processes of *defining* property rights must be played out before market interactions can begin. Concerned primarily with issues of resource allocation via impersonal markets, conventional economists are content to view property rights as simply 'evolving' or 'emerging'. For institutionalists, they are consciously and actively created. They result from the play of contending forces. Arising from legislative acts and judicial decisions, forms of property rights and their assignment to individuals are subject to all of the influences that can be brought to bear on government. Property rights are dynamic and endogenous. Institutional analysis sees property rights and power joined in two distinct ways: they are a form of power, and they are created by the exercise of power (Samuels, 1971).

The form of power most easily recognized by all schools of social scientists is an ability to get one's way in a social decision when others are opposed. When a conflict is joined, some win and others lose. The ability to determine the outcome in the face of opposition has been called 'one-dimensional power' (Lukes, 1974). It arises from control, whether 'official' or informal, over political resources. Such power may arise from holding established office, as with a federal judge able to call on armed might to support his or her will. Coercion or the threat of coercion is certainly power, and political decisions made via the institutions of the state ultimately have that sanction. Power over social decisions may be less formal. It may be based on social connections, control over crucial resources, or access to means of communication (Mills, 1956). It may arise from asymmetries in access to, and control over, information. Knowledge alone is not power; it becomes power only when others do not also have it (Bartlett, 1989).

Many institutionalists see a connection between the discretionary power of large organizations in markets and the ability of those who control the institutions to influence social choices. They see a 'privileged position' for business corporations in modern democratic states. The investment, production and employment decisions of corporations are essential elements of social performance. An unwillingness to undertake those responsibilities leads to poor economic performance and threatens the political survival of those in office. Policy decisions must ensure adequate incentives for corporate performance. That, in short, is power held by those in control of business corporations (Lindblom, 1977). When conflicts arise in the public arena, it is power that determines who will win. Economic structures often determine who has that power.

There is also an even more subtle type of power over social decisions, sometimes called 'two-dimensional' power (Lukes, 1974). Not all potential conflicts make their way onto the political agenda. For those that do not, no overt process of social decision making takes place. Policy is made by default rather than deliberation. Thus there is no observable exercise of power affecting outcomes. Neither proponents nor opponents come forth. To the extent that some actors can restrict the scope of debate to 'safe' issues, power has been exercised. The ability to avoid decisions can be as important as the ability to affect them.

Power over personal values
Neoclassical economics sees persons as utility functions, essentially given in content and constant in form. Such persons transact in society but are not fundamentally changed or affected by social interaction. Institutionalism sees persons as relational. Social contexts do not merely define constraints within which maximization can occur; they also define the very content of persons. The values to be pursued, the authority to be accepted, the rights to be respected, the ideology to be internalized – all are part of endogenous social interaction. This is power not just to affect what people do, but to

determine what they are. It adds a third dimension to power (Lukes, 1974; Bartlett, 1989).

This control over values need not be a conscious manipulation. Neither those exercising nor those experiencing power need be aware of it. The forces of acculturation seem natural, and may be inevitable. Values supportive of dominant institutions are taught and learned, and become internalized by teacher and pupil alike. Power can then be held to be strongest when no coercion is apparent at all. When values have been so thoroughly internalized that Americans 'naturally' support American institutions, French citizens 'naturally' support French institutions, and so on, power is most firmly entrenched. When the process of value creation is weakest, the need for overt coercion becomes greatest (Dugger, 1980).

RANDALL BARTLETT

See also:

Administered Prices; Class, Social, in Institutional Economics; Corporate Hegemony; Democracy, Economic; Galbraith, John Kenneth; Game Theory and Institutions; Hale, Robert Lee; Law and Economic Policy; Law and Economics; Means, Gardiner C.; Power (II); Property; Public Sector, Role of the; Rothschild, Kurt Wilhelm.

Bibliography

Bartlett, Randall (1989), *Economics and Power: An Inquiry into Human Relations and Markets*, Cambridge and New York: Cambridge University Press.
Dugger, William (1980), 'Power: An Institutional Framework of Analysis', *Journal of Economic Issues*, **XIV**, (4), pp. 897–907.
Galbraith, John Kenneth (1952), *American Capitalism: The Concept of Countervailing Power*, Cambridge, Mass.: Houghton Mifflin.
Galbraith, John Kenneth (1967), *The New Industrial State*, New York: Houghton Mifflin.
Lindblom, Charles E. (1977), *Politics and Markets: The World's Political–Economic Systems*, New York: Basic Books.
Lukes, Steven (1974), *Power: A Radical View*, London: Macmillan.
Means, Gardiner C. (1935), *Industrial Prices and Their Relative Inflexibility*, Senate Document No. 13, 74th Congress, 1st Session.
Mills, C. Wright (1956), *The Power Elite*, London and New York: Oxford University Press.
Samuels, Warren (1971), 'Interrelations Between Legal and Economic Processes', *Journal of Law and Economics*, **14**, October, pp. 435–50.
Schmid, A. Allan (1987), *Property, Power, and Public Choice: An Inquiry into Law and Economics*, 2nd edn, New York: Praeger.
Simon, Herbert A. (1957), *Administrative Behavior*, 2nd edn, New York: Macmillan.
Williamson, Oliver (1985), *The Economic Institutions of Capitalism*, New York: Free Press.

Power (II)

'Power', as a sociologist once said (Martin, 1977, p. 35), is like 'Love', one of those phenomena which are both highly relevant and at the same time difficult to define. This is perhaps even more true for 'Power' than for 'Love', because power is an all-pervasive element in human relationships

which can occur in many different forms and aspects. Consequently, delineations and definitions of power are legion, ranging from Max Weber's clear
and simple description of power as the ability of a person or group of
persons to bring about desired consequences even (but not necessarily)
against the resistance of others, to highly sophisticated game-theoretical
mathematical treatments. In view of this multitude of aspects and viewpoints, no general 'authentic' definition of power can be given. Indeed, as
Steven Lukes has convincingly shown, definitions of power 'are inextricably
tied to a given set of (probably unacknowledged) value-assumptions which
determine the range of its empirical application' (Lukes, 1974, p. 26). Quite
generally, however, the scope and problematic of the power problem can be
indicated by drawing attention to some of the more important elements
which have to be considered when the term 'power' is used and a decision
has to be made where – depending on the problem under discussion – the
differentiating line *vis-à-vis* other phenomena is to be drawn.

To begin with there is a multitude of *forms* which power can take, with
brute force and coercion on the one end, and then stretching to 'milder'
forms like control, authority, influence and persuasion at the other end.
These different forms of power can have different *bases*: force, constitutions
and authority, status and hierarchies, wealth, knowledge, charisma and so
on. Definitions and importance of power are also concerned with the *uses* to
which the power potentialities are directed, such as political ends, economic
ends, private or community targets.

In addition to decisions with regard to the forms, bases, and ends to be
included in a power analysis, questions of *motivation*, *relevance* and *valuation* also play a part. Power can be defined very widely to include all causal
influences of A on B irrespective of A's intentions and B's 'suffering'. This
corresponds roughly to Talcott Parsons's power concept in relation to the
workings of a social network. At the other end, power can be defined rather
narrowly to cover only a selected field of important items where A deliberately enforces actions on B which B would not have taken otherwise. It is
obvious that the latter case has stronger normative associations than the
former. In between these two extremes all sorts of combinations of intentions, forms and scope of interpersonal relations can be described as power
relations, including the question whether only *exercised* power should be
counted or also the mere *possession* of power which can lead to 'voluntary'
adaptation of B's behaviour ('anticipatory surrender').

This short indication of the many different aspects of the power problem
should suffice to explain why a sociologist has called power a 'messy term'
(Philp, 1985, p. 636). But that and the great difficulty of making power (in
whatever definition) operational in empirical investigations does not prevent
power from being an important ingredient for all social sciences, though its

delineations may have to be adjusted, depending on the problem under discussion. That power plays a predominant role in political science goes without saying; and in sociology it also finds a secure place. Since the economic sphere, though highly specialized in the scientific division of labour, is a subsystem of politics and sociology, one should expect power also to loom largely in economic theory, even if one does not go as far as Bertrand Russell who, in his 1938 book on *Power*, wrote: 'Economics as a separate science is unrealistic, and misleading if taken as a guide in practice. It is one element – a very important element, it is true – in a wider study, the science of power'. In fact, it is not difficult to think of 'economic power' in general or of specific examples of power in special economic relationships such as hierarchies in firms, unequal relationships in international trade, positional differences in respect to wealth, monopolies and oligopolies, asymmetric information in wage/profit or manager/owner relations, persuasion in advertising, influence through lobbies and, and, and ... There seems to be no lack of power problems in economics. Yet in contrast to other social sciences there is a strange lacuna of power themes in mainstream (neoclassical) economic theory. This requires comment.

Though economic theorizing has a long history, the main roots of modern economic theory can be traced back to Adam Smith and the classical literature of his time. Now from our point of view it is important to see that two different strands can be distinguished in Smith's grand opus, *The Wealth of Nations*. To some extent the book presents a grand picture of human economic action as an important aspect of social and political life, while at the same time providing a general and abstract scientific analysis of the mechanisms of free markets characterized by division of labour and decentralized individualistic decision making. Both these perspectives are essential elements in the classical school which for this reason regarded and named itself quite properly 'Political Economy'. In the works of that school the phenomenon of power both as an individual and group motive and as an important element in distributional matters was by no means neglected. It comes up again and again in Smith, Ricardo and other writings and, of course, took pride of place in Marx's work, which also built on the classical foundations.

The switch from the classical theory to neoclassical equilibrium theories of different descriptions which set in in the second half of the nineteenth century was accompanied by an increasing isolation of the market-mechanics aspects of earlier theories and a neglect of the linkages between economic processes and other aspects of sociopolitical activities. 'Political Economy' turned into a highly sophisticated but narrowly specialized 'Economics' which – attracted by the methods and achievements of mechanical physics – aims at modelling as exactly as possible the mechanics and equilibria of free market exchange and production processes.

Important as such studies are in order to elucidate the intricate chains and consequences of market processes, they can only contribute certain elements for a complete analysis of economic phenomena and developments. But the tendency in neoclassical economics has been to regard its methods and results as the basic elements for economic analysis in general. With this tendency it has become a serious obstacle to a fuller understanding of the socioeconomic universe. For, in order to make the complicated interdependent market processes tractable for 'exact' and solvable equilibrium analyses, the neoclassical theories have been under constant pressure to adopt and maintain radical simplifications in their basic axioms. To give a 'reliable' picture of market mechanics as such, all 'disturbing' elements had to be reduced to a minimum. The complexities of human motivation and decision making were reduced by creating the utility-maximizing *homo economicus*, and the various sociological influences emanating from group and political action were 'tamed' through a methodological individualism which permitted making the *homo economicus* (or even an isolated Robinson Crusoe) the main actor on the scene. Perfect atomistic competition, with the state providing merely a framework for the workings of individual exchange and production, thus became the *basic* model, not because it comes nearest to socioeconomic realities, but because it meets best certain methodological (and also ideological) requirements.

But in a world of atomistic competition and weak states, where individuals can only passively adjust to an economic environment in which all prices and conditions are given, is a world in which power does not exist. Thus in a way the prototype of neoclassical theory is on the one hand a useful abstraction for the study of market mechanisms and, on the other hand, the utopian picture of a society in which economic power is so dissipated that it has ceased to exist. In more extended and applied neoclassical studies power problems are, of course, mentioned and treated. But with the exemption of monopoly power, which gets full attention as the outcome of a special *market* form, the diverse power phenomena – power as motive force, economic position as power base, extra-market actions for achieving economic power and so on – do not properly fit into the basic theoretical framework and therefore tend to be neglected or to be treated as secondary or exogenous factors. This problematic has been mitigated but not removed with the appearance 50 years ago of game theory, which has laid stress on the importance of the problems of strategic action.

In contrast to the neoclassical (equilibrium) theories, practically all other 'schools', whatever their differences may be, have a more conscious and direct access to the power problem. This follows from their usually wider and more interdisciplinary approach. Whether we turn to historical 'schools', where politics and power turn up quite naturally; to a return to classical perspectives,

as in the case of Neo-Ricardians and Neo-Marxists; to institutional economics, where institutions as sources of power have their proper place; to evolutionary economics, which cannot escape the discussion of changing social and
power patterns; or indeed to most other 'unorthodox' views: they all normally
give more weight to the problems of economic *and* political power and their
mutual relationships than is characteristic for mainstream economics. Names
such as Veblen, Schumpeter and Galbraith stand out as famous examples and
representatives of a broader spectrum of approaches and theories in which
power in its various forms and aspects has an established place.

KURT W. ROTHSCHILD

See also:

Class, Social, in Institutional Economics; Galbraith, John Kenneth; Law and Economics;
Power (I); Property; Rothschild, Kurt Wilhelm; Smith, Adam.

Bibliography

Lenski, G. (1966), *Power and Privilege*, New York: McGraw-Hill.
Lukes, S. (1974), *Power: A Radical View*, London: Macmillan.
Martin, R. (1977), *The Sociology of Power*, London: Routledge & Kegan Paul.
Mills, C. Wright (1956), *The Power Elite*, New York: London and Oxford University Press.
Philp, M. (1985), 'Power', in *The Social Science Encyclopedia*, edited by A. and J. Kuper,
    London: Routledge.
Rothschild, K.W. (ed.) (1971), *Power in Economics*, Harmondsworth: Penguin.
Street, J.H. (1983), 'The reality of power and the poverty of economic doctrine', *Journal of
    Economic Issues*, **XVII**, June, pp. 295–313.

Prigogine, Ilya

Ilya Prigogine, born in Moscow in 1917 but a resident of Belgium after
World War II, was educated at the Free University of Brussels and awarded
the Nobel prize in Chemistry in 1977. Along with a number of co-research-
ers at the Solvay Institute in Brussels, he pioneered the application of nonequilibrium thermodynamics to understand the behaviour of structures considered to be 'dissipative' in character. The most accessible non-specialist
introduction to Prigogine's work and its general scientific relevance is
Prigogine and Stengers (1985), while Nicholis and Prigogine (1977) provides a more formal statement of his thermodynamic approach.

   Since all types of structure, whether chemical, biological or social, include dissipative examples in the face of the second law of thermodynamics
(the entropy law), Prigogine and his associates lay claim to having discovered a general scientific paradigm, capable of displacing the prevailing mechanical approach to dynamics in the natural and social sciences. Since
much of the criticism of mainstream economics amounts to a rejection of the
underlying mechanical analogy used (see Mirowski, 1988), Prigogine's pres-

entation of a competing paradigm ought to be of considerable interest to economists.

Prigogine challenges conventional attempts to model processes as 'clockwork' mechanisms that obey timeless functional laws and are discoverable using a reductionist experimental method. However, he also attacks the kind of thermodynamics developed in the nineteenth century, characterizing all structure as tending irreversibly towards a thermodynamic equilibrium state of maximum disorder. This 'heat death' view, Prigogine argues, had a profoundly pessimistic effect, in both science and art, which has lingered on to the present day. In economics, such pessimism took early shape in Stanley Jevons's application of thermodynamic thinking in *The Coal Question*.

In Prigogine's view, there are many examples, both in the natural and social worlds, which contradict both the static mechanical and the thermodynamic disordering notions of process. Processes at all levels, he argued, often seem to be characterized by increasing, not static or decreasing organization. Dissipative structures, far from thermodynamic equilibrium, are able to achieve a degree of 'self-organization' (or autopeosis) which enables them to export entropy and import free energy to maintain themselves and, in the biological domain, to facilitate development and reproduction. Thus the irreversibility implied by the entropy law is countered by organization, which leads to the formation of complex structure that also contains irreversible features. Because of the entropy law, a structure must acquire a degree of inflexibility in a spatial sense and a degree of irreversibility in a temporal sense. Consequently, a dissipative structure cannot simply go into reverse in the face of exogenous shocks, as is the case in mechanical models: it must either evolve or face destruction.

Prigogine defines a dissipative structure as a thermodynamic system whose behaviour is determined by its boundary conditions, in contrast to what he defines as a dynamic system which is determined by its initial conditions. Thermodynamic systems are open, yet partially closed by boundary conditions. The exportation of entropy alters the boundary conditions and creates an 'entropy barrier' (time irreversibility) which ensures that past history influences the future behaviour of the structure. Such a dissipative structure can only be understood macroscopically because it contains initial conditions which are random. Only structures which are dynamic, with non-random initial conditions, can be analysed microscopically.

Prigogine's characterization of structure and process echoes that of many institutionalists in economics. In particular, both Georgescu-Roegen (1971) and Boulding (1981), independently of Prigogine, employ the entropy law in their 'systems approach' to evolutionary/ecological economics. Of course, both these economists had a more expansive approach to entropy and evolution, asserting the importance of human creativity, cooperation and forward planning. Indeed, their approaches do raise questions as to the extent to which economists can use the Prigoginian metaphor, despite its obvious superiority over the mechanical metaphor.

Questions have already been raised in biology, most notably by Brooks and Wiley (1986), as to the relevance of the Prigoginian variant of self-organization beyond strictly chemical applications. They identify two main stumbling blocks. First, biological organisms do not always simply have free energy imposed upon them; they actively seek out specialized forms of free energy. This leads them to argue that it is information, not energy value, which is relevant in identifying entropy production and exportation. Increasing organization involves more information embodied in structure and it is this which offsets the rise in entropic potential associated with increasing complexity. Second, they argue that initial conditions are not entirely random in many biological structures; therefore Prigogine's distinction between dynamics and thermodynamics is not very clear-cut in biology. Thus self-organization is influenced by the internal history of a structure as well as by its boundary conditions. Consequently, history is given a much more direct role to play than in the Prigoginan approach.

It is clear that this greater emphasis upon information and history would seem to apply also in the case of economic processes. Indeed, it may be necessary to go even further and add teleological considerations related to forward planning before we can have a self-organization approach suitable for economic application. Be that as it may, Prigogine remains the originator of the self-organization paradigm and its widespread adoption in the natural sciences will, undoubtedly, lead to the removal of the mechanical metaphor from mainstream economics at some future date. Then the hope expressed by Alfred Marshall in successive editions of his *Principles of Economics* a century ago, that economics might be able to progress from its initial mechanical stage to a science of 'life and decay', embodying time irreversibility and employing biological metaphor, might finally come to pass. In this regard, institutional economists already seem to be far ahead of their more conventional colleagues.

JOHN FOSTER

See also:

Atomism and Organicism; Biology and Economics; Chaos Theory and Economics; Entropy and Economics; Evolution, Theories of Economic; Georgescu-Roegen, Nicholas; Spontaneous Order.

Bibliography

Boulding, K.E. (1981), *Evolutionary Economics*, London: Sage.
Brooks, D.R. and E.O. Wiley (1986), *Evolution as Entropy: Towards a Unified Theory of Biology*, Chicago: University of Chicago Press.
Georgescu-Roegen, N. (1971), *The Entropy Law and the Economic Process*, Cambridge, Mass.: Harvard University Press.

Mirowski, P. (1988), *Against Mechanism: Protecting Economics from Science*, Totowa, NJ: Rowman and Littlefield.
Nicholis, G. and I. Prigogine (1977), *Self-Organisation in Nonequilibrium Systems: From Dissipative Structures to Order through Fluctuations*, New York: Wiley.
Prigogine, I. and I. Stengers (1985), *Order out of Chaos*, London: Fontana.

Property

William Blackstone, in his *Commentaries on the Laws of England*, postulated the right of property as 'that sole and despotic dominion which one man claims and exercises over the external things of the world, in total exclusion of the right of any other individual in the universe'. One of the 'absolute rights', says Blackstone, 'inherent in every Englishman, is that of property: which consists in the free use, enjoyment, and disposal of all his acquisitions, without any control or diminution, save only by the laws of the land' (II.I.2). This understanding pervades the mentality of modern Western civilization, as belief in private property and the autonomous individual replaced the institutions and mind-set of medieval feudalism. Yet the Blackstonian conception obscures some fundamental aspects of the nature and operation of private property in modern economy and society.

Property is one complex form of participation in economic decision making; it is therefore a form of power understood as participation in decision making and/or the bases thereof. Property rights, accordingly, are interests given legal protection as property. To have property is to have one's interests (however identified by the individual) defined and protected as property and thereby to participate in economic decision making. Property, or the system of property, including its distribution, is part of the larger social system. The law of property is part of the constitution of society. Indeed, in the absence of a written constitution, the law of property becomes for many practical purposes the constitution of society.

Property is not an absolute; it is a bundle of rights and obligations or duties. Each right, or each bundle of rights, is relative to other rights, or other bundles of rights, and to legal and non-legal (for example, customary) determinations of limitations on rights. Moreover, although in principle it is better for the individual to have property rights than not to have rights (rights represent protected interests), the economic significance of property rights is of contingent, problematic significance: the economic value of a right is dependent upon market and other conditions, including the legally protected interests of others which permits them to compete and thereby potentially to reduce the economic value of one's property (the very nature of competition).

Thus the meaning of private property can change with a changing system of economic organization. Adolf Berle and Gardiner Means argued in *The*

Modern Corporation and Private Property (1933) that the rise of the modern corporation, and its management, have been accompanied by a fundamental change in the locus and nature of private property. Berle and Means demonstrated centrifugal dispersion of ownership and centripetal concentration of control. The discretion of legal holders of equity interests is confined to holding or selling stock. The managerial class has discretion over the issuance of stock and the acquisition, use and disposition of corporate assets. The stockholders have only pro forma control over management. Formal ownership of property may or may not provide for participation in economic decision making – a view also stressed, in the context of central planning, by Milovan Djilas in *The New Class* (1957).

Property is not protected by government because it is property; it is property because it is protected by government. The slogan, 'the role of government is to protect property', is misleading because it fails to acknowledge that what is thereby understood as property is an already established protection of interests and that it was government which made property what it is in the first place by selectively protecting interests. One of the functions of government is to determine, in the case of conflicting interests and claims, which interest is to be recognized and protected as property.

The putative exclusive nature of rights and the ubiquitous conflicting interests and claims pertaining to property underscore the importance of the dual nature of rights, notably property rights. Whenever economic actors are in the same social space, for one actor to have a right is for all other actors to have a non-right and thereby to be exposed to the exercise by the actor of his or her rights. The dual nature of rights underlies the reciprocal nature of externalities: whether Alpha is allowed to harm Beta or Beta is allowed to harm Alpha, and thereby the substance of the realized externality, will depend on who has what rights and whose interests are protected by rights.

Property rights can be defined, mistakenly, as if they existed independently of the regulatory or police, and tax, powers of government, in which case the exercise of those powers by government becomes a fundamental infringement on and loss of property rights. Alternatively, property rights can be defined so as to recognize and encompass the continuing role of the regulatory or police and tax powers of government, in which case the exercise of those powers is a constituent part of the nature of property itself, and no such fundamental infringement or loss occurs. In this regard, regulation is the functional equivalent of deregulation; each is a mode of protecting interests as rights, albeit the interests of opposite parties.

Thus the Blackstonian formulation of a 'sole and despotic dominion ... without any control or diminution, save only by the laws of the land' commences by seemingly affirming the first definition but effectively adopts the second. In Adam Smith's *Lectures on Jurisprudence*, he utilizes the concept of the impartial spectator as a mode through which social control exercised by changing beliefs in what constitutes property and the use of property is administered. In modern society and economy, property rights are what the law says they are, granted within the penumbra of belief and customary usage, a penumbra which is heterogeneous, thereby permitting and indeed requiring the exercise of legal choice. Conflicts arise typically, not over whether there will be a covering body of law, as there always is, but over legal change of law and thereby legal change of the interests for which government is to be used to give its protection.

A distinction needs to be drawn between the institution of private property and particular property rights. To have the institution of private property does not necessarily mean that some particular private property rights are to be adopted, or that there cannot be change of property rights and thereby of the interests to which government gives its protection.

Private property rights have sometimes been juxtaposed, often in a pejorative manner, to human rights. The juxtaposition is incomplete and misleading, although perhaps of rhetorical value in the mobilization of political psychology. Property rights are the rights of human beings, either as individuals or in organizations, such as corporations. Apropos of the corporation, the corporation as a legal entity is juxtaposed between management decision making and those who feel the effects of decisions. Corporations arose in part as a legal buffer for owners and, eventually, for management. This permits evasion of public accountability for decision makers on most, but not all, issues, yet this insulation applies to most if not all private property, corporate and individual.

Moreover, inasmuch as property signifies the selective protection of interests and thereby established participation in economic decision making, it is necessary to recognize other modes of legal protection of interests and establishment of participation in decision making. These modes, for example labour relations and protective labour legislation, social insurance and various other 'entitlement' programmes, not recognized *de jure* as property rights, constitute private property equivalents in performing the same functions as property rights, albeit often, if not typically, for different individuals.

The genesis of extant property rights can be comprehended in two ways, ways which appear to be contradictory but which are both nonetheless historically true, although they give rise to two different legitimations of property as an institution and of particular property rights. In one respect, property rights can be seen as deriving from the control of government by those otherwise in a position of power or influence, such that they are able to get their interests protected as property by government. In this case, property is established through the control of government power. In another respect, property rights can be seen as emerging from efforts to protect private interests against government, or against the use by others of government to have an adverse effect upon the interests already protected as property. In this case, property is a limitation on government, not a consequence of the absence of government. One can argue that different particular rights arose in each of these contexts, although it is not always clear in which context a particular right fits. It is also important that, even when understood as protection against government, private property is in fact a matter of legal rights; thus, in both respects, property rights are a matter of law, even when the law is understood to limit government law itself. Moreover, also even when understood as protection against government, private property rights function to structure private power; that is, particular private rights are relative both to government and to other private rights.

Property rights have, therefore, a dual private and public character. They eminently are private rights but they have a public, that is, legal, character to them; the private rights that are of economic significance are public or legal in origin and status. Moreover, property rights have the technical public-good character of all rights: determination of private rights for one party is not only a matter of public or legal action, but applies to all other relevant parties, without ability to exclude and without additional cost.

There are theories that explain and theories that legitimize (and others that denigrate) property as an institution and property rights in general, and a fundamental distinction must be drawn between them. Theories which purport to explain property are concerned with how and why particular private property arrangements have arisen and deal with what is, or has been, the case. Theories which propose either to legitimize or to delegitimize particular private property arrangements are normative in character and deal with questions of desirability, of what ought to be the case. Inasmuch as one cannot derive an 'ought' from an 'is' alone, but only with additional normative premises, there is a fundamental disjunction between theories of description–explanation and theories of legitimation–delegitimation. Nonetheless, in practice the two are often conflated. In the conventional interpretation and use of John Locke's theories of property and government, for example, one finds that his labour appropriation theory of property is taken to be both explanation of the origin and legitimation of the existence of property in the state of nature, though these are two quite different matters, and that the labour appropriation theory is cavalierly applied to civil society, whereas Locke himself argued that in civil society the rights that count are a function of civil law itself.

In conventional microeconomic theory, property (and arguably all other) rights constitute the initial entitlements on the basis of which trade takes place, leading to Pareto optimal resource allocations. A central thesis of institutionalist theory (if not also that of other schools) is that there are no unique Pareto optimal allocations, only power structure- or rights structure-specific outcomes. In such a context, the allocation of resources is a function of the initial determination – definition and assignment – of rights, including property rights. Broadly, resource allocation is a function of market demand and supply, which is in turn a function of power, which is a function of property rights (understood as a mode of participation in decision making, or power), which are a function of law, which is a function of government, which is a function of the results of the contest over the control of government to use it to protect certain interests rather than others.

Government and property, therefore, are interdependent variables; each is both dependent and independent relative to the other; each is formed and influenced by the other. The ineluctable problems are always which, or whose, interests are to count; through which institutional or power structure they are to be defined so as to count; and with what legal change of law legal rights are to be revised.

WARREN J. SAMUELS

See also:
Commons, John R.; Law and Economics; Market, Institutionalist View of the; Power; Transaction.

Bibliography
Commons, John R. (1924), *Legal Foundations of Capitalism*, New York: Macmillan.
Ely, Richard T. (1914), *Property and Contract in their Relations to the Distribution of Wealth*, 2 vols, New York: Macmillan.
Schmid, A. Allan (1987), *Property, Power and Public Choice*, 2nd edn, New York: Praeger.
Wunderlich, Gene and W.L. Gibson, Jr. (eds) (1972), *Perspectives of Property*, University Park: Institute for Research on Land and Water Resources, Pennsylvania State University.

Public Choice

Institutional and evolutionary economics (I&EE) has as its core a theory of collective action, that is, public choice. The domain of public choice or governance includes both public and private corporate bodies. It involves the formation of groups and the evolving process of coordination and settling of conflicts. These processes work out the distribution of power and freedom. Public choice is the process of aggregating individual preferences, including constitutional issues such as voting and the structure of government. I&EE observes the political–economic nexus. Institutions are both independent and dependent variables, being influenced by the economy as well as shaping the economy. Market exchange begins with a set of rules which defines who is buyer and who is seller and what each may do to obtain the consent of others. Thus the market cannot be an independent reference upon which governance is to be modelled. In other words, the purpose of governance is not to emulate the market when it fails. Governance is itself subject to rules. Change the constitutional rules for making rules and you get different results in terms of market and administrative rules. The institutional research agenda is to illuminate sources of power and trace the substantive consequences of alternative rules for governance.

Group formation and action
We are all born into existing groups with instituted rules and we often seek to change these and form new ones as we learn new preferences. This is a costly process. People sometimes calculate the benefit–cost ratio of their participation in terms of narrow self-interest (instrumental or consequential analysis). In this mode people would not bother to be informed or vote, since their vote makes no difference and the result cannot be denied to non-participants. The paradox of actual voting results because people are also rule-governed and have learned a habitual response to certain perceived situations (Ostrom, 1991; Hodgson, 1988). People are also moved by a sense of injustice and righting wrongs. These non-instrumental behaviours prevent some people from being free-riders, who try to benefit from group formation to provide high exclusion cost goods without paying any of its costs (Hirschman, 1984). In any kind of cooperative behaviour, people learn whom they can trust even when opportunism is possible (Frank, 1988). This reasoning can be applied to citizens and bureaucrats. While bureaucrats are self-interested, attention must be given to the way in which the self-image is learned.

The forms of collective action which the state chooses to make legal are instrumental in determining whose interests count. For example, organized labour can be labelled a conspiracy or legitimate. Rules governing contributions to finance political campaigns determine the power of small special interest groups as against more diffuse general interests.

Institutionalists have long been concerned with the separation of ownership and control in private corporations when the stockholders lose control to the hired management. The same issue arises in government. Bounded rationality and high information costs mean that voters and elected officials cannot monitor all actions of bureaucrats, giving them some scope for independence. But there is more to the problem than shirking. Where the voters have different preferences among themselves there is a continuing struggle to work out both ends and means. It is popular to portray bureaucrats as imposing their will over the electorate, but the issue is more often the struggle within the electorate and between different bureaucrats who identify with different parts of the electorate.

Institutional Change

Where is institutional change headed and where should it head? Can change to improve allocative efficiency be distinguished from redistribution? I&EE is marked by an evolutionary perspective rather than seeking equilibrium determined by some prior overarching values (Adams, 1990). Institutional change is something to be worked out and chosen by participants and not something to be deduced. Change is path-dependent and heavily influenced by existing political rules (March and Olsen, 1984). Nowhere is cumulative causation clearer than where the present majority party determines voting jurisdictional boundaries to further its future interests.

Efficiency cannot be a guide to institutional change, since efficiency has no conclusive normative meaning unless the distribution of income and opportunities is legitimate. Thus it is not possible to condemn the use of resources to change institutions as wasteful rent seeking without making a judgement on the acceptability of a particular distribution (Samuels and Mercuro, 1984). It is more descriptive to speak of efficiency set one versus efficiency set two than efficiency versus distribution (Bromley, 1989).

Institutions can facilitate exchange among parties so that they can reach the contract curve (exhaust mutually beneficial trades). But each starting place rights distribution will result in the parties reaching equally efficient but different points on the contract curve.

Power

The unit of analysis in I&EE is the transaction. When interests conflict and only one can have the opportunity and the other party has an exposure, there is necessarily the exercise of power. To own an economic resource or civil right is to have decision power. Markets begin after decision power is distributed. Control of the agenda is an important source of power in governance, as is influence on perception and learning of preferences and what rules are seen as possibilities (Bartlett, 1989; Galbraith, 1983). Individual choice takes place in a context of meaning and symbolic action.

Freedom

The transaction view of human interdependence has implications for such issues as freedom and the size of government. We all want to be free, but, in an interdependent world, the issue for collective choice is whose freedom counts when individuals conflict. One person's freedom is another's constraint. Freedom in the aggregate is a shibboleth and provides no dispositive standard against which to judge political institutions.

The size of government is coterminous with the scope of human interdependence. If people can get in each other's hair, there is government giving order to opportunities and exposures. Externalities are ubiquitous. Government can sift them from one party to another, but never eliminate them. It is analytically incorrect to measure the size of government by the size of public spending. Private property rights and public regulations are substitutes and complements for public spending. For example, government can provide a public hospital for those injured in industrial accidents (public spending), change the regulation of the workplace by a public agency, or the courts may reinterpret private liability for industrial accidents (private property). While different, the government is no smaller or less present in any of these, nor is freedom in the aggregate any more or less.

From individual preferences to aggregated outcomes
I&EE has always understood what Kenneth Arrow proved formally (Impossibility Theorem), that you cannot begin with some hopefully widely acceptable abstract procedural principles and derive market or voting institutions (social welfare function). Rather, this is something that has to be worked out in the context of the historical moment with its particular institutions and the existing passions and interests. This is the essence of the evolutionary perspective.

The Arrow conditions are quite abstract without any reference to end states with real people winning and losing. The conditions expose a conflict between consumer sovereignty and the Pareto principle. In a world of scarcity each cannot be free of the effects of others and still be bound by a rule that no one loses. Politics is the process that chooses the mix of who wins and who loses. Any political rule has a substantive end state distribution embedded in it and cannot be judged independent of that end state. I&EE scholars trace out the substantive consequences of alternative rights, including those of constitutions, and hold peoples' feet to the fire of choosing when to compromise and when to fight and provide no psychic balm to relieve citizens of this existential burden.

Constitutional analysis
I&EE scholars have a long history of inquiry into voting rules. John R. Commons in his *Proportional Representation*, originally published in 1892, analysed the result of many elections in the USA and Europe under district winner-take-all rules versus proportional representation. He showed who lost and who won under different rules without trying to justify this by any abstract principle.

Another constitutional issue is the structure of government. The consequences of federalist versus unitary governance have received much attention from public choice analysts. The decision-making boundary influences whether a person is part of a winning coalition. In a unitary system, a person can be in the minority on many issues while, if some kinds of decisions are reserved for a local government, the same person may be in the majority. It is a mistake, however, to regard federalism as minimalist government. If the effect of a local choice has external effects on other localities, choice of level of government is tantamount to choice of whose interests count. It is not helpful to label some interest as meddlesome or to speak of victimless crimes. This is just an expression of the preferences of the speaker as to whose freedom counts. The decision as to what choice to place at what level of government is a choice of the distribution of opportunities and income.

I&EE emphasizes the need collectively to choose substantive end states in the distribution of opportunities. There may be more agreement on general procedures for collective choice than on substantive end states, but every specific procedure has a result whose fairness must be judged. Any procedure which favours the status quo requires that the status quo be morally grounded.

Gordon Tullock (1987) summarized what he regards as the implication of public choice research for improving government: more direct voting on issues, larger legislatures, proportional representation, more than simple majority for more issues, more control of the bureaucracy by political leaders, more competition among agencies and more privatization (contracting out) of services. Institutionalists have helped to trace out the consequences of these and other reforms for whose preferences count but avoid speaking of improvements in the aggregate as if there were a self-evident single public interest to be served.

A. ALLAN SCHMID

See also:
Cooperation, The Evolution of; Cumulative Causation; Democracy, Economic; Dewey, John; Hale, Robert Lee; Law and Economics; Power; Public Sector, Role of the; Transaction.

Bibliography
Adams, John (1990), 'Institutional Economics and Social Choice Economics: Commonalities and Conflicts', *Journal of Economic Issues*, **XXIV**, (3), pp. 845–59.
Bartlett, Randall (1989), *Economics and Power*, Cambridge: Cambridge University Press.
Bromley, D.W. (1989), *Economic Interests and Institutions*, Oxford: Basil Blackwell.
Commons, J.R. (1907), *Proportional Representation*, 2nd edn, New York: Macmillan.
Frank, Robert (1988), *Passions Within Reason*, New York: Norton.
Galbraith, J.K. (1983), *The Anatomy of Power*, Boston, Mass.: Houghton Mifflin.
Hirschman, A.O. (1984), 'Against Parsimony: Three Easy Ways of Complicating Some Categories of Economic Discourse', *American Economic Review*, **72**, (2), pp. 89–96.
Hodgson, Geoffrey (1988), *Economics and Institutions*, Philadelphia: University of Pennsylvania Press and Cambridge: Polity.
March, James G. and Johan P. Olsen (1984), 'The New Institutionalism: Organizational Factors in Political Life', *American Political Science Review*, **78**, (3), pp. 734–49.
Ostrom, Elinor (1991), 'Rational Choice Theory and Institutional Analysis: Towards Complementarity', *American Political Science Review*, **85**, (1), pp. 237–43.
Samuels, W.J. and Nicholas Mercuro (1984), 'A Critique of Rent Seeking Theory', in D.C. Colander (ed.), *Neoclassical Political Economy*, Cambridge, Mass.: Ballinger.

Schmid, A.A. (1987), *Property, Power and Public Choice*, New York: Praeger.
Solo, R.A. (1974), *The Political Authority and the Market System*, Cincinnati: Southwestern Publishing.
Tullock, Gordon (1987), 'Public Choice', in John Eatwell *et al.* (eds), *The New Palgrave: A Dictionary of Economics*, New York: Stockton Press and London: Macmillan.

Public Policy: Contributions of American Institutionalism

Institutionalists have always been interested and active in the area of public policy formation and the crafting of reasoned and pragmatic responses to public problems. Central to the institutionalist philosophic approach is the belief that policies that enhance the reasoning ability of the population, enlarge the scope of public discourse, and protect and reinforce the domain of the democratic process are to be furthered.

There are two components to this view that distinguish the institutionalist from the neoclassical position, both revolving around the role of markets. The first is that, since citizens are more than *homo economicus*, leaving the market to be the arbiter of public decision making would be to reduce all decisions to the level of economic decisions; such a reduction would be unattainable and absurd. Moreover, even if markets could produce public decisions they would still not be democratic decisions, since markets weight decision-making power by wealth – which would no doubt be a proper standard for the 'public interest' in a plutocracy, but is far from the one person, one vote standard of democratic decision making.

The second point is that real-world markets cannot accomplish what the neoclassicals often claim for them because of the existence of powerful corporate and governmental institutions which affect outcomes through their organizational or market power.

The rejection of markets as the foundation and standard of decision making on issues of public consequence is replaced in institutionalism by the study and design of ways to improve community decision making reflected in education, legislation and enforcement. Consistently, throughout the 100 years of American institutionalism, certain problems have been a focus of interest and effort by its public policy wing. By way of illustration, the institutionalist contribution and approach in three of these areas (the control of monopoly power and holding companies; regulation of public utilities; and mobile home rent control) will be described in the sections that follow.

The control of corporate power

American institutionalists have always been sceptical of monopoly power. Beginning with the work of Richard Ely, but maturing in the work of Thorstein Veblen, there was a realization that the desire of the great corporate and financial empires for power and profit would rarely coincide with the goals of society at large other than by chance.

However, the consensus over the nature of the problem did not extend to an agreement over the character of the solution. Some institutionalists, following Brandeis, were for resolving the problem by pulverizing the trusts, conglomerates and monopolies so as to reopen monopoly-dominated sectors of the economy to smaller-scale enterprise, eliminate anti-competitive 'coordination' and reduce the anti-democratic use of corporate political power (Hovenkamp, 1990). Other institutionalists were for controlling the organizational power of the great financial empires in the public interest. Their view was that this could be done through a combination of incentives and regulation.

In the New Deal these two forces contended for the US president's ear. The result was that some legislation and programmes attacked the trusts (antitrust enforcement, the Public Utility Holding Company Act of 1935, the Tennessee Valley Authority, Rural Electrification Administration programmes in the 1930s, for example), while others sought to harness the corporations through a system of national planning and regulation (Hawley, 1966). The legislation and programmes of this latter group included the National Industrial Recovery Act and the National Recovery Administration, minimum wage laws and the creation of government-sponsored countervailing interests (for example, labour, via the National Labor Relations Act), the creation of the Securities and Exchange Commission and the Banking Acts of 1933 and 1935.

Recent work of institutionalists in this area has been of two kinds. The first is the development of the idea that major private economic institutions in US society are not independent of one another in their decision making. John Munkirs, Greg Hayden and others have shown a high degree of interconnection, rising to the level of coordination and perhaps joint planning, between large groupings of corporations and financial institutions. This work constitutes a significant attack on the doctrine that the fierce independence of, and unbridled competition among, major corporations result in a cancelling out of their power to injure the public. Moreover, Hayden's case studies at the state level show that this interconnectivity is to be found not just among corporations, but also between corporations and government. The works of Dugger, Samuels and especially Brock and Adams support these conclusions.

These developments have led to a critique of the forms and management of US government (especially on the state and local level) which allows this high degree of more or less invisible corporate cooption. As might be expected, the result has been that the social control of business has been dramatically weakened in the areas of regulation and especially antitrust enforcement. The average citizen sees this phenomenon in the creation of two strata of government with separate working rules. The first deals on a privileged and largely private basis with large corporations, while the other deals on an unprivileged basis with citizens at large.

The penetration of corporations into US government has gone beyond biasing the process of public decision making; it now draws off substantial public resources to aggrandize the corporations, leaving the public sector of the economy notably underfunded. The policy conclusions reached by institutionalists have been that the role of corporations in US society needs to be rethought with an eye to eliminating the abuses and correcting the weaknesses in the social control of business.

This stance is in sharp juxtaposition to the Chicago School and other economists who continue to argue that further deregulation, further weakening of the antitrust laws and further inroads of corporations into the public fisc ('economic development programmes', 'public–private partnerships' and so on) are all in the public interest.

Public utility regulation

Institutional economists have been involved in initiatives in the USA to control corporate utilities in the public interest. In the early days, economists like John R. Commons were instrumental in the design and passage of reforms meant to reduce the power of these combines *vis-à-vis* their regulators and the public. Two of these major reforms were establishment of state public utility commissions and the creation and imposition of the Uniform System of Accounts to standardize utility bookkeeping and financial reporting practices.

Notwithstanding these advances, by the late 1920s and 1930s the abuses of the utilities and their giant holding companies had become a cause for concern. To correct these problems, many institutionalists assisted with the formulation of legislation at the federal level to break up the holding companies, and at both the state and federal level to provide alternatives to the corporate utilities in the form of federal power agencies at the national level, and municipal and cooperative utilities at the local level.

With the nationwide loosening of commission control over utilities in the 1980s, under pressure for deregulation from large utility combinations, there has been a renewal of work by institutionalists including Harry Trebing, Edith Miller, Peter Fisher, Doug Jones and others. This work has been particularly notable in the areas of cost allocation and pricing, the use of Ramsay pricing to apportion overhead costs, and the problem of cross-subsidization between monopoly and competitive services using the same plant. Currently there is also work being done on Bell Corporation proposals to implement 'incentive regulation' and to relocate behind closed doors most of the commission decisions over cost allocation and pricing.

The clash of ideas has been most resounding in the telecommunications area, where the regulatory structure is at present most fluid. This fluidity has been the result in large measure of lobbying by the Bell holding companies in support of deregulation, incentive regulation and other regulatory changes. These changes are motivated by the corporations' desire to socialize the cost and risk of their planned and exceedingly expensive move into new services (such as cable television and broadband and two-way video) while privatizing as much of the potential gains as possible. The situation in cable television provides a good illustration of the character of these controversies. As their systems are currently configured, the Bell holding companies would have to make a very large investment (estimates range from $40 billion to $1 trillion) in their current telephone lines and switches to allow them to offer cable television. Once this new investment was in place, however, the new equipment would carry both the pre-existing telephone and the new cable television traffic.

From a marketing perspective, once the new plant and equipment was installed, the price for the new services would have to be low enough to allow successful competition against the other cable television companies. Market penetration of the Bell's cable television service would be low in the initial years, but it would be much lower still if the full incremental cost of the new investment had to be borne primarily by the new cable television customers. In these circumstances the Bell Corporation has a clear incentive, given their desire to be in the cable TV business, to force as much as possible of the cost of the new investment onto captive local telephone users. Were the Bell successful, this would be costly for both the captive telephone customers and the competing cable television providers, who would fall victim to cross-subsidization and predatory pricing, respectively.

Bell executives, supported by the usual team of well-paid economic advisers, have been pushing hard to convince commissions and legislatures to allow them to shift the bulk of these costs onto captive telephone customers, citing Ramsey pricing, marginal cost pricing, competitive pressures and 'workable competition'. Institutionalists have responded that the companies' 'analysis' has masked the real problem, which is one of investment planning: who is to decide what is to be built, when it is to be built, and who is going to pay for it?

In the investment planning calculus allocation of costs is crucial, since it is clear that the decision on who is to pay for the investment will determine in most cases whether these investments will be made. The reason for this is that, if Bell's cost recovery is limited to the target class of customers for whom the investment is ostensibly being made – in our illustration, cable television users who sign up for the Bell service – with Bell shareholders as the residual cost bearers, then the price will be too high to be competitive.

This will mean that the investment will most often not be made, or at least not as soon, with the result that society will be saved from large losses in scarce infrastructural dollars.

The conclusion of the institutionalists has been that there is no reason to facilitate bad planning on the part of the Bell Corporation by providing the companies with a guarantee of cost recoupment to be paid by captive customers receiving no direct benefit from the service.

Mobile home rent control

With the rise of a more conservative federal judiciary in the Reagan–Bush years and the evolution of an economic activism by the Chicago School and its allies, there has been a general offensive in the courts attacking government for limiting the rights of property. One such series of suits sought to eliminate mobile home rent control (control of pad rents charged by park owners to park tenants who own their own mobile homes) on the grounds that such laws constitute a Fifth Amendment 'taking' of park owners' property rights without compensation.

A number of institutionalists became involved in these cases, either as academic commentators, attorneys or expert witnesses in the federal district courts or before the Supreme Court in the recently decided case *Yee* v. *City of Escondido*, 112 S.Ct. 1522 (1992). On the opposite side were neoclassical economists with their standard critique of all rent control ordinances: rent control makes matters worse because it means that profits will be lower than the level necessary to attract new investment, and maintenance will decline because park owners will move their capital to enterprises where returns are higher.

In these cases institutionalists were able to show that none of this was true. The City of Los Angeles's ordinance in question, in one of the two main cases, takes as its base rent the rent that was being charged by each landlord in the period *preceding* the imposition of the rent control and then adjusts it upward for inflation year by year. Further adjustments are made for landlords that have had cost increases which are out of the ordinary. Furthermore, for the park in question in the *Azul Pacifico* v. *Los Angeles* case, the forensic accountant employed by the city found that the park's rate of return *under rent control* was no less than 31 per cent (in the earlier years) and ranged upwards to 170 per cent (in more recent years). Moreover, there was no disagreement that the park in question was very nicely maintained on a continuing basis.

The analysis by the institutionalists reached the following conclusions: there is no necessary connection between any particular rent control ordinance and variations in new investment – this is purely an empirical question. Secondly, the neoclassical position on maintenance is also, as an empirical matter, entirely without foundation as a general proposition. Finally, rent control is an appropriate tool to consider whenever the monopoly power of the corporations owning these properties gives rise to substantial abuses and generalized hardship among essentially captive tenants. Both the City of Escondido and the City of Los Angeles have been successful in defending their ordinances.

Conclusion

American institutionalists have been a substantial force in public policy formation in the United States, through service in government and reform organizations, as well as through their scholarly writing. Their attempts to improve the standard of living and quality of life of the general population have often put them at odds with the vested interests demanding the right to exploit their market or political power at the public expense. Yet, in spite of these pressures, institutionalist contributions have been significant in many areas, as demonstrated in the three illustrations provided above.

MICHAEL F. SHEEHAN

See also:

Commons, John R.; Corporate Concentration and Interdependence in Europe; Corporate Hegemony; Corporate Interdependence in the United States; Full Cost Pricing; Habits; Hale, Robert Lee; Hamilton, Walton Hale; Industrial Structure and Power; Institutions; Instrumental Value Theory; Law and Economics; Means, Gardiner C.; Power; Property; Public Sector, Role of the; Public Utility Regulation, Institutionalist Contribution to; Regulation, Theory of Economic; Social Change, Theory of; Trebing, Harry M.; Veblen, Thorstein; Witte, Edwin Emil.

Bibliography

Hawley, Ellis (1966), *The New Deal and the Problem of Monopoly*, Princeton: Princeton University Press, Part III and especially Chapter 15.
Hovenkamp, Herbert (1990), 'The First Great Law & Economics Movement', *Stanford Law Review*, **42**, April, pp. 993–1058.

Public Sector, Role of the

Virtually from the outset, American institutionalists have recognized that their view of the operation of the modern economy robbed them of the comfort and relative simplicity mainstream economists drew from competitive markets and the convenient assumptions surrounding them. Critical allocative decisions could not be entrusted to any putative 'invisible hand'. Modern large-scale production units were required by modern technology, but virtually guaranteed that critical monitoring of all market allocation would be required. From this early recognition, the institutionalist view of the role of the public sector has logically developed.

Conventional economics and the public sector
It is easy to forget that even the most unrelievedly mainstream non-interventionist economic view would have a place for a public sector. Milton Friedman, for example, has written:

> A government which maintained law and order, defined property rights, served as a means whereby we could modify property rights and other rules of the economic game, adjudicated disputes about the interpretation of rules, enforced contracts, promoted competition, provided a monetary framework, engaged in activities to counter technical monopolies and to overcome neighborhood effects widely regarded as sufficiently important to justify governmental intervention, and which supplemented private charity and the private family in protecting the irresponsible, whether madman or child – such a government would clearly have important functions to perform. The consistent liberal is not an anarchist. (Friedman, 1962, p. 34)

The field of public finance, which is the principal mainstream economics subdiscipline dealing with 'the public sector', begins with many of the trappings of its mainstream origins: it begins by suggesting that Pareto optimality is the goal and that, under the explicit conditions often specified in connection with mainstream competitive theory, the operation of such an economy would permit Pareto optimality. This in turn would obviate the need for a public sector, except for the areas Friedman enumerated. The major exception of this characterization of the public sector is that economists working in this field grant that individual economies may opt for additional public goods and services for reasons that are either in violation of the rules for efficiency, based on murky notions of equity which defy 'rational' analysis, or are otherwise defined to be outside the analytical compound.

Furthermore, argues the mainstream, whatever the rationale, if one adds that government failure is about as likely to occur in the public sector as market failure in the private sphere, there is no certainty that governmental activity will do any better than private activity in improving economic performance and so the effort in the public sector is called into question before it has even been put into operation.

Institutional economics, power and the public sector
Institutionalists suggest explicitly that economic analysis based on narrow efficiency is, from the outset, inadequate. They insist that the economy in general – and its public sector in particular – is itself a valuable instrumentality involved interactively in influencing, being influenced by and achieving the allocative objectives that any particular society strives for at any one time. Consequently, the operational question is always, given the resources

and the technology of any given system, are its resources being deployed in such a way as to move the system maximally (hence optimally) towards the total objectives which its participants, ideally informed, would wish? Thus the social value principal is always in process of reinterpretation for a new era.

Critical here is the institutionalist recognition that the development of concentrated power throughout the economy is always a factor in the way resources are directed. A major reason for the welfare implications of the competitive model being so inadequate in the real world is that concentrated economic power has profound implications for the way the system in fact operates. Institutionalists argue that a dynamic objective – 'the higher efficiency' (Klein, 1984) – requires that the system be judged by employing all the criteria that are relevant, including certainly 'narrow' or conventional efficiency, but also security, equity, freedom and compassion. The 'higher efficiency' is being served when one can say that resources are being deployed at any given time so that, given full information on the part of the participants – unclogged information channels, no deliberate misinformation or self-interest-motivated persuasive measures on the part of sellers to influence tastes – the resources are totally utilized so as to enhance the life process optimally.

But, of course, it is the factors just mentioned, as such, through which concentrated power is most likely to affect the system (Galbraith, 1973). The technologically necessary departures from structurally pure competition (not to mention other factors) constitute a major reason for a public sector charged with the constant and conscious monitoring of resource allocation being a basic necessity in any democratic political economy. It follows that in all times and all societies there is a discrepancy between the full implications of resources allocated totally by the private sector and resources affected by inclusion with private allocation of public provisioning. The public sector is defined by that optimal role the government can play in moving resource allocation along towards optimal fulfilment of all these criteria.

With this general perspective in place, we may consider briefly the size of the public sector and the major functions institutionalists would assign to it.

The size of the US public sector

In recent years there has been much public discussion concerning the size of the public sector. By way of illustration, we may refer to recent debate in the United States. (There has been a similar debate offering many parallels in Thatcherite Britain.) In the late 1970s, the debate became particularly heated, and Ronald Reagan was elected President in large part because of his oft-stated conviction that the government was too large. In particular, he argued that the federal government was too large and that more should be done by state and local governments. In connection with the changes initiated during these years, often called 'the Reagan Revolution', it is instructive to consider what in fact happened to the size of the public sector during the Reagan presidency. In fact, federal expenditures constituted 22.5 per cent of GNP in 1980, the year Reagan became President. In 1988, at the end of the Reagan presidency, the federal government constituted 22.9 per cent: rather than shrinking, it had in fact increased very slightly relative to GNP. State and local government remained essentially unchanged at slightly more than 13 per cent of GNP. This suggests that Reagan's effort to shift expenditure burdens from the federal to the lower levels of government was largely ineffectual. A major path for this redistribution of activity from the federal to other levels of government as urged by Reagan was to have been greater emphasis on 'revenue sharing' – return of federal tax revenues to the states for spending. In fact, this programme, in the form of grants-in-aid from the federal to the state and local governments, declined from just over 3 per cent of GNP in 1980 to about 2.5 per cent of GNP in 1988.

These figures suggest that there is conflict between mainstream and institutionalist economists over what the role of the public sector should be. Even more, we can see what in fact happens when an effort is made to implement change in that role to accommodate a different theory. The conclusion is inescapable that many, if not most, public expenditures are extremely intractable. We may conclude that there is considerable institutional support for many of the major extant public programmes of the various levels of government and that shrinking the overall size of the federal government is not easy to manage; nor is increasing the scope of the lower levels of government. Indeed, in the wake of changes emanating from Washington in the 1980s, lower levels of government found it increasingly difficult to maintain, let alone increase, taxes. The result was that, while there was no perceptible diminution in public demands for public services (they do, after all, tend to become institutionally sanctioned), there was increased difficulty in paying for them. (Violent public objection to existing tax rates, let alone increases in them at any level of government, for a time took on all the characteristics of a Veblenian fad or fashion.) As such, this institutional characteristic was at odds with the technological necessity to raise or at least maintain tax rates so as to maintain the existing level of public services.

In sum, the size and activity of the public sector, as it in fact operates in the US economy, has proved to be quite resistant to change. Similarly, there is a significant public sector still in Britain. Indeed, the public sector accounts for at least as large a percentage of GNP as is the case for the USA in most other market-oriented economies.

The public sector as regulatory agent

What of the second function of the public sector, namely regulating activity in the private sector? As has been pointed out (Trebing, 1984) the original move in the USA to regulate industry was spearheaded in large part by institutional economists. But by the late 1980s the move to deregulate much industry had grown in mainstream circles – both in the USA and elsewhere – which charged to regulation many economic difficulties including inflation, inefficiency and obstacles to innovation.

As Trebing notes, it is too simple to charge that mainstream economists were impervious to all the reasons for regulating industry, in particular natural monopolies, but they were also – here as in many other areas – less than ideally sensitive to the dangers of concentrated economic power. In this area, as elsewhere, institutionalists, in making regulatory recommendations, have argued that we must face such dangers head-on. The lists of US industries deregulated in the 1980s is long (airlines, road haulage, rail traffic and so on). Today it is fair to say that institutionalists on both sides of the Atlantic favour activist proactive policy and are unwilling to accept that unfettered market solutions can safely be assumed to provide ideal operation. They argue, therefore, that much non-competitive industry requires regulation. Once again, competitive theory, even as 'benchmark theory' proves less useful to institutionalists than to mainstream economists. It requires regulation to avoid the evils of monopoly, to promote efficiency and to curb the use of concentrated power in which institutionalists continue to see danger lurking in unregulated firms.

In short, in the area of regulation, institutionalists find that the results of resource allocation require constant monitoring to spot areas where private resource allocation conflicts with the evolving values of the community. The views of institutionalists, therefore, stand in some contrast to those of mainstream economists typified in the area of regulation by, for example, Alfred Kahn, who declared that the market economy is 'a manifestly inefficient system that is better than any of its alternatives' (Kahn, 1971). Institutionalists here, as elsewhere, argue that the instrumental value theory and the social value policy which is derived from it suggest ways of judging whether or not market allocation needs to be filtered through a regulatory network in order to conform at an given time to what is then seen as socially optimal.

Provision of public goods

A third function of the public sector, of course, is to provide for 'public goods'. In the realm of national defence, the existence of 'externalities' is non-controversial. Mainstream economists do not dispute the legitimate role of the public sector, therefore, in providing for national defence. 'Security'

and 'efficiency' are the two criteria for judging economic performance customarily recognized by neoclassical economists.

Institutionalists, however, have always viewed the task of monitoring
economic performance in broader terms. The criteria are enumerated in
various ways but, as noted earlier, along with narrow efficiency and security,
institutionalists are concerned with such matters as equity, freedom and
compassion; in short, they judge economic performance again in terms of a
'higher efficiency'. As such the higher efficiency therefore involves the
public sector in two more functions – making direct public expenditures and
acting as guarantor of minimal societal welfare standards for all participants
in the economy. In connection with the former, the public sector can become
involved in building infrastructure, in the direct creation of some resources
(such as an appropriately trained labour force), providing for jobs and so on.

Setting welfare standards
Finally, the public sector is intimately concerned with both setting and
enforcing societal welfare standards. As always, the economic units are
engaged interactively with the public sector in setting welfare standards and
subsequently with monitoring them and planning remedial action where they
are found wanting. That the public sector is viewed here in radically different terms by institutionalists is clear. For mainstream economists welfare
standards involve 'non-economic criteria'. Such variables as infant mortality
ratios, basic educational opportunities, job training programmes and job
possibilities through education and reeducation in the light of changing
technology, health care facilities and so on can be regarded as measurable
only by non-economic indicators – social indicators. For institutionalists
these may all be subsumed under economic indicators because, for example,
the degree of compassion exhibited by an economy is part of what determines the character of the economy. All economies exhibit some degree of
compassion in their operation (between none at all and a good deal) and so,
as with the other dimensions of economic performance, its manifestation
becomes part of the performance which must be instrumentally monitored.

The public sector and emergent value
In the final analysis, therefore, as was indicated in our preliminary consideration of institutionalist views, the public sector plays a critical role in
transmitting emergent value to economic performance. But it also plays a
role, in the face of technological change, in creating emergent value. In the
process of its operation the public sector is an actor in public debate. In this
way institutionalists would not necessarily disagree with Friedman's characterization of the government as rule maker and umpire (Friedman, 1962), but

they would add that the government is also sometimes player, manager and coach as well.

Conclusion

In the end, therefore, it is clear that, in viewing the role of the public sector, institutionalists are neither for nor against intervention *per se*. They are concerned with assessing the economic potential of a society and with positioning the mechanisms of the economy, including the public sector, to optimize the 'higher efficiency'. This is what Ayres had in mind in calling for 'a reasonable society'. It has elsewhere been given other names (a Great Society and so on). In Britain it was once called the Welfare State. In the USA the Scandinavian approach was often called 'the middle way'.

However it is called, the public sector becomes a critical link between the economy as merely a market allocation mechanism and the economy as governing total resource allocation in the service of the process of valuation, which is the ultimate task of the economy. As such, the role of the public sector is vital in 'enhancing the life process', to use Veblen's telling phrase for the task of the economy.

PHILIP A. KLEIN

See also:

Corporate Concentration and Interdependence in Europe; Corporate Hegemony; Hamilton, Walton Hale; Institutional Theory of Economic Policy; Instrumental Value Theory; Law and Economics; Planning, National Economic; Planning, Theory of; Power; Public Policy: Contributions of American Institutionalism; Regulation, Theory of Economic.

Bibliography

Friedman, Milton (1962), *Capitalism and Freedom*, Chicago: Phoenix Books, University of Chicago Press.

Galbraith, John Kenneth (1973), *Economics and The Public Purpose*, Boston, Mass.: Houghton Mifflin.

Kahn, Alfred (1971), *The Economics of Regulation*, New York: Wiley.

Klein, Philip A. (1984), 'Institutionalist Reflections on the Role of the Public Sector', *Journal of Economic Issues*, **XVIII**, (1), March, pp. 45–68.

Trebing, Harry (1984), 'Public Control of Enterprise: Neoclassical Assault and Neoinstitutional Reform', *Journal of Economic Issues*, **XVIII**, (2), June, pp. 353–68.

Public Utility Regulation, Institutionalist Contribution to

For more than a century the public utility concept has been synonymous with the regulation of prices and earnings of privately owned firms supplying electricity, gas, telecommunications, water, and to a lesser degree, air and surface transport. This largely American concept was the product of individual actions by courts and legislatures as they sought to constrain the behaviour of firms that provided essential services, possessed market power and required grants of privilege (such as franchises and the right of eminent domain) to operate. These firms were deemed to be affected by the public interest and were required to provide adequate service at just and reasonable rates. The institution of control was to be the independent regulatory commission, which would implement a broad mandate to regulate in a fashion that would promote the public interest. Hence the term, 'public interest regulation'.

Since the 1960s, public interest regulation has come under increasing attack from historical revisionists, proponents of the interest group theory of government intervention, large buyers seeking to exercise monopsony power, and neoclassical economists who believe that unfettered markets provide a superior option for promoting efficiency. The result of these attacks has been to accelerate economic deregulation of air and surface transport, significantly diminish regulation in energy and telecommunications and raise questions about the legitimacy of public control of enterprise.

Institutional and neoclassical economists have been sharply divided over the role and content of regulation and the underlying market structure of these industries. For the most part, institutionalists have favoured economic regulation. Their contribution covers two periods: 1920–61, when they attempted to give content and meaning to public interest regulation, and the years since 1961, when they built upon this earlier work to propose reforms consistent with the evolving structure of the public utility industries and demonstrate the adverse effects of deregulation. In contrast, the neoclassical literature has sought to minimize direct government intervention by introducing peripheral constraints that would complement rather than displace market forces. Each of these approaches will be examined.

Institutionalist contribution, 1920–61
While early institutionalists like R.T. Ely and J.R. Commons were active in promoting the creation of state commissions, it was the next generation of institutionalists who were particularly influential in formalizing the nature and content of public interest regulation. From the 1920s to 1961, M.G. Glaeser, J.M. Clark, J.C. Bonbright, J. Bauer, E.W. Clemens and C.E. Troxel were principal contributors to the institutionalist literature in this area. Their work covered (a) the need for regulation, (b) control of the market, (c) cost characteristics and pricing, (d) rate-making reforms and (e) organizational and institutional reform.

With regard to the need for regulation, Glaeser (1927) distinguished between public functions, quasi-public functions (public utilities) and private functions. A unique characteristic of the quasi-public functions was the ability to recover special benefits that accrue to individual users through prices charged for services. But, for this sector, he believed that collective interests and common benefits remain dominant and collective action, through regulation, serves to liberate individual action and choice. Glaeser noted (1957) that there is a transitional zone between public utility functions and competitive markets where the industry structure is primarily oligopolistic. Here, he stated, 'we meet some of the most perplexing problems of modern capitalism' (1957, p. 11).

Clark (1939) believed that neither the essential nature of the service nor the theory of natural monopoly was sufficient to designate an industry susceptible to government regulation. He stated that the concept of natural monopoly failed to consider a number of those businesses affected by the public interest. According to Clark, a more comprehensive justification for regulation was 'afforded by the theory advanced by Professor Tugwell: that of consumers' disadvantage ... The essential fact seems to be that the nature of the business is such that competition, for one reason or another, does not afford the protections to buyers and sellers that it is supposed to afford' (1939, p. 178). Significantly, Clark noted that 'a public interest of this sort need not apply to an entire industry but to only certain relations or functions' (1939, p. 179).

Bonbright (1961) believed that an enterprise is not regarded as a public utility unless it is subject to direct controls over the rates charged for service. But price control alone was not sufficient to confer public utility status. Bonbright emphasized that the primary purpose of regulation must be the protection of the public in the role of consumer rather than in the role of producer or taxpayer. In effect, a public utility is any enterprise subject to price regulation of a type designed primarily to protect consumers. 'What must justify public utility regulation is the necessity of regulation and not merely the necessity of the product' (1961, p. 9).

All of these writers accepted the public interest theory of regulation and, as Clemens (1950) noted, the interests of the public transcend those of the individual. Private interests must yield to a greater public interest and the firm accordingly accepts a unique set of obligations and rights which differentiate it from other enterprises.

As for control of the market, Glaeser (1927, 1957) believed that competition would be self-destructive in the public utility sector. Firms would have great difficulty estimating costs, and in the long run the struggle to avoid losses would result in mergers and consolidations. On balance, he believed that monopoly was the best form of organization. When an industry was monopolized, the producer would have control over a common necessity and the economic power of the producer must be curbed by the application of the political power of the state.

Clark (1923) was sceptical of the idea that big business, with high fixed costs, would be ruined by cut-throat competition. On the other hand, he expressed doubts about the effectiveness of potential competition in such industries. About 50 years before the theory of contestable markets, Clark noted that potential competition 'is a slow and wasteful check, especially where the new plant has to be large and expensive [and] it is inherently impossible to have an industry effectively governed by potential competition alone' (1923, pp. 444–5).

Bonbright (1961) took a view similar to Glaeser, noting that, although public utility enterprises may face severe competition in selective markets, they are still essentially monopolistic. What favours monopoly status, according to Bonbright, is not that it operates under increasing returns, but rather that it involves a close connection (via networks) between the plant and the consumer.

Glaeser (1927, 1957) emphasized four dimensions of the economy: the load factor, diversity factor, economies of scale and economies of joint cost, all of which he considered to be uniquely important in the utility industries. He gave particular attention to the economies of joint production where 'it would be cheaper to turn out two or more services from one central process or structure than to produce them separately' (1957, p. 177), thus anticipating by two decades the discussion of economies of scope.

Commenting on the cost characteristics of public utilities, Bonbright clearly anticipated sub-additivity by noting that a single company may supply a given market more cheaply than two or more companies operating in direct competition, even when the utility supplies output under conditions of increasing unit costs, for 'the single company can secure the maximum advantages of economies of scale and density, while ... it is no more subject to the diseconomies of enhanced output ... than would be two or more companies ... called upon to supply the region with the same total output' (1961, pp. 15–16). On the question of pricing behaviour, Bonbright responded to the critics of regulation who argued that rates in the long run are higher with regulation than without regulation, and that profit-maximizing firms would experiment with rate reductions, which are impeded because of regulation. Bonbright argued that, when freed from controls, utilities would not follow a practice of lowering prices to maximize profits. Instead, it will be more apt to follow a policy of price discrimination with high prices for inelastic markets and low prices for elastic markets. There would be no incentive to make this type of rate structure conform to cost-of-service standards.

Troxel (1947) and Clemens (1950) accepted the importance of joint production economies and scale effects and focused more attention on price discrimination. The case for and against price discrimination was developed at length by these two institutionalists. While Clemens argued that price discrimination can conceivably approximate the long-run equilibria of perfect competition, Troxel was much more critical of the evolving structure of prices for classes of service. He noted that a system of differentiated prices that reflect different demand elasticities is essentially discriminatory pricing by customer class. As Troxel observed, 'when private managers control price changes, cost economies are translated primarily into price reductions for large buyers or new buyers. Inelastic markets receive no price reductions' (1947, p. 592). Troxel argued that commissions must limit demand-based exploitation of small buyers and that effective control of price discrimination and buyer class discrimination requires control over earnings.

For Glaeser (1927) the answer was to impose rate base/rate-of-return regulation on the public utility industries, using the Uniform System of Accounts as a data base, together with supplemental monitoring for quality of service. Where excess profits appeared because of differential prices, then prices on all units sold should be reduced, output should be expanded, or prices should be lowered for existing customers and output extended to new customers at a lower price. Glaeser believed that any increase in capacity should be approved by the regulator but, once consent has been given, 'it is not thereby implied that the state underwrites the risk' (1927, p. 636).

Bonbright distinguished between a total revenue requirement reflecting historic and current costs, and the design of rates reflecting anticipated or escapable costs. To determine revenue requirements, he would rely upon rate base/rate-of-return regulation. To design prices, he would rely upon marginal cost analyses. Bonbright noted that between revenue requirements and rate design there should be an intermediate standard reflecting the cost of serving a particular class or group of customers. This would be called a class rate standard. Class rate standards would determine whether charges for a specific service were compensatory or non-compensatory, and accordingly would become a standard for judging internal cross-subsidization. For Bonbright, class rate standards should be based on differential or incremental costs and not absolute accounting costs. However, if a total cost apportionment were required, then Bonbright suggested that 'fully apportioned costs ... should reflect cost relationships, not absolute costs ... a relationship of direct proportionality suggests itself, and is perhaps the most generally useful one for rate-making purposes' (1961, pp. 340–41). In effect, an apportionment of total costs or revenue requirements should reflect relative or proportional relationships rather than an estimate of absolute cost by service.

In a broader context, all of these economists would appear to concur with Bonbright and Means (1932) that the holding company system was conducive to waste and inefficiency, financial manipulation, and excessive service company fees that could be shifted forward to the consumer. Bonbright and Means also argued that diversification by utilities into non-utility activities was held to be potentially damaging to the ratepayer because it was a menace to the credit of the public utilities. The solution involved extending regulation to the holding company, discouraging the formation of holding companies that could not demonstrate engineering and economic gains through improved performance, and the divestment of non-utility enterprises. Bonbright and Means desired an industry structure composed of autonomous operating entities, unencumbered by holding company affiliates and diversification programmes.

John Bauer (1950) held similar views regarding an optimal utility structure. Integration and consolidation would be promoted only to achieve economies of operation. With this goal in mind, Bauer believed that commissions should be turned into positive planning agencies. Giving the commissions appropriate powers and duties, raising the professional status of staff and commissioners, and providing adequate financing would improve regulatory planning. With these resources commissions could focus on improving all phases of regulation, including integrating utility properties and operations whenever justified by economies of scale. This planning process, he noted, would be greatly strengthened by broader public participation, since consumers had been under-represented in the past.

Planning became even more significant for Glaeser (1957). Building upon the economies of joint development and technical coordination, he looked towards the development of regional river basin projects, new public power authorities and coordinated large-scale systems based on efficiency gains. Indeed, the last epoch in the evolving public utility process was the shift from monopoly regulation to one of comprehensive public planning.

To summarize, for Glaeser, Clark, Bonbright, Bauer, Troxel and Clemens, the public utility concept defined a unique sector of the economy having distinctive features that required regulation for protection of the consumer. While there might exist highly competitive submarkets, the basic core of public utility service reflected monopoly control which, in turn, required cost-based pricing. Further, the control of prices could not be divorced from the review of profits. They perceived nothing inherently inconsistent between a regulatory system that had these objectives and the promotion of efficiency and equity objectives.

Neoclassical critique and institutionalist rebuttal
At the outset it is important to differentiate between the mainstream neoclassical literature dealing with regulation and the ideological critics of all forms of economic and social regulation. Mainstream thought accepts natural monopoly as a special case but is critical of much of the content and application of public utility regulation. Five points deserve particular mention.

First, neoclassical economists accept the Averch–Johnson thesis, notably that rate base/rate of return regulation introduces an incentive to overinvest in capital at the expense of other inputs when the allowed rate of return is greater than the cost of capital. This has been generalized into a belief that regulatory constraints on earnings divert management from the pursuit of X efficiencies towards asset and expense padding that serve to camouflage economic rents and promote allocative inefficiency.

Second, neoclassical analysis rejects all attempts to allocate common, joint and shared costs through fully distributed cost pricing. Full cost allocations are criticized as arbitrary and perverse and are held to culminate in sending the wrong price signals to consumers, further aggravating resource misallocation.

Third, marginal cost pricing is the first-best choice for setting price under conditions of natural monopoly, but where this is impractical because of the need to cover the firm's total revenue requirement, Ramsey pricing (or the inverse elasticity rule) is the preferred choice. Under Ramsey pricing, prices are increased substantially above marginal cost in markets where demand is highly inelastic, while prices are set at or slightly above marginal cost in markets where demand is highly elastic. Cumulative revenues from both types of markets equal the total revenue requirement of the firm. This supposedly avoids any need to allocate costs for a multi-product firm under increasing returns to scale.

Fourth, neoclassical analysis, primarily building on the work of Faulhaber (1975) and Baumol (1983), has developed a test for cross-subsidization that allegedly avoids common cost allocations. For monopoly markets, price ceilings would be based on the stand-alone cost of providing a specific monopoly service. For competitive price markets the minimum price would be long-run incremental cost (LRIC). If price were to exceed stand-alone cost, profit levels would increase or prices would fall below incremental cost in competitive markets. Either tactic could be detected without recourse to elaborate common cost allocations.

Fifth, moving from the simple case of natural monopoly to highly concentrated public utility industries, many neoclassicists would argue that there is no reason to fear bigness *per se*, or vertical/conglomerate diversification. Corporate power would be constrained by potential entry (the Baumol, Panzar and Willig theory of contestable markets, 1982), so that price discrimination and excessive earnings would be transitory at best. Similarly, proponents of transactions cost analysis would argue that vertical and conglomerate diversification merely represent the application of the efficiency criterion to the procurement process. That is, acting on the desire to minimize transactions costs, the firm will make a basic decision whether to incorporate the production of an input or product within the framework of management control (vertical/conglomerate diversification) or go to the open market to secure that input or product. Acceptance of this argument would serve as a rationale for dismissing much of the concern over holding company practices.

Finally, neoclassical economists have tended to avoid fixing prices and earnings directly in favour of bounded limitations within which management would exercise substantial freedom. Ramsey pricing and the stand-alone test are examples and, more recently, pure price caps have been advocated as a stimulus for efficiency. Pure price caps involve setting ceiling prices for market baskets of services based on a general inflation index and a productivity offset. Management would be permitted to set prices at any level below these ceilings. Neoclassicists are also inclined to promote franchise bidding, auctioning and similar market-oriented solutions for services produced under conditions of natural monopoly. For example, pipeline transmission capacity would be auctioned on the assumption that those able to pay the highest price derive the greatest value from that service.

Institutional economists currently working in the field are highly critical of each of the above points. They argue that inefficiencies and potential abuses are far more complex than indicated by the A-J thesis and that Ramsey pricing sets demand-based rates in monopoly markets which violate the basic public utility concept that prices for necessities should be cost-based. Fisher (1991) has also extensively criticized the application of marginal cost pricing. Similarly, virtually all institutionalists believe that the common costs of a network must be addressed directly and that incremental costs are often indeterminate or zero for many services. On the question of market power, institutionalists from Clark to the present (including Bolter *et al.*, 1984, and Trebing, 1989), have argued that potential entry (that is, contestability) has little applicability for capital-intensive public utilities. Continuing, Edythe Miller (1992) has shown that the transactions cost rationale for vertical/conglomerate diversification ignores corporate power and the dynamics of corporate strategies, while White and Sheehan (1992) demonstrate that holding company abuses are still much in evidence in telecommunications. Price caps are criticized as ineffectual because of both the method of calculation and the nullification of the tie between prices and earnings. Furthermore, Ramsey pricing is shown to be inconsistent with price caps since the former can only function once a revenue requirement (including the appropriate level of earnings) has been established. Finally, institutionalists such as Ray *et al.* (1991) argue that competitive bidding has only a supportive role within a regulatory planning context and is not a substitute for regulatory oversight.

The institutionalist contribution, 1962 to the present

It would be a mistake to assume that institutionalists currently working in the field of regulation have done little more than respond negatively to neoclassical proposals. Institutionalists still perceive the central problem to be the persistence of economic power and the need to develop a system of social control that constrains the exercise of that power while promoting higher levels of social efficiency than would otherwise be associated with highly imperfect markets.

The control of price discrimination, cross-subsidization and risk shifting are central features of any programme of regulatory reform. Melody (1971) is willing to accept marginal cost pricing and peak/off-peak pricing as a contribution to rate design, but argues that cost causation is the proper basis for assigning depreciation and common costs to particular services – whether these costs are sunk or current. Loube (1991) has argued that risk shifting facilitates corporate strategies which transfer the burden of obsolescence and past corporate errors to monopoly markets, thereby permitting both overinvestment in and underpricing of new services that would not be supported by market demand.

The remedial step is to address the problem of common and joint cost allocation in heavily capital-intensive public utility industries. Melody (1971) vigorously analysed and defended common cost allocations. Bolter *et al.* (1984) and David and Richard Gabel (1987) have argued that the stand-alone test presents the best option, while Loube (1991) and Trebing (1989) have recommended applying Glaeser's alternative expenditures theory on the grounds that the benefits from joint development accruing to individual services should serve as the basis for assigning such costs. The stand-alone concept, of course, denies joint production savings to monopoly markets. All of these approaches essentially build upon Bonbright's class rate standard and may be viewed either as a relative assignment of common and joint costs (to be followed by specific rate designs) or as an allocation of revenue requirements.

Equally important, present-day institutionalists focus attention on the evolving structure of energy and telecommunications as a basis for new forms of regulatory intervention. In electricity and natural gas, transmission and distribution networks hold the potential for bringing together a myriad of new supply options and a range of different types of customers. It becomes imperative, as David Penn (1990) notes, that free access and non-discriminatory pricing be maintained for these networks. In telecommunications, the information/computer revolution has created the prospect of global networks and the transformation of both national and international economies. Estabrooks (1988) believes that global networks will create opportunities for both the exercise of greater monopoly power and greater competition and will eventually lead to conflicts between national policies that will culminate in new forms of international regulation. At the same time, deregulation in domestic American telecommunications has not produced the hoped-for highly competitive markets, but rather appears to be pointing towards natural oligopoly in both local and long-distance markets. Trebing (1989) believes that future regulation must deal with new issues such as price leadership among facility-based carriers, the establishment of quality of service standards that respond to the demands of the computer revolution and the prospect that pricing for efficiency will promote even greater concentration.

Finally, institutionalists believe that regulation must move from adjudication towards a greater reliance on rulemaking and planning. Ray *et al.* (1991) have argued that least-cost planning is needed to integrate demand-side management (conservation) and supply-side management in a fashion that achieves efficiency while at the same time minimizing social costs and other negative externalities in electricity supply. Loube (1991) has criticized efforts to upgrade the telecommunications infrastructure as little more than an attempt to buttress the market power of incumbent firms and he believes that least-cost planning must also be applied to telecommunications. At a more theoretical level, Tool (1990) and Samuels (1978) have explored the strengths and weaknesses of instrumental value theory as a guideline for regulators in making judgements regarding social policy.

HARRY M. TREBING

See also:

Administered Prices; Clark, John Maurice; Corporate Concentration and Interdependence in Europe; Corporate Hegemony; Corporate Performance; Firm, Boundaries of the; Full Cost Pricing; Game Theory and Institutions; Industrial Structure and Power; Information Theory in Economics; Law and Economics; Means, Gardiner C.; Power; Public Policy: Contributions of American Institutionalism; Public Sector, Role of the; Regulation, Theory of Economic; Trebing, Harry M.

Bibliography

Bauer, John (1950), *Transforming Public Utility Regulation*, New York: Harper & Bros.
Baumol, W.J. (1983), 'Minimum and Maximum Pricing Principles for Residual Regulation', in A.L. Danielsen and D.R. Kamerschen (eds), *Current Issues in Public Utility Economics*, pp. 177–96, Lexington, Mass.: Lexington Books.
Baumol, W.J., J.C. Panzar and R.D. Willig (1982), *Contestable Markets and the Theory of Industry Structure*, New York: Harcourt Brace Jovanovich.
Bolter, Walter *et al.* (1984), *Telecommunications Policy for the 1980s: The Transition to Competition*, particularly chs 3 and 6, Englewood Cliffs, NJ: Prentice-Hall.
Bonbright, J.C. (1961), *Principles of Public Utility Rates*, New York: Columbia University Press.
Bonbright, J.C. and G.C. Means (1932), *The Holding Company, Its Public Significance and Its Regulation*, New York: McGraw-Hill.
Clark, J.M. (1923), *Studies in the Economics of Overhead Costs*, Chicago: University of Chicago Press.
Clark, J.M. (1939), *Social Control of Business*, 2nd edn, New York: McGraw-Hill.

Clemens, Eli W. (1950), *Economics and Public Utilities*, New York: Appleton-Century-Crofts.

Estabrooks, Maurice (1988), *Programmed Capitalism: A Computer-Mediated Global Society*, Armonk, NY: M.E. Sharpe.

Faulhaber, Gerald (1975), 'Cross-Subsidization: Pricing in Public Enterprises', *American Economic Review*, **65**, December, pp. 966–77.

Fisher, Peter S. (1991), 'The Strange Career of Marginal Cost Pricing', *Journal of Economic Issues*, **XXV**, (1), pp. 77–92.

Gabel, David and Richard Gabel (1987), *A Study of the Stand-Alone and Incremental Costs for Michigan Bell's Major Categories of Service*, Lansing, Mich.: Public Interest Research Group in Michigan.

Glaeser, Martin G. (1927), *Outlines of Public Utility Economics*, New York: Macmillan.

Glaeser, Martin G. (1957), *Public Utilities in American Capitalism*, New York: Macmillan.

Loube, Robert (1991), 'Institutional Conditions for Technological Change', *Journal of Economic Issues*, **XXV**, (4), pp. 1005–15.

Melody, William H. (1971), 'Inter-Service Subsidy: Regulatory Standards and Applied Economics' in H.M. Trebing (ed.), *Essays on Public Utility Pricing and Regulation*, pp. 167–210, East Lansing, Mich.: Michigan State University..

Miller, Edythe S. (1992), 'The Economic Imagination and Public Policy: Orthodoxy Discovers the Corporation', *Journal of Economic Issues* (forthcoming).

Penn, David W. (1990), 'Electric Supply Industry Regulation', *Journal of Economic Issues*, **XXIV**, (2), pp. 545–53.

Ray, D., R. Stevenson, M. Hanson and S. Kidwell (1991), 'Electric Utility Least Cost Planning', *Journal of the American Planning Association*, **57**, (1), pp. 34–44.

Samuels, Warren J. (1978), 'Normative Premises in Regulatory Theory', *Journal of Post Keynesian Economics*, **1**, Fall, pp. 100–13.

Tool, Marc R. (1990), 'Social Value Theory and Regulation', *Journal of Economic Issues*, **XXIV**, (2), pp. 535–44.

Trebing, Harry M. (1989), 'Telecommunications Regulation – The Continuing Dilemma', in K. Nowotny, D.B. Smith and H.M. Trebing (eds), *Public Utility Regulation*, pp. 93–130, Boston Mass.: Kluwer Academic Publishers.

Troxel, C. Emery (1947), *Economics of Public Utilities*, New York: Rinehart & Co.

White, Evan D. and Michael F. Sheehan (1992), 'Monopoly, Asset Stripping, and the Yellow Pages', *Journal of Economic Issues*, **XXVI**, (1), pp. 159–82.

Rational Actor Models

Rationality has been understood in many different ways in Western social thought, but one of the most influential contemporary usages is to identify rationality with behaviour that maximizes the satisfaction of preferences. Models of maximizing behaviour are widely used in economic theory, and rational choice analysis can be understood as proposing to extend that 'economic approach' to other areas of social life. It is in this spirit, for example, that Gary Becker insists that the economic approach 'is applicable to all human behaviour, be it behaviour involving money prices or imputed shadow prices ... rich or poor persons, men or women, adults or children, brilliant or stupid persons, businessmen or politicians, teachers or students' (Becker, 1976, p. 8). Becker and other advocates of the economic approach insist that it is rigorous, capable of great technical sophistication and able to generate powerful explanations across a wide range of situations. Influential examples can be found outside economics proper in the literature on public choice, in political science and sociology, and even in academic Marxism.

The presumption that the greater part of social life can be explained as the outcome of the rational choices of individuals involves a commitment first, to a distinctive view of the individual actor and, second, to a rigorous methodological individualism; that is, to the view that behaviour is not to be explained in terms of the actions of large-scale social forces such as the interests of classes or the needs of capitalism. On the first point, the fundamental assumption is that action follows rationally from the beliefs and desires of the actor concerned. Given a situation of action, the actor selects those beliefs and desires that seem to be relevant, and uses them to decide on a course of action. The 'economic approach' usually involves the further utilitarian assumption that actors' desires (preferences) are such that an optimal outcome can be defined in most situations. Actors, then, may be considered rational to the extent that they seek to maximize the satisfaction of their preferences. Since they are concerned to maximize their own preferences, actors are necessarily regarded as self-interested. However, their self-interest might also concern the welfare of others. Sympathy, for example, may be regarded as a condition in which the sufferings of others may be upsetting, thereby directly affecting one's welfare.

Rational choice analysis does not pretend that self-interested action is always rational in this sense or that self-interest is the only motivation of human action. Its claim, rather, is that the assumption of rational self-interest is the essential starting-point for the analysis of human behaviour. The rational choice literature has been dominated by more or less sophisticated versions of Friedman's well known assertion that models 'should be tested primarily by the accuracy of their predictions rather than by the reality of their assumptions' (Friedman, 1953, p. 21). The point of constructing rational actor models, then, is not to present a realistic portrayal of human behaviour but rather to generate successful predictions – or else, in the event of predictive failure, to provide means of identifying the place of non-rational elements in human behaviour. As an example of the latter, consider the case of electoral behaviour. In most circumstances there is little incentive for anyone to vote in national elections: the vote of one individual will have little effect on the outcome; and the consequences of the outcome for the realization or otherwise of the preferences of that individual will also be small. On the assumption of individual maximizing behaviour, then, hardly anyone would bother to vote in such elections. Hardin therefore concludes that rational actor models 'help us to understand why half of eligible Americans do not vote, but it does little to help us understand the other half' (Hardin, 1982, p. 11).

The 'free-rider' problem provides another example of the heuristic use of rational actor models. Public goods are those that cannot be provided for one individual without also being made available to others: clean air and national defence are obvious examples. Since, if they are provided at all, such goods are provided to a public, any rational individual will choose to be a free-rider, leaving others to bear the costs of their provision. If there are sufficient such individuals then the public good will not be provided at all. Olson has extended this argument to suggest that, even if all members of a group share a common interest, it need not follow that they will organize to pursue that interest. Collective action by large groups therefore depends on the existence of selective incentives for activists, and sometimes also on an element of compulsion. Olson also argues that the situation of small groups is significantly different: its members can bargain with each other to reach an agreed course of action.

Applying these arguments to the analysis of national economies, Olson (1982) maintains that there will be too many organized interests for the conditions of small group bargaining to obtain, and that many interests will not be organized at all. Such bargaining as does develop can be expected to further special interests rather than serve the interests of society as a whole; that is, it will tend to reduce efficiency and aggregate income. However, given time and some degree of political stability, some of the larger groups can be expected to develop organizations for collective action. Politically stable societies will tend to develop more collusions and organizations for collective action over time. Olson uses these points to account for the differential growth rates of parts of the USA and for the fact that Britain, throughout the twentieth century, has had a lower rate of economic growth than France, Japan or West Germany, all of whom have had their special-interest organization devastated by war and political instability.

Since the 'economic approach' does not claim to be realistic, it will not be greatly damaged by the appeal to evidence of significant cases of irrationality in human behaviour. More serious critical approaches tend to retain the analytical commitment to a presumption of human rationality while insisting that economic theory operates with too simple a view of what that rationality consists in. Two lines of argument have been particularly influential here. One, most clearly presented in Sen's 'Rational Fools' (1977), insists that economic theory takes too little account of moral and other commitments. His argument makes an important distinction between sympathy and commitment. Both suggest that individual preferences may be more than purely self-interested, but the former can be integrated within the rational choice approach without much difficulty. Commitment is another matter, since it provides a motive for choices that may run counter to the welfare of the chooser.

The second line of argument follows from the observation that decision making frequently involves deliberation, which in turn involves specific techniques of framing the issue under consideration and of calculation within the chosen frame. Some of the most influential versions of such arguments and orthodox responses to them are contained in a special issue of the *Journal of Business*. Simon (1986), for example, argues that the requirements of rationality demand too much of the cognitive and computational capacities of human individuals. Other authors refer, in addition, to various external limitations on the knowledge available to actors in the absence of equilibrium, perfect competition and completeness of markets. They suggest that actors have no alternative but to make use of a variety of satisficing and framing devices for making decisions within their limitations.

Unfortunately, like all too many authors in this tradition, Simon tends to present techniques of framing and satisficing in negative terms; that is, as responses to the imperfect character of human knowledge, a view that can also be found at the heart of Hayek's well known arguments against the very possibility of governmental economic planning. In fact, the argument from imperfection concedes too much to the rational choice approach. Deliberation is a normal feature of decision making in all but the most simple cases, and it is a feature that is ignored in standard economic accounts of rationality.

To say that we should take deliberation seriously is also to say that we should treat the techniques of framing and the forms of economic calculation employed by individuals as objects of investigation. We should certainly not assume that they can be derived simply from the assumption of maximizing behaviour. It is not difficult to show that distinct modes of economic calculation may be employed by firms operating within a single national economy, or that there are significant differences in this respect between one national economy and another. These points suggest that what has to be investigated is the commitments of and the forms of calculation employed by the actor or actors in question. The 'economic approach' takes a different view: it asks us to investigate what would motivate hypothetical rational actors to perform the actions we wish to explain. However, in the absence of further assumptions concerning the character of their preferences, the shape and dimensions of their utility functions, and so on, the assumption of rationality tells us little about what actors can be expected to choose. It tells us that there will be a certain consistency in their behaviour, but nothing about the substance of their motivations.

The explanation of aggregate economic phenomena, or of structural features of social life, in terms of the rational actions of large numbers of individuals therefore depends on auxiliary hypotheses concerning the content of those motivations. The usual procedure here is to assume that actors' concerns reflect their membership of one of the social categories employed by the model in question: for example, that capitalist entrepreneurs are profit maximizers in a sense that involves a single well-defined notion of what is to count as capital and as profit, and the same types of decision procedures and timescale of calculation.

This dependence on auxiliary hypotheses raises two rather different problems for the claims of rational choice analysis. First, there is the question of how far the assumption of rationality plays a significant explanatory role in the model in question. Taking examples both from economics and from Becker's extension of the 'economic approach' to other areas, Simon demonstrates that 'almost all the action, all the ability to reach non-trivial conclusions, comes from the factual assumptions and very little from the assumptions of optimization' (Simon, 1986, p. 212). Secondly, the auxiliary hypotheses themselves commonly derive actors' concerns and perceptions from their social location (Olson's account of the character and deleterious effects of organized interests is a particularly clear example); that is, they invoke a surreptitious structural determinism which contradicts the overt commitment to methodological individualism.

BARRY HINDESS

See also:

Atomism and Organicism; Cognition, Cultural and Institutional Influences on; Determinism and Free Will; Formalism in Economics; Game Theory and Institutions; Habits; Human Nature, Theory of; Leibenstein, Harvey; Methodological Individualism; Need, Concept of; Neoclassical Microeconomic Theory, Critique of; Olson, Mancur; Rationality and Maximization; Rules; Simon, Herbert Alexander.

Bibliography

Becker, G.S. (1976), *The Economic Approach to Human Behaviour*, Chicago: University of Chicago Press.

Elster, J. (ed.) (1976), *Rational Choice*, Oxford: Blackwell.
Friedman, M. (1953), 'The methodology of positive economics', *Essays in Positive Economics*, Chicago: University of Chicago Press.
Hardin, R. (1982), *Collective Action*, Baltimore, Md.: Johns Hopkins Press.
Hindess, B. (1988), *Choice, Rationality and Society Theory*, London: Unwin-Hyman.
Hodgson, G. (1988), *Economics and Institutions*, Cambridge: Polity Press, esp. Part Two.
Olson, M. (1982), *The Rise and Decline of Nations*, New Haven, Conn.: Yale University Press.
Sen, A. (1977), 'Rational fools: a critique of the behavioural foundations of economic theory', *Philosophy and Public Affairs*, **6**, pp. 317–44.
Simon, H.A. (1986), 'Rationality in Psychology and Economics', *Journal of Business*, **59**, (4), pt.2; also in R.M. Hogarth and M.W. Reder (eds) (1987), *Rational Choice: the contrast between economics and psychology*, Chicago: University of Chicago Press.

Rationality and Maximization

Rationality is frequently associated with the selection of the most efficient means to achieve a given end. Thus agents in economics are motivated by objectives such as utility or profit generation and they are deemed (instrumentally) rational because they calculate what action(s) will maximize utility/profits (or more generally expected utility/profits when there is uncertainty). This apparently simple hypothesis regarding rationality has proved extremely powerful both in economics and in other social sciences, but it also has drawbacks and these cast doubt over whether it can serve as the exclusive rationality hypothesis for social science.

Before these strengths and weaknesses are discussed, a word should be said about the related axiomatic approach to decision making. This approach suggests that rationality is revealed in choices which satisfy certain axioms. For instance, the conditions placed on individual preferences with respect to different commodity bundles when there is no uncertainty are: *reflexivity* (any bundle must be rated as good as itself); *completeness* (any two bundles can always be compared and ranked, where ranking entails a relation either of preference and/or indifference); *transitivity* (this entails that if bundle A is preferred to B and B is preferred to C, then A must be preferred to C); and usually, although for many purposes it is not necessary, *continuity* (which has the effect of ensuring that no bundle is absolutely necessary in the sense that it cannot be traded off at the margin for another bundle). These axioms define rationality and it can be shown that choices satisfying these axioms could be represented 'as if' they came from a process of maximizing a utility function.

The utility function is arbitrary, however, in the sense that any number of utility functions which are positive monotonic transformations of each other could be used to represent these choices. In this way 'utility maximization' is a heuristic gloss on action which accords with the axioms of rational choice. This is an important observation because it helps sever the traditional and controversial connection between economics and utilitarian explanations of action. However, it should not be thought that it thereby also dispenses with the need for an instrumental or maximizing account of rationality. To appreciate why this still might be needed, consider what it is about rationality under the axiomatic approach which makes it rational to follow these axioms. In particular, why should 'transitivity' recommend itself to rational agents? The point of the question is that it is difficult to think of an answer which does not rely on the instrumental conception of rationality. After all, intransitivity is worrying when you have objectives which you wish to satisfy because it means you could be traded into poverty. (A person starting with C, who prefers A to B, B to C, and C to A rather than A to C, will pay to swap C for B, and B for A, and A for C; and thus pays at each stage in a cycle which returns him or her back to holding C.)

At first sight, instrumental rationality may not seem a very promising or rich motivational hypothesis. It takes objectives as given and turns rationality into no more than a calculating skill; and one might suspect that it would be more interesting and revealing to know something about the way agents come to hold particular objectives. Nevertheless it has proved extremely fertile. The applications and insights are legion in economics (for instance in consumer theory and in the 'invisible hand' theorems of neoclassical general equilibrium theory); and it has spread from economics to politics, as in the economics of democracy, of bureaucracy and other related literatures, and from the mainstream to Marxism, where it underpins the so-called 'rational choice' or 'analytic' Marxism. So, for instance, in the application to democracy, individuals have preferences over parties, they vote so as to satisfy best those preferences and the Arrow impossibility theorem has been used to generate a variety of insights with respect to the resulting political process.

Furthermore, instrumental rationality is capable of generating surprisingly complicated types of behaviour. Two are worth mentioning to avoid creating the impression that maximization simply tells us in a rather banal way that a person did something because that is what he or she wanted. In both cases, action becomes more complex because what is best in the short run conflicts with long-run interests, with the result that the individual may cunningly foresake immediate gratification. The first relates to settings where individuals knowingly interact with others. Such situations are known as games and when repeated they can produce a distinctive sort of strategic action where the individual acts in a way that conflicts with his or her immediate self-interest so as to generate a change in the beliefs of the other individuals in the game. This action makes sense from the individual (agent)'s instrumental perspective because the change in the belief of the others facilitates utility maximization in future interactions. An obvious example of this type of reputation-building behaviour is the monopolist who fights entry in one market even though it is more costly than acquiescing to that entry because it fuels a reputation for bellicosity which deters entry in other markets (later plays of the game).

The second is exemplified by the tale of Ulysses and the Sirens. It again involves a temporal twist. Ulysses, it will be recalled, instructed his men to tie him to the mast and to plug up their ears. This was uncomfortable at the time for Ulysses, but it had the virtue of enabling him later to listen to the Sirens without following their suggestion to guide the ship towards the rocks. Such a strategy is sometimes referred to as self-command and it will be familiar to anyone who has attempted to do something like stopping smoking that is painful in the short run but which offers outweighing long-run benefits.

Against this background, what at first seemed a weakness in the instrumental/maximizing account, the silence with respect to the provenence and type of objectives pursued, begins to look like a strength. Indeed, the results appear promisingly general precisely because so little has been assumed about the nature of the agent's objectives/preferences. However, some care is required here. There remain significant gaps in the instrumental/maximizing account of rational action. Two will be mentioned which point us in an institutional direction. Firstly, there seem to be a variety of plausibly human objectives which are not sufficiently 'well-behaved' to admit representation by a utility function (in other words, choices based on them do not satisfy the standard axioms). Literature is a ready source for individuals who entertain objectives which entail the kind of conceptual impossibility we find in Hegel's discussion of the lord and his bondsman and in Sartre's discussion of love – indeed it is the stuff of tragedy. Likewise, there are reasons for believing that ethical objectives cannot be represented by a well-behaved set of preferences (as in Sen's impossibility of being a Paretian liberal). The economist may shrug at these examples, but they are a testament to the difficulty of accepting generally that individuals have well ordered objectives and it would be strange if these difficulties did not surface in economic life. Indeed, anthropologists such as Mary Douglas argue that consumption cannot be properly understood unless it is recognized that people are groping to make sense of their world and the objectives which they pursue within it. Intelligibility and coherence simply cannot be taken as given. Instead, coherence has to be worked at and, on Douglas's account, consumption plays a vital role. In particular, people use goods as a non-verbal form of communication in what is a continuing dialogue with others over how to make sense of one's world and the objectives pursued within it.

This is a tempting line of thought. It echoes early institutional ideas like those of Veblen on conspicuous consumption and it may help explain why there is little evidence of satiation in our consumption behaviour. But, if the line is to be pursued, then it will bring us up against institutions because Douglas's communicative consumption, like Veblen's conspicuous consumption, depends on a very public, if invisible institution – society's culture, in the form of the unwritten rules governing how to interpret particular acts of consumption.

Secondly, there is a ticklish question of where the beliefs come from which aid instrumental calculation. Economics has typically offered two explanations of the origin of belief which appear to be consistent with instrumental rationality. One is subjective and has the effect of turning belief into a type of preference. No more will be said on this since it seems likely that rational agents would demand more of their beliefs than mere subjective coherence. In particular, and this is the second approach, it seems that rational agents would want their beliefs to be 'objective' in the sense of corresponding loosely to what will happen because this enables them to make 'correct' calculations about what best serves their interests. This is the approach taken by those who argue for rational expectations and for the Nash (and the related perfect equilibrium) concept in game theory. The difficulty with this approach is that it often fails to narrow down sufficiently the range of admissible beliefs, as when there are multiple rational expectations equilibria or Nash or perfect equilibria. In these circumstances, there are a number of self-confirming beliefs and so something in addition to 'objectivity' is required to firm up the choice of belief.

Institutionalists firm up beliefs by locating individuals more deeply in a social and historical context. Individual behaviour on this account is as much bound up with custom and (creative) role play as it is with instrumental calculation because individuals inherit and can draw upon what Veblen referred to as the 'customs, canons of conduct, principles of right and propriety' of time and place. These are some of the institutions that, in Commons's words, form part of the 'collective action in control of individual action'. In short, it is institutions in the form of the shared ways of doing and thinking about things, that are the legacies of an evolutionary history, which 'firm up' those otherwise dangling beliefs.

It may help in appreciating this institutional claim to recognize that the problem of selecting a belief, when there are many which potentially satisfy the condition of 'objectivity', involves solving a coordination game. For instance, consider a setting where there are multiple rational expectations equilibria. Any of these equilibria will become 'the' rational expectation for an individual to entertain, provided all others select the same equilibrium. Equally, no equilibrium from within the potential set will be rational if others do not entertain it. The trick of selecting 'the' correct belief, then, is simply to coordinate your choice with that of others.

The coordination may be achieved formally and unmysteriously through explicit collective action within a well defined institution. Alternatively, it may be achieved informally and spontaneously by each individual conditioning his or her beliefs on what contemporary orthodox economists sometimes refer to as 'shared sources of extraneous information'. In this case, it is the fact of 'sharing' sources which provides the coordination and by definition the source must be extraneous to the conventional way in which market interaction is defined, otherwise it will not provide a source for distinguishing one equilibrium from another (since that is the whole problem of multiple rational expectations equilibria: under the conventional definition of what is relevant and the presumption of instrumental rationality, there is no way of distinguishing one equilibrium from another).

Of course, contemporary orthodox economists may prefer to talk of 'shared sources of extraneous information' in these circumstances – so be it. But it is difficult to escape the conclusion that they may be rediscovering some old institutional insights regarding the part played by 'customs, canons' and so on in economic life!

SHAUN P. HARGREAVES HEAP

See also:
Cognition, Cultural and Institutional Influences on; Consumer Behaviour; Culture; Formalism in Economics; Habits; Human Nature, Theory of; Methodological Individualism; Rational Actor Models; Realism, Philosophical; Rules; Veblen, Thorstein.

Bibliography
Douglas, M. and Baron Isherwood (1978), *The World of Goods*, Harmondsworth: Penguin.
Elster, J. (1983), *Sour Grapes*, Cambridge: Cambridge University Press.
Hargreaves Heap, S. (1989), *Rationality in Economics*, Oxford: Basil Blackwell.
Hargreaves Heap, S., M. Hollis, B. Lyons, R. Sugden and A. Weale (1991), *The Theory of Choice: A Critical Guide*, Oxford: Basil Blackwell.
Hodgson, G. (1988), *Economics and Institutions*, Cambridge: Polity and Philadelphia: University of Pennsylvania Press.

Realism, Philosophical

Any position can be designated a *realism*, in the philosophical sense of the term, that asserts the existence of some disputed kind of entity (such as causal laws, class interests, economic equilibrium, events, material objects, numbers, probabilities, social structure, universals, utility and so on). Realism, then, is typically an ontological thesis about the nature of being. In recent years, Mäki (1988, 1989, 1990a) has suggested extending its coverage so as also to reflect variations in the semantic properties of theories. Specifically, perspectives which allow that linguistic expressions can (a) refer to existing entities, or (b) not only refer to but provide representations of existing entities, or (c) not only refer to and represent existing entities but be adjudged to be true or false by virtue of the way the world is, are identified as referential, representational and veristic realisms, respectively (see also Lawson, 1988, on direct and representative realism). In philosophy, however, realism remains most usually an ontological doctrine and, as Bhaskar (1986, 1989) identifies, normally connotes a position in: (a) the theory of perception – a perceptual realism – where, opposed to (subjective) idealism, it holds that material objects exist independently of our perceiving them, and in the domain of the social sciences that the conceptual and empirical do not jointly exhaust the real; (b) the theory of universals – a predicative realism – where, opposed to nominalism, conceptualism and Wittgensteinian resemblance theory, it stands for the existence of universals independently (like Platonic realism) or as the properties (like Aristotelian realism) of material things; and (c) the philosophy of science – a scientific realism – where, opposed to varieties of irrealism, it asserts that the objects of scientific knowledge (such as causal laws) exist and act, for the most part, independently of the enquiry of which they are the objects.

It is as a position in all three categories, but especially as one in the philosophy of science, of course, that realism is of most obvious concern to economics. In consequence it is insightful, here, to dwell upon the recent growth of both interest in, and of, scientific realist contributions concerned with the nature of social material, much of it inspired by the work of Bhaskar in particular, and referred to as transcendental realism or, in its elaboration with respect to the social sphere specifically, critical realism (see, for example, Bhaskar, 1978, 1979, 1986, 1989; Collier, 1989; Chalmers, 1988; Lawson, 1989a, 1989b, 1990; Sayer, 1984). In what follows we shall refer to this specific project only as critical realism.

A scientific realism, as noted, is a theory of being, of some object – that is a theory of ontology – not primarily a theory about the knowledge of that object, or of method, or truth and so on (although it will necessarily entail epistemological and other implications). But any scientific realism must explicitly acknowledge two realms, that of the object of analysis and that of knowledge about the object, dubbed by Bhaskar the intransitive and transitive dimensions, respectively. It is, of course, a condition of the possibility of science that objects exist and act independently of their identification, that is, as intransitive objects. But it is only when both dimensions are recognized that we can understand how changing knowledge of (possibly) unchanging objects is feasible. To be a fallibilist about knowledge is to be a realist about its object.

Does all this, however, relate to the study of economic and other explicitly social mechanisms? The results of economists are always open to appropriation by lay agents, thus affecting the operation of the economic mechanisms that economists seek to understand. Does it then make sense to talk of the objects of economic science as existing intransitively? The answer is yes in the sense that, at the time specific research is undertaken, or indeed at any *given* moment of time, economic mechanisms exist and act independently of the economist's knowledge of them. Indeed, even the knowledge mechanisms of the economists can themselves become the intransitive objects of a meta-epistemic inquiry; and so on ad infinitum.

Now it is clear that any philosophy, discourse, substantive economic analysis, method, practical activity and so on presupposes a realism in the sense of some ontology or general account of being, some premise concerning the nature of the object of study. Realists, then, are disposed to ask the transcendental question: 'What must be the case, given that X occurs?' In the context of examining existing economic contributions, this transcendental question takes the form of 'What must the economists in question be presupposing about the nature of social reality, given their substantive analyses?' In the context of examining the world in which we live the question posed is 'What must be the nature of reality, given that certain observed scientific and other practices and generalized features of experience actually occur?'

In the first of these types of activity, realists are engaged in teasing out the implicit ontological presuppositions of existing (especially mainstream) substantive contributions and dominant methods and so on, and assessing their intuitive plausibility and empirical and other support. An often cited example of this sort of reasoning is Veblen's (1898) identification of the economic agent of classical theory as 'a lightning calculator of pleasures and pains, who oscillates like a globular of desire of happiness under the impulse of stimuli that shift him about the area, but leave him intact' (p. 73). Keynes (1933, p. 285) also employs this mode of transcendental reasoning to identify, among other things, the conditions (atomism and closure) that must prevail if the techniques of econometrics are to receive endorsement (Lawson, 1985, 1989b). More recently, this form of reasoning has also been wielded to reveal the implicit presuppositions of prominent economic 'rhetoricians' (see Mäki, 1988), various Austrians (Mäki, 1989, 1990a, 1990b), Friedman (Lawson, 1992; Mäki, 1992), Haavelmo (Lawson, 1989b), Kaldor (Lawson, 1989a), Koopmans (Lawson, 1989b) and Machlup (Mäki, 1989) among others.

It is essentially through the second more positive thrust of analysis, however, involving a questioning of what the world must be like, given various generalized features of experience, that critical realism in particular has been elaborated. Specifically, through a transcendental analysis of experimental and other scientific practices, and of the nature of human agency in general, a set of insights have been systematized under the label of critical realism, constituting a position in (a) the theory of perception which insists that the empirical is only a subset of the actual, which itself is but a subset of the real; from this perspective, the world consists not only of such actualities as 'falling' leaves, puppies turning into dogs, people from low-income families being under-represented in higher education and so on, and of our experiences of them, but also of 'deeper' structures such as gravitational forces, genetic codes and class relations that govern them; (b) the theory of universals that holds that some classes or ways of classifying objects constitute natural kinds (such as copper or dogs) but that most do not (such as hi-fis or dog-collars); and (c) the philosophy of science that articulates the general character of natural and social material, respectively. Thus, for example, the world is characterized not only by *structure* and *change* but also, among other things, by *openness* and *stratification* (presupposing *emergence*). The world is open in the sense that social, and most natural, phenomena are the product of, or governed by, a plurality of deeper structures and mechanisms. In consequence significant empirical regularities are rarely achievable. Only when one mechanism or structure is isolated from all others – when a closed system is engineered (typically through methods of experimental control) – can an empirical regularity be legitimately predicted; that is, can a non-empirical mechanism be empirically identified. In short, not only are structures irreducible to the patterns of events, discourses or practices that they govern, but they are rarely immediately apparent or manifest in them. In consequence, their identification can be achieved only through the practical and theoretical labour of science. The world is stratified (or layered) in the sense that the reasons for phenomena identified at any one stratum or level are located at a deeper one. At issue, in fact, is a theory of emergence, whereby entities or powers found at some level of organization are said to have arisen out of some 'lower' level being conditioned by and dependent upon, but not predictable from, properties found at the lower level. In particular, human agents and social objects are each conceived of as possessing certain powers that lie only at their own levels, thus prohibiting the reduction of either psychological or social sciences to some other, perhaps all embracing biological or physicalist level.

Now any theory of social ontology, of the nature or generic qualities of social life of concern to economics, must (a) identify the nature of major constituents of the social realm, and (b), given the human agency, including concept, dependent nature of social forms, elaborate the nature of connection between agency and structure. In opposition to individualists, on the one hand, and collectivists, on the other, critical realism emphasizes an essentially *relational* conception of the social. And in opposition to structuralists and subjectivists alike, critical realists elaborate a *transformational* conception of the agency/structure relation whereby neither element can be identified with, explained completely in terms of, or reduced to, the other.

On the relational conception of the social all social forms, structures, systems and so on – the economy, the state, international organizations, trade unions, households – depend upon, or presuppose, social relations. And of special concern are the relational positions into which individuals essentially slot, with their associated, relationally defined, positioned practices, tasks, rights, obligations, prerogatives and so forth. On the transformational conception of social activity the existence of social structure is the often unacknowledged but necessary condition for an individual act, as well as an often unintended, but inevitable outcome of, individual actions taken in total. Social structure, in short, is the unmotivated condition of our motivated productions, the non-created but drawn upon and reproduced/transformed condition for our daily economic/social activities.

On this critical realist conception, then, the objective of economics is to identify the structures governing some economic phenomenon of interest. Essentially, this entails identifying and understanding certain practices of relevance to the phenomenon in question; that is, identifying the unacknowledged conditions of these practices, unconscious motivations and tacit skills drawn up, as well as unintended consequences. In short, while society and the economy are the skilled accomplishment of active agents, they remain to a degree opaque to the individuals upon whose activities they depend. The task of economics, then, is to describe the total process (whether or not adequately conceptualized by the agents involved) that must be going on for some manifest phenomenon of interest to be possible.

Note also that the essential mode of inference required here is not induction (particular to general) or deduction (general to particular) but retroduction or abduction (from the manifest phenomenon, at any one level, to the 'deeper' conditioning structure). For example, this essential movement of science is captured not by starting from, say, the observation of a few black ravens and inferring that all ravens must be black (induction), nor by starting with the claim that all ravens are black and deducing that the next one to be observed must be black (deduction), but by starting with the observation of one or more black ravens and identifying a causal mechanism intrinsic to ravens which disposes them to being black. As Peirce, arguably a significant influence on the American institutionalism of Veblen and Commons (Mirowski, 1987) recognized: induction 'never can originate any idea whatever. Nor can deduction. All the ideas of science come to it by way of Abduction. Abduction consists in studying the facts and devising a theory to explain them' (Peirce, 1967, Vol. V, p. 146).

Finally, three considerations bearing upon method, policy and scope also warrant emphasis. First, because critical realists identify the economic world as open and the aim of science as the identification and elaboration of the deeper structures that govern surface phenomena, the criterion of theory assessment must be exclusively explanatory, and not predictive, power (see Lawson, 1989a, 1989b, 1990). Second, because critical realists recognize that (with the world being open, and human choice real) significant empirical regularities are not to be found in the economic sphere, and that the aim of economic science is instead to identify relatively enduring underlying structures, they hold that economic policy is properly concerned *not* with predictive control – with manipulating values of variables in the hope of controlling future events, with the attempted amelioration of states of economic affairs – but with emancipation, through the knowledgeable transformation of structures that govern and facilitate human action. Third, it must be emphasized that critical realism does not, and cannot, license any specific substantive theory, or a set of substantive practices. In any given context, for example, the scope of, say, human choice may be significant, in others it may not be. It all depends. The identification and understanding of any given structure, mechanism, set of practices and so on, as well as the explanation of concrete phenomena, are the tasks of economic science. From this perspective, if criticism is to be levelled at those economists, such as Veblen, who have made ontological considerations explicit, it is through their having tied such considerations too closely to specific substantive claims. In Lockean fashion, critical realism is essentially an under-labourer for science including economics, a ground-clearing device or tendency. It does not exist apart, or detached, from science, and it deals with the same reality. But its task is primarily to facilitate a set of perspectives on the *nature* of the economy and society, and on how to understand them. It is never a substitute for, but an essential aid to, or a meta-theoretical moment in, the empirically controlled investigations of science into the real structures that generate and govern the equally real phenomena of economic and social life.

TONY LAWSON

See also:
Cartesianism in Economics; Econometrics, The Limits of; Methodology.

Bibliography
Bhaskar, R. (1978), *A Realist Theory of Science*, Brighton: Harvester Press; 2nd edn, first published 1975, Leeds: Leeds Books.
Bhaskar, R. (1979), *The Possibility of Naturalism*, Brighton: Harvester Press.
Bhaskar, R. (1986), *Scientific Realism and Human Emancipation*, London: Verso.
Bhaskar, R. (1989), *Reclaiming Reality*, London: Verso.
Chalmers, A. (1988), 'Is Bhaskar's Realism Realistic?' *Radical Philosophy*, **49**, pp. 18, 23.
Collier, A. (1989), *Scientific Realism and Socialist Thought*, Hemel Hempstead: Harvester Wheatsheaf; Boulder, Colo.: Lynne Rienner.
Keynes, J.M. (1933), *The Collected Writings of John Maynard Keynes*, Vol. XIV, *The General Theory and After: Part II Defence and Development*, London: Macmillan.

Lawson, T. (1985), 'Keynes, Prediction and Econometrics', in T. Lawson and H. Pesaran (eds), *Keynes Economics: Methodological Issues*, pp. 116, 133, London and Sydney: Croom Helm.

Lawson, T. (1988), 'Probability and Uncertainty in Economic Analysis', *Journal of Post Keynesian Economics*, 11, Fall, pp. 38–65.

Lawson, T. (1989a), 'Abstraction, Tendencies and Stylised Facts: A Realist Approach to Economic Analysis', *Cambridge Journal of Economics*, 13, (1), March, pp. 59–78; reprinted in T. Lawson, G. Palma and J. Sender (eds), *Kaldor's Political Economy*, London and San Diego: Academic Press.

Lawson, T. (1989b), 'Realism and Instrumentalism in the Development of Econometrics', *Oxford Economic Papers*, 41, (1), pp. 236–58; reprinted in N. De Marchi and C. Gilbert (eds), (1990), *The History and Methodology of Econometrics*, Oxford: Oxford University Press.

Lawson, T. (1992), 'Realism, Closed Systems and Friedman', *Research in the History of Economic Thought and Methodology*, 10, pp. 149–70.

Mäki, U. (1988), 'How to Combine Rhetoric and Realism in the Methodology of Economics', *Economics and Philosophy*, 4, (1), pp. 89–109.

Mäki, U. (1989), 'On the problem of realism in economics', *Ricerche Economiche*, 43, (1–2), pp. 176–98.

Mäki, U. (1990a), 'Scientific Realism and Austrian Explanations', *Review of Political Economy*, 2, (3), pp. 310–44.

Mäki, U. (1990b), 'Mengerian Economics in Realist Perspective', *History of Political Economy*, 22, pp. 289–310.

Mäki, U. (1992), 'Friedman and Realism', *Research in the History of Thought and Methodology*, 10.

Mirowski, P. (1987), 'The Philosophical Bases of Institutionalist Economics', *Journal of Economic Issues*, XXI, (3), September, pp. 1001–38.

Peirce, C.S. (1967), in C. Hartshorne and P. Weiss (eds), *Collected Papers of Charles Sanders Peirce*, Cambridge, Mass.: Harvard University Press.

Sayer, A. (1984), *Method in Social Science: A Realist Approach*, London: Hutchinson.

Veblen, T. (1898), 'Why is Economics not an Evolutionary Science?', *Quarterly Journal of Economics*, xii, July, pp. 373–97; reprinted (1919) in *The Place of Science in Modern Civilisation and Other Essays*, New York: Huebsch.

Regulation, Theory of Economic

Economic regulation is a hybrid form of industrial structure that combines private ownership and direct public control. It originated in the USA as a means of restraint of private economic power in the energy, communications and transport industries. The underlying theory finds its basis in a blend of the facts of historical experience and the tug of two disparate national value systems that historically have vied for dominance in popular thought.

One of these systems is centred in a concept of social efficiency founded upon a sense of community and mutual obligation, a somewhat extraneous imagery for a nation largely lacking in traditions of *noblesse oblige*. The other apprehends efficiency in a strictly singular and private sense, and is individualist to the point of atomism. The systems may be viewed as models, alternatively, of economic interdependence and economic independence. They are primarily the work, respectively, of US institutional economists and of economists working in the dominant neoclassical tradition. The patterns of belief reflect antagonistic perspectives about freedom, equity, efficiency, power and the appropriate role of government. In the first instance, a governmental role is viewed as integral to the process; in the latter, it is perceived as an unavoidable add-on under certain highly restrictive conditions and, more generally, as an intrusion that is detrimental to social well-being. The systems may be designated, respectively, as a public interest theory of regulation and an individualist theory of welfare.

It is important to recognize that, irrespective of prevailing ideology and nominal economic structure, all economies are, and historically have been, blends of public and private authority. In a contemporary 'free enterprise system', for example, 'private' ownership is hedged about with myriad strictures and mandates governing use and disposition, set forth in bodies of law respecting contract, taxation, inheritance, malfeasance and so forth. Commercial codes direct and restrain business activity. Aggressive or passive fiscal and monetary policy affect the wax and wane of private fortune. Even many supposed highly personal career and family decisions are circumscribed by rule of law. That is, irrespective of prevailing ideal, government action permeates daily living.

In a sense, economic regulation is a strand in that interwoven web of government action. Moreover, it is clear that the part takes on the coloration of the whole: popular attitudes about economic regulation reflect more general beliefs about public activity; the deregulation movement is one aspect of a national and worldwide campaign to privatize, and generally to circumscribe government. But, in another sense, economic regulation is distinguishable in terms of rationale, procedures, practices and the formal mechanism developed for application to an industrial sector with unique cost and demand characteristics. That is to say, the theory of economic regulation is not an all-embracing model for government intervention, but a subset of the larger subject that is both linked to the wider issue and a topic unto itself.

Strictly speaking, the theory of economic regulation does not squarely address global economic issues. It looks, not to the macroeconomy, but to the viability of certain of its key micro-underpinnings. Thus it might be said, for example, that Keynesian and Post Keynesian economics directly address issues of overall economic stability and growth and prescribe demand management and monetary policies to that effect, acting upon issues of social efficiency and equity only indirectly. Economic regulation, in contrast, directly confronts issues of social efficiency and equity through the direct setting of prices, profits, service quality standards, and entry and exit limitations in particular core industries, affecting overall economic stability and growth only indirectly.

Public utility regulation in the USA is an illustration of the symbiosis of law and economics in social affairs. Regulation can be traced back to ancient and medieval religious concepts of just price, but the major original form of control was judicial, rooted in the English common law. Indeed, the 'affected with a public interest' distinction goes back at least to the seventeenth-century British common law case of *De Portibus Maris* in which Lord Chief Justice Hale held that when private property is so affected it ceases to be private only, and a measure of social constraint is indicated (Glaeser, 1957, p. 202). The modern history of US economic regulation begins in the Progressive era in the late nineteenth century. The milieu out of which it evolved included both state-sponsored promotional incentives to development and legislative deterrents to abuse. States vacillated between reliance upon competition and statutory restraint to control abusive power. Legislative remedy, however, was primarily a matter of periodic response to protest rather than continuous surveillance, although several states established railroad commissions.

The development of a legal code for social control in the USA was uneven, reflecting conflicting beliefs about freedom and private property. The Supreme Court decision in *Munn* v. *Illinois* (1877) is generally credited with beginning the modern era of regulation in the USA. In *Munn*, the court acknowledged an 'affected with a public interest' category of business and upheld the authority of states to limit rates when the position of a business at the 'gateway of commerce', enables it to exact tolls from those who pass. The *Munn* case stands for recognition of the coercive potential of certain forms of private property. It is of interest that *Munn* was decided at the threshold of the deployment of the large-scale technology of such major public utilities as electricity and the telephone. The *Munn* decision rests, not upon economies of scale, but upon control over access to an essential service.

In successive cases the court shifted authority from the judiciary, to the legislature and, finally, to administrative agencies. It attempted from time to time to issue methodological guidelines, ending by accepting 'end result' as criterion. A 1934 case threw open the type of business subject to social control, finding that the category of business affected with a public interest is not a closed one. There were also periods of retreat. For example, the court limited sharply the exercise of social control during the 1920s (Glaeser, 1957, pp. 206–15, 342–4).

The growing body of regulatory law provided the framework of rules within which the substantive body of economic theory evolved. That institutional economics would have so profound an effect upon the development of economic regulation in the USA reflects two dimensions of its thought: the scepticism with which the school generally views the working of unfettered market forces in the light of the existence of centres of concentrated power; and the emphasis it places upon pragmatic experimentation, as opposed to reliance upon ideal states, to accommodate change and achieve social purposes. The advocacy of public utility regulation by institutionalism is but one aspect of its general acceptance of the need for social intervention to smooth the rough edges of market capitalism.

From the start, institutional regulatory theory was fact-based. Henry Carter Adams developed an accounting system that would serve as the basis for the uniform system of accounts, essential for comprehension and comparability of utility data. John R. Commons, whose interest in social action had been quickened during the course of his studies with Richard T. Ely, all but invented the subfield when he offered the first course in public utility economics at Wisconsin in 1907. Apprehending the necessity for continuous monitoring by an expert body, Commons was instrumental in establishing one of the two first state regulatory commission in the USA. Most states quickly followed suit after Wisconsin and New York formed commissions in 1907. The system of federal regulation did not exhibit similar growth until the Depression decade of the 1930s.

The positions of institutional public utility economists and of the neoclassical mainstream in regard to social control of private power have consistently been disparate, a difference that, if anything, has widened in recent decades. The mainstream dichotomizes the economic world into competitive and naturally monopolistic segments. It concedes that non- or extra-market measures are necessary to deal with natural monopoly, a sphere that it views, however, as anomalous, insignificant, subject to containment and, on the whole, uninteresting. Accordingly, it concentrates upon the formulation and elaboration of models of competition, viewed as capable of achieving the highest possible degree of Paretian or Kaldor–Hicksian individual efficiency. Social efficiency is viewed as the strict summation of individual results. In another, and an even more fundamental sense, the rejection of government restraints upon private power rests upon grounds of freedom of contract and the sanctity of private property.

The institutional view of the economic world is less sanguine; its model more subtle and complex. It sees the economic world as a continuum, rather than a dichotomy, and as characterized by varying degrees of market power along the spectrum of industrial organization. That is, in its view many of the markets perceived by the mainstream as competitive are permeated by significant oligopoly elements.

Institutionalism substitutes for the individualism that the mainstream apprehends as organizing principle and motive force of the economy a view of an economy marked by persuasion, manipulation and coercion of the less by the more powerful. In place of the end (presented as means) of individual efficiency, it postulates a goal of social efficiency that contains significant equity elements. Commons points out that the privileges and responsibili-

ties, even the definitions, that attach to property and contract are not transcendental divinations but, rather, human creations subject to human control
and change (Commons, 1959, pp. 318–21). Adolf Berle and Gardiner Means,
in a pathbreaking work of the 1930s, reveal the profound transformation in
the concept of private property that attended the growth of the modern
corporate form (Berle and Means, 1933, *passim*).

Institutional regulatory economists, in focusing upon market power and
its tools of control, formulate a public interest theory of regulation that is
essentially centred in concepts of community and social efficiency. They see
market failure as including, but not limited to economies of scale. Additional
technical conditions that inhere in the organization and operation of modern
industrial economies conduce to concentration in markets. Such combinations of conditions, for example, as the requirement of high threshold levels
of investment and the existence of localized markets, of monopoly control
over access, of persistent externalities, of degrees of industrial interdependence that make necessary coordination and joint planning, and of economies
of joint production generally, also contribute to market concentration and a
concomitant market power (Trebing, 1974, pp. 224–5).

It is contended that the necessity for social control stems from the nature
and technical requirements of the activity; that the legal restriction upon
entry and attendant regulation is not the cause but the result of the existence
of a market containing significant monopoly elements. The absence of social
control in these monopoly, or tightly oligopolistic, markets will result, in
various stages of development, in costly duplication of facilities, excess
capacity, price warfare, incentives to takeover and merger, extortionate,
discriminatory and cross-subsidized pricing of essential services, and limit-
entry pricing.

The institutional public utility literature develops the technical apparatus
of rate base, rate of return regulation and treats contested areas of regulatory
methodology (Bonbright, 1961, pp. 147–58, and *passim*). Public utility responsibilities and rights are set forth: the obligation to provide satisfactory
service to all comers at reasonable, non-discriminatory cost-based rates; the
opportunity to earn, but no guarantee of, a fair return; the right of eminent
domain.

Until the 1960s, the climate of opinion in the USA in regard to economic
regulation might be termed one of qualified consensus, albeit with some
disagreement about boundaries. In the immediate aftermath of World War II,
public utilities had sustained strong technological advance, and continuous
productivity and demand increases. Economies of scale translated into declines in real prices; falling prices induced a sense of tranquillity in the
public, and complacency in regulators. Academically, an informal
intradisciplinary general division of responsibilities existed: the mainstream,

in a sense, owned the ideal world of competition; the institutionalists, the real world of imperfect markets. During the 1960s and 1970s, a convergence of forces subjected this limited consensus to severe strain.

First of all, beginning in the late 1960s, the economy experienced a series of shocks having generally adverse effects, but with particular impact upon utilities. In electricity, a combination of inflation and attendant increases in capital costs, sharp fuel price increases accompanying an oil embargo, decreased rates of technological progress and demands for the internalization of externalities resulted in rapid price increases. Problems were compounded in the years that followed. Price increases and mandated rate structure reform had the effect of flattening demand. The industry, confident in its vision of past as prologue, expanded to satisfy former growth rates, culminating in costly excess capacity.

The gas industry was also encountering problems. Congress, anticipating shortages, implemented policies of price indexing and deregulation. The result was fuel switching, decreased usage and the generation of a seemingly interminable 'gas bubble'. The 'law of supply and demand' appeared to have been suspended. Supply was abundant, demand was down, yet prices continued to increase. Nor was the condition of the sector vastly improved when gas prices eventually began to decline. Problems seemed rather to be compounded. For example, most gas transmission companies were locked into high fixed-rate, long-term 'take-or-pay' contracts with producers. The flight of their industrial customers to lower-cost spot markets left transmission companies with high fixed obligations and a decimated customer base.

The economic experience of utilities influenced public attitudes towards economic regulation. Previously primarily a target of political conservatives, regulation now encountered opposition from groups that ranged over the political spectrum. Environmentalists faulted it for intransigence; consumers saw a regulatory system incapable of control. Their voices were added to those of large volume users, seeking to exploit oligopsonistic advantage, and new entrants waiting in the wings.

Throughout this period, the neoclassical perspective was gaining ground within the economics discipline generally. It took possession of the academy and cornered the professional journals. In public utility economics, also, the neoclassical presence increased, while that of institutionalism declined. Courses in the 'Social Control of Business' were transmogrified into the study of 'Industrial Organization', in the process becoming little more than applications of price theory. A stream of books and articles in support of a view of regulation as ineffective, unnecessary and perverse in its effects found ready publication. The attitude was echoed in the popular media. The message was repetitive and insistent.

The academic work is two-pronged. One line focuses upon the nature of regulation, the other upon market structure. Examples of the former are behavioural explanations, such as that found in capture and life-cycle theories. A lack of or decline in regulatory vigour is associated with natural human or bureaucratic tendencies (see, for example, Stigler, 1971, pp. 3–4). An Averch–Johnson effect; that is, a tendency towards overinvestment under rate base regulation if rates of return are in excess of capital costs, is widely adduced and accepted (Averch and Johnson, 1962, pp. 1053–69).

The second line of criticism rests upon grounds of the nature of markets. These criticisms take three major forms. First, the boundary of the competitive sector is enlarged beyond even the orthodoxy's prior generous assessment; that of the abnormal is accordingly reduced. Next, regulation is rejected even for many highly concentrated markets. For example, monopoly is pictured as ephemeral and transitory, vulnerable to technological advance and the assault of entrepreneurial energies. Contestability theory perceives potential competition as capable of eliciting competitive responses from concentrated markets, rendering removal of entry barriers sufficient unto the cause (Baumol, 1982, pp. 14–15). In such a scenario, actual market data such as market concentration ratios to measure market power, or empirical appraisals of minimum viable scales of production to indicate the number of firms a market will sustain, become unnecessary. And finally, within the small core of regulated activity that remains, the use of such competitive tools as bidding and auction, and the application of marginal cost and Ramsey pricing, is recommended, to maximize individual efficiency and innovation.

It is difficult to assess whether, or the extent to which, the juncture of current events and aggrandizing orthodoxy forged a new public consensus. Political leaders were evidently sufficiently convinced to effectively deregulate much of the transport industry. Oil and natural gas production were also deregulated. Much of the rate structure reform adopted for electricity reflected neoclassical principles. In telecommunications, administrative and judicial deregulation and relaxed entry at the federal level was followed by extensive state deregulatory activity.

Subsequent patterns of activity in telecommunications are instructive. In interstate markets, the deregulation and relaxation of entry barriers, in combination with AT&T's continued market dominance, resulted in excess capacity and price leadership. The seven regional holding companies (RHCs) created by divestiture for intra-exchange and short-distance toll mirror the control over access and retain the incentives to action that previously typified AT&T. Moreover, their holding company structure tends to position them increasingly beyond regulatory control. At both the inter- and intra-exchange levels, companies operate in segmented markets, serving classes of customers with different demand elasticities. Prices are set on the basis of relative demand elasticities. Under such conditions, the existence of a captive customer base provides companies with a source of cross-subsidization. The existence of significant joint costs allows discretion (in the name of cost-causative pricing, a major precept of neoclassical economics) in cost allocation among customer classes.

At the federal level, and in a large and growing number of states, rate of return regulation is replaced with one or another version of incentive regulation, effectively removing limits on earnings and profits. Relaxation of prohibitions against diversification furnishes a cover for excess earnings. At the same time, the cessation of profit limitation provides almost costless entry into related and unrelated fields, and subsidizes limit entry pricing in these endeavours. Diversification increases enterprise risk, adversely affecting capital costs and also compounding the potential for a creative cost allocation that deprives captive customers of benefits of joint production (Trebing, 1989, pp. 114–20).

Incentives such as these are present generally in unregulated public utilities. They have consistently been articulated by institutional public utility economists. They are classic examples of the asocial effects of the exercise of power that public control was established to prevent. The reality of unregulated concentrated markets is not competition, but oligopoly unrestrained.

Recent public policy has been driven by an unqualified acceptance of deregulation in disregard of market realities. These policy measures have received the strong support of neoclassical economics. In its place, institutional economics substitutes a programme based upon the formulation of public policy in the light of the facts, rather than one of tailoring the facts to conform to cherished principle. The institutional programme does not preclude outright deregulation, if this is warranted. It actively advocates regulatory reform, while broadening its meaning beyond the currently fashionable view of it as regulatory relaxation only, to include increased regulatory assertiveness where that is indicated. That is, instead of viewing market form as an end in itself, institutionalism apprehends market structure as a means to achieve such goals of public policy as efficiency, security and equity, and as subject to examination and debate along those lines.

More specifically, and in the light of the prevalence of market power and of concomitant opportunities to abandon principles of cost-based rates and otherwise to adopt questionable pricing practices, institutional economics advocates a programme that would include measures to reverse the decline in accountability implicit in increases in concentration, diversification, and the spread of the holding company structure in these core industries; to arrest the movement from tariff to contract; to restrict the potential to exploit control over access; and to ensure equitable allocation of the costs and benefits of joint production.

The public utilities that traditionally have been subject to economic regulation provide an important integrative function. The power, communications and transport industries help to knit together potentially fragmented and isolated communities. They facilitate individual performance by reducing the frictions and obstructions that impede its flow. Consequently, they foster a social efficiency that is greater than the simple sum of isolated individual effects.

John R. Commons recognized the potential of collective action both to enhance and to restrain individual action. In the view of the mainstream, the only purpose and result of collective action is oppression; its liberating effects are ignored. The tool of economic regulation was conceived because the unrestrained exercise of the substantial power with which technical and operational realities imbue particular forms of business enterprise has the potential to transform the power of integration into a force for polarization and disintegration.

EDYTHE S. MILLER

See also:
Commons, John R.; Hale, Robert Lee; Law and Economics; Power; Property.

Bibliography
Averch, Harvey and Leland Johnson (1962), 'Behavior of the Firm under Regulatory Constraint', *American Economic Review*, **52**, December, pp. 1053–69.
Baumol, William J. (1982), 'Contestable Markets: An Uprising in the Theory of Industry Structure', *American Economic Review*, **72**, (1), pp. 1–15.
Berle, Adolf A. and Gardiner C. Means (1933), *The Modern Corporation and Private Property*, New York: Macmillan.
Bonbright, James C. (1961), *Principles of Public Utility Rates*, New York: Columbia University Press.
Commons, John R. (1959), *Legal Foundations of Capitalism*, Madison: The University of Wisconsin Press; first published 1924.
Glaeser, Martin G. (1957), *Public Utilities in American Capitalism*, New York: Macmillan.
Stigler, George J. (1971), 'The Theory of Economic Regulation', *Bell Journal of Economics and Management Science*, **2**, pp. 3–21.
Trebing, Harry M. (1974), 'Realism and Relevance in Public Utility Regulation', *Journal of Economic Issues*, **VIII**, (2), pp. 209–33.
Trebing, Harry M. (1989), 'Telecommunications Regulations – The Continuing Dilemma', in Kenneth Nowotny, David B. Smith and Harry M. Trebing (eds), *Public Utility Regulation*, Boston, Dordrecht, London: Kluwer Academic Publishers.

Régulation Theory, French

There are several regulation theories. The best known of these is the self-styled but rather heterogeneous *école de la régulation* ('regulation school'), originating in Paris. Two other French schools exist, one promoted by several Marxist political economists based in Grenoble, the other by some communist theorists. Similar approaches to regulation have also emerged outside France, sometimes independently, sometimes under French influence (on other schools, see Jessop, 1990). This entry only discusses French regulation theory, however, especially the Parisian School.

All three French schools are inspired by the general method and substantive claims of Marx's *Capital*. They also take institutions seriously and emphasize the transformative potential of social action. In this context they are interested in the way in which long waves of capitalist expansion and contraction are mediated through particular institutions and practices which modify the general laws and crisis tendencies of capitalism. All three schools try to show – empirically as well as theoretically – that relatively stable capitalist expansion over any extended time period depends on quite specific *extra*-economic, as well as economic, institutions and practices. They stress that the co-presence and coherence of these institutions and practices cannot be taken for granted but depend on a varying mixture of chance events, conscious class struggle and social action, and economic tendencies which operate 'behind the backs of the producers'. Accordingly, all three schools argue that capitalist reproduction is both contingent and precarious: it proceeds smoothly (albeit cyclically) only so long as its inherent tensions, conflicts and contradictions can be contained through a suitable mode of regulation.

Much the most extensive and well-known body of research adopting such views has been produced by the Parisian School. This includes Aglietta's pioneering historical account of regulation in the USA (Aglietta, 1979), Boyer's prolific output on topics ranging from labour markets through inflation and growth dynamics to possible future modes of regulation (for example, Boyer, 1988, 1990) and Lipietz's critical analyses of monetarism, peripheral Fordism, global capitalism and the prospects for ecologically sound, alternative socialist economic strategies in the face of the current capitalist restructuring (for example Lipietz, 1986, 1989). Other members of this school have examined technological change, the labour process, spatial reorganization, state intervention, changing international regimes and state socialism. The range, volume and power of such studies have brought the Parisian School wide acclaim in many disciplines around the world. But such popularity has also led to a dilution of some of its key original lessons and aims. In particular, its approach is too often simply equated with an interest in Fordism, its crisis and the rise of post-Fordism. But not all work on these issues is regulationist, nor does all regulationist work deal with these issues. Thus, to discover what the Parisian approach entails, we should look at its broad conceptual concerns rather than specific empirical studies.

The Parisian School was developed in the mid-1970s in opposition to structural Marxist and neoclassical views of the *reproduction* of capitalism.

These suggest that capitalism somehow reproduces itself automatically, impersonally and immutably. To this essentially static account, Parisian theorists counterposed the dynamic notion of *régulation*. This highlights the changing economic and extra-economic mechanisms which lead economic agents to act in accordance with changing objective requirements of capitalist reproduction. By the mid-1980s, the Parisian School had developed the core concepts most appropriate for exploring these changes. Thus each stage of capitalism is analysed as a long wave of economic expansion and contraction with its own distinctive industrial paradigm, accumulation regime and mode of regulation which together endow it with its own cyclical patterns and forms of structural crisis. As a long *wave* (rather than long *cycle*) theory, the regulation approach treats the succession of stages as discontinuous, creatively destructive and mediated through class conflict and institutional change.

Four key terms are used in the Parisian regulation approach. Firstly, an *industrial paradigm* is a model governing the technical and social division of labour. One such paradigm is mass production. Secondly, an *accumulation regime* is a complementary pattern of production and consumption which is reproducible over a long period. Accumulation regimes are sometimes analysed abstractly in terms of their typical reproduction requirements; but, specified as national modes of growth, they can be related to the international division of labour. Thirdly, a *mode of regulation* is an emergent ensemble of norms, institutions, organizational forms, social networks and patterns of conduct which can stabilize an accumulation regime. It is generally analysed in relation to five dimensions: the wage relation (the organization of labour markets and wage–effort bargaining, individual and social wages, life styles); the enterprise form (its internal organization, the source of profits, forms of competition, ties among enterprises, links to banking capital); the nature of money (its dominant form and its emission, the banking and credit system, the allocation of money capital to production); the state (the institutionalized compromise between capital and labour, forms of state intervention); and international regimes (the trade, investment, monetary settlements and political arrangements that link national economics, nation states and the world system). And, fourthly, when an industrial paradigm, an accumulation regime and a mode of regulation complement each other sufficiently to secure for a time the conditions for a long wave of capitalist expansion, the resulting complex is often analysed more inclusively and comprehensively as a *model of development*. Each of these concepts is typically defined to take account of the conflictual and antagonistic character of capitalist social relations. This explains why four complementary concepts are used, why the Parisian regulation school insists on the provisional, unstable and contradictory character of capitalism and, of course, why the very concept of *régulation* was developed in the first place to modify that of *reproduction*.

Using such concepts, early regulationist work identified two main stages: an extensive accumulation regime associated with liberal, competitive capitalism, and an intensive regime accompanying monopoly capitalism. These were linked in the inter-war years by an unstable transition period when the intensive regime emerged without a suitable mode of regulation. The stagflation of the 1970s was held to signify the structural crisis of intensive accumulation and its mode of regulation. At first, regulation theorists examined attempts to resolve this crisis and restabilize the intensive regime through 'neo-Fordist' techniques. More recently, their work has reexamined the conditions underpinning the postwar model of development (nor clearly identified as Fordist rather than as monopolistic) as well as considering possible new development models under the rubric of post-Fordism.

A second French regulation school is based on the 'Groupe de Recherche sur la Régulation des Économies Capitalistes' at Grenoble. Its leading theorist is de Bernis, whose work has only recently become generally available in English (for example, de Bernis, 1988). It has a somewhat narrower, more specifically economic account of regulation than the Parisian School. It argues that stable capitalist expansion requires successful mobilization of counter-tendencies to the rate of profit to fall as well as tendential equalization of profit rates through capitalist competition. This depends in turn on extra-economic adjustment processes which can secure the stable, coherent and simultaneous realization of these two tendential laws and ensure their consistency with other economic processes. Another feature of this approach is its stress on the plurinational character of the productive systems in which such tendential laws and regulatory mechanisms operate. For the Parisian School, in contrast, Fordism was initially seen as essentially autocentric (or national) in nature.

The third French regulation school (linked to Paul Boccara and the French Communist Party) is also concerned with long-term fluctuations and discontinuities in capitalism. It explains them through the law of 'overaccumulation–devalorization'. Essentially this means that capital's drive for profit leads periodically to an overaccumulation of capital relative to available opportunities for profitable investment. If this impasse cannot be removed via normal, short-term cyclical mechanisms, part of total capital investment must be devalorized (destroyed, written down or obliged henceforth to accept subnormal profits) and changes must occur in the structural conditions affecting productivity and profitability so that the profit rate for leading firms or branches increases. This will help to recreate the conditions for long-run growth. But social restructuring must also occur in such fields as family and generational patterns, training and education, industrial relations, political institutions and cultural values. Together with the changing economic factors, these comprise a mode of regulation; that is, a particular configuration of wage relations, competition, state intervention and hierarchical relations in the international economy, which secure the conditions for renewed accumulation.

The regulation approach has been criticized on six main grounds. Firstly, it is accused of functionalism; that is, of assuming that capitalism has certain functional needs which are satisfied through modes of regulation and that the latter come into being in order to satisfy these requirements. Regulationists would counter that modes of regulation are contingent discoveries that codetermine the course of capital accumulation and do not emerge in order to secure already given economic objects of regulation. Secondly, regulationists are said to ascribe an objective and immutable logic to capitalism; this allegedly implies either that this logic cannot be affected by class struggle or that such struggle is simply a mechanism through which it is realized. In fact, regulation theory has tried to overcome the false polarity informing this criticism by showing how so-called economic laws are always mediated in and through specific institutions and practices and why the elements of a mode of regulation cannot contain class struggles for ever. The same reply is relevant for a third criticism: that even the regulation approach is still too static because it seems to imply an alternation between stable, crisis- and conflict-free stages of capitalism punctuated by unstable transition periods. Taking these various criticisms and possible responses together it is not hard to see the similarities between much of the Parisian regulationist approach and the more general arguments of evolutionary and institutional economics. For, while rejecting an abstract, teleologically driven functionalism, French *régulation* theory certainly promises an institutionally specific and historically contingent account of economic evolution.

Fourthly, one finds claims that regulation theory is too voluntarist, that the very idea of 'regulation' implies that conscious action (notably state intervention) can suspend capital's contradictions and guide its accumulation in a crisis-free manner. This criticism stems from the problems of translating the French notion of an emergent social *régulation*, leading to its confusion with legal or state regulation. Fifthly, it has been argued that regulation theory is simplistic because it limits the past to the inevitable rise of Fordism and the future an equally inevitable transition to post-Fordism. This criticism ignores both the initial methodological arguments and the later empirical scope of French regulation work and would be better aimed at its superficial reception abroad. Finally, it is charged that, because regulation theorists have speculated about new forms of compromise which might help to restabilize capitalism after the crisis of Fordism, they are political reformists desirous of saving capitalism rather than moving beyond it. There is no obvious single political message entailed in the regulation approach, however; and it would certainly be mistaken to sacrifice the major heuristic potential of this approach simply because of secondary disagreements over political issues.

BOB JESSOP

See also:

Fordism and Post-Fordism; Institutional Economic Thought in Europe; Keynes, John Maynard; Long Waves; Macroeconomic Theory; Marx, Karl; Regulation, Theory of Economic; Schumpeter, Joseph Alois; Technical Change and Technological Regimes; Veblen, Thorstein.

Bibliography

Aglietta, M. (1979), *A Theory of Capitalist Regulation: the U.S. Experience*, London; Verso; first published in French, 1976.
de Bernis, G.D. (1988), 'Propositions for an analysis of the crisis', *International Journal of Political Economy*, **18**, (2), pp. 44–67.
Boccara, P. (1983), 'Cycles longs: mutations technologiques et originalité de la crise de structure actuelle', *Issues*, **16**, pp. 5–60.
Boyer, R. (ed.) (1988), *The Search for Labour Market Flexibility*, Oxford: Clarendon Press; first published in French, 1986.
Boyer, R. (1990), *The Regulation School: a critical introduction*, New York: Columbia University Press; first published in French, 1986.
Boyer, R. (1991), 'The Eighties: the search for alternatives to Fordism', in B. Jessop *et al.* (eds), *The Politics of Flexibility*, pp. 106–32, Aldershot: Edward Elgar.
Brenner, R. and M. Glick, (1991), 'The regulation approach: theory and history', *New Left Review*, **188**, pp. 45–119.
Jessop, B. (1990), 'Regulation Theories in Retrospect and Prospect', *Economy and Society*, **19**, (2), pp. 154–216.
Lipietz, A. (1986), *Mirages and Miracles*, London: Verso.
Lipietz, A. (1989), *Choisir l'audace*, Paris: la Découverte.

Richardson, George B.

George B. Richardson was born in 1924 in London. Any account of his work will inevitably focus attention on his *Information and Investment*, first published in 1960. This is now recognized as a major contribution to the study of economic adjustment and a deep critique of the theory of perfectly competitive equilibrium. It is important, however, also to recognize a stream of other writings, spread over a period of some 20 years (1953 to 1972), which first sketched the arguments presented in that book and subsequently refined them into a mature statement of the complex and subtle institutional arrangements which made competition possible in modern capitalist economies. In this regard Richardson is very much a Marshallian and he is rightly seen as standing within a theoretical tradition which also includes P.W.S. Andrews, J. Downie and E. Penrose. This Marshallian connection is made even more explicit when we recognize that the problems addressed by

Richardson are either problems of long-period adjustment under given technical conditions or problems of secular adjustment when the set of commodities is variable: the 'filling up of uncharted economic space' as it is expressed (1990, p. 103). Analysis of short-period equilibrium is not his concern; the conditions under which investment becomes possible are.

The central issue throughout his work is how the efficient long-run allocation of resources is to be achieved when the knowledge of individuals in general, and entrepreneurs in particular, is incomplete and fragmented. It is the presence of ignorance which denies the possibility of appropriate future markets, so transforming the economic problem from one of allocating known means to fully comprehended ends to one of creating and distributing knowledge so that individuals can act in an economical way. The concept of a perfectly competitive equilibrium, based on *anonymous* transactions between a large number of agents freely able to dispose of their resources, is, according to Richardson, quite inadequate to the task of understanding how equilibrium is to be achieved or restored following changes in fundamental data. The striking theoretical failure is to not explain how individuals form reliable beliefs as a basis for action. Current prices do not contain the appropriate information and expectations of future prices cannot be conjured up arbitrarily: they must be rationally based on adequate evidence, and the possibility of such evidence depends on the information-generating and disseminating properties of the prevailing set of market institutions. From this perspective, perfect competition does not generate the information on which investments can be reliably made and it therefore rules out the very activity, efficient long-run resource allocation, which could create a competitive equilibrium. Paradoxically, it is the large number of anonymous agents required for perfect competition which contributes to the impossibility that knowledge might adjust to changing circumstances.

Here it must be made clear that the desirability of competition is not being questioned, quite the opposite. Rather it is the nature of competition which is the issue, with attention switched from competition as a state of equilibrium to competition as a process of adaptation. Richardson's principal claim is that this process can only operate in the presence of certain restraints: restraints which from a static perspective are undesirable frictions and market imperfections but which from a dynamic point of view are necessary if appropriate information is to be made available to entrepreneurs.

In considering the investment decision, a careful distinction is made between competitive and complementary investments and the general problem is typically presented as follows. How, under conditions of perfect competition, is a firm to respond to a general increase in demand when that increase will also be perceived by rival producers? How, in these circumstances, is an individual entrepreneur to know how much investment his actual or potential rivals are also planning? This information is not contained in current prices, yet without such knowledge the profitability of an investment programme cannot be determined, for the profit opportunities facing any one entrepreneur depend on the unspecifiable actions of rivals. A profit opportunity which is available to everyone turns out in fact to be available to no one in particular. Consequently, under perfect competition plans to adapt cannot be formed rationally, with the ever-present possibility of under- or overinvestment and the consequent wastage of resources.

In practice it is the restraints which make possible an effective process of adaptation. Some of these involve explicit collusion, others are more subtle and involve the imperfect distribution of information concerning investment opportunities or differential access to the resources to invest – indeed, capital market imperfections facilitate the process of adaptation. Such restraints create a phased response to changes in data and permit the gradual accumulation of the necessary information to guide investment decisions. Equally important are arrangements which attach customers to each firm, and ensure that its share of any general increase in demand can be assessed with some confidence. Product differentiation, inertia and reputation are examples of the factors which so segment markets, as are cartel arrangements which are simply an explicit, planned form of an information-generating restraint. Similar considerations apply with respect to complementary investments, but with different kinds of restraints, ranging from information sharing, through subcontracting to vertical integration. Such restraints, by making markets more secure, increase market information and the predictability of the entrepreneurial environment (1990, p. 68). In short, they replace anonymity and ignorance with commitment and knowledge.

Problems of information and coordination become particularly acute when we turn to matters of innovation. This reaches to the core of the competitive process, for the state of competition is not to be assessed in terms of the cross-elasticity of demand between different firms, but rather by their ability to innovate and so 'enlarge the field for active competitive warfare' (1990, p. 106). Even less is price information now available to the process of coordination and so voluntary consultation and agreement between firms (as with the setting of technical standards or the pursuit of collaborative development programmes) are likely to be essential to the effective conduct of innovation. To the extent that such restraints promote the creative imagination of each entrepreneur they are to be welcomed, not condemned.

The Marshallian influences underlying the above are clear. All cases of restraint are to be judged on their balance of merits and drawbacks, not in terms of an overarching principle of static efficiency. A trade-off is nonetheless involved between the generation of information and the possible inhibiting effects of restraints on the process of competition. As befits a one-time member of the British Monopolies Commission, Richardson insists that each market situation is to be judged in terms of its own, unique complex of circumstances. Studies of the electrical engineering industry (1966) and open price agreements (1967) exemplify this approach. Characteristically, Richardson summarizes the real problem in these cases as the invention of 'arrangements that permit the manufacturers and their customer to work together as a *team* without sacrificing the objectives for the attainment of which price competition is a useful device' (1966, p. 89, my emphasis). In further contributions (1964, 1965), an explicit theory of investment is developed, with the rate of growth of the firm jointly limited by the ability to manage growth and the availability of finance from an imperfect capital market. But it was in 1972 that Richardson outlined a mature version of his main concerns. Here it is argued that the distinction between planning within firms and coordination through anonymous market transactions is far too simple-minded, for it ignores the immense variety of intermediate arrangements by which firms coordinate activities in formal and informal networks. These arrangements are particularly important for the coordination of technical progress between firms defined by differential capabilities, and it is precisely the element of innovation which drives the competitive process in the long term.

For many years Richardson's work remained virtually unnoticed: it presented too fundamental a challenge at a time when Arrow–Debreu theory was thought capable of revealing the inner structure of competitive economy. This is no longer the case. In Richardson's work are found clear insights into modern debates on markets v. hierarchies, the stability of prices, the economics of information, the basis for rational expectations and the economic reform of socialist economics. More significantly, by emphasizing competition as a process based upon differentiated firms, Richardson anticipated many of the questions credited to modern evolutionary economic theory. To weave together, albeit implicitly, the patterns of thought of Marshall, Hayek and Schumpeter in this way is an achievement of considerable and enduring importance.

J.S. METCALFE

See also:

Administered Prices; Capital Theory; Corporate Hegemony; Firm, Boundaries of the; Firm, Theory of the; Formalism in Economics; Game Theory and Institutions; Industrial Structure and Power; Information Theory in Economics; Institutional Economic Thought in Europe; Market, Institutionalist View of the; Marshall, Alfred; Means, Gardiner C.; Microfoundations of Macroeconomic Competitiveness; Neoclassical Microeconomic Theory, Critique of; Power; Rationality and Maximization; Transaction.

Bibliography
Richardson, G.B. (1953), 'Imperfect Knowledge and Economic Efficiency', *Oxford Economic Papers*, **5**, June, pp. 136–56.
Richardson, G.B. (1956), 'Demand and Supply Reconsidered', *Oxford Economic Papers*, **8**, June, pp. 113–26.
Richardson, G.B. (1959), 'Equilibrium, Expectations and Information', *Economic Journal*, **69**, June, pp. 223–37.
Richardson, G.B. (1960), *Information and Investment*, Oxford: Oxford University Press.
Richardson, G.B. (1964), 'The Limits to a Firm's Rate of Growth', *Oxford Economic Papers*, **16**, March, pp. 9–23.
Richardson, G.B. (1965), 'Ideal and Reality in the Choice of Techniques', *Oxford Economic Papers*, **17**, July, pp. 291–8.
Richardson, G.B. (1966), 'The Pricing of Heavy Electrical Equipment: Competition or Agreement?' *Bulletin*, Oxford University Institute of Statistics, **28**, May, pp. 73–92.
Richardson, G.B. (1967), 'Price Notification Schemes', *Oxford Economic Papers*, **19**, November, pp. 359–69.
Richardson, G.B. (1971), 'Planning Versus Competition', *Soviet Studies*, **22**, (3), pp. 433–47.
Richardson, G.B. (1972), 'The Organization of Industry', *Economic Journal*, **82**, September, pp. 883–96.
Richardson, G.B. (1990), *Information and Investment*, Oxford: Oxford University Press, reprint of 1960, together with a new Introduction, and the 1971 and 1972 papers above.

Robinson, Joan

Joan Robinson (1903–83) was born into an upper middle-class English family with a tradition of dissent. She read history at school and economics at Cambridge because she wanted to know why poverty and unemployment occurred. She graduated in 1925. In 1926, she married Austin Robinson, the economist. After two years in India they returned to Cambridge, their base for the rest of their lives.

Joan Robinson was an outstanding teacher and an exemplary supervisor of research students, demanding but supportive. She lectured all over the world to students, often at their request. She spent many (northern) summers in India, making many trips to China after 1949. She said she came to learn, not to teach; in fact, in her papers are notes of lectures which she gave on the economics of planning a newly emerging nation. She inspired the Western young and irritated the old (and not so old) with her lectures and articles on China. There was a leaven of advocacy in her views, offsetting what she saw as basic hostility from others.

Joan Robinson passionately hated injustice, whether it was the by-product of a class-ridden society such as the UK or a caste-ridden one such as India. She searched for ways of creating a just, equitable society, analysing and criticizing trenchantly societies she knew and theories about them. She had a passion for truth and was as hard on herself as on others, changing her views, yet at any moment fiercely defending them. Sometimes harsh and unfair, she was also warm-hearted, a loyal friend, quixotically courageous, an indomitable free spirit who never gave up, nor ever accepted the limitations of age and ill health.

As an undergraduate, Joan Robinson absorbed Marshall's *Principles* from Pigou and Shove. That she was eager to criticize his views because of their increasing inability to square with the unfolding experiences in UK industry is borne out by the publication of *The Economics of Imperfect Competition* (1933). Writing it was a group effort; it brought together ideas in the air in the UK (and the USA, with the concurrent publication of Edward Chamberlin's *The Theory of Monopolistic Competition*). Marshallian/Pigovian theory predicted that a sustained fall in demand would close down the least efficient firms, the rest operating at full capacity with price equal to marginal cost. In fact, most firms operated at less than capacity with prices greater than marginal costs. In a famous paper in the *Economic Journal* Piero Sraffa (1926) suggested that firms should be analysed as mini-monopolies operating in a competitive environment, constrained by demand, not rising marginal costs. This idea, the invention of the marginal revenue curve (by Charles Gifford), Richard Kahn's 1929 dissertation, 'The Economics of the Short Period', and Shove's lectures led to Joan Robinson's book. She herself saw it at the time as a critique of the benefits of laissez-faire capitalism – a denial of the beneficial purging of the unfit in a slump. Later, she said her analysis undermined the simple statements and the normative implications of the marginal productivity theory of distribution. With Kahn, James Meade, Austin Robinson, Sraffa and the bright undergraduates of the 'Cambridge Circus', she became absorbed in arguing out the *Treatise on Money* and helping Keynes to develop *The General Theory*, the theory of the level of employment as a whole in a monetary production economy. The analysis revealed another more damning indictment of laissez-faire, the failure to provide full employment. Joan Robinson played an important role, criticizing drafts of the book and Keynes's lectures, which led up to it, and, following its publication, publishing her 'told to the children' version, *Introduction to the Theory of Employment* (1937).

In the mid-1930s, another major influence emerged – her interest in Marx, sparked by reviewing Strachey's *The Nature of Capitalist Crisis* (1935) and the beginnings of her friendship with Kalecki. He came to Cambridge just after *The General Theory* was published and amazed Joan Robinson by knowing all about its contents and more. Kalecki had a lasting effect on the direction of her thought for the rest of her life. In *An Essay on Marxian Economics* (1942) she distilled out for the orthodox the economic structure of Marx's thought, comparing his results with orthodox teaching on various issues. She showed that Marx operated on a larger scale and was interested in problems that had been expunged by the advent of neoclassical preoccupation with value, distribution and resource allocation theory within a static framework.

The Keynesian revolution, Marx and Harrod's growth theory focused her major efforts for the postwar period on two separate but related endeavours: first, a critique of the orthodox theory of value and distribution and of what she took to be its basic method; second, her attempt, with Kahn, Kaldor and others, to bring about the generalization of *The General Theory* to the long period, going over classical preoccupations with institutions, distribution and accumulation, in the light of insights gained from the Keynesian revolution. She analysed the choice of technique in the economy as a whole as part – in her view, a secondary part – of the accumulation process. To do this she went back to Wicksell, Marshall and Hicks (1932). The result was her best known postwar article, 'The Production Function and the Theory of Capital' (1953–4). Alongside this issue was her increasing preoccupation with the way she thought neoclassical economists handled time. Her basic criticism was that there was no place for time on a plane diagram. This was often ignored in discussions of existence, uniqueness and stability of equilibrium. Her most comprehensive statement is 'History versus Equilibrium' (1974). She attacked the use of comparisons of equilibrium positions to analyse processes following a disturbance – failing to distinguish between differences and changes. A favourite analogy was a pendulum. Its ultimate resting place is independent of whether it is given a slight nudge or arbitrarily lifted high and let go – not so for analogous disturbances in markets or economies.

However, the issue latched onto in her 1953–4 article was the meaning and measurement of capital within the neoclassical framework. Can we say the rate of profits is high or low partly because we have a 'little' or a 'lot' of 'capital'? Do we mean something when we talk of 'its' marginal product? She said later that Veblen had anticipated these criticisms in his critique of J.B. Clark. In the positive aspects (Robinson, 1956, 1962b), she dealt with real issues, using a model of an unregulated free enterprise economy in which firms 'within the limits set by their command of finance determine the rate of accumulation', while members of the public, constrained 'by their command of purchasing power, are free to make the rate of expenditure what they please'. It was used 'to analyse the chances and changes of development of an economy as time goes by'. Much of the analysis is comparative dynamics, often interpreted as applying to real economies. They do not. They are statements of consistency conditions bringing out how rarely, in actual economies, they are likely to be brought about.

The central model incorporated Keynesian, Kaleckian, Marxian and classical ideas. The distribution of the product between classes determined the saving ratio, because wage-earners effectively do not save and profit-receivers do. This affected the determination of profits by the rate of accumulation, reflecting Kalecki's maxim that capitalists receive what they spend, itself constrained by their access to finance. The Keynesian 'animal spirits' function expressed the dependence of planned accumulation on expected profitability. If accumulation induced by given expectations of profitability creates an income distribution which implies that this profitability is achieved, a sort of economy equilibrium is obtained. The business people are happy (the growth rate is akin to Harrod's warranted rate) but the wage-earners may not be – there may be considerable unemployment. It is not a stable, long-period or sustainable equilibrium. The mere passage of time, during which replacements associated with past accumulation become due and new methods of production emerge, can rupture the 'equilibrium' by changing the positions of the underlying functions.

In 'What are the Questions?' (1977), Robinson argued that ideology and analysis are indissolubly mixed, that the dominant ideology exerts disproportionate power in the discipline at any moment of time, developing themes she discussed in *Economic Philosophy* (1962a). She deplored the distinction made between macro and micro in modern economics, arguing that one cannot exist without the other. In her later years, Joan Robinson became pessimistic, even nihilistic. Her last substantial paper was originally called 'Spring Cleaning' (1980b). Here she urged us to start again. She set out what she still believed valuable in Sraffa's critique of neoclassical economics and the structure he put upon the surplus approach in his attempted revival of classical political economy. She despaired of ever obtaining a satisfactory long-period theory, sensing that Keynes's short-period analysis (in its Kaleckian form) was as far as we could go, giving us a theory of cyclical growth in the form of linked short periods, the happenings of each helping to determine what happens next.

Joan Robinson *may* have been too pessimistic. More balanced is the following statement: 'In reality, all the interesting and important questions lie in the gap between pure short-period and pure long-period analysis' (1973). Her own example will inspire those who are now trying to implement this agenda.

G.C. HARCOURT

See also:

Capital Theory; Kaldor, Nicholas; Keynes, John Maynard; Marx, Karl.

Bibliography

Joan Robinson published with Basil Blackwell five volumes of *Collected Economic Papers* (I, 1951; II, 1960; III, 1965; IV, 1973; V, 1979) and two volumes of (mainly) selections from them: *Contributions to Modern Economics* (1978) and *Further Contributions to Modern Economics* (1980a). In the references below usually appear places and dates when the papers were first published and then where in these seven volumes they may also be found.

Gram, Harvey and Vivian Walsh (1983), 'Joan Robinson's Economics in Retrospect', *Journal of Economic Literature*, **XXI**, pp. 518–50.

Harcourt, G.C. (1979), 'Joan Robinson', in David L. Sills (ed.), *International Encyclopaedia of the Social Sciences. Biographical Supplement*, Vol. 18, New York: Free Press; an expanded version is in G.C. Harcourt (1982), *The Social Science Imperialists. Selected Essays*, pp. 346–61, edited by Prue Kerr, London: Routledge & Kegan Paul.

Harcourt, G.C. (1990), 'On the Contributions of Joan Robinson and Piero Sraffa to Economic Theory', pp. 35–67, in Maxine Berg (ed.), *Political Economy in the Twentieth Century*, Baltimore, Md.: Barnes and Noble.

Hicks, J.R. (1932), *The Theory of Wages*, London: Macmillan.

Kahn, R.F. (1929), *The Economics of the Short Period*, reprinted 1989, London: Macmillan.

Robinson, Joan (1936), 'Review of John Strachey, *The Nature of Capitalist Crisis* (1935)', *Economic Journal*, **XLVI**, pp. 298–302.

Robinson, Joan (1937), *Introduction to the Theory of Employment*, London: Macmillan.

Robinson, Joan (1942), *An Essay on Marxian Economics*, London: Macmillan.

Robinson, Joan (1953–4), 'The Production Function and the Theory of Capital', *Review of Economic Studies*, **xxi**, pp. 81–106; partly reprinted in Vol. II, 1960, pp. 114–31.

Robinson, Joan (1956), *The Accumulation of Capital*, London: Macmillan.

Robinson, Joan (1962a), *Economic Philosophy*, New York: Watts.

Robinson, Joan (1962b), *Essays in the Theory of Economic Growth*, London: Macmillan.

Robinson, Joan (1973), 'Ideology and Analysis', in *Sozialismus, Geschichte und Wirtschaft, Festischift für Edward Marz*, pp. 53–60, Euro paverlag H.G. Weiss; reprinted in Vol. V, 1979, pp. 254–61.

Robinson, Joan (1974), 'History Versus Equilibrium', *Thames Papers in Political Economy*, London: Thames Polytechnic; reprinted in Vol. V, 1979, pp. 48–58.

Robinson, Joan (1977), 'What are the Questions?', *Journal of Economic Literature*, **XV**, pp. 1318–39; reprinted in Vol. V, 1979, pp. 1–31.

Robinson, Joan (1980b), 'Spring Cleaning', mimeo, Cambridge, published as 'The Theory of Normal Prices and Reconstruction of Economic Theory', in George R. Feiwel (ed.) (1985), *Issues in Contemporary Macroeconomics and Distribution*, pp. 157–62, London: Macmillan.

Sraffa, Piero (1976), 'The Laws of Returns under Competitive Conditions', *Economic Journal*, **XXXVI**, pp. 535–50.

Strachey, John (1935), *The Nature of Capitalist Crisis*, London: Victor Gollancz.

Rothschild, Kurt Wilhelm

Kurt W. Rothschild was born in 1914 in Vienna. He studied law at the University of Vienna, but soon he became interested in problems of economic policy and theory. However, he was not able to deepen his economic knowledge in Austria. When he completed his doctorate in law in 1938, he was one of the last Jewish students to get their degree in an 'unofficial' ceremony. Being aware of the growing danger, Rothschild applied for a scholarship at the University of Glasgow. He had to flee to Switzerland, from where he was able to emigrate to the UK. For almost ten years, from the end of 1938 to 1947, he benefited from British hospitality, first as a student of political economy and political philosophy (until 1940, when he gained his MA) and then as assistant lecturer and lecturer in economics at the University of Glasgow. In 1947, Rothschild returned to Austria to work as a research fellow at the Austrian Institute for Economic Research. He remained there until 1966, at which time he became full professor at the University of Linz, Austria. He retired from his professorship in 1985.

A number of experiences in Rothschild's life have had a decisive influence upon his work and character. To begin with, the terrible experience of mass unemployment in the 1930s stimulated a profound interest in matters of labour and employment policy, which was to become a major theme in Rothschild's later research activities. Furthermore, the sudden change from the study of marginal utility economics in Vienna to Keynesian economics in Glasgow contributed to the development of Rothschild's well known interest in the coexistence of rival schools (Rothschild, 1989). Upon reading Rothschild's articles and books, and following his contributions in scholarly discussions, one observes his tolerance towards rival ideas and theories: his ability to examine paradigms he does not and cannot share seems to mirror British tolerance and liberalism. Furthermore, he has a clear and concise style of writing and an impressive ability to find short and understandable explanations for difficult matters.

Finally, his fellowship at the Austrian Institute for Economic Research, where he worked for almost 20 years, was a decisive experience. Here, the daily routine required him to become thoroughly familiar with empirical data and statistical methods. Being forced to use economic reasoning for practical purposes and political advice, Rothschild's already critical stance towards elegant but useless theories was reinforced. Theories have to be regarded as tools to be selected according to the questions to be tackled.

A selective presentation rather than a full account of Rothschild's work follows (but see Rothschild, 1990, for a comprehensive list of publications). Brought up in two quite different economic schools, it is not surprising that Rothschild developed his own independent way of economic thinking: 'He can hardly be classified as belonging to one school in economics' (Laski, 1987). Judged by his *macroeconomic* writings he may be called Keynesian, albeit not in the American tradition of Tobin and Samuelson, but in the more fundamentalist tradition of Joan Robinson and Kahn. On the other hand, Rothschild's *microeconomic* work has been quite substantial.

Probably the single most important microeconomic contribution was his 1947 article on 'Price Theory and Oligopoly', a pathbreaking work which seems to be neglected to this very day. In concert with a generation of young economists – Chamberlin, Joan Robinson, Triffin – Rothschild tried to develop a 'more realistic' theory of prices (Rothschild, 1947). He argued that oligopoly is by far the most important market structure, yet oligopoly is treated in a cavalier fashion and as a special case in our textbooks. The latter verdict seems still to be true for most microeconomic textbooks (with some notable exceptions, for example Koutsoyiannis, 1975).

To explain prices and price movements observed in oligopolistic markets, the methodological perspective has to be changed from purely economic models to strategic behaviour models, for example to models of military thinking and planning. The behaviour of large oligopolies is guided by considerations of securing profits and of survival in the medium and long term, not necessarily by maximizing profits in the short run. These firms are conscious of their *interdependence*, and of a wider range of *economic and political actions* at their disposal that are used to achieve their goals. The resulting uncertainty about the behaviour of this important part of economic agents precludes the existence or at least the uniqueness of an equilibrium price system (Rothschild, 1981, p. 20).

Hence Rothschild is very clear about the methodological status of general equilibrium: the model of general equilibrium is a sophisticated formalization of Adam Smith's idea of the 'invisible hand'. But it is neither a positive description of the real world nor a normative model for the real world: prevailing oligopolistic markets render general equilibria impossible, and pareto optimality is unlikely to satisfy notions of equity and social justice (Rothschild, 1981).

When the existence of large oligopolies as a prevailing feature of modern economies is accepted, the notion of 'power' has to be introduced into economic reasoning (Rothschild, 1971). Rothschild was extremely successful in showing that considerations of power, social institutions and psychological elements are also necessary to understand macroeconomic phenomena. Among others, the fields of macroeconomics, international economics, the theory of distribution and the labour market in general and unemployment in particular have been central topics of Rothschild's research interest. He never tired of emphasizing the crucial difference between the goods market and the labour market: whereas goods may be separated from the producer and their transactions may be looked at as independent of their suppliers, labour is a genuine part of the producer's life; it cannot be separated from the supplier. Hence price differentials in the labour market, that is, wage differentials, do not necessarily make a worker change his job, his home and country. The market mechanism is therefore of reduced relevance in labour markets and wage flexibility is not necessarily a remedy for unemployment.

Finally, Rothschild convinced his students to regard economics as an instrument which should *ultimately* be socially relevant and not just *l'art pour l'art*, and he reminds us that economics, or rather political economy, is both a *social science* and a *positive science* (Rothschild, 1989). It is therefore acceptable neither that economics fall back to a mere formal science, nor that political economy abstains from public life and discussion.

WOLFGANG BLAAS

See also:

Administered Prices; Corporate Concentration and Interdependence in Europe; Corporate Hegemony; Corporate Interdependence in the United States; Full Cost Pricing; Keynes, John Maynard; Power; Robinson, Joan.

Bibliography

Koutsoyiannis, A. (1975), *Modern Microeconomics*, London: Macmillan.
Laski, K. (1987), 'Rothschild, Kurt Wilhelm', in J. Eatwell, M. Milgate and P. Newman (eds), *The New Palgrave*, London: Macmillan.
Rothschild, K.W. (1947), 'Price Theory and Oligopoly', *Economic Journal*, **57**.
Rothschild, K.W. (1954), *The Theory of Wages*, Oxford: Blackwell.
Rothschild, K.W. (1971), *Power in Economics*, Harmondsworth: Penguin.
Rothschild, K.W. (1981), *Einführung in die Ungleichgewichtstheorie*, Berlin: Springer Verlag.
Rothschild, K.W. (1989), 'Political Economy or Economics? Some Terminological and Normative Considerations', *European Journal of Political Economy*, **5**, pp. 1–12.
Rothschild, K.W. (1990), 'Arbeitslose: Gibt's die?', in R. Buchegger, M. Hutter and B. Löderer (eds), *Ausgewählte Beiträge zu den ökonomischen und gesellschaftspolitischen Aspekten der Arbeitslosigkeit*, Marburg: Metropolis.
Rothschild, K.W. (1991), 'Glimpses of a Non-Linear Biography', *Banca Nazionale Del Lavoro*, 176, March.

Routines

Neoclassical economists see individual and organizational action as largely the consequence of optimizing choices. Institutional and evolutionary economists see action as largely the consequence of following habits or customs (Veblen, 1919), or rules of thumb (Cyert and March, 1963) or routines (Nelson and Winter, 1982) appropriate to the particular decision context. There are at least two reasons for the difference.

First, as a 'starting place' for theorizing, neoclassical economists assume that individuals and organizations have an accurate understanding of the circumstances they are in, and the options they face, and have the cognitive capabilities and the opportunity to assess the actual best action. Institutional and evolutionary economists, in contrast, stress the limits of human cognitive capabilities relative to the real-life decision problems they face, and the real time involved in thinking through any problem. The former means that human understanding of a situation tends to be at best oversimplified, and in some cases mistaken in important regards. The latter means that the amount of cognitive attention that can be given to most problems is severely limited.

Second, neoclassical economists 'back up' their starting place theory about maximizing choice by proposing that, even if individuals and organizations do not really think through their problems but actually use rules of thumb or other routines, these routines can be assumed to be optimal. There are two 'back up' arguments: (a) trial and error learning converges to an optimal choice, and (b) competitive selection eliminates those that do not learn.

Institutional and evolutionary economists see no good theoretical reason for simply assuming either of these, and much empirical evidence against the propositions.

The issue is akin to the one in biology about whether biological evolution optimizes. Biologists do acknowledge constraints and random elements that are endogenous to the evolutionary process itself, and thus that evolution is a path-dependent process, and any optima achieved local ones. Some biologists argue that the very term 'optimizing' carries the wrong connotation. At best what survives is viable and at that only in the context of prevailing ecology. The question, then, of why prevailing species, or routines, are what they are thus needs an explicit historical accounting, paying attention to the forces that have shaped them over time. This theoretical position is basic to institutional and evolutionary economists.

An important implication is that the only way to understand behaviour, to the extent that it is routine-driven, is by identifying the operant routines. One cannot deduce or rationalize them from any simple model, although one may be able to deduce some of the qualitative properties they must have if they are to be viable. This is a heavy research agenda. It only makes sense if it can be argued that routines have a certain element of stability to them. Why would this be the case? There are several reasons. First, routines (as contrasted with more or less random behaviour, or highly deliberative behaviour) tend to come into existence when certain ways of doing things consistently give results that are at least satisfactory, in the sense of not triggering conscious cognitive problem solving to find something better to be doing. That is, the existence of routines implies that they are 'satisficing' if not 'maximizing'.

Second, when routines do 'satisfice', behaviour according to routine can become a conscious target, with deviations leading to attempts to get back to the routine. In organizations like business firms where people come and go, and this will be the context assumed in the rest of this account, new people are taught the routines appropriate for particular circumstances. It is the routines that characterize 'how we do it'. Problems with operations can usually be ascribed to deviation from routines. In such a multi-person context, the routines also define what 'everybody has agreed to do' and have the character, therefore, of an implicit (sometimes explicit) contract, and may require renegotiation if they are to be changed.

Also there are strong forces pressing for standardization of certain types of routines across organizations employing them. This facilitates the carrying of learned skills relevant to a particular routine from one organization to another. It also serves to make expectations and norms similar across organizations where the members of each can compare theirs with those of others. And there are extra pressures for standardization regarding what might be

called 'interface' routines, those that govern the interaction of an organization with its customers, suppliers and other external parties. Standard 'interface' routines greatly reduce transaction costs (see Williamson, 1985).

Thus, while many routines are organization-specific, many are common
across organizations, defining the way a particular kind of activity is performed in the society at large. It is the widespread generally accepted routines that are often called 'institutions' (Hodgson, 1988). An observer looking at accounting offices in different firms will find considerable standardization regarding just how accounting is done. Boards of directors of large
corporations do similar things in similar ways. The admissions offices of
virtually all Ivy League universities and colleges operate pretty much the
same way. Most universities and colleges in the United States begin the
academic year in late August or early September, and go through until mid-
May or early June. As I suggest above, some routines have the force of an
implicit contract: some are codified in contracts; some carry the force of law,
as various regulations, and forms one must fill in and other procedures one
must go through in order to be eligible for unemployment compensation;
most do not, but none the less have stability for the reasons discussed above.

Routines do not operate alone but in a system. At any time particular
routines tend to be supported by a set of others. Thus, in his *Theory of
Economic Development* (1934), Schumpeter describes a 'circular flow of
economic activity', with each actor (firm) doing its customary thing, and
being supported by the complementary customary actions of others (suppliers and demanders) so as to make the whole system mesh. In a well working
organization, such as a firm or a university, the various routines need to
mesh, although, as any perceptive observer knows, some may be at odds
with others. In an economy, routines of interacting organizations need to
mesh. This meshing of routines is another reason for their stability. But
customs and standards and routines are not stable forever. Almost all change
over time as conditions change and require some adaptation, as a result of
successful innovations that lure others to follow in the change, and because
of random drift. It is apparent that different kinds of routines evolve with
different speeds and in very different ways.

As noted, some routines are mandated and enforced by law, and cannot
change much unless the law changes. At the same time, changes in law, for
example, a sharp tightening of environmental regulatory constraints, can
force an across-the-board rapid change in routines. In other cases one sees
changes in routines in response to problems or challenges, as in the US
motor industry today in the face of challenges from the Japanese. This
example illustrates several things. First, routine changes in one organization
are often in the nature of mimicking the perceived practices of more successful ones. Second, complex organizational routines may be very difficult to

imitate, in part because it may not be clear what is essential about the routines and what is peripheral; the American companies are struggling to find out. Third, while once an effective new routine comes into existence in one organization it may be the object of emulation by others, it may have come into existence under special circumstances in the first place. It would appear that many of the 'routines' that are now argued to lie behind the greater efficiency and quality of Japanese motor car production were originally put in place for reasons that were quite particular to the Japanese scene, and that many of their advantages were not anticipated.

Perhaps the most rapid and continuing changes in routines are in those associated with particular technologies which are themselves changing rapidly. Thus the advent of the modern computer has revolutionized parts of the accounting routine. However, more generally it can be argued that technical advance is today the most important force driving changes in routines, by far. Some of the changes are directly tied to new technologies that replace older ones. Thus the way one produces semiconductors is totally different from the way the older vacuum tubes were produced. Powerful computers based on semiconductors have changed the nature of the 'routines' involved in the design of products and their production: CAD, CAM. On the other hand, new technology may lend advantages to certain pre-existing routines and disadvantage others. The opportunities opened by computers for flexible manufacturing turned out to lend special advantages to other routines that had been adopted by Japanese motor companies, and to disadvantage those associated with American mass production.

Thus the analysis of the way routines change is complex, in large part because they do not stand as independent entities but as part of systems and, further, may often be parts of several. Understanding how they fit together and how they coevolve is much of what lies at the heart of institutional and evolutionary economics.

RICHARD R. NELSON

See also:

Evolution and Optimality; Habits; Institutions; Nelson, Richard R.; Rational Actor Models; Rationality and Maximization; Rules; Technology, Theory of; Winter, Sidney G., Jr.

Bibliography

Cyert, R. and J. March (1963), *A Behavioral Theory of the Firm*, Englewood Cliffs, NJ: Prentice-Hall.

Hodgson, G. (1988), *Economics and Institutions: A Manifesto for Modern Institutional Economics*, Cambridge: Polity.

Nelson, R. and S. Winter (1982), *An Evolutionary Theory of Economic Change*, Cambridge, Mass.: Harvard University Press.

Schumpeter, J. (1934), *The Theory of Economic Development*, Cambridge, Mass.: Harvard University Press.

Veblen, T. (1919), *The Place of Science in Modern Civilisation and Other Essays*, New York: Huebsch.
Williamson, O. (1985), *The Institutions of Modern Capitalism*, New York; Free Press.

Rules

Introduction
How can we explain the administration of postal service or refuse collection by the state when productivity would be greater if such services were privatized? Why would a society outlaw the trade in human organs, babies or sexual services which apparently decreases the welfare of the consenting adults? Why would certain constraints on property rights and predatory public finance persist in a society when they are proved to be sub-optimal? In a similar fashion, why are treaties and codes of honesty ignored, to the long-term detriment of the organization of production?

At the risk of oversimplification, social scientists have offered two broad answers for the persistence of inefficient rules. The first, associated with old institutional economists (OIE) who are inspired by Thorstein Veblen, such as Geoffrey Hodgson (1989), maintains that there are moral principles, ideological commitments and sociocultural norms which are *not* devised, to start with, to attain greater efficiency. Rather, OIE contends, norms and principles are part of the moral fabric of social cohesion and, hence, outside the scope of allocative efficiency. This thesis is focused on here. As a corollary to this thesis, individual tastes – contrary to the reductionist postulate of methodological individualism – are to a great extent shaped by enculturation and socialization processes (see Hodgson, 1988, ch.3). This aspect of the debate is ignored here.

The second answer, associated with new institutional economists (NIE), such as Ronald Coase and Oliver Williamson, holds that there are hidden reasons which, after all show that inefficient rules are efficient or optimal. As put by an advocate of NIE, Thrainn Eggertsson who, along with Douglass North (1990), champions a moderate version close to OIE, there is a clear strategy, consisting of three steps, to explain rules in terms of efficiency:

> First, it is assumed as a *working rule* that low-cost organizations tend to supersede high-cost ones ...
> Second, when high-cost organizations appear to persist and it seems that reorganization would increase net output, we search for hidden benefits at unexpected margins. Such offsetting benefits may involve a reduction in supervision costs or an increase in output in a related activity when a nexus of contracts ties several activities, or a host of other factors. ... Finally, if the search for hidden benefits ... is in vain, we search for political constraints that block the rearrangement of property rights. It is recognized that the polity may not adopt output-

maximizing property rights if the new structure might cause *distributional losses* for those who control the state. And, according to Neoinstitutional Economics, high (transaction) costs of collective action are the principal reason why the members of a community cannot agree on new rules that would increase the community's aggregate output. (Eggertsson, 1990, pp. 213–14)

That is, economists should look at the high cost of collective action (as a result of free-riding), rather than exogenous cultural norms or ideological commitments, in order to explain the persistence of sub-optimal rules. In this sense, NIE is an extension of the neoclassical hard core, rather than a revolutionary research programme, as some presume.

What does 'rules' denote?
There is a more fruitful way to think about rules than exclusively as either shorthand for efficiency or moral dicta. To start with, however, the term 'rules' has become ambiguous. It has been employed to denote everything other than Walrasian exchange. It has been used loosely, along with 'transaction cost', with regard to institutions, organization of production, firms, games constrained by rules, structures of incentives, standards (conventions) of weights and measures, uniform medium of exchange (money), ideology, cultural norms, informal constraints, formal restrictions, political order, family structure, constitutions, political parties, the state and its organs, rules of election, habits, customs concerning fairness, regulations of industry, consumer safety standards, property rights, enforcement tactics, contracts, legal framework, trust, reputation, moral principles and probably other things.

In order to clear up somewhat the terminological mess, a taxonomy of the questions involved might help. The word 'canons' might help in serving as the broadest possible term. As Table 1 shows, there are two axes with regard to differentiating canons. Following John Rawls's (1955) distinction between binding and non-binding canons, the horizontal axis is concerned with formality. Following Ronald Dworkin's (1977, pp. 43–9; 1972) delineation between rules and principles, the vertical axis focuses on rationality. In practice, it is usually difficult to draw a clear line dividing formal and informal canons. However, it is important to differentiate between the two. To start with, the question of formality has usually been framed by the supposed binary opposition between state-sanctioned (formal) laws and spontaneously generated (informal) customs. Such a distinction is the gist of the work of Friedrich Hayek (1967), especially with reference to his notion of 'spontaneous order'. Such order is presumably the result of the multitude of economic exchanges constrained by evolved universal rules of conduct as opposed to state-designed rules. That is, the state is not ultimately viewed as part of the evolutionary process, but rather as antithetical to it. This implies that prohibitions against theft, free-riding and breach of contracts are formal

Table 1   The nomenclature of canons

		Formality	
		Formal	*Informal*
	Principles	Binding duty, Commitments, Justice, Property rights	Prudence, Beneficence, Kindness, Customary/moral obligations
Rationality			
	Rules	Voting method, Traffic rules, Deadlines, Conventions of measure	Etiquette, Courtesy, Propriety, Taste in consumption

in so far as they are enforced by the state, which holds the monopoly over the dispensation of force. This would imply that stateless societies have no formal canons against theft and murder; the prohibitions against such acts fall within the same category as other spontaneously engendered customs.

To correct such failing, formal canons should be considered obligations and prohibitions whose violation invites imprisonment or ostracism in *any* kind of society. That is, for canons to be considered formal, they need not presuppose the state. One could view the canons which, for example, prohibit overfishing in a tribal lake as the embryonic form of modern state licences. The tribe and the state are political communities which attempt formally (that is, strictly) to prevent the overuse of a common resource. In contrast, informal canons constitute non-binding limitations on actions which would ease social life and make it more pleasant. The violation of informal canons does not invite punishment, but, at worst, disapproval. Stated differently, while informal canons are usually obligatory, they are not binding like formal ones. Informal canons are obligatory only in a moral sense or in the light of propriety and good taste. While most formal canons also reflect informal restrictions, most informal restrictions do not become formal. This means that formal canons derive their legitimacy from much wider customary attitudes and general public opinions. However, it is possible for formal canons, as under a revolutionary regime, to reach beyond what is informal and successfully steer society into a new constitution.

While every society has a different definition of the line dividing formal from informal canons, it nonetheless recognizes the difference. In section four, part seven of *The Theory of Moral Sentiments*, Adam Smith criticizes medieval, casuistic moralists for treating, what he considers, informal virtues as strict, formal canons of justice – as if all canons are commands. In the text, Smith does not reject the distinction; he only wants to draw it elsewhere. Following Kant's distinction between hypothetical and categorical imperatives, philosophers, who might as well subscribe to deontology in ethical theory, generally make the distinction between norms concerning etiquette and kindness, on the one hand, and moral prohibitions and obligations, on the other. In this sense, the Ten Commandments and criminal law fall within the formal category.

While the formality dimension is important, more attention is given here to the vertical axis of Table 1, the rationality question. Following Max Weber, there is a difference between canons as rules or means of efficiency and canons as principles or goals. Principles express deep or, to borrow Amartya Sen's lexicon, higher-order tastes, such as freedom of speech, right to choose, right to life, privacy, right to a job, the wrongness of benefiting from one's crime, and so on. Dworkin (1977, pp. 43–4) identifies the category 'policies' as a subspecies of principles; that is, policies amount to intermediate goals which could be practically pursued. To translate the distinction into economics, at the level of the firm, a policy could be the pursuit of profit or community service. At the level of the agent, a policy could be the pursuit of fame, knowledge or higher pecuniary utility. While Dworkin's distinction between principles and policies is useful, it is not observed here because they are part of the same species. Nor do we observe H.L.A. Hart's (1961) distinction between 'primary' and 'secondary' principles. They correspond, respectively, to *substantive* views about the good society and *procedural* canons (such as democratic processes or dictates by the representatives of God's will) which provide legitimacy to substantive principles (see Khalil, 1989, pp. 43–4).

In order to distinguish between principles or policies of various kinds, on the one hand, and rules, on the other, one needs to identify the range of restrictions which they impose. While rules reduce one's budget constraint, principles articulate one's tastes and valued pursuits, ranging from honesty, beneficence, price and commitment, to clothes and leisure. Classroom lectures, for example, have rules about the deadline and style of papers, schedule of meetings, methods of asking questions and so on. None of these rules provide a *raison d'être* for having education and, hence, the rules restrain students only from actions they *can already do*. What is needed in order to explain the organization is the set of principles on excellence in the acquisition of knowledge and skills. Such principles articulate the goals of action and, hence, motivate students to act in ways *they otherwise could not have done*. Likewise, team spirit or clear property rights as to the distribution of pecuniary rewards help the crystallization of motivation which acts as the spring of novel behaviour.

The difference between rules and principles was noted, without using the terminology employed here, in the core parts of Smith's *The Theory of Moral Sentiments* (Khalil, 1990). In part one, Smith discussed one type of judgement concerning the propriety of, for example, a degree of crying, given the occasion. This kind of judgement, for Smith, is different from the evaluation of the merit or demerit of human conduct, which he discussed in the second part of the book. The question of merit deals with formal principles like justice and informal principles like prudence and beneficence.

In short, given the two axes, we have at hand four major types of canons: formal principles, informal principles, formal rules and informal rules. The classification might help us clarify the difference between OIE and NIE. But first we need to examine whether moderate NIE has been successful in solving the anomalies facing orthodox NIE.

Orthodox new institutionalism

An eloquent exposition of orthodox NIE is the work of Nicholas Rowe (1989; see also Ault and Ekelund, 1988). Rowe carefully attempts to explain, within the neoclassical framework, non-optimizing behaviour: why would a person who was cheated in a contract undertake the cost of vindication even when the cost is greater than the restored gain? Why does an agent pay back a loan, even when it is most advantageous not to honour the promise? Fear of law enforcement is not an answer since, according to Rowe, we are trying to explain why law enforcement – a canon itself – exists in the first place. Furthermore, using law enforcement as the explanation is close to functionalism because the existence of such a rule would be taking an institution's efficiency (function) as the reason for its existence. The task, according to Rowe, is to provide an *endogenous* account of canons, rather than treat them as exogenously imposed constraints on games, as Robert Axelrod does.

According to Rowe, non-maximizing practices would remain problematic if neoclassical analysis continued to view each act as isolated from other acts. In fact, acts are interrelated, since an agent is continuously interacting with a community of agents over time in repeated transactions. If an agent failed to keep a promise, he or she would tarnish his or her reputation, and an agent with a blemished reputation would have more difficulty or incur greater cost entering future transactions. Therefore, as put by Rowe, rational agents do not maximize returns at each instant. Rather, they constrain their behaviour with rules in order to convey to other actors that they are trustworthy. Such rules are not physical constraints, such as the endowment of beer and apples given prior to exchange, but are rather social constraints which arise spontaneously among agents involved in exchange. Rules such as the observance of property rights and the carrying out of responsibilities make no sense in a Robinson Crusoe economy. In this manner, one does not need to abandon methodological individualism, according to Rowe. The agent follows an apparently non-optimum rule in order to influence the expectations of others as to his or her future behaviour. Thus principles of honesty and commitment are optimum rules of efficiency. They are not, in the final analysis, the outcome of public spirit, conscience or self-respect.

The instrumental view of reputation may explain expenditures on good will. The cost of advertisement and investment in brand-names, what Williamson calls 'hostages', are ways by which the seller assures the buyer that it is not worthwhile to cheat him and sell him a 'lemon' (see Eggertsson, 1990, pp. 195–203). High commitment costs or hostages are noticed when information about the quality of the product is not free at the point of purchase; that is, as put by George Akerlof, when information is asymmetrical. The asymmetry is solved when the buyer realizes that the cost of hostages exceeds the momentary benefit of cheating.

Moderate new institutionalism
The attractive feature of orthodox NIE is its ability to provide an endogenous account of rules. However, the persistence of rules beyond their supposed economic usefulness is anomalous for orthodox NIE. For example, one could point at many inefficient arrangements of property rights in history which failed, contrary to Harold Demsetz's (1967) theory, to internalize externalities and hence encourage investment. In this regard, the University of Washington perspective – a term suggested by North (1990, p. 27n) to distance it from Williamson's approach – generally views Demsetz's theory of property rights as naive (Eggertsson, 1990, pp. 249–62). It does not take into account the asymmetry between the special interest groups and the public with regard to the cost and benefit of changing the regime of property rights. Furthermore, the initiation of a collective action to change inefficient property rights is expensive because of free-riding. In addition, following Brian Arthur's (1988) work, North argues that such a transaction cost increases over time because of the path dependency of regimes of property rights. That is, regimes become entrenched and inertial because of 'increasing returns'. Thus North and his colleagues at the University of Washington take a moderate NIE position and accept that, in the light of limited cognitive processes, inefficient rules and property rights could persist (see Khalil, 1992).

Apart from brief caveats (for example, North, 1990, pp. 8–9), there are three major problems with North's moderate NIE agenda. First, while such explanations may account for the delay of change, they cannot account for the long persistence of inefficient institutions. North and Eggertsson recognize this failing and try to correct it by recognizing the pertinence of ideological and cultural norms. This makes them come close to OIE. However, the OIE agenda provides an account of the persistence of canons which flows consistently from its vision of human action as embedded within sociocultural processes. To elaborate, Veblen's emphasis on prestige and conspicuous behaviour provides a good reason why, for example, a small country in the South Pacific insists on subsidizing its bankrupt airlines or refuses to enter into a monetary union with its neighbours. OIE have pointed out that such persistence is not only the result of costly switching to more efficient practices, but also ultimately of people deriving pride and identity from such constraints. Another example, the resistance of the Japanese government to the demolition of trade obstacles against the importation of rice, which is six times cheaper in the world market, could be explained better within the OIE framework. Rice in the Japanese culture has enormous religious and national value: it symbolizes independence and communal cohesion; but it is possible to attribute the legal rules restricting the importation of rice to the pressure of special interest groups. However, and this would be an empirical issue, the Japanese public might favour the legal rules in order to guard itself against the temptation or counter-preferential choice of individuals to buy the cheaper, imported rice. While North and Eggertsson are ready to appeal to values such as national identity and pride, the appeal is abrupt; that is, it does not flow smoothly from the neoclassical hard core. But their appeal might build a bridge between OIE and NIE because there is a need to go beyond Veblen and provide an endogenous theory, based on modern cognitive psychology, of prestige, identity, pride, sociocultural processes and so on.

Second, moderate NIE cannot deal successfully with cases, such as the Anglo-American tradition of property rights, when collective action succeeds in overcoming inefficient regimes. North resorts, in an ad hoc fashion, to the ideology of the separation of powers to explain why Britain was able to break away from the self-perpetuation cycle of predatory public finance. In contrast, according to North, such pro-efficiency ideological fervour failed to take root in Spain to loosen the grip of the absolute monarch.

Third, it amounts to a 'reification of regimes' to think that economic growth is the result of a 'correct' set-up of property rights. A good illustration of such reification is James Buchanan's (1991) advocacy of strict constitutional rules against deficit spending. Buchanan thinks that the passage of such rules ensures that rent-seeking behaviour will be stabilized in the post-constitutional game of self-pursuits. Likewise, North thinks that the instituting in the seventeenth century of a secure regime of property rights in Britain, as opposed to Spain, is mostly responsible for the divergence of the British–North American and the Spanish–Latin American developments. This neglects the fact that the Spanish were very successful in driving out the Moors in the fifteenth century, that there was economic expansion in the sixteenth century and the continuation of the empire in Latin America in the following two centuries. Also the 'correct' British–North American regime of property rights has not secured a lasting superiority for the British or, as we witness today, the US economy.

As admitted by Eggertsson, actual or operational behaviour is not necessarily guaranteed to be cooperative once we have erected the correct regime of constraints. Evidence shows that 'similar rules can create different behaviour and outcomes' (Eggertsson, 1990, p. 310). What seems fundamentally important is not only the erection of the correct regime of property rights, but also the prevalence of high regard for trustworthy conduct at every level of interaction. Otherwise, an efficient regime would not be able to help economic growth withstand stagnation and collapse.

In short, apart from resorting to ad hoc reasoning, moderate NIE cannot explain why efficient regimes break down, any more than why inefficient ones persist. A good explanation demands the articulation of an endogenous theory of principles and ideology to match the endogenous theory of rules offered by NIE. So far, however, as recognized by Eggertsson (1990), 'NIE does not have a workable theory of ideology'.

Reconciling new and old institutionalism
The rule/principle distinction suggested earlier may offer a way out of North's appeal to ad hoc auxiliary statements in order to salvage NIE. To achieve this, a rational reconstruction of the differences between NIE and OIE is needed. OIE maintains that principles do not lower the budget constraint in order to achieve greater efficiency. They are not adopted, to start with, in order to maximize returns in the long run. Principles are not shorthand for minimum risk and transaction cost. Rather, principles are part of the preference set. That is, the observance of contractual commitments, trustworthy behaviour and the pursuit of self-respect are values in themselves. Thus the persistence of principles in the face of price change is not anomalous for the OIE framework. However, OIE is weak when it comes to providing an endogenous theory of the origin of such principles and why they change.

In contrast, the offering of an endogenous theory of the origin and change of principles is fundamental to the NIE framework. This is the mark of the transaction cost approach. However, in the process, NIE treats principles as mere rules which lower the budget constraint in order to maximize non-myopic returns. Given such treatment, NIE is baffled when it comes to providing an endogenous theory of the persistence of inefficient principles and regimes of property rights in the face of new circumstances.

If one may simplify, the weakness of each institutional camp is the strength of the other. North's solution has been to incorporate in an unsystematic fashion many of the theses and insights of OIE in the light of the fact that NIE faces enormous difficulties when confronted with history. A more fruitful way could be found by starting afresh with a cognitive theory of the self and its psychological parameters. It seems that agents are predisposed to transform rules, designed originally to minimize transaction cost, into moral values, principles and ideological convictions. What start as optimum rules of efficiency and pragmatic legal canons of contingent character become, over time, part of the set of moral values justified on the ground of what seem intrinsic, inalienable natural rights.

Jack Hirshleifer, in his evolutionary theory of law, maintains that moral values such as privacy and cooperation, which originated from efficiency consideration, have become part of the 'hard-wiring' of our genetic make-up. A good example is the evolution of sex. While it evolved, inter alia, to enhance the ability of organisms to resist diseases, it is pursued even by sterile organisms for its own sake, that is abstracted from its function. Likewise, moral canons, such as respect for life or love of liberty, probably originated in functional/efficient considerations. Thus they are not natural in the sense of residing in some immutable Platonian realm or revealed to man by a deity. But neither are they ephemeral or contingent, as orthodox neoclassical economists and positivist legal theorists, such as Richard Posner, stipulate.

Stated differently, rules tend to outlive their original function and become principles of action. This is the case because they become, through the process of habituation, part of one's identity and even part of the biological repertoire. In such cases, we have vestigial customs or what the anthropologist E.B. Tylor calls 'survivals': the loss of function, but the persistence of the underlying framework – equivalent to what biologists call 'structure' or the underpinning anatomy. The structure/function rift means that rules start acting as principles of motivation and policies to be pursued; they become symbols of power, honour and even the meaning of life. For example, a national currency which replaced local currencies in the infancy of capitalism has certainly allowed, through the lowering of transaction cost, the capturing of greater benefits of trade. However, a country might refuse to surrender its currency for a greater union, which defies the stipulation of NIE, because the national currency has become a principle which inculcates a taste for nationalism. Thus the adherence to national currency persists not simply because of the cost of switching. The rule itself has become part of the set of tastes and principles.

The relationship between rules of efficiency and principles of tastes is symbiotic enough to complicate standard economic reasoning. For example, a professor may decide to work for university X rather than university Y because of the total package of benefits. However, the choice engenders a by-product, commitment, which prevents him or her from moving to a more attractive university located in the same vicinity. While such a commitment is not at the same level as the pecuniary benefits, it is still a taste which one might eventually give up if the attractive alternative is too intense to handle.

Conclusion
Given the precursory proposal of reconciliation, there still remains a major philosophical difference between OIE and NIE. Advocates of NIE may agree with the promoters of OIE that there might remain a residual resistance to changing behaviour in the light of new circumstances which cannot be explained by transaction cost or any of its derivatives. Promoters of OIE argue that such quasi-inflexibility arises because agents are more or less set in their ways, that is, semi-prisoners of habits and customs. In contrast, advocates of NIE explain it as the result of the taste for risk aversion. On the surface, the difference between risk aversion and being a prisoner of habits amounts to a linguistic one, but, at a deeper level, the division is along the rift which divides behaviourism and neoclassical economics from what Richard Day (1975) calls 'existentialist' economics. Each camp provides a different answer to whether action consists only of revealed preferences in the fashion of behavioural psychology or whether it is also underpinned by a deeper, underlying personality who, in Herbert Simon's words, is concerned with 'satisficing' and involved in 'bounded rationality'.

Armed with the concept of 'social norms', Jon Elster (1989, p. 99) confuses the existential/behavioural question with the one we ignored at the outset: whether individual tastes are the outcome of the deliberation of 'a self-contained, asocial atom' or are a 'mindless plaything of social forces'. Furthermore, the existential/behavioural question is distinct from the question whether pride, shame, commitment and moral principles are commensurable with pecuniary benefits. The existential/behavioural question, which is the playground of phenomenological sociology as practised by Alfred Schutz and other followers of Edmund Husserl, asks whether humans stand outside life and reexamine – as long as transaction costs allow – the totality of their consumption set in the light of changes of circumstances, or whether they are part of the natural world, and hence *experience* life from their particular matrix of space and time. Martin Heidegger calls such experience 'enframing', that is, the formation of personality through the process of everyday life. For example, the preference for a particular software for word-processing depends greatly on the software with which the person was initiated. Such a phenomenon, also widespread among animals, is called by ethologists 'imprinting' – the tendency to prefer what one experienced first. Psychologists identify the same tendency and call it the 'primacy effect'. These traditions dispute the behaviourist view of human personality. They argue that it is not shallow and given by stimuli, as B.F. Skinner argues, but rather is deep and experiential.

The point of contention has a long history and has caused a deep rift in philosophy, dividing realists (sometimes called universalists or essentialists) and nominalists. Apart from important differences in outlook and detail, realists from Plato to Aristotle and Husserl believed that there are deep essences which regulate surface phenomena. In contrast, nominalists from Hobbes to Hume and Skinner believed that culture and other supposed deep essences are just names (*nomina*). Thus, whatever likeliness exists among particular agents, or among traits within the same agent, could be explained in the manner of superficial resemblance theory. This conviction is based on the thesis that the appeal to deep essences would be 'non-scientific'. To put it tersely, the current struggle between old and new institutional economics is another battle between realism and nominalism.

ELIAS L. KHALIL

See also:
Cooperation, The Evolution of; Culture; Habits; Institutionalism, 'Old' and 'New'; Methodological Individualism; North, Douglass C.; Property; Realism, Philosophical; Routines; Spontaneous Order; Trust; Williamson, Oliver E.

Bibliography

Arthur, W. Brian (1988), 'Self-Reinforcing Mechanisms in Economics', in Philip W. Anderson, Kenneth J. Arrow and David Pines (eds), *The Economy as an Evolving Complex System*, pp. 9–31, Redwood City, CA: Addison-Wesley.
Ault, Richard, W. and Robert B. Ekelund (1988), 'Habits in Economic Analysis: Veblen and the Neoclassicals', *History of Political Economy*, **20**, (3), Fall, pp. 431–45.
Buchanan, James (1991), *The Economics and the Ethics of Constitutional Order*, Ann Arbor: University of Michigan Press.
Day, Richard H. (1975), 'Orthodox Economists and Existential Economics', *Journal of Economic Issues*, **IX**, (2), June, pp. 229–35.
Demsetz, Harold (1967), 'Towards a Theory of Property Rights', *American Economic Review*, **62**, pp. 347–59.
Dworkin, Ronald M. (1972), 'Social Rules and Legal Theory', *Yale Law Journal*, **81**, pp. 855–90.
Dworkin, Ronald M. (1977), 'Is Law a System of Rules?' in R.M. Dworkin (ed.), *The Philosophy of Law*, Oxford: Oxford University Press.
Eggertsson, Thrainn (1990), *Economic Behaviour and Institutions*, Cambridge: Cambridge University Press.
Elster, Jon (1989), 'Social Norms and Economic Theory', *Journal of Economic Perspectives*, **3**, (4), Fall, pp. 99–117.
Hart, H.L.A. (1961), *The Concept of Law*, Oxford: Oxford University Press.

Hayek, F.A. (1967), 'Notes on the Evolution of Systems of Rules of Conduct: The Interplay between Rules of Individual Conduct and the Social Order of Actions', *Studies in Philosophy, Politics, and Economics*, pp. 66–81, Chicago: University of Chicago Press.

Hodgson, Geoffrey M. (1988), *Economics and Institutions: A Manifesto for Modern Institutional Economics*, Cambridge: Polity and Philadelphia: University of Pennsylvania Press.

Hodgson, Geoffrey M. (1989), 'Institutional Economic Theory: The Old versus the New', *Review of Political Economy*, **1**, (3), November, pp. 249–69.

Khalil, Elias L. (1989), 'Principles, Rules and Ideology', *Forum for Social Economics*, **18**, (2)/**19**, (1), Spring/Fall, pp. 41–54.

Khalil, Elias L. (1990), 'Beyond Self-Interest and Altruism: A Reconstruction of Adam Smith's Theory of Human Conduct', *Economics and Philosophy*, **6**, (2), October, pp. 255–73.

Khalil, Elias L. (1992), 'Between Culture and Efficient Rationality: A Review of Douglass C. North's *Institutions, Institutional Change and Economic Performance*', *Journal of Evolutionary Economics*, **2**, (4).

North, Douglass C. (1990), *Institutions, Institutional Change and Economic Performance*, Cambridge: Cambridge University Press.

Rawls, John (1955), 'Two Concepts of Rules', *Philosophical Review*, **69**, pp. 3–32.

Rowe, Nicholas (1989), *Rules and Institutions*, Ann Arbor: The University of Michigan Press.

Sahlins, Marshall

The early work of the economic anthropologist, Marshall Sahlins (born 1930, PhD Columbia University, 1954) was an attempt to restore interest in an evolutionary perspective in anthropology. When anthropologists abandoned the task of classifying cultures in a simple and linear evolutionary scheme in favour of description of the particular, interest in cultural evolution fell into disfavour. A purpose of all of Sahlins's work has been to combine knowledge of the specific adaptations of cultures with a revived focus on the general evolution of which these specific adaptations are part.

For Sahlins, interest in general cultural evolution was combined with a strong commitment to empiricism and a specific interest in comparing economies across time and space, and it is this latter task that has dominated his work since the 1970s. This combination of interests and method has led, in turn, to his rejection of several key elements of an implicit scheme of general economics that has long been part of economic thought and of popular understanding as well. The most striking of his rejections is the notion that primitive (paleolithic) humans were barely able to eke out a living from niggardly nature. In the standard view, human wants have always exceeded means, especially for our ancestors who, armed only with stone tools, had to work so hard to feed themselves that they were unable to find time or 'surplus' production to create cultural niceties. Only as tools improved and specialization occurred did mankind become capable of enough 'leisure' and sufficient 'surplus' to begin building cultures. And, the story continues, our plight today remains the same: the struggle to produce enough to satisfy unlimited wants continues, as does progress towards larger output. The evolutionary chain is unbroken.

The anthropological record tells a different story. Sahlins found that accounts of hunting and gathering economies that have survived into modern times show that these people – working with traditional tools – have substantial leisure time. Indeed, they feed themselves by working four to five hours a day. Their diets are often quite good and varied. What observers have often taken as variety brought on by near-starvation turns out to be keen appreciation of the tastiness of a wide variety of foodstuffs that modern people have never tasted, and cannot taste without a revulsion that is a product of their culture. Sahlins is aware that it may not be legitimate to draw conclusions about our stone-age ancestors from observations of modern remnants of paleolithic cultures; the modern ethnographies of hunters and gatherers are, he reminds us, records of 'incomplete cultures'. However, the fact remains that the subsistence problem is solved easily by these people, using stone-age tools in much less hospitable environments than those that stone-age people inhabited millennia ago.

The key to the paradox that stone-age people may have enjoyed the 'original affluent society' is that their material wants were limited. Successful hunting and gathering meant frequent moves and material possessions for nomadic people did not therefore constitute wealth. Even when given the opportunity, modern nomads do not want goods that we prize highly and, given the opportunity, modern nomads reject a settled, agricultural life as 'involving too much work'.

Sahlins also found that the anthropological literature indicates substantial under-utilization of labour in most agricultural societies. He concludes that in both non-agricultural and agricultural societies production is not only low but – and this is the important point – it is low relative to existing possibilities. Not only did the wants of the earliest humans probably not exceed their capacity to produce, but for most of mankind the capacity to produce has probably exceeded production. It should be made clear that Sahlins is not arguing a romantic point that people in the past have been happier with fewer goods than we are with more, and that we should give up wanting more. He draws no conclusions about relative happiness, for the evidence is not available. Rather, his point is that the standard scheme in which systems are driven by an excess of wants over means is not supported by empirical evidence. Sahlins proposes instead that the key to understanding economies and their evolution is to understand social and political relations; the production and distribution of goods follows from patterns of sociopolitical relationships.

Sahlins also concludes that the evidence is overwhelming that wants are culturally determined, not inborn and insatiable. We would not consider eating dogs, he reminds us, but we will eat other animals with relish. But his point is more subtle as well. The fact that we can conceive of wants as being unlimited is also part of our culture. Our most fundamental conceptions of the economic problem and of human behaviour are culturally determined. These conclusions lead directly to Sahlin's concern with the relationship between 'culture and practical reason' and with conceptions of societies as agglomerations of individuals who produce culture through 'practical reason'. Sahlins argues that Marxists and many anthropologists believe that cultures can be understood as natural human reaction to nature, a proposition fundamental to bourgeois (neoclassical) economics. What we have done, he says, is to think of human social action as derived from nature but, at the same time, to conceive nature in the terms in which we understand human social action. This reinforces the belief that our behaviour is derived from nature through 'practical reason'. But empirical evidence indicates that all that we do and sense is so fundamentally mediated by culture that it is difficult to imagine how any reactions to natural conditions can be conceived as 'natural' or common to all people, and difficult to accept that we can 'see' nature except through a cultural lens.

Sahlins's work offers support for important institutionalist propositions about economies as aspects of culture, about the cultural rather than the natural nature of 'the economic problem' of unlimited wants and limited means, and about the importance of redistribution and reciprocity as socially embedded forms of economic integration. Sahlins was a member of the 'Polanyi Group' at Columbia University; he was a contributor to Polanyi's legacy to institutional economics and has been strongly influenced by that legacy. His work is also relevant to the continuing efforts to formulate an empirically sound theory of the evolution of economic systems.

ANNE MAYHEW

See also:
Culture; Evolution, Theories of Economic; Law and Economics; Polanyi, Karl.

Bibliography
Sahlins, Marshall (1972), *Stone Age Economics*, Chicago: Aldine-Atherton.
Sahlins, Marshall (1976a), *Culture and Practical Reason*, Chicago: University of Chicago Press.
Sahlins, Marshall (1976b), *The Use and Abuse of Biology*, Ann Arbor: University of Michigan Press.
Sahlins, Marshall and Elman R. Service (eds) (1960), *Evolution and Culture*, Ann Arbor: University of Michigan Press.

Schotter, Andrew

Andrew Schotter was born in 1947 in the USA. He has reached prominence on the basis of one major work: *The Economic Theory of Social Institutions* (1981). Although this is generally regarded as part of the so-called 'new institutional economics', it has a number of features which demarcate it from the work of others of that genre. Schotter (1981, p. 5) claims to be influenced by the account of the emergence of money and social institutions in the economics of Carl Menger. Taking a cue from Edna Ullmann-Margalit's (1977) use of mathematical game theory to analyse the emergence of norms, Schotter attains high standards of rigour, clarity and elegance. His work differs from that of other game theorists such as Martin Shubik (1982) who takes rules as fixed. Instead, Schotter sees rules as solutions to repeated games. Furthermore, Schotter develops a forceful and innovative critique of 'free market' economics, unlike the conservative and apologetic flavour of much 'new institutionalism'.

However, in at least two respects, Schotter shares common presuppositions with other 'new institutional'; economists. First, as in all game-theoretic models, the abstract individual, attempting to optimize with given preferences, is retained. Second, Schotter adopts the 'new institutionalist' project to attempt to explain the existence of political, legal, or more generally social, institutions by reference to a model of individual behaviour, tracing out the unintended consequences in terms of human interactions. In Schotter's models, agents have the choice of different strategies to obtain the maximum payoff. The conception of the agent is still that of maximizing 'economic man': the only slight difference is that there is not necessarily a single, determined outcome. Agents maximize, but they may, for example, mix strategies randomly in certain proportions as they seek to optimize.

Schotter's argument is based on games that are played over and over again. It is argued that, as the games 'are repeatedly played, the players develop certain societally agreed to rules of thumb, norms, conventions and institutions which are passed on to succeeding generations of players' (Schotter, 1981, p. 12). Within this framework, Schotter shows that institutions and routines – far from being market 'imperfections' – are actually necessary to supply vital information, particularly about the future stratagems of other actors, upon which agents can develop expectations regarding the future. In contrast, if action was unstructured and completely fluid, it would be much more difficult to form such expectations. The orthodox model of price adjustment under perfect competition is a case in point. In this ideal case, information is signalled principally through the price system. In contrast, with market restrictions and 'imperfections', much more information is transmitted, and other than through price. The web of institutions within and around the market-place serve as 'mechanisms that supply information about the potential actions of other economic agents' (Schotter, 1981, p. 157).

Consequently, the rigidities in a market system should not be treated as a restrictive assumption to be imposed upon a 'more general' model. Institutions and routines are actually necessary to supply vital information, particularly about the future stratagems of other agents. 'Perfect competition' does not signal this information other than through the restrictive mechanism of the price system. 'Imperfect' markets enable much more information to be transmitted, and other than through price: 'economies contain an information network far richer than that described by the price system. This network is made up of a whole complex of institutions, rules of thumb, customs and beliefs that help to transfer a great deal of information about the anticipated actions of agents in the economy' (Schotter, 1981, p. 118).

Hence rigidities are not a 'special case'. These so-called 'imperfections' help to impose coherence and order on the market system. Markets function coherently *because of* these 'imperfections', and not *despite them*, as mainstream theorists presume. However, Schotter does not refer to other theorists such as G.B. Richardson (1959) who have reached a similar conclusion.

In a later work, Schotter (1990) highlights the important policy conclusions of his theory, in terms of a critique of the 'free market' economics of the New Right. Clearly, his argument that institutions and rigid conventions are actually functional to the decision-making process, both inside and outside the market, is a counter to the New Right view that, as much as possible, all such rigidities and conventions should be dissolved. In this later (1990) work his analysis is described as an 'immanent critique' of orthodox theory, because it shares some of its basic assumptions but draws untypical conclusions. Arguably, game theory cannot serve as a wider foundation for an economic theory of social institutions, partly because of its continuing adoption of the assumptions of maximizing 'economic man'. Thus there is a tension in Schotter's work between his adoption of orthodox assumptions and his attempt to describe some of the informational functions of institutions.

For instance, despite a brief reference to bounded rationality, Schotter (1981, pp. 148–9) underlines a standard assumption of game theory that agents make use of '*all* relevant information', and nothing is ignored in the determination of their optimal strategy (1981, p. 160). However, as Herbert Simon argues, such global calculations are impossible because of the limited computational capacity of any computer or human brain. A function of institutions that is not encompassed by Schotter' model is that they facilitate actions when such global calculations are impossible. Furthermore, as G.L.S. Shackle has pointed out, game theory presents known payoffs and thereby excludes such factors as tactical surprise.

In game theory the factors influencing the formation of the individual's purposes and goals are not taken into account. Preferences are taken as given. Schotter thus considers the evolution of institutions in a non-cumulative manner. In contrast to the work of Thorstein Veblen and other 'old' institutionalists, there is no cumulative evolution by further feedback and alteration of people's preferences. In addition, Schotter's game-theoretic study of the emergence of institutions assumes the 'rules of the game' at the outset, without considering their emergence. It is thus vulnerable to Alexander Field's (1979) critique. Importantly, markets are themselves social institutions which have to be explained. In sum, we can never reach a primary, institution-free state from which explanation in the 'new institutionalist' vein can begin. The game-theoretic explanation of the emergence of institutions thus suffers from a problem of infinite regress.

In the subsequent explosion of activity in game theory, the examination of different types of games and repeated 'supergames' has shown that the very definition of the concept of rationality is problematic. As Philip Mirowski (1986, p. 257) puts it in his critique of Schotter and Shubik: 'Game theorists have opened the Pandora's Box marked "rationality", and do not know how to close it again.'

Nevertheless, despite these problems in Schotter's work, it marks an important theoretical milestone. Both its negative and its positive features should be taken into account in the development of non-neoclassical institutional economics.

GEOFFREY M. HODGSON

See also:

Cognition, Cultural and Institutional Influences on; Cooperation, The Evolution of; Cumulative Causation; Evolution, Theories of Economic; Game Theory and Institutions; Institutionalism, 'Old' and 'New'; Money, Evolution of; Richardson, George B.; Rules; Shackle, George Lennox Sharman; Simon, Herbert Alexander; Ullmann-Margalit, Edna; Veblen, Thorstein.

Bibliography

Field, A.J. (1979), 'On the Explanation of Rules Using Rational Choice Models', *Journal of Economic Issues*, **XIII**, (1), March, pp. 49–72.

Mirowski, P. (1986), 'Institutions as a Solution Concept in a Game Theory Context', in P. Mirowski (ed.), *The Reconstruction of Economic Theory*, Boston, Mass.: Kluwer-Nijhoff.

Richardson, G.B. (1959), 'Equilibrium, Expectations and Information', *The Economic Journal*, **69**, pp. 223–37.

Schotter, A. (1981), *The Economic Theory of Social Institutions*, Cambridge: Cambridge University Press.

Schotter, A. (1990), *Free Market Economics: A Critical Appraisal*, 2nd edn, Oxford: Basil Blackwell.

Shubik, M. (1982), *Game Theory in the Social Sciences*, Cambridge, Mass.: MIT.

Ullmann-Margalit, E. (1977), *The Emergence of Norms*, Oxford: Oxford University Press.

Schumacher, E.F.

Ernst Friedrich 'Fritz' Schumacher was born in 1911 into a bourgeois family in Bonn; his father was a professor of economics. He was educated at Bonn, Cambridge, Oxford and Columbia Universities, but did not take a degree. At first Schumacher worked in business in Germany and (after 1937) in England. For much of World War II he was a researcher at the Institute of Statistics in Oxford, publishing several well received papers on the application of Keynesian theory to the international economy. From 1950 until his retirement in 1970, Schumacher was employed by the National Coal Board in Britain, and wrote prolifically on energy policy, the economic development of the third world and on the liberation of work. *Small is Beautiful*, the collection of essays which appeared in 1973, became an international bestseller. Schumacher was awarded the CBE (Commander of the British Empire) in the following year. He died in September 1977.

Schumacher's hostility to orthodox economics originated in his experience at the Coal Board. As early as 1954, he was predicting a global energy shortage and he strongly opposed the rapid rundown of the British coal industry which began at the end of the decade. Economists had failed, Schumacher argued, to take seriously the crucial distinction between renewable and non-renewable goods; the discounting principles embodied in the slogan 'best seams first' were wholly inappropriate to energy production. At first his criticisms were those of a mainstream economist berating the incompetence of his colleagues, but increasingly Schumacher turned against what he came to regard as 'the prevailing dictatorship of economics' and 'the spurious verisimilitude which borders on mendacity' of econometric forecasts of energy supplies. By 1967, he had become a voluble opponent of nuclear power, on environmental and medical grounds. Instead, he advocated the development of decentralized renewable energy sources, which were safe, sustainable and conducive to the alternative life style which he now believed to be essential for human survival and sanity.

The second major influence on Schumacher's thinking came from his spells as economic adviser to the governments of Burma and India in 1955 and 1961. Attempts by poor countries to imitate the Western way of life were bound to fail, he discovered. In the long run they were doomed by insufficient energy resources; more immediately, by inadequate levels of saving and investment. The only result of this abortive emulation was economic dualism. For Schumacher the relationship between traditional and modern sectors was one of 'mutual poisoning', in which urban industry destroyed village handicrafts but also prompted an unmanageable flood of city-bound migrants from the neglected and increasingly depressed rural areas. Job creation, he argued, must be the overriding goal of economic development, with efforts concentrated in the villages and small towns. In opposition to both neoclassical and Stalinist thinking, Schumacher urged that Western production techniques be renounced in favour of 'appropriate' or 'intermediate' technology, with much lower capital–output and capital–labour ratios. This would stimulate small-scale production and promote local self-reliance. Schumacher favoured a fundamentally egalitarian development process, both for its own sake and because, by involving the great mass of the population rather than a small urban elite, it was much more likely to succeed.

His emphasis on employment was not confined to the third world. Drawing on Marxism, Buddhism, the teachings of Mahatma Gandhi and on Christian theology, Schumacher maintained that creative, fulfilling and socially useful work is a prerequisite for human self-realization. Orthodox economists treat labour merely as an input, a source of disutility, a necessary evil to be minimized; for Schumacher it is very much more than this. 'Good work' produces and reproduces healthy people, in addition to marketed output; 'bad work' degrades and stunts the human personality. It follows that conventional economic criteria for the appraisal of production techniques are wholly inadequate. Technology is not ideologically neutral; its impact on the autonomy, dignity and self-esteem of the worker is no less important than its contribution to output. Schumacher argued that modern technology is inherently repressive, as it requires an authoritarian hierarchy inside the workplace and engenders a violent and alienated society outside. Thus, in Schumacher's vision of the world, there are both natural and social limits to growth: natural, since stocks of fossil fuels are finite; social, because increasing greed and envy, and the accompanying collapse of human intelligence, render the prevailing economic system unsustainable. Small is indeed beautiful, on spiritual no less than ecological grounds.

There is no evidence that Schumacher considered himself to be part of the institutionalist tradition, and his (very numerous) followers today are drawn largely from the 'green' and Christian Socialist movements. His affinities are, however, easily identified: an unashamed eclecticism in sources of ideas and citation of authorities; a disdain for the narrowness of neoclassical analysis; a deep suspicion of formal modelling, and especially of econometric techniques; a transcending concern for the formation of preferences and the moulding of character and personality. Indeed, these very qualities have been seized on by orthodox and Marxian critics as a source of weakness, as with Wilfred Beckerman's sardonic counter-slogan, 'small is stupid', and Arghiri Emmanuel's scathing attack on 'underdeveloped technology'.

It is true that Schumacher's ideas were themselves often vague and underdeveloped, making it possible for them to be – in the words of a *Times* editorial on the day of his memorial service – 'almost dissolved into conventional wisdom'. There is some justice, too, in the charge frequently levelled by mainstream resource and environmental economists that he was simply a neoclassical economist gone to seed. A more balanced verdict would allow for the fact that neoclassical theorists came late to some of the questions which Schumacher raised, such as the dangers of economic dualism in poor countries and the legitimacy of discounting when the welfare of future generations is at stake, while they remain oblivious to others. A satisfactory theory of work, above all, will owe more to Schumacher than to the heirs of Walras, Hicks and Samuelson.

J.E. KING

See also:

Development Policy; Development Theory; Growth, Limits to; Technical Change and Technological Regimes; Technology in Development Policy; Technology, Theory of.

Bibliography

King, J.E. (1988), *Economic Exiles*, London: Macmillan, ch.10.
Schumacher, E.F. (1973), *Small is Beautiful: Economics As If People Mattered*, London: Blond and Briggs; New York: Harper & Row.

Schumacher, E.F. (1979), *Good Work*, London: Cape.
Wood, B. (1984), *Alias, Papa: a Life of Fritz Schumacher*, London: Cape.

Schumpeter, Joseph Alois

Joseph Alois Schumpeter was born in Trest (Triesch), Moravia in 1883. He studied law and economics at the University of Vienna, and in Berlin and London. In 1909 he was appointed assistant professor at the University of Czernowitz, which is today in Ukraine. There he was known as an *enfant terrible* and the faculty was in fact delighted when he left for Graz as full professor in 1911. Schumpeter taught at Graz from 1911 until 1919, spending one year (1913–14) as visiting professor at Columbia University, New York. After that he tried his luck as minister of finances in the Austrian government, and then as the head of the private Biedermann Bank in Vienna. In neither occupation, however, was he a success. In 1925, he accepted a position at the University of Bonn and in 1932, just before Hitler came to power in Germany, he moved to Harvard University. From 1937 until 1941, Schumpeter was president of the Econometric Society; in 1948, he served as president of the American Economic Association; in 1949, he was elected president of the International Economic Association. Schumpeter died at his home in Taconic, Connecticut, in 1950.

Schumpeter's work

Schumpeter's scientific work amounts to 30 books and pamphlets and 260 articles, reports and book reviews (Augello, 1990). Basically it can be divided into three main sections. The first part covers his critical discussion of current economic theory. It begins with *Das Wesen und der Hauptinhalt der theoretischen Nationalökonomie* (The Nature and Substance of Theoretical Economics) (1908) and ends with *History of Economic Analysis* (1954). A second collection of Schumpeter's scientific contributions deals with the theory of social and institutional change, starting with *Die Krise des Steuerstaates* (Crisis of the Tax State) (1918) and ending with *Capitalism, Socialism and Democracy* (1942) and 'The March into Socialism' (1950). The third field of Schumpeter's research concentrates on the theory of economic development of market economies. This section may be considered as the core of Schumpeter's work. His first and most significant publication in this respect is *Die Theorie der wirtschaftlichen Entwicklung* (Theory of Economic Development) (1912), followed by numerous other contributions, ending with his *Business Cycles* (1939).

Schumpeter's main contributions and significance for modern economic theory

Schumpeter's core scientific work centres around the explanation of the development of the capitalistic market system. As his view of society is based on the integration of historical facts and of philosophical and socio-logical considerations, he saw this development as not solely determined by economic factors. In addition, his lack of mathematical ability may be an-other reason why his research was presented largely in a theoretical form rather than in a more formal fashion.

Schumpeter gained most recognition for his work on the factors and the process of economic development, starting with the famous *Theorie der wirtschaftlichen Entwicklung* (hereafter *TED*). He understood this work to be a necessary supplement to *Das Wesen und der Hauptinhalt der theoretischen Nationalökonomie* and therefore to current neoclassical eco-nomic theory. The latter is only able to show how, within a given system, economic resources are put to their best use, how the system adapts when one or several parameters are changed exogenously – for example, popula-tion growth, consumer preferences and so on – and how the endless circular flow of such a static system works. This, however, has nothing to do with economic development as Schumpeter understands it. He recognizes eco-nomic development as a process which originates from within the system itself. Consequently, he does not aim at purely adaptive behaviour reactive to exogenous changes or shocks, but, to the contrary, emphasizes a process whose driving forces are inherent to the system. Thus, whereas the dynamics of the static system, that is the circular flow, is stationary, the technical term 'evolutionary' can be used for the dynamics of development. This view of economic life must be seen as a major attack on orthodox neoclassical theory as the conditions, data and parameters of the static system now change *continuously* or even *discontinuously*, and time can no longer be treated as the theoretical and reversible variable of a mechanistic theory. It rather has the character of a historical and irreversible parameter, which implies that in an evolutionary context the concept of equilibrium is un-known. These elements of the new approach are being taken up currently in the research branches of neo-Schumpeterian and evolutionary economics.

Schumpeter based his *TED* on microeconomic fundamentals as he asks for the *object* and the *subject* of such a development process. The objects in Schumpeter's concept of change are innovations and the initiators of devel-opment are the entrepreneurs who provide innovations. Innovations are de-fined as the success of new combinations. With this definition Schumpeter covers the following five cases: new products or products with new quali-ties, called product innovations, new production processes, called process innovations, access to new markets, exploitation of new sources of raw materials and semi-finished products, and implementation of new organizational structures. As to the subject promoting the development process, Schumpeter claims that this is always a leader characterized by imagination, creativity and the striving for power – over others. This concept of leadership applies not only to economic development but also to the political sphere, as stated in his *Capitalism, Socialism and Democracy* (hereafter *CSD*). In an economic context, leadership refers to the entrepreneur as someone who does something new, who succeeds with new combinations. The entrepreneur's motivation to break the circular flow and to perform something new is determined by the pursuit of (temporary) profits or quasi-rents on innovations; his actions are creative and risky and they are the reason why new things are created and the old will be destroyed. Schumpeter's entrepreneur is therefore deeply involved in a process of *creative destruction* and he stands in striking contrast to the so-called static-oriented managers whose activities are mainly devoted to the circular flow and can thus be characterized as conservative and administrative. Schumpeter also discussed the role of credit and money expansion in the development process. In a static world, credits and money creation are not necessary but in an evolutionary context they enable the entrepreneur to reallocate resources from old productions to new ones.

Based on these concepts of innovations and the entrepreneur, market competition gains a new dimension. It is not only price competition, as in the neoclassical framework, that counts, but competition in terms of doing things in a totally new manner; that is, competition by innovation and imitation. Not only the best adaptation to specific (exogenously) given economic conditions but the destruction and change of such conditions, and not solely the notion of the 'invisible hand' but also that of creative destruction characterize the capitalistic market and its evolution. And, finally, for this kind of competition the chances for yielding profits are not signalled solely by prices and market relations but are also to be seen in the imagination and creativity of single actors.

In his *Business Cycles* (1939), Schumpeter tackles the question of the ups and downs of economic development and of the continuity of the endogenous, micro-based economic development elaborated in the *TED*. The wave-like movements in economic activity which can be observed empirically are the result of the appearance of swarms or bursts of entrepreneurs. Since the appearance of one entrepreneur facilitates the appearance of others, an upswing in economic development occurs. As chances for making profit are reduced by imitation and diffusion, the economic downswing follows necessarily. For these ups and downs Schumpeter distinguished three different cycles, the length of each depending on the disturbance that created it and each consisting of four phases: upswing, recession, depression and recovery.

The three-year *Kitchin cycle* may be identified by inventory accumulation and deaccumulation. The *Juglar cycle* (8–11 years) is related to individual innovations such as the dynamo, electric motor and so on. Finally, the longest cycle, the *Kondratieff cycle* (50–60 years), is caused by the appearance of major innovations such as railroads, electricity or the microchip. Today this Schumpeterian concept of business cycles is discussed and further elaborated in the theory of long waves.

Of Schumpeter's sociological writings the most significant are *Capitalism, Socialism and Democracy* (1942) and 'March into Socialism' (1950). His prediction of the transformation of capitalism into socialism became a topic of debate in the early 1990s as the transition processes in Eastern Europe failed to confirm Schumpeter's forecast. Schumpeter's vision of an inevitable march into socialism and the doom of the capitalistic system is based (a) on changes in the social and institutional sphere and (b) on the very success of the capitalistic system itself. His approach is clearly in contrast to the quite similar Marxian one where the final dominance of socialism is related (a) entirely to economic forces and (b) to the failures of capitalism which will bring about its destruction. Schumpeter's explanation for this transition process – again micro-oriented – focuses on the function of and the institutional conditions for entrepreneurs as the very subject of economic progress, for two reasons: on the one hand, with the prosperous development of the capitalistic system, the importance of the entrepreneur will decline as he will be more and more displaced by large, management-driven enterprises. For this reason Schumpeter develops in *CSD* a model of the management of innovation, where huge research laboratories are engaged to bring about the innovative activities in a controlled, routinized and impersonal manner. In competition, small and medium-sized firms are outperformed; in consequence, the firms' size will increase and competition decrease. Thus development from single entrepreneurial firms to gigantic, manager-driven and bureaucratic enterprises will pave the way for socialism. On the other hand, capitalism itself will have a psychological and sociological impact on society since, with the destruction of the bourgeois class actually protecting entrepreneurial activities, an intellectual class will emerge that rejects the bourgeois values essential to the operation of the economic system.

The reform processes in Eastern Europe suggest that the Schumpeterian forecast was in error. Of course, since small and medium-sized firms remained healthy under capitalism, Schumpeter underestimated capitalism in its persisting ability always to creatively destroy old structures. Thus the idea of the collapse of capitalism because of the supposed loss of bourgeois support collapses itself.

Besides his enormous work on the development of market economies, Schumpeter also contributed significantly to other related fields. For public choice theory his *methodological individualism* is very important in its claim that the description of social, political and economic processes must begin with the action of individuals. Moreover, Schumpeter is to be seen as a forerunner of the (economic) theory of democracy. Here he introduced the idea that democracy is a type of horizontal coordination in the public sector which is comparable with the role of the market mechanism in the private sector. Democracy is then best understood as a method for the selection of leaders. This view appears to be similar to that of the successful entrepreneur selected by the market.

Finally, Schumpeter's work includes contributions to the history of economic science, the most prominent being the *History of Economic Analysis* (1954) and the *Epochen der Dogmen- und Methodengeschichte* (Economic Doctrine and Method) (1914). Here Schumpeter repeatedly tried to explain that economic theories develop in the same manner as theories in science; that is, they are not self-contained but develop cumulatively.

Joseph A. Schumpeter has to be considered one of the greatest economists of our century. He made his scientific contributions at the same time as John M. Keynes, who appeared pre-eminent in the second and third quarter of the twentieth century. However, since the 1980s, Schumpeterian ideas have begun to assume an importance similar to those of the Keynesian heritage and the decades to come may have a good chance of becoming what could be called the 'Age of Schumpeter'.

UWE CANTNER AND HORST HANUSCH

See also:

Corporate Performance; Culture; Development Theory; Evolution, Theories of Economic; Growth, Limits to; Hirschman, Albert O.; Innovation, National Systems of; Long Waves; Marx, Karl; Methodological Individualism; Rationality and Maximization; Social Change, Theory of; Technical Change and Technological Regimes; Technology, Theory of.

Bibliography

Allen, L. (1985), *The Life and Work of Joseph Schumpeter*, New York: Harper & Row.
Angello, M. (1990), *Joseph Alois Schumpeter. A Reference Guide*, Heidelberg: Springer-Verlag.
Oakley, A. (1990), *Schumpeter's Theory of Capitalist Motion* Aldershot: Edward Elgar.
Schumpeter, J.A. (1908), *Das Wesen und der Hauptinhalt der theoretischen National ökonomie*, München und Leipzig: Duncker & Humblot.
Schumpeter, J.A. (1912), *Die Theorie der wirtschaftlichen Entwicklung*, Leipzig: Duncker & Humblot.
Schumpeter, J.A. (1914), *Epochen der Dogmen- und Methodengeschichte*, Tübingen: J.C.B. Mohr (Paul Siebeck).
Schumpeter, J.A. (1918), *Die Krise des Steuerstaates*, Graz und Leipzig: Leuschner & Lubensky.
Schumpeter, J.A. (1939), *Business Cycles*, New York and London: McGraw-Hill.
Schumpeter, J.A. (1942), *Capitalism, Socialism and Democracy*, New York: Harper.
Schumpeter, J.A. (1950), 'The March into Socialism', *American Economic Review*, **40**, (5), pp. 446–56.

Schumpeter, J.A. (1954), *History of Economic Analysis*, London and New York: Allen & Unwin.
Stevenson, M.I. (1985), *Joseph Alois Schumpeter. A Bibliography*, Westport, Conn.: Greenwood Press.
Swedberg, R. (1991), *Joseph Alois Schumpeter. His Life and Work*, Oxford: Blackwell.

Selection, Units of Evolutionary

In his best-selling book, Richard Dawkins (1976) sustains a forceful polemic against the idea of biological 'group selection' advanced by V.C. Wynne-Edwards and others. The relevance of this issue for socioeconomic evolution is shown by the fact that similar arguments have been used by Viktor Vanberg (1986) to undermine theories of cultural group selection and to promote methodological individualism. Vanberg's main target of criticism is actually Friedrich Hayek, who, strangely, supports the principle of group selection with simultaneous allegiance to the methodological individualist idea.

The prominent argument against group and cultural selection is that there is no clear mechanism to ensure that an advantageous pattern of behaviour for the group will for some reason be replicated by the actions of the individuals concerned. In particular, such a mechanism must ensure that 'free-riders' do not become dominant in the groups that exhibit socially useful altruistic behaviours. Free-riders would have the benefits of being members of a group whose other members perform socially useful and self-sacrificial acts, but would bear no personal costs or risks in terms of self-sacrificial behaviour themselves. Consequently, in the absence of any compensating mechanism, it is likely that free-riders within the group will expand in numbers, crowd out the others, and alter the typical behaviour of the group as a whole.

Thus, despite the possible benefits to the group of self-sacrificial behaviour, it appears that there is no mechanism to ensure that groups with these characteristics will prosper above others. What seems crucial is the selection of the constituent individuals and not the groups as a whole. Vanberg (1986, p. 97) thus concludes that the 'notion of cultural group selection is theoretically vague, inconsistent with the basic thrust of Hayek's individualistic approach, and faulty judged on its own grounds'.

However, as argued elsewhere (Hodgson, 1991), the arguments of Dawkins and others against group selection are not entirely satisfactory. A number of biologists now propose that there are levels of selection other than the gene. Biologists such as Niles Eldredge, Stephen Jay Gould, Richard Lewontin and Ernst Mayr have all taken issue with such single-level or 'genetic reductionist' explanations in which it is assumed that animal behaviour can be explained exclusively in terms of the appropriate genes. It is proposed that selection operates simultaneously on different types of unit, depending on the timescale and the type of selection process. Such ideas reflect a widespread, but non-universal, acceptance of non-reductionist and hierarchical views of selection in biology.

Arguments for and against group selection
When group selection occurs, all the organisms in the same group are bound together by a common fate. Although members of the group may not have identical fitness values, group selection works via a uniform effect. It may be that all such information about ostensible group selection may be reduced to and represented by selection coefficients of organisms or genes. But, contrary to Dawkins, such a formal reduction does not imply that the concept of group selection is invalid or that it is individual or genic selection which is occurring: 'In particular, the computational adequacy of genetic models leaves open the question whether they also correctly identify the causes of evolution' (Sober and Lewontin, 1982, p. 158).

Genetic reductionists respond that the gene is the single unit of replication. However, as Elliott Sober (1984, p. 205) argues, group selectionists 'do not deny that the gene is the mechanism by which biological objects pass on their characteristics ... this shared assumption about the unit of replication simply cuts no ice. That genes are passed along leaves open the question as to what causes their differential transmission.' David Sloan Wilson and Elliott Sober (1989) go so far as to argue that to settle on the individual as the unit of selection involves an inconsistency. Simple reduction to the individual level is unacceptable because the same arguments concerning reduction from groups to individuals apply equally to reduction from individual to gene. To avoid this 'double standard' one must either accept multiple levels of selection or reduce everything to the lowest possible level: the gene or even below. Thus Vanberg's attempt to support methodological individualism by citing the genetic reductionists is open to objection.

Some of the major detailed arguments against group selection emanate from the mathematical work of John Maynard Smith and his collaborators. However, mathematical expressions of evolutionary dynamics are highly complex and notoriously intractable. In order to build Maynard Smith's 'basic selection model' a number of necessary simplifications had to be made, excluding several non-linearities and environmental interdependencies. Michael Wade (1978) demonstrates that the mathematical selection models in the literature are based on oversimplifying and restrictive assumptions. He argues that, when these assumptions are relaxed, group selection is much more plausible.

David Sloan Wilson (1983) points out that all such models assume a spatial homogeneity in the genetic composition of populations. Although this assumption is mathematically convenient, it is neither necessary nor realistic. Once again, the assumptions upon which the basic selection model is founded are shown to be over-restrictive and oversimplified.

The possibility of multiple and higher levels of selection is considered by a number of biological theorists. They have argued that, whilst evolutionary theory has already acknowledged the utility of hierarchical structure in describing biological phenomena, it should move on to incorporate hierarchical structure in its conventional modes of explanation. Multiple levels of selection, including that between such 'high level' entities as species or ecosystems, are accepted by a number of biological theorists.

Concluding remarks

Given the possibility of group selection in biology, it can be conjectured that the same phenomenon occurs in the socioeconomic sphere. Economic evolution could work through the selection of habits, individuals, routines, institutions and even whole socioeconomic systems and subsystems. Furthermore, cultural processes of 'emulation' (Veblen) or of conformism may engulf any individualistic 'free-rider' effects. Accordingly, there is no reason why selection should be confined to entities within the framework of the market. It is desirable to consider selection both between different types of market and between market and non-market forms of allocation. A selection process in this context would involve a mixed economy, of whatever type or hue. Given this, Hayek should be criticized, not for embracing group selection and eschewing a consistent individualism, but for failing to incorporate additional processes of selection above the group level, involving the selection of different types of institution, including both market and non-market forms. To work at such higher levels, evolutionary selection must involve different types of ownership structure and resource allocation mechanisms, all coexisting in a mixed economy.

An evolutionary theoretical framework with multiple levels of selection provides an alternative to the prominent reductionism of modern economics. Neoclassical economics is preoccupied with the attempt to found macroeconomics on 'sound microfoundations'. In this effort it mimics the reductionism of classical physics, in trying to build up models from the allegedly fundamental particles of the system. But biology is developing hierarchic and non-reductionist modes of thinking in which entities at several levels can be considered. This suggests both the possibility and the legitimacy of a macroeconomics that enjoys some autonomy from microeconomics and does not have to be based on the axiom of the maximizing individual.

GEOFFREY M. HODGSON

See also:

Biology and Economics; Darwinism, Influence of Economics on; Evolution, Theories of Economic; Hayek, Friedrich A.; Lock-in and Chreodic Development; Macroeconomic Theory; Methodological Individualism; Natural Selection, Economic Evolution and.

Bibliography

Dawkins, R. (1976), *The Selfish Gene*, Oxford: Oxford University Press.

Hodgson, G.M. (1991), 'Hayek's Theory of Cultural Evolution: An Evaluation in the Light of Vanberg's Critique', *Economics and Philosophy*, **7**, (1), March, pp. 67–82.

Hodgson, Geoffrey M. (1993), *Economics and Evolution: Bringing Life Back into Economics*, Cambridge: Polity.

Sober, E. (ed.) (1984), *Conceptual Issues in Evolutionary Biology: An Anthology*, Cambridge, Mass.: MIT.

Sober, E. and R.C. Lewontin (1982), 'Artifact, Cause, and Genic Selection', *Philosophy of Science*, **49**, (2), pp. 157–80; reprinted 1984 in Sober.

Vanberg, V. (1986), 'Spontaneous Market Order and Social Rules: A Critique of F.A. Hayek's Theory of Cultural Evolution', *Economics and Philosophy*, **2**, pp. 75–100.

Wade, M.J. (1978), 'A Critical Review of the Models of Group Selection', *Quarterly Review of Biology*, **53**, pp. 101–14; reprinted 1984 in R.N. Brandon and R.M. Burian (eds), *Genes, Organisms, Populations: Controversies Over the Units of Selection*, Cambridge Mass.: MIT.

Wilson, D.S. (1983), 'The Group Selection Controversy: History and Current Status', *Annual Review of Ecology and Systematics*, **14**, pp. 159–88.

Wilson, D.S. and E. Sober (1989), 'Reviving the Superorganism', *Journal of Theoretical Biology*, **136**, pp. 337–56.

Shackle, George Lennox Sharman

G.L.S. Shackle was born in Cambridge in 1903 into a middle-class family. However, financial problems prevented him from going straight to university after school. Instead he took a series of office and teaching jobs, but found time to complete successfully a part-time degree. In the early 1930s he had read Keynes's *Treatise on Money* and Hayek's *Prices and Production*, and was so stimulated by these works that he decided to pursue economics as a career.

This ambition was fulfilled in 1935 when a Leverhulme Scholarship enabled him to study, under Hayek, for a PhD at the London School of Economics. He completed this in 1938 and it was published a year later as *Expectations, Investment and Income*. After that he spent some time at Oxford working with Sir Henry Phelps Brown. A period in government service was followed by two academic positions culminating in his obtaining the Brunner Chair of Economics at Liverpool University in 1951. He remained there until his 'retirement' in 1969. He died in 1992. Shackle made contributions to areas such as entrepreneurial theory, business cycles, Keynesian scholarship and decision making under conditions of uncertainty. We shall be concentrating on the latter two aspects.

Shackle, although an adept mathematician, was very unhappy with the slavish way in which so many economists sought to imitate the natural sciences. This too easily led to a type of economics that was very mechanical and deterministic. He constantly emphasized the role of free will and imagination in the human sciences. This viewpoint was greatly to influence his theory of decision making, which was first fully elaborated in 1949 in *Expectation in Economics*. By this time he had become particularly unhappy with the way economists were using the frequency theory of probability. This approach essentially depends upon generating values from a large number of trials conducted under similar conditions. If we were to toss a coin 100 000 times we would discover that we have a fifty–fifty chance of obtaining a head or a tail. From such trials seemingly reliable probabilities for the occurence of different events could be established. Many economists have employed this reasoning, believing it to be a reliable guide to social phenomena. However, Shackle has argued that this is not so. He contends that there are a large number of decisions that we make where appeal to any kind of frequency distribution is not possible. For example, making an investment is largely a move into uncharted territory. These uncertainties are further compounded when we take notice of the element of time. The decisions we make today are likely to have their full consequences some time in the future. Consequently, many of our decisions are clouded by a significant degree of uncertainty which appeals to the frequency approach will not mitigate.

This consideration led Shackle to develop his alternative theory of decision making based upon the notion of *potential surprise*. Many of the choices we are forced to make do not lead to unambiguously good or bad outcomes. Therefore we have to determine the likely alternative results of our decisions. For example, suppose an academic is offered a job in Tasmania and his existing position has become increasingly less attractive. The Tasmanian position offers more money, less teaching and better facilities. Superficially it appears that the choice is straightforward. If the academic stays in his existing position, things could deteriorate further. However, the benefits of going to Tasmania could be diluted by the loss of easy contact with America and Europe. To help make the decision, Shackle developed the notion of potential surprise. Here we would imagine bad and good outcomes, ranging from unsurprising to astonishing. Using sophisticated mathematical techniques, Shackle demonstrated how individuals could imagine different scenarios and then decide what action to take. Despite some early interest on the part of economists his approach did not prove generally popular. However, corporate strategists thought it of value and the techniques of scenario planning were developed as the result of the inspiration of Shackle's contribution.

Such methodological considerations led Shackle to reevaluate Keynes's work in a way that was seen as heretical in the early 1960s, but is now regarded as quite respectable. Since the late 1950s, a growing group of economists, known as Post Keynesians, had argued that the IS/LM interpretation of Keynes's *General Theory* did scant justice to the subtlety of that book. The IS/LM framework reduces Keynes's work to a comparative state, mechanical equilibrium framework where there is little room for time, uncertainty and expectations. Shackle had read Keynes's *Treatise on Probability* and noticed that Keynes had criticized the frequency approach along similar lines to his own. This made Shackle consider how Keynes had mentioned the importance of expectations in the *Treatise on Probability*. Could Keynes have endorsed IS/LM?

The problem, in part, is that he appeared to do so, in a letter written to John Hicks in 1937, endorsing the famous article that spawned IS/LM analysis. However, Shackle noticed that in the same year Keynes published a response to critics of the *General Theory* in the *Quarterly Journal of Economics*. Here Keynes explained time, uncertainty and expectations in a way suggesting a fundamental incompatibility with the IS/LM interpretation of his work. Shackle argued that this apparent contradiction was resolved if we distinguished between the *method* and the *meaning* of the *General Theory*. The method was dependent upon equilibrium analysis, but once we endeavour to interpret the meaning of the book a different picture emerges. Recent scholarship has done much to support the view that Keynes's intentions were considerably more radical than many interpreters realized. This recent work on understanding Keynes owes much to the pioneering efforts of Shackle.

In recent years, his methodological position has been labelled 'nihilistic' by certain critics. They argue that, by dismissing econometrics and mathematics, he does not leave much for economists to do. Furthermore, his emphasis upon free will and imagination renders any kind of predictive economics impossible. Such claims are greatly exaggerated. Shackle was certainly unhappy with the routine and unthinking use of mathematics and econometrics that is so widespread today. However such techniques had some place, albeit a considerably more modest one, in his thinking. The second charge raises the interesting issue of institutions in Shackle's writings. He was not familiar with pragmatic philosophy or the institutionalists. However, he did view institutions as being a vital element in our analysis. He recognized that the law, the Church and moral sanctions all played vital roles in establishing order. Although he emphasized uncertainty, he was also concerned with the way in which decisions could be made within an orderly framework. There is much useful work to be done in synthesizing the work of the institutionalists and Shackle.

JOHN PHEBY

See also:
Cognition, Cultural and Institutional Influences on; Consumer Behaviour; Determinism and Free Will; Econometrics, The Limits of; Institutions; Keynes, John Maynard; Macroeconomic Policy; Macroeconomic Theory; Monetary Policy; Monetary Theory; Planning, Theory of; Rational Actor Models; Rationality and Maximization; Time; Uncertainty; Unemployment.

Bibliography
Boehm, S., S. Frowen and J. Pheby (eds) (1993), *Essays in Memory of G L S Shackle*, London: Routledge.
Frowen, S. (ed.) (1990), *Unknowledge and Choice in Economics*, London: Macmillan.
Shackle, G.L.S. (1958), *Time in Economics*, Amsterdam: North-Holland.
Shackle, G.L.S. (1979), *Imagination and the Nature of Choice*, Edinburgh: Edinburgh University Press.
Shackle, G.L.S. (1988), *Business, Time and Thought*, London: Macmillan.

Simon, Herbert Alexander

The award of the 1978 Nobel Prize in economics to Herbert Simon (born 1916) surprised many economists. Despite having published in leading economics journals, Simon is actually Professor of Computer Science and Psychology – not economics – at Carnegie-Mellon University in Pittsburgh. Even the three disciplines so far mentioned do not exhaust the range of this remarkable polymath: his work also embraces sociology, philosophy, production engineering, operations research and other human sciences. This range of scholarship should not be taken to imply that his work has only a passing relevance for economics. On the contrary, its view of the way systems function and how people make decisions strikes at the core of mainstream theorizing.

As far as system functioning is concerned, a key notion in Simon's work is decomposability, in other words, the extent to which a system can be broken down into a hierarchy of independent subsystems. Modular or cellular systems are likely to stand a bigger chance of surviving in environments that are liable to suffer from shocks. If part of a decomposable system fails, the system as a whole may survive; by contrast, in systems whose elements are interconnected, a disruption in one area may spread to threaten the viability of the system as a whole. This thinking seems significant in relation to innovations, financial failures and, of course, to diseases such as AIDS: whether or not they spread very far will depend on the pattern of linkages between system elements. Although perfect decomposability may be rather rare, Simon suggests that many decision environments are 'nearly decomposable': it is safe in the short run to engage in partial analysis, even though elements are somewhat linked together. Systems that survive with little change in the long run are likely to be ones in which linkages between subsystems act, like ripples on a pond, to dissipate disturbances, rather than producing compounding effects.

Simon emphasizes that decision makers actually need to be able to act as if the world is highly decomposable because they suffer from 'bounded rationality': the complexity of the choice environment outstrips their ability to frame and solve decision problems in ways that take account of all relevant possibilities and interdependencies. If nothing is defined at the outset, the computational requirements for choice appear overwhelming; far from being able to handle all the information that might be relevant to a problem, the boundedly rational decision maker will be stretched in terms of short-term memory capacity by anything much more complex than a seven-digit telephone number. Mainstream theorists often play down the potential for information overload because they assume that a set of possible options and constraints has already been defined, and that the characteristics of the rival opportunities have been assayed. In reality, decision makers must first work out whether they have a problem to solve, then generate options and size them up, before somehow making a choice.

Logic and empirical research led Simon to argue that people cope with the world, not by trying to comprehend it as an integral system, but by trying to build workable partial models and identify recurrent patterns. Instead of looking far ahead in terms of a variety of conflicting objectives, people tend to worry about only one thing at a time, shifting their focus between problems in a priority manner as particular thresholds are crossed (for example, we do not normally worry about our need for food if we are out searching for a suitable used car, but, beyond a certain point, hunger will make us redirect our search from cars to food). Mental tunnel vision and myopia lead decision makers to filter out much information that might be relevant but at the same time this helps reduce information overload.

Obviously, such a response to complexity might be portrayed as optimization – a trade-off between the advantages of a more complex model of the choice problem and the danger that information overload will lead to processing errors. Likewise, it could be claimed that search is undertaken until its expected marginal benefit equals its marginal cost. However, Simon opts not to do this and argues instead that it may be better to view many decisions as 'satisficing' acts. His rejection of the notion of maximizing behaviour arises because the suggestion that maximization can be carried out subject to costs of gathering and processing information begs questions that end up in an infinite regress. For example, people may suspect that they are responding optimally in a particular situation, and their hunches may even be correct. But they will be unable to confirm this without consuming resources that could have been used to do other things; they must also grapple with the question of how to discover the best way of checking that they are doing the best thing.

When 'satisficing', choosers set themselves targets that define the situations in which they would like to find themselves. (If they are working in a firm, they may have a variety of personal goals and only be interested in profitability when they perceive that this is in danger of falling below levels necessary to let them meet these goals.) They then use simplifying rules of thumb or behavioural routines to seek out and appraise possible ways of putting themselves in these desired situations. Once they have discovered an option that their appraisal rules leads them to judge as 'OK' they select this option unless other rules lead them to believe that further search could be worthwhile (for example, if it is unexpectedly easy to find something that is OK according to one set of criteria, the chooser may bring into play another routine which might allow further search until, say, something 10 per cent better is discovered, subject to some time limit for search). Decisions may be arrived at with no attention being paid to some of the possible trade-offs that a detached observer might judge to be relevant to the problem at hand; instead, the chooser may simply appear to be acting in a matter akin to a computer running a program which stops once a particular pattern is identified.

This view of behaviour makes no presumption that equilibrium will be attained. A decision is not necessarily the end of the chooser's problems: although most people develop mental models that fit events well enough to permit them to avoid major crises, some may get into difficulties because they fail to perceive a need for action soon enough or find themselves surprised, owing to their failure to explore possible linkages between system elements. They may then need to form and test new hypotheses about the challenges with which they are dealing. If the choice environment is not static, life becomes a matter of muddling though by experimenting with new rules of thumb, aspiration levels and objectives, one of discovering and then sticking to the best ways to obtain utility or profits.

Some of Simon's most recent work uses the idea of bounded rationality to explain how the evolution of an economy may come to benefit from altruistic acts by individuals. It is not obvious why people may opt to behave in ways that impose costs on themselves even if they help strengthen the economy as a whole. Simon suggests that free-rider behaviour that would interfere with socially beneficial outcomes may be precluded because of people acting in a 'docile' manner. They conform with social information about what constitutes knowledge and 'proper behaviour' because they feel guilt or shame at the prospect of acting in a deviant manner and, more importantly, lack the expertise to evaluate social wisdom or assess whether socially prescribed behaviour is in some way beneficial to themselves or whether it involves altruism. It is often far easier to live life on the basis of social wisdom and norms rather than acquire knowledge by possibly painful experience, but social norms may also be used in judging what constitutes an appropriate amount of experimental, risk-taking behaviour.

PETER E. EARL

See also:

Boulding, Kenneth Ewart; Cognition, Cultural and Institutional Influences on; Consumer Behaviour; Human Nature, Theory of; Information Theory in Economics; Neoclassical Microeconomic Theory, Critique of; Rational Actor Models; Rationality and Maximization; Realism, Philosophical; Rules.

Bibliography

Simon, H.A. (1945), *Administrative Behavior*, New York: Free Press.
Simon, H.A. (1959), 'Theories of decision-making in economics and behavioral sciences', *American Economic Review*, **49**, June, pp. 253–83.
Simon, H.A. (1969), *The Sciences of the Artificial*, Cambridge, Mass.: MIT.
Simon, H.A. (1982), *Models of Bounded Rationality: Volume 1, Economic Analysis and Public Policy; Volume 2, Behavioral Economics and Business Organization*, Cambridge, Mass.: MIT.
Simon, H.A. (1990), 'A Mechanism for Social Selection and Successful Altruism', *Science*, **250**, 21 December.

Smith, Adam

Adam Smith was one of the three or four leading members of the Scottish School of Moral Philosophy in the mid-eighteenth century and has to be understood in that light, but, along with John Locke, the other founding philosopher of modern Western civilization, he was a man for the ages.

Smith is best known for his theory of the way in which self-interest, regulated by the price mechanism in open markets, could lead to the growth of the wealth of nations. *An Inquiry into the Nature and Causes of the Wealth of Nations* postulates that wealth consists of consumable commodities, and the capital goods useful for their production. The book's central technical argument concerning the growth of wealth centres on the division of labour as the source of increased production and on the conditions which promote the division of labour, namely, the wide extent of the market, the use of money, and domestic and international free trade. All this could take place in an orderly, relatively spontaneous and even relatively harmonious manner, and without the close and extensive supervision of the allocation of resources by central authorities. In its emphasis on self-interest, a self-regulating, even optimizing, system of production and exchange, individual autonomy and opportunity, non-interventionism by government, and so on, Smith's philosophy – some would call it an ideology – both reflected and projected the self-images of the middle class, the leading social group in the modern urban, industrialized, market economy which was already to some extent in place by the mid-eighteenth century in England and Scotland and even on the continent.

Together with this general explanation of what would promote the growth of wealth, so defined, Smith presented an array of economic theories required to explicate the operation of markets. Some of these theories were ambiguous, some were defective, some were incomplete, and some were the progenitors of later theoretical work. They include the labour theory of value, and theories of market price, competition, national income, productive and unproductive labour, capital, money, wage rates, profits and taxation. But there is much more to Adam Smith's total system of thought than his technical economics and economic philosophy, as important as they certainly are. His is an attempt at a comprehensive, indeed, synoptic and synthetic, theory of psychology, society, economy and polity; a complete system of social science. The comprehensiveness of Smith's total system renders his analyses extremely complex and subtle. It also renders highly problematical any generalizations based upon his technical economics alone, and especially any implications with regard to policy.

There is still another respect in which Smith's analyses engender interpretative difficulties. Smith has elements in his analysis, or at least in his modes of discourse, of quite contradictory philosophy: supernaturalism, naturalism, utilitarianism, empiricism, historicism, and so on. Just as 'facts' take on meaning only within the theoretical contexts in which they are used, Smith's ideas and theories acquire quite different signification depending on the philosophy in which they are located. Different readers can, therefore, see quite different stories being told in Smith's work.

Smith's largest model of society – and he himself tells us this – is tripartite: it encompasses the realms of the moral sentiments, the market and jurisprudence. Smith's economics, surveyed above, deals with the second. The other two deal with moral and legal social control and constitute the framework, as it were, within which production and exchange in markets can be carried on. But it is Smith's central argument, at a certain level of generalization, that the three spheres interact, so that, for example, the formation of moral and legal rules both influences and is influenced by market behaviour.

In his *Theory of Moral Sentiments*, Smith indicates that human nature encompasses self-interest, benevolence, and sympathy, meaning by the last the ability to put oneself in another's place, thereby to feel the pain and pleasure which the other undergoes. Self-interest is not only channelled by social control; it is also informed. Smith argues that individuals are driven by the principles of approbation and disapprobation to examine critically both their own behaviour and the behaviour of others; that on the basis of the working of these principles moral rules of behaviour are worked out; and that these moral rules are internalized as social control – with respect to which Smith uses the metaphor of the Impartial Spectator (conscience). It will be noticed that moral rules are artefacts: their origin is within the processes of social life – though the principles of approbation and disapprobation are given to mankind by Nature, an interesting admixture of empiricism and naturalism, and even supernaturalism in the form of Providence or the Benevolent Author of Nature.

Operative within the processes which produce the moral rules is what later came to be called status emulation. People respect and emulate those of higher rank, not least in respect to their ideas and their life styles. The desire for greater wealth, largely in the quest for status, is the great stimulus to industry. Yet, says Smith, people do often come to sense that the desire for wealth is a Great Deception, that wealth and even status is not everything that they had thought it to be so far as human happiness is concerned, albeit a socially functional desire, inasmuch as it sets industry in motion. Be that as it may, the field of the moral sentiments constitutes for Smith, in modern terms, the source of the moral and customary rules which function as social control.

In lectures which he gave on law and government, Smith explored the nature and role of law, also as social control. In the *Wealth of Nations* Smith addresses the functions of government in a straightforward but also cursory fashion, limiting government to the administration of justice, national defence and the provision of public works. In the lectures on jurisprudence we see that the 'administration of justice' is a euphemism for the processes through which are developed and continually revised the rights of economic significance which determine people's individual place and participation in markets and therefore whose interests will count therein. Smith's 'simple and obvious system of natural liberty' is to be juxtaposed to the predations of government under such systems as mercantilism; it does not rule out a wide range of necessary activities of government, not least those which determine whose interests will count when private interests conflict, as they often do.

Government for Smith is not exogenous to the economy. It is part of the total social system, government officials and agents interacting with economic actors and agents. What government does is not so much centrally planned as the result of uses to which government is put by those in a position to use government. Not the least of those users were businessmen, who stood ready to use government to promote their own interests rather than the interests of consumers. Nor was the market necessarily neutral: markets could be formed which skewed performance in favour of certain groups and not others; Smith presented labour markets as examples in which buyers of labour, in part through their use of government, could dominate sellers of labour.

Smith, then, was very much a realist, in the sense that he understood that the general theory of a market economy which he was advancing neither reached nor prescribed the details of the economy; it did not stipulate whose interests were to count when those of buyers and sellers conflicted; such would have to be worked out through legal–economic processes. And he was very much aware, therefore, that public statements about public interest were often used to mask the pursuit of private interest in politics.

In the *Wealth of Nations* Smith writes of an 'invisible hand' which leads those who seek their self-interest so to act as to promote, though no part of their intention, the social welfare. There have been in the subsequent literature some three dozen identifications of what is the invisible hand; and some dozen or so specifications of precisely what it is that the invisible hand does or signifies. But perhaps the most widely cited identifications are the market, the price system and competition (though there are several quite contradictory specifications as to just what constitutes competition), often in combination. Yet a reading of Smith's system as a whole suggests that the social control mechanisms of society are many and varied, and include both the competitive market with its price mechanism and the institutions, including those of government, which form and operate through both markets and self-interest. Neither individuals nor markets nor economies nor polities are autonomous, self-subsistent phenomena; and it is in the nexus formed by all of these (and still other spheres, especially the moral and customary) that economic performance is worked out in Smith's total system.

'Non-interventionism' therefore conveys both much less force and much less specificity (of interests to be protected as rights) than the typical laissez-faire interpretation of Smith would have it. Moreover, there is an even more transcendental respect in which the operation of law and government is problematic in Smith's system: Smith envisioned a sequence of stages of the evolution of human society and thereby an evolution of law and government.

It is conventional to speak of Smith's mechanistic philosophy when discussing his static economic theory. But his philosophy is broader and more complex, and his economics encompasses more than the mechanics of supply and demand. There is in Smith evolutionism both within a stage of law and government and between stages, an institutionalism in conjunction with the market mechanism. Any analysis or application of Smith which neglects any important facet of Smith's total system is bound to be myopic and selective, and analytic myopia was one malady which Smith decidedly did not have. Smith the great philosopher of the modern economic system was more sophisticated and subtle than most, if not all, of his interpreters.

That for Smith human behaviour and the evolution of markets, and of both legal and non-legal institutions had spontaneous (and therefore unintended and unforeseen) as well as deliberative elements, and that the relevant processes served a selection function, has long been understood, although subject to varying formulations. Recent study of the notebooks of Charles Darwin, moreover, has shown that, along with Thomas Robert Malthus, Smith's economics was a major inspiration for Darwin and his theory of natural selection – the foremost theory of evolution in the natural sciences.

WARREN J. SAMUELS

See also:

Darwinism, Influence of Economics on; Development Theory; Evolution, Theories of Economic; Growth, Limits to; Habits; Institutions; Law and Economics; Market, Institutionalist View of the; Spontaneous Order.

Bibliography

Campbell, R.H. and A.S. Skinner (1982), *Adam Smith*, New York: St Martin's Press.
Samuels, Warren J. (1973), 'Adam Smith and the Economy as a System of Power', *Indian Economic Journal*, **20**, January–March, pp. 363–81.
Samuels, Warren J. (1977), 'The Political Economy of Adam Smith', *Ethics*, **87**, April, pp. 189–207.
Skinner, Andrew S. (1979), *A System of Social Science: Papers Relating to Adam Smith*, New York: Oxford University Press.

Social Change, Theory of

Among the various approaches to social change to be found in the American institutionalist literature, the most coherent emerges from the works of Thorstein B. Veblen (1857–1929). Veblen sought to explain social change as an evolutionary process of 'cumulative causation', which he described in terms of the impact of 'technology' on 'institutions'. Subsequent generations of institutional economists have modified and refined Veblen's original formulation. The discussion that follows briefly sketches the evolution of the theory and the form it currently takes in the literature.

In the course of his analysis, Veblen emphasized the difference between behaviour based on 'invidious' distinctions and behaviour that was not. He defined an invidious distinction as a comparative judgement of the presumed inherent worth of human beings. The 'ceremonial' practices embedded in the institutional structure of society warrant behaviour on invidious grounds to the extent that such practices sanction class and caste systems which provide differential advantages to some members of the community while denying them to others. In contrast, non-invidious behaviour benefits the community at large without regard to status or differential advantage. Applying this distinction to an analysis of the economy, Veblen differentiated between what he called the 'industrial' and 'pecuniary' employments. The industrial employments, which are non-invidious, arise from the application of science and technology to the production of goods and services that meet the needs of the community as these needs are impersonally considered. The pecuniary employments, which are invidious, spring from predatory habits of thought and are preoccupied with the acquisition of differential advantage and the preservation of existing patterns of status and power.

According to Veblen, technological innovations arising in the industrial employments require changes in habits of thought and behaviour, not only in the industrial employments, but also in the pecuniary employments. More often than not there will be considerable ceremonial resistance to changes in habitual modes of behaviour when it is recognized that innovations will upset invidiously warranted patterns of status and power. The resistance to techno-logical innovation will occur at all levels of society. The rich and the powerful will resist changes that threaten their privileged position within the commu-nity. Those of lesser status and income may also resist change because they emulate the conservative temperament of the 'leisure class'. At the very bot-tom of the social and income scale, the impoverished are resistant to change because they are exhausted by the day-to-day struggle for survival and have little or no capacity to consider alternative ways of doing things. As a conse-quence of these retarding influences, the (invidious) pecuniary employments tend to dominate the (non-invidious) industrial employments.

In spite of these retarding influences, institutional change does take place as a form of selective adaptation to technological innovation. Veblen viewed institutional change as a continuing process. At any point in time, the institu-tional structure is composed of habits of thought and behaviour that emerged from earlier adaptations to changes in the objective circumstances of the community. Institutions of the present period are, therefore, determined by past patterns of adaptation. Consequently, the institutional structure is al-ways in a sense obsolete with respect to the current technological situation, and further adaptation is required. But the adaptation itself produces a new set of circumstances that requires further adaptation, and so forth. It is in this continuous process of institutional change that Veblen captures the notion of cumulative causation.

Veblen stressed the point that the evolution of institutions is not teleologi-cal; that is, there is no natural law or 'invisible hand' guiding the process to some ultimately desirable, final form. Institutional change is a process of adaptation to changing circumstances, and the mode of adaptation is a mat-ter of human volition. There is no *a priori* reason for believing that the adaptation will be well done. This is particularly true when the pecuniary employments dominate the industrial employments of the community. In-deed, Veblen tended to be pessimistic about mankind's ability to make the institutional changes necessary to achieve progress in human affairs.

Clarence E. Ayres (1891–1972) combined Veblen's seminal contributions with philosopher John Dewey's (1859–1952) instrumental value theory to produce a theory of economic progress. Ayres elaborated on the Veblenian dichotomy between 'technology' and 'institutions' by shifting the focus to the technological and ceremonial aspects of 'organized behaviour' and examining the value structure of each. Ayres argued that both the progressive character of technology and the retarding character of ceremonial behaviour are traceable to the different modes of valuation upon which the social warrant of each depends. According to Ayres, instrumental (non-invidious) valuing is the foundation of the technological processes (which incorporate all of the arts and sciences). This mode of valuation *tests* values through the consequences of their use. The ceremonial practices of the community, on the other hand, are based upon an invidious mode of valuation that entails what Dewey called the 'quest for certainty'. This mode of valuation is embedded in the myths, rituals and ideology of the community and seeks to *authenticate* existing patterns of behaviour by reversion to claims of authority, the immemorial practices of the community, the word of God and so forth. It is in the examination of these two conflicting modes of valuation that we find the explanation of the way technological processes generate change in human behaviour and how ceremonial practices inhibit it. Ayres argued that 'progress' occurs when technologically warranted behaviour displaces ceremonially warranted behaviour in the conduct of human affairs.

In the main, Ayres was more optimistic than Veblen concerning the possibilities for progress in the adaptation of institutions to technological innovation. Although a careful reading of his total work clearly indicates that he did not believe progress was inevitable, critics have pointed out that he appears to have slipped occasionally into the very kind of teleological reasoning that Veblen sought to dispel from social analysis.

Ayres's treatment of the instrumental–ceremonial dichotomy was refined by one of his leading students, J. Fagg Foster (1907–85). Foster eliminated a continuing source of confusion in the institutionalist literature by locating both instrumental and ceremonial patterns of behaviour *within* the institutional structure of society. He defined institutions as socially prescribed patterns of correlated behaviour. He further identified values as standards of judgement by which behaviour is correlated within the institutional structure. Combining this conception of the role of values in the institutional structure with the instrumental–ceremonial dichotomy, Foster was able to show that behavioural patterns are either instrumentally or ceremonially warranted.

Foster's approach considerably enriches institutional analysis and makes it more robust. According to Foster, the 'tool–skill nexus' that is at the heart of the technological process is itself a set of socially prescribed patterns of correlated behaviour. The key insight is that those behavioural patterns that form the tool–skill nexus are instrumentally warranted; that is, they are socially warranted through a process of instrumental valuation wherein the values that function as standards for the correlation of behaviour are tested by their consequences in furthering the problem-solving processes of the community. In contrast, those values that function as standards of judgement in the correlation of ceremonial patterns of behaviour are shielded from critical scrutiny and tests of experience. Ideologies, myths and rituals block inquiry into their origins and validity. From Foster's analytical perspective the institutional dichotomy cannot be meaningfully viewed as a matter of technology and institutions occupying two different domains in social space. Instrumental and ceremonial patterns of behaviour are found in all institutions and are interlinked in complex ways. The essence of the institutional dichotomy is to be found in the two fundamentally different value systems that provide the social warrant for each type of behavioural pattern.

Foster set forth three 'principles' of institutional change. The first he called the 'technological dynamic'. This principle embodies the views of Veblen and Ayres concerning the inherent dynamics of science and technology. The evolution of human institutions is driven by the dynamic processes of continuing inquiry and innovation in 'turning material things to account' (to use Veblen's phraseology). The second principle Foster called 'recognized interdependence'. This principle is also clearly alluded to in the works of both Veblen and Ayres. It calls attention to the fact that society is, to use an apt cliche, a seamless web. An institutional change in one area of the social structure has the potential for generating changes in other areas. The third principle, which is implicit in the conceptual schemes of Veblen and Ayres, is clearly delineated by Foster; he calls it the principle of 'minimal dislocation'. This principle takes account of the fact that technological innovations may not only dislodge ceremonial patterns of behaviour, but may also dislocate other instrumentally warranted patterns of behaviour. Minimal dislocation of instrumentally warranted patterns of behaviour is required if the institutional change is to take hold in the community. In other words, people cannot be expected to change habits of thought and behaviour beyond the range of activities that they comprehend as being part of the problem. They will not be inclined to give up instrumentally warranted behaviour in other domains of their experience not perceived to be part of the problem; thus, the institutional change must involve a minimal dislocation of instrumentally warranted patterns of behaviour.

Two of Foster's students, Louis J. Junker (1927–81) and the present writer, formulated the concept of 'ceremonial encapsulation' for the purpose of examining more closely the process by which innovations in the arts and sciences are absorbed into the institutional structure. The basic thesis is that ceremonial values tend to dominate the institutional structure and encapsulate technological innovation in such a way as to diminish its impact on existing patterns of power and status. This means that, at any point in time, the community possesses ceremonially encapsulated knowledge that cannot be brought to bear on the problem-solving processes. In order for such encapsulated knowledge to be utilized, there must be a 'progressive' institutional change (under conditions of minimal dislocation) that involves the displacement of ceremonially warranted patterns of behaviour by instrumentally warranted patterns of behaviour. There are, then, potentially two phases in the adjustment of institutions to technological innovations: ceremonial encapsulation, and progressive institutional change. The word 'potentially' is used to indicate that progressive institutional change is by no means inevitable. As the present writer has attempted to demonstrate, ceremonial encapsulation can take such a form as to induce 'regressive' institutional change in which ceremonial patterns of behaviour displace instrumental patterns of behaviour in response to technological innovation.

Marc R. Tool has produced a body of work that offers the most coherent restatement of the Veblen–Ayres–Foster approach to evolutionary economics. Tool's analysis rests explicitly on Dewey's theory of instrumental valuation. It culminates in his formulation of the 'social value principle', which captures the normative implications of progressive institutional change under conditions of minimal dislocation. According to this principle, progressive institutional change occurs when the instrumental use of knowledge 'provides for the continuity of human life and the noninvidious re-creation of community'. In recent years, many American institutionalists have explored the policy implications of Tool's social value principle and have applied it in policy analysis across a spectrum of political–economic issues.

PAUL D. BUSH

See also:

Ayres, Clarence E.; Culture; Cumulative Causation; Dewey, John; Foster, J. Fagg; Institutions; Instrumental Value Theory; Technology, Theory of; Veblen, Thorstein; Veblenian Dichotomy and Its Critics.

Bibliography

Ayres, Clarence E. (1978), *The Theory of Economic Progress*, 3rd edn, Kalamazoo: New Issues Press; originally published in 1944 by the University of North Carolina Press; the 3rd edn is preferred because it contains a foreword and an addendum written by Ayres.
Bush, Paul D. (1987), 'The Theory of Institutional Change', *Journal of Economic Issues*, **XXI**, September, pp. 1075–1116; reprinted in Marc R. Tool (ed.), *Evolutionary Economic: Foundations of Institutional Thought*, Volume 1, Armonk, NY: M.E. Sharpe, 1988, pp. 125–66.
Dewey, John (1929), *The Quest for Certainty*, New York: G.P. Putnam's Sons, particularly chs 1 and X.
Foster, J. Fagg (1981), 'The Papers of J. Fagg Foster', *Journal of Economic Issues*, **XV**, December, pp. 851–1012, particularly pp. 907–13, 923–35, 937–42, 997–1006.
Tool, Marc R. (1979), *The Discretionary Economy: A Normative Theory of Political Economy*, Santa Monica, CA: Goodyear, particularly chs 8 and 15.

Veblen, Thorstein B. (1965), *The Theory of the Leisure Class*, New York: Augustus M. Kelley, particularly ch. VIII; first published 1899.

Spontaneous Order

Although the notion, if not the term, of a spontaneous order of things may claim an impressive pedigree in the social sciences (Hamowy, 1987), which is usually traced back to the Scottish moral philosophers (with intimations present in Aristotle and Aquinas), current usage of the term is so closely identified with the work of F.A. Hayek that it seems expedient to limit the following considerations to a discussion of his thought on the subject. Likewise, more recent parallel developments in the sciences surfacing under various names such as dissipative structures, self-organization, self-regulation, autopoiesis and homeostasis will not be pursued here.

It is arguably fair to say that the conception of spontaneous order informs Hayek's distinctive approach to economic theory, social and political philosophy jurisprudence and theoretical psychology. Given its significance in Hayek's work, it is all the more remarkable that the scope and meaning of the concept are by no means assured. Whilst not a woefully under-theorized concept, the limits of the application of the idea are nevertheless a matter of considerable and continuing controversy. In Hayek's own work the concept figures more prominently from the early 1960s onwards, although a case could be made that the basic idea was there 'from the beginning': in his excursion into theoretical psychology in the early 1920s (to be published some three decades later as *The Sensory Order*); in his studies on 'knowledge' published in the 1930s and 1940s; and in his criticism of the role of 'scientism' in the study of society presented in the early 1940s. What was novel in his later work was a more systematically elaborated distinction between different kinds of order and an increasingly realist understanding of the existence of social order sustained by the observance of rules on the part of its elements.

The kind of order contemplated by Hayek is not a response to what has come to be enshrined as 'the Hobbesian problem of social order'. In Hayek's account, social order is not narrowly viewed as a peaceful state of affairs in which the security of persons and their property is assured. That is to say, it is not some variant of a coercion explanation of social order according to which men's impulses have to be restrained by those entrusted with the monopoly over the means of physical coercion in order to avert Hobbes's vision of life in the state of nature as 'solitary, poor, nasty, brutish and short'. The obsession with the problem of order in modern social theory, 'the quest for order', with 'order' being conceived as something to be deliberately designed, imposed, controlled, manipulated, orchestrated, engineered or ad-ministered, is clearly derived from Hobbes's authoritarian conception of order – an order that had to be imposed to contain and hold in check what appeared to be the natural state of the world, a world in flux (see Bauman, 1991, pp. 5–7).

According to this view, then, society is artificially created by power and force: an artificial mechanism meant to impose predictability on the contin-gency of human agency in the aftermath of the collapse of medieval society. It should be noted that the inexorability of an externally constraining social system – a notion so congenial to the sociologist's frame of mind and one that is shared, ironically, by neo-Walrasian general equilibrium theory – paradoxically derives from particularly narrow views of human nature and social action. Indeed, Hobbes's mechanistic and atomistically individualistic schema archetypally represents the idea of man as a machine moved by utterly egoistic passions served by instrumental rationality only (see the splendid contribution by Dawe, 1978, p. 383).

Because Hayek does not identify order with the means of social control, he does not juxtapose order to absence of cooperation, disintegration, or political turmoil and confusion. Social order in Hayek's account is not a non-excludable, public good (although the provision of public goods may certainly contribute to it); hence there is no 'problem' of its provision. Hayek's claim concerning the existence of social order is a claim about the world we inhabit. Given the deeply social nature of human beings (as op-posed to figments of an atomistic imagination), social order must be as-sumed to be a normal feature of the world and the normal mode of existence for humans. While political systems may be highly unstable, social order as such, at least at the community level, is neither problematical nor random. People usually live in structured, cooperative relationships sustained by rules, institutions and practices. It is up to social theory to explain the emergence, maintenance and transformation of the variety of institutions and practices that social order has actually encompassed.

The central task for social enquiry according to Hayek is not the search for a solution to the problem of social order as canonically articulated by Hobbes; it is rather the tracing out of the orderly patterns and regularities that we do find to exist in society. Taking up a cue from Menger, who had been prompted to consider how it happens that institutions necessary and salutary for the achievement of conscious purposes arise without having been deliberately aimed at by any single human being, Hayek is concerned with those enduring patterns in social relationships which are anything but cloud configurations without stability of structure. To this end Hayek seeks to transcend the 'natural' versus 'artificial' dichotomy handed down from Greek philosophy, inserting a distinct third category allowing for the explication of the orderliness which is, in Adam Ferguson's celebrated, often misquoted words, 'the result of human action, but not the execution of any human design'. There is no difficulty in identifying what Hayek finds so congenial about what he takes to constitute the 'Mandeville–Hume–Smith–Ferguson tradition': (a) the notion that many, if not most, of the institutions and practices on which human achievement depends have arisen and operate independently of a directing mind; and consequently, (b) a sceptical attitude, grounded in inherent limitations of human intelligence to penetrate the intricacy and opacity of social life, towards the feasibility of comprehensive schemes of social and political reform. While Hayek heaps praise on the Scottish contribution to the emerging social theory as exemplary of 'true' individualism and evolutionary rationalism, he is equally dismissive of what he takes to be the pernicious effects emanating from the tradition of 'false', or social-contract individualism and 'constructivist rationalism' (chiefly associated with Descartes, Hobbes and Bentham) – a particularly sinister manifestation, according to Hayek, of grand social engineering ambition, exalting reason and intelligence at the expense of custom, tradition and 'grown' institutions.

Hayek defines an *order* as 'a state of affairs in which a multiplicity of elements of various kinds are so related to each other that we may learn from our acquaintance with some spatial or temporal part of the whole to form correct expectations concerning the rest, or at least expectations which have a good change of proving correct' (Hayek, 1973, p. 36; emphasis deleted). Hayek is adamant that no society can do without persistent social structures being taken for granted and forming the conditions of our experience. An orderly, non-contingent and non-random world is a world in which one knows how to get by, or knows how to find out how to get by; only in such a world does our capacity for learning and memorizing make sense.

What ignites Hayek's intellectual curiosity is whether the order thus conceived comes about as a result of spontaneous formation or of deliberate construction. He therefore draws a sharp distinction between two kinds of order which he variously casts as the difference between (a) an endogenous, self-generating, grown or *spontaneous order* (*cosmos*); and (b) an exogenous, made, created, artificial order, a deliberate arrangement, construction or an *organization* (*taxis*). Drawing on the work of Michael Polanyi (1951), who is usually credited with having coined the phrase 'spontaneous order', Hayek occasionally appeals to the contrast between a polycentric and a monocentric order. It should be noted that the element of predictability inherent in the concept of order would seem to suggest randomness, chance or a lack of predictability as its antithesis. But large-scale disorder is none of Hayek's concern; rather, the emphasis is on the contrast between spontaneous orders and organizations. More correctly, the emphasis is on the distinctiveness of spontaneous orders relative to organizations. The latter is a rather shadowy concept in Hayek; it is merely reactive to, or parasitic upon, the former.

Orders in the above sense are generated by adherence on the part of their elements to systems of rules governing conduct. Since orders exhibit a distinct patterning of relationships among their elements as a result of behaviour conforming to rules, and since we cannot talk about social institutions without mentioning rules, it turns out that orders are nothing but social institutions. Hence spontaneous orders are an important class of institutions. But, as Hayek warns, one has to distinguish carefully between the rules of conduct according to which individual members of a group (or the elements of any order) behave and the overall order, or pattern, of actions forming itself for the group as a whole. Not every system of rules of conduct will produce an orderliness of the system of actions among group members; rule-observing behaviour on the part of the elements may very well produce violent disorder.

The paradigm cases of the spontaneous formation of order in society invariably invoked by Hayek are language, money, markets, morals and the common law. What are the distinguishing features of such spontaneous orders in contradistinction to non-spontaneous orders or organizations? Hayek is by no means unambiguous on this point. At times he conveys the impression that the mode of origin is the sole criterion for the juxtaposition; but on closer inspection it transpires that what really matters is that spontaneous orders rest on abstract rules of just conduct (*nomoi*), enabling individuals to use their knowledge for their own ends, rather than on specific commands – the rules required to run an organization (*theseis*). But there is a snag here, as Hayek notes: the distinction between the two kinds of order in accordance with two kinds of rules they require for their operation collapses when the spontaneous formation of an order is confounded with the spontaneous origin of the rules on which it is based. It is certainly feasible that a spontaneous order may arise from deliberately designed rules. This points to a frequently overlooked aspect of Hayek's theory of spontaneous order, somewhat paradoxically stated: (a) even when individuals coalesce to form organizations with specific, limited ends, such as business partnerships, political parties or schools, there will invariably be involved a patterning of relationships bearing features of a spontaneous order; and (b) the establishment of organizations may only occur within the limits set by the rules associated with extant institutions (whether spontaneous orders or organizations). While his critics would maintain that pure spontaneous orders hardly exist (apart from language, perhaps), Hayek turns the burden of argument on the former, objecting that there are no pure organizations either. While the 'free' society will always include many organizations (indeed, it could not do without them), it is itself never an organization; the coordination between organizations is left to those ordering forces making for a spontaneous order.

There is an ambiguity in Hayek's usage of 'rule' that needs to be cleared up. Occasionally, he conceives of a rule simply as a statement describing regularity of conduct; but usually he means a prescription of a proper course of action. Rules understood in the first sense would not, of course, sustain a distinction between spontaneous and created orders. Rules understood in the second, normative sense are typically abstract and negative when they apply to spontaneous orders, and concrete and positive when they govern behaviour in organizations. Again the distinction is fluid: spontaneous orders can be transformed into created orders by modifying rules to the extent that individual (rule-governed) discretion is reduced to such a degree that the negative rules become in effect positive commands.

John Gray (1986, pp. 33–4) has valuably delineated three distinct aspects of Hayek's theory of spontaneous order. First, there is the thesis that social institutions emerge as the unintended by-product of action rather than from design (invisible-hand thesis). Second, there is the idea that our knowledge of the social world is primarily embodied in practices and skills rather than in theories and that a great deal of this practical knowledge cannot be articulated and communicated. This thesis bolsters Hayek's claim concerning the superior use of knowledge in a market order and puts severe limits on the feasibility of 'interference' and 'control'. Third, there is the controversial claim that the rules (of action and perception) and practices on which a spontaneous social order rests may themselves be the result of cultural evolution by natural selection.

Among those who harbour doubts concerning the general presumption of the beneficence of social evolutionary processes is James Buchanan (1986), whose constitutional political economy comes close to what Hayek pejoratively dubs 'constructivist rationalism'. According to Buchanan, Hayek does not sufficiently heed the distinction between the constitutions, rules and processes, on the one hand, and the end states emerging within this procedural framework, on the other, thereby illegitimately extending the notion of the market as a spontaneous order to the institutions constraining (or, rather, enabling) it. Despite the validity of this sort of criticism, it is surely to Hayek's lasting credit that he resuscitated the dormant idea of spontaneous order which, stripped of its normative excess luggage, provides a powerful explanatory framework for the complex phenomena of the social world.

STEPHAN BOEHM

See also:

Cartesianism in Economics; Cumulative Causation; Determinism and Free Will; Evolution and Optimality; Evolution, Formal Models of Economic; Evolution, Theories of Economic;

Hayek, Friedrich A.; Methodological Individualism; Money, Evolution of; Natural Selection, Economic Evolution and; Prigogine, Ilya; Property; Realism, Philosophical; Rules; Smith, Adam; Social Change, Theory of; Uncertainty; Veblen, Thorstein.

Bibliography

Bauman, Zygmunt (1991), *Modernity and Ambivalence*, Cambridge; Polity.
Buchanan, James M. (1986), 'Cultural Evolution and Institutional Reform', ch.8 in his *Liberty, Market and State: Political Economy in the 1980s*, Brighton: Harvester.
Dawe, Alan (1978), 'Theories of Social Action', in Tom Bottomore and Robert Nisbet (eds), *A History of Sociological Analysis*, London: Heinemann.
Gray, John (1986), *Hayek on Liberty*, 2nd edn, Oxford: Basil Blackwell.
Hamowy, Ronald (1987), *The Scottish Enlightenment and the Theory of Spontaneous Order*, Carbondale and Edwardsville: Southern Illinois University Press.
Hayek, F.A. (1967), *Studies in Philosophy, Politics and Economics*, London: Routledge.
Hayek, F.A. (1973), *Law, Legislation and Liberty: A New Statement of the Liberal Principles of Justice and Political Economy, Vol 1: Rules and Order*, London: Routledge.
Kukathas, Chandran (1989), *Hayek and Modern Liberalism*, Oxford: Clarendon.
Polanyi, Michael (1951), *The Logic of Liberty: Reflections and Rejoinders*, Chicago: University of Chicago Press; Midway reprint 1980.
Sugden, Robert (1989), 'Spontaneous Order', *Journal of Economic Perspectives*, **3**, (4), Fall, pp. 85–97.
Vanberg, Viktor (1982), *Markt und Organisation: Individualistische Sozialtheorie und das Problem des Korporativen Handelns*, Tübingen: J.C.B. Mohr (Paul Siebeck).

Steindl, Josef

Josef Steindl was born in Vienna in 1912 and died in 1993. The significance of his contribution to economics comes from his connecting the process of competition, the distribution of income and wealth, and the problem of macroeconomic stagnation. His starting-point was the work of Michał Kalecki, whom he met at the Oxford Institute of Statistics, where Steindl had come in order to flee the Nazi takeover of his native Austria. In 1950, he returned to Vienna and resumed his prewar position at the Austrian Institute for Economic Research.

Steindl's earliest work was on questions of competition and the growth, size and profitability of firms. His findings, contained in Steindl (1945; 1990, ch.2), were that larger firms hold advantages from economies of scale and greater access to finance, which in turn gives them higher profits. Steindl saw these profits as 'differential rent', owing to the scarcity of accumulations of significant wealth. These profits cannot be competed away, and in fact small firms only survive because of their abilities to draw on cheaper labour, the attachment of a loyal clientele ('goodwill') and the willingness of entrepreneurs to stay in business at negligible profit rates in order to maintain a social position and be one's own boss.

Steindl's concern for the relations between firm size, firm growth and the distribution of wealth later led him to apply the statistical theory of random processes to the matter. This work can be found in Steindl (1965; 1990, chs 22–6). The basic idea is to deal with issues of distribution and growth in an evolutionary, or non-ergodic, fashion, since the ergodic theorem is only valid for a stationary state. Steindl's work explores the applicability of the Pareto distribution and illuminates questions concerning the stability of the distribution of firms by size and of income over time.

After his initial work on issues of firm size, Steindl turned to the question of the relation of monopoly to the stagnation of the industrialized economies leading to the Great Depression. This resulted in his most influential book, *Maturity and Stagnation in American Capitalism* (1976). Applying his theories to the behaviour of the US economy in the last half of the nineteenth century and the first half of the twentieth, Steindl followed Kalecki's reasoning that fluctuations in output and employment occur because of the interactions among investment, profits and productive capacity when price–cost margins are inflexible. Investment spending increases profits by increasing aggregate demand, but it also adds to capacity, which can depress further investment if it becomes sufficient to meet current plus anticipated product demand. If the margin of price above cost (which is mainly labour cost) at a given degree of utilization of capacity should fall, however, real wages would rise, increasing consumption demand, eliminating the excess capacity and spurring more investment. If the margin does not fall, the excess capacity remains as a deterrent to investment until it becomes worn out or obsolete.

Steindl argued that an industry with a spectrum of producers with differing production costs would see the larger, lower-cost firms cut prices relative to costs if faced with undesired excess capacity. As the larger firms were able to price below the costs of their smaller rivals, the smaller firms would not be able to match the lower prices without losing money and so would lose business or be forced out of business, while the bigger firms would eliminate their undesired excess capacity with the sales they gained.

Once an industry reached what Steindl called the stage of 'maturity,' however, in which the 'marginal' firms had been eliminated by the cost and profit advantages of the large firms, cost differentials across firms would become too small for price cutting to work as a competitive tool. Every firm would be large enough to have sufficient financial reserves to match a price cut, and none would have a significant enough cost advantage to withstand a lower margin better than the others. Now if undesired excess capacity emerged, it would not be eliminated by price cutting.

The stage of 'maturity' is thus the stage of 'monopoly', or, better, of oligopoly. The average level of investment spending becomes permanently lowered, and consumption demand from real wage growth does not sufficiently take its place. Steindl held that the process of the emergence of maturity had largely occurred in the US economy by 1890. Its effect on long-term growth, however, had been offset for a while by improvements in the US capital market. The major advance was the increased ability to market shares to the public, which functioned much like a lowering of the rate of interest in channelling saving into increased investment. By the 1920s, however, share yields had become so low that there was bound to be an adverse reaction. This occurred in the stock market crash of 1929, which in turn ushered in the Great Depression, as the force of the inevitable growth slowdown was felt.

In recent years, Steindl has sought to amend the ideas of *Maturity and Stagnation* in the light of self-criticism and to extend the analysis to explain post-World War II developments. Because he felt that the ability of business to exploit innovations took a long time, Steindl assumed in *Maturity and Stagnation* that firms invest only in their own industries. This assumption also enabled him to avoid having his derivation of an endogenous trend contaminated by exogenous innovations. He has since realized that there are innovations with commercial potential which are also scarce enough to attract a significant amount of investment (Steindl, 1976; 1990, ch.9). Though the effect of innovations increases economic growth, Steindl (1990, ch.10) still sees them overtaken by the endogenous forces of the interaction among investment, profits and capacity, along with the longer-run consequences of the rise of oligopoly.

Steindl (1976; 1990, chs 9–17) attributes the revival of prosperity in the industrialized world after World War II and the subsequent downturn since the mid-1970s largely to governmental policy. Tax-financed government spending and technological spillovers plus application backlogs from earlier innovations led to the prosperity. The decline arose in the context of a weakening of technological stimuli and emerging environmental and energy problems, but was largely due to the political reaction in favour of tighter money and of a willingness to tolerate greater unemployment and less social spending to fight inflation. The inequality in the income distribution and the concern of big capital with takeovers and financial and real estate speculation also contributed to depressing aggregate demand.

The evolutionary aspects of Steindl's work come out most strongly in his notion of a distribution of firms by size and cost structure and the implications of this for growth patterns. This has been appreciated by economists such as Stan Metcalfe (for example, 1988), concerned with attempts to apply analogies from the theory of natural selection to the analysis of economic growth and change. Steindl's work was also an important stimulus to the Marxian theory of 'monopoly capital'. Like that of Kalecki, it unites Marxian and Keynesian perspectives. It belongs to the type of economics which explains the economy as a process of self-development.

TRACY MOTT

See also:

Administered Prices; Evolution, Theories of Economic; Kalecki, Michał; Keynes, John Maynard; Marx, Karl; Microfoundations of Macroeconomic Competitiveness; Natural Selection, Economic Evolution and.

Bibliography

Metcalfe, Stan (1988), 'Evolution and Economic Change', in Aubrey Silberston (ed.), *Technology and Economic Progress*, London: Macmillan.

Shapiro, Nina (1988), 'Market Structure and Economic Growth: Steindl's Contribution', *Social Concept*, **4**.

Steindl, Josef (1945), *Small and Big Business: Economic Problems of the Size of Firms*, Oxford: Basil Blackwell.

Steindl, Josef (1965), *Random Processes and the Growth of Firms*, London: Griffin.

Steindl, Josef (1976), *Maturity and Stagnation in American Capitalism*, 2nd edn, with new introduction, New York: Monthly Review Press; first published 1952, Oxford: Basil Blackwell.

Steindl, Josef (1990), *Economic Papers 1941–88*, New York: St Martin's Press.

Tax Theory and Policy

A discussion of institutionalist theories of tax policy must begin with John R. Commons's canon of taxation: 'Taxes should be proportioned *directly* according to a person's ability to pay, and *inversely* according to his ability to serve the commonwealth' (Commons, 1934, p. 819). While the first part of this canon represents an idea that long preceded Commons and that enjoys widespread acceptance to this day, the second part bears close examination, both for its foundation in institutionalist thought and for the implications of such a rule for tax policy.

Commons refers to his 'ability to serve' principle as an expression of the 'police power of taxation': 'Even when not consciously intended to be regulative, taxes nevertheless regulate, for they ... determine the directions in which people may become wealthy by determining directions in which they may not become wealthy. ... Taxation is, in fact, a process of obtaining public revenue by proportioning inducements to obtain profits' (Commons, 1934, p. 820). He also says: 'If we look at a tax from the police-power standpoint of what may be expected as the economic results of the tax, then we shall inquire: What will be the best inducements to individuals to increase the commonwealth by increasing their own wealth?' (Commons, 1934, p. 819).

The idea that tax policy should be designed to provide incentives to individuals to engage in productive behaviour that maximizes public benefits is supported by the writings of Thorstein Veblen, in his distinction between ceremonial and instrumental behaviour. If one accepts the validity and significance of this Veblenian dichotomy, one is led to acknowledge the importance of making distinctions between productive and unproductive activity or uses of wealth in the design of tax policy. The tax system should reward productive, instrumental activity that adds to the commonwealth, and penalize mere speculation or the accumulation of idle wealth to provide for conspicuous consumption. It is also important to note that, in the writings of Commons, policy decisions distinguishing productive from unproductive activity are to be made through collective action; the public is to define what constitutes a public benefit.

This institutionalist approach to tax policy contrasts sharply with neoclassical orthodoxy. Ever since neoclassical economists pronounced as invalid the interpersonal comparison of utility, they have been unabashed in their agnosticism on the issue of the correct or optimal degree of progressivity or regressivity – that is, exactly how taxes are to be proportioned to ability to pay. On the other hand, neoclassical theory elevates 'neutrality' to the status of a canon of taxation above all others. A neutral tax is one which is stripped entirely of any elements of the police power of taxation; for precisely as a tax induces the taxpayer to behave in one fashion rather than another, it is non-neutral and therefore causes inefficiencies and deadweight losses. It is worthwhile counterpoising the institutionalist views on progressivity and neutrality.

Institutionalists have made a variety of arguments in favour of substantial progressivity in the tax system. First, there is the obvious concern for a more egalitarian distribution of income on grounds of fairness. Second, a progressive tax system plays an important macroeconomic role as one of the automatic stabilizers. Third, it is a convenient device for taxing unearned income or economic rent more heavily than earned income, since unearned income and rents account for a larger share of the total income of those in the highest brackets. Fourth, a progressive tax reduces the ability of the wealthy to buy political influence. Fifth, it enhances the commonwealth to the extent that it contributes to the alleviation of poverty and hence promotes greater health and productivity and fuller participation of all members of society. Finally, progressivity is consistent with the idea that ability to pay is best measured, not by total income, but by discretionary income, income above that needed to purchase the basic necessities of life. This is the notion behind the 'credit income tax' as proposed by Wallace Peterson (1982) and others; income is measured comprehensively and taxed at a low flat rate, but a large credit is allowed for each household member reflecting the non-discretionary income that should remain free of tax. Modern institutionalists, in other words, feel no need to resurrect formal notions of cardinal utility and interpersonal comparisons of utility to justify taking a higher portion of the incomes of the rich on the grounds that the last dollar earned by the rich yields less utility. Nor do they cling to the fiction that economic science can or should be value-free. Instead, their defence of progressivity is based on pragmatic grounds and on basic egalitarian values.

The second major point of difference between neoclassical and institutional theories of taxation is the issue of neutrality. The principle of tax neutrality is founded on an assumption that markets of all kinds are everywhere perfectly competitive, or at least close approximations thereof. Only in such a competitive general equilibrium can one justifiably assert that a departure from neutrality is inefficient. If we have attained the best of all possible worlds, then there is nothing left for tax policy to regulate; its role must be to raise revenue without disturbing that perfect equilibrium. This leads to an important corollary of the neoclassical canon; departures from non-neutrality are justified if and only if the tax would correct a market failure such as an externality or the exercise of monopoly power. Again, competitive markets are presumed, and the burden of proof is on those who assert that a certain product or activity is underpriced or overpriced, underproduced or overproduced, and that this can be corrected through tax policy.

Institutionalists start from no such presumption of competitive general equilibrium. They see instead a world where perfect competition is the exception, where prices are determined and resources allocated through the exercise of market power, in varying degrees, where external or social costs are pervasive, and where any assumption about the social optimality of the existing set of prices and production levels and the existing distribution of income is simply absurd. In such a world, the canon of neutrality is not only useless, it is pernicious, for its application reinforces the inequities and irrationalities of the status quo. Much better is the pragmatic principle that, on grounds of fairness, taxes should extract more from those with greater ability to pay, and that, on the grounds of promoting the commonwealth or of enhancing the economy's ability to sustain and expand the material standard of living, taxes should 'regulate' economic activity away from unproductive and wasteful uses of society's resources and in the direction of productive uses. Such a position leads to support for, among other things, a shift in property taxation away from improvements that add to the stock of society's productive wealth and towards land, whose increase in value is socially created, unearned and often speculative.

This is not to say that institutionalists would reject the prescription that follows from the neoclassical market failure corollary: tax external costs and subsidize social benefits, so that market prices reflect total social costs of production. But the institutional approach is broader and more flexible; the concept of taxing to promote the public good encompasses much more than production and consumption externalities and does not begin with a presumption that markets are perfect unless proved otherwise. The public good is an evolving concept, defined by the legal system and by the collective process of establishing laws, appropriating funds and levying taxes.

Justice Louis Brandeis exemplified this institutional view of the police power of taxation in an opinion regarding a Florida statute that imposed discriminatory taxes on chain stores:

> The purpose of the Florida statute is not, like ordinary taxation, merely to raise revenue. Its main purpose is social and economic. ... The citizens of the State. ... may have believed that the chain store, by furthering the concentration of wealth and of power and by promoting absentee ownership, is thwarting American ideals; that it is making impossible equality of opportunity; that it is converting independent tradesmen into clerks; and that it is sapping the resources, the vigor and the hope of the smaller cities and towns. [The State] may exempt from taxation kinds of business which it wishes to promote ... and may burden more heavily kinds of business which it wishes to discourage. (Reprinted in Groves, 1947, pp. 320–21)

Clearly the kinds of public purposes cited by Brandeis cannot easily be subsumed under the neoclassical concept of 'externalities'.

How would institutionalists approach the current debates over the uses of the tax system to promote investment and economic development? One might infer from Commons's canon that policies such as the investment tax credit or the capital gains preference or local property tax abatements for industry are just the sort of policies that he had in mind when he wrote of inducements to promote the commonwealth. If so, Commons would be at odds with many contemporary institutionalists who have argued for income tax reform that eliminates all tax preferences and loopholes (Galbraith, 1973; Peterson, 1982) and instead imposes a lower uniform rate on a comprehensive income base.

The empirical and pragmatic bent of institutionalists of whatever stripe, including Commons, would lead them to view quite critically the particular form that investment incentives have taken in recent practice. There is in fact little evidence that such incentives have benefited the economy. The capital gains preference may play a minor role in encouraging high-risk investments in new ventures, but it also subsidizes a panoply of unproductive and purely speculative investments and is fundamentally a redistribution to the very rich. Commons himself recognized clearly the potential abuses of the police power of taxation and his 'ability to serve' principle:

> It can always be objected that such a maxim opens the door to the prejudices, passions, and struggles for power of individuals and classes. ... Well, it is already being done ... consciously, unconsciously, blindly, ignorantly, by greed and camouflage. ... It is better to recognize this openly than to deceive ourselves. We can then base our case ... on whether or not its economic effect will be what it is asserted to be, a public benefit. (Commons, 1934, p. 821)

Harold Groves has argued that the influence of institutional economics on public finance has been profound (Groves, 1964). This influence is reflected in (a) an emphasis on empirical research and on the historical development of institutions, (b) a pragmatic approach to the use of government to promote the public good, (c) a view that economists should earn their keep by contributing to the development of public policy, (d) a concern with the promotion of real productivity rather than merely pecuniary interests, and (e) the identification of the importance of the intangible element in property and the concept of the value of an asset as forward-looking rather than derived from historical costs, a crucial issue in the valuation and taxation of property

Institutionalist thought contributes importantly to current debates on tax policy. The institutionalist defences of progressivity, and the public benefit rationales for 'non-neutral' tax expenditures, find little support in orthodox economics principles texts, yet these institutionalist rationales can often be found in statements of legislative intent and in populist and progressive positions on tax issues. Perhaps most importantly, institutional theory demolishes the 'value-free' and 'objective' basis for the neoclassical concept of neutrality and exposes it as a rationalization for the status quo distribution of wealth and economic power. Institutionalism substitutes a collectively determined public good, or the promotion of the commonwealth, as the standard to judge the economic effects of taxation.

PETER S. FISHER

See also:
Commons, John R.; Distribution Theory; Law and Economics; Macroeconomic Policy; Power; Public Sector, Role of the; Veblen, Thorstein; Veblenian Dichotomy and Its Critics; Welfare Economic Theory.

Bibliography
Brandeis, Justice Louis D. (1947), Dissenting opinion in *Liggett* v. *Lee*; reprinted in Harold M. Groves (ed.) *Viewpoints on Public Finance*, pp. 318–25, New York: Henry Holt and Company.
Commons, John R. (1934), *Institutional Economics: Its Place in Political Economy*, New York: Macmillan.
Galbraith, John Kenneth (1973), *Economics and the Public Purpose*, Boston, Mass.: Houghton Mifflin.
Groves, Harold M. (1964), 'Institutional Economics and Public Finance', *Land Economics*, **40**, (3), August, pp. 239–46.
Peterson, Wallace (1982), *Our Overloaded Economy*, Armonk, NY: M.E. Sharpe.

Technical Change and Technological Regimes

Not only 'evolutionary' economists but virtually all economists have recognized technical change as the principal source of dynamism in capitalist economies. Differences of approach and disagreements arise, not with respect to the importance of technical change for productivity growth and the introduction of new products, processes and services, but in relation to the measurement of technical change and its role in economic analysis and models. The notions of technological trajectories, technological paradigms and technological regimes attracted particular attention from evolutionary economists in the 1980s, but were almost completely neglected by orthodox theory. For many twentieth-century economists their acknowledgement of the importance of technical change amounted to little more than lip-service. Having given it a deferential nod they then proceeded to ignore it in most of their work. Thus, for example, Keynes, whilst once acknowledging that Schumpeter's explanation of the main trends in investment behaviour could be 'unreservedly accepted' (Keynes, 1930) generally ignored technical change in his later work on business cycles and employment.

Schumpeter was almost alone among economists in the first half of the twentieth century in placing technical change at the very centre of his entire analysis. He linked his theory of the long-term evolution of the capitalist system to the diffusion of waves of technical and organizational innovations, which he described as 'successive industrial revolutions' (Schumpeter, 1939). But even Schumpeter devoted relatively little attention to specific innovations and their diffusion and to the analysis of ordered patterns of technical change. Jewkes *et al.* (1958) attributed the tendency of mainstream economists to disregard technical change to their preoccupation with other problems, especially unemployment and cyclical phenomena. To the neo-Schumpeterian economist this explanation is revealing. Jewkes and his colleagues (1958) were among the few economists in the 1950s who did indeed concentrate on technical change in their classic *The Sources of Invention*, but it is clear that they regarded this study as an *alternative* to the study of business cycles and economic development. For Schumpeter and neo-Schumpeterians, technical change is at the heart of their analysis of economic growth and development itself including cyclical phenomena. However, Jewkes *et al.* also offered another more convincing explanation of the neglect of technical change by most twentieth-century economists. They pointed to the extraordinary difficulties of measurement in this field and to the fact that most economists were not at home with natural science and technology and therefore preferred to consign technical change to a 'black box' to be opened sometimes by technologists and historians, but not by economists.

There are indeed acute problems of classification and measurement when we come to open the black box and look inside it. For example, there are tens of thousands of patents for inventions taken out every year and although we can enumerate them and classify them in various useful ways (for example, Pavitt, 1988) there are persistent problems of reconciling the technological classification systems used by most patent offices with the industrial classifications used by most economists and government statisticians. Anyone who has worked with patent statistics (as many evolutionary economists have) knows that the dynamics of technologies do not respect conventional industry boundaries and may give rise to entirely new industries, so that statistical systems lag far behind new developments in technology.

When it comes to *innovations* the problems are even more formidable. With patents we do at least have an enormous international statistical data base, with a very long time series, which can with care and ingenuity be used for a wide variety of comparative studies between industries and technologies (see, for example, Schmookler, 1966; Achilladelis *et al.*, 1990). In the case of innovations and their diffusion there are no comprehensive statistics for firms, industries or countries. There are a growing number of academic research projects, including doctoral dissertations, which have attempted to measure and classify innovations in particular sectors (for example, Hufbauer, 1965) and to analyse the diffusion of specific innovations. There are also a few attempts at more comprehensive measurement of innovation in many sectors over long time periods, such as the SPRU Data Bank on Innovations (Pavitt and Townsend, 1987). This Data Bank has proved very valuable for many purposes, especially the assessment of the contribution of small firms to innovation. It has also proved useful for the study of inter-industry technology flows but it still falls far short of what is needed.

Neither in the case of inventions, nor in the case of innovations and their diffusion, do we have any generally agreed method of assessing and measuring their *relative* importance. Yet they clearly vary enormously in their technical and economic significance. For some purposes, as Schmookler (1966) argued, these differences can be disregarded. The aggregation of large numbers of patents makes it possible to develop useful comparisons despite the varying significance of individual patents. It is also possible to 'weight' or rank individual patents or innovations in terms of certain characteristics. Thus, for example, a number of authors (for example, Baker, 1976) have used the concept of 'key patents' or 'master patents' and have shown that numerous other 'minor patents' or 'secondary patents' have been either derivative or follow-up inventions based on these primary inventions or have been designed to establish the position of competitive firms without direct legal infringement of the original inventions (sometimes known as 'me-too patents'). An historical approach is thus essential to the interpretation of patent data and much can also be learnt about technological trajectories from patent citations (Narin, 1986).

Once evolutionary economists began to open the black box and study the development of technology, using patent data and other historical sources, they became increasingly aware of the importance of clustering phenomena and of the emergence of ordered patterns of change. It was quite evident to historians of science and technology, as to evolutionary economists, that the activities of scientists and technologists have their own internal dynamics even though the way in which a particular technology develops is heavily influenced by economic circumstances and by the social milieux (often described as the 'selection environment'). Thus Nelson and Winter (1977) in their seminal paper 'In Search of a Useful Theory of Innovation', which set the research agenda for a whole generation of neo-Schumpeterian economists, spoke of 'natural trajectories' in technology and of generalized natural trajectories for some especially influential technologies. Dosi (1982) systematically developed both the idea of natural trajectories and the concept of 'technological paradigms' by analogy with Kuhn's (1962) scientific paradigms. Sahal (1985) followed a parallel path in developing his concepts of 'technological guideposts' and 'innovation avenues'. These and other authors point to such examples as aircraft technology and microelectronic technology where, over a considerable period, new developments followed a relatively ordered (and to some degree predictable) pattern. 'In microelectronics technical change is accurately represented by an exponential trajectory of improvement in the relationship between density of the electronic chips, speed of computation, and cost per bit of information' (Dosi, 1984).

Moore's law of the annual doubling of the number of components in successive new generations of microchips was first formulated in 1964 and proved reasonably accurate for at least 30 years from the first planar process transistor in 1959. Even in areas where the pattern of technical change is less clearly evident and regular, it is fairly obvious that the search for new advances is not completely unconstrained but starts from the neighbourhood of past achievements and present knowledge. However, the idea that such trajectories are in some sense 'natural' or predetermined has been effectively criticized by sociologists, especially Donald MacKenzie (1990). He pointed out that, while the idea that a trajectory shows a persistent pattern is unexceptionable, a trajectory can never have a momentum 'of its own'. Patterns are persistent partly because scientists, technologists, designers and others believe they will persist and act accordingly. Trajectories are self-fulfilling prophecies based on the actors' expectations of the future. Like any institutions they are sustained not by 'naturalness' but by the interests that develop in their continuance and the belief that they will continue. This belief of course is not arbitrary but is founded on previous knowledge, experimental work and discoveries.

This insistence by sociologists on the role of beliefs and institutions in sustaining trajectories is an important corrective to the economists' tendency to classify observed regularities and patterns as 'natural', whether it be the rate of unemployment, the rate of interest or a technological trajectory. It is all the more important when we come to consider the interrelationships between a variety of trajectories and the prevailing social institutions governing the behaviour of the system as a whole. A satisfactory evolutionary theory in economics has to be 'Lamarckian' rather than 'Darwinian' and take into account the role of purposive action and beliefs of individuals and social groups. Furthermore, it must take into account that the 'selection environment' for technical change involves not only firms in competition, but the internal workings of the science and technology system. That is not all; it must also include both the natural environment and the built environment comprising the capital stock embodying past innovations, and the interaction between this capital stock, social institutions and new technological trajectories (Freeman, 1991). Thus it must go well beyond the selection of individual 'mutations' and deal with new technological systems and the conditions under which they emerge to dominance.

One such attempt to develop a more comprehensive evolutionary theory on these lines was that of Carlota Perez (1983, 1985). She advanced the notion of 'technoeconomic paradigms' which affect not one industry or sector but many and sometimes all. Examples of extremely pervasive technologies are steam power, electric power or computer technology. In her conceptualization such technologies are associated with Schumpeter's long waves of economic development, offering numerous new applications both in product and process design throughout the economic system. A technoeconomic paradigm is a set of commonsense guidelines for technological and investment decisions as pervasive new technologies mature. It introduces a strong bias in both technical and organizational innovations which are increasingly embodied in capital equipment and software. This cumulative bias tends to lock out alternative technological innovations and trajectories. The advantages of conforming to a particular pattern of technical change are related to the falling costs and scale economies of key inputs to the productive process, such as steel in the 'Third Kondratieff Wave' (1880s–1930s), oil in the Fourth Wave based on Fordist mass production (1930s–1980s) and microelectronics in the present wave. Some aspects of the locking-in mechanisms which tend to reinforce an established technology have been analysed by Brian Arthur (1988) and Paul David (1985). Their work and that of Perez show why the combined influence of standards, textbooks, availability of low-cost components and materials, fashions, training systems, management routines, technological expectations, advantageous infrastructure and scale economies is so great that, once established, a technoeconomic paradigm becomes a dominant technological regime for several decades (corresponding to the upswing and boom period of the Kondratieff long waves). The new paradigm is so strongly entrenched that it appears as the only 'natural' commonsense path of development.

The dominance of each regime is reinforced by a variety of political and social institutions, including government policies to promote particular infrastructures, research programmes, sectoral privileges, management systems, educational and training activities and so forth. However, ultimately any technological regime approaches diminishing returns and both the rate of productivity improvement and profit margins tend to be eroded. Diminishing returns frequently arise from social and organizational problems, as well as from limits to particular trajectories of technical advance. The combined effect leads to a structural crisis of adjustment of the regime. A new technoeconomic paradigm emerges at first within the old regime, attempting to overcome its limitations. But gradually it becomes apparent that the displacement of the old paradigm involves a profound process of institutional change, since social institutions have been adapted for a long time to match the characteristics and developmental potential of the older technologies. The mismatch between the old institutions and the potential of the newly emerging technoeconomic paradigm is thus the source of the recession and depression phases of the Schumpeterian long wave and the intense efforts at social, political and managerial reform associated with such periods. Ultimately, a variety of solutions are found to the mismatch problems at regional, national and international levels and once more a new technological regime is consolidated.

Evolutionary economists, historians of technology, sociologists and other disciplines have only begun the difficult work of classifying, measuring and interpreting the dynamics of technical change, but many suggestive insights developed once the black box was opened.

CHRISTOPHER FREEMAN

See also:
Ayres, Clarence E.; Evolution, Theories of Economic; Innovation, National Systems of; Lock-in and Chreodic Development; Long Waves; Nelson, Richard R.; Schumpeter, Joseph Alois; Technology in Development Policy; Technology, Theory of; Veblen, Thorstein; Winter, Sidney G., Jr.

Bibliography
Achilladelis, B., A. Schwarzkopf and M. Cimes (1990), 'The Dynamics of Technological Innovation: the Case of the Chemical Industry', *Research Policy*, **19**, (1), pp. 1–35.

Arthur, B. (1988), 'Competing Technologies: an Overview', ch.26 in G. Dosi, C. Freeman, R.R. Nelson, G. Silverberg and L.L.G. Soete (eds), *Technical Change and Economic Theory*, London: Pinter.

Baker, B. (1976), *New and Improved – Inventors and Inventions that have Changed the Modern World*, London: British Museum Publications Ltd.

David, P. (1985), 'Clio and the Economics of QWERTY', *American Economic Review*, **75**, (2), pp. 332–7.

Dosi, G. (1982), 'Technological Paradigms and Technological Trajectories', *Research Policy*, **11**, (3), pp. 147–62.

Dosi, G. (1984), *Technical Change and Industrial Transformation*, London: Macmillan.

Freeman, C. (1991), 'Innovation, Changes of techno-economic paradigm and biological analogies in economics', *Revue Economique*, **42**, (2), pp. 211–31.

Hufbauer, G. (1965), *Synthetic Materials in International Trade*, London: Duckworth.

Jewkes, J., D. Sawers and J. Stillerman (1958), *The Sources of Invention*, London: Macmillan.

Keynes, J.M. (1930), *A Treatise on Money*, Vol. 2, p. 86, London: Macmillan.

Kuhn, T. (1962), *The Structure of Scientific Revolutions*, Chicago: University of Chicago Press.

MacKenzie, D. (1990), 'Economic and Sociological Explanation of Technical Change', paper given at Manchester Conference on Firm Strategy, 27–8 September (mimeo), Sociology Department, University of Edinburgh.

Narin, F. (1986), 'Identifying Areas of Leading Edge Japanese Technology', report to National Science Foundation, Washington, DC.

Nelson, R.R. and S. Winter (1977), 'In Search of Useful Theory of Innovation', *Research Policy*, **6**, (1), pp. 36–77.

Pavitt, K.L.R. (1988), 'Uses and Abuses of Patent Statistics', ch.16 in A. van Raan (ed.), *Handbook of Quantitative Studies in Science and Technology*, Amsterdam: Elsevier.

Pavitt, K.L.R. and J. Townsend (1987), 'Technological Accumulation, Diversification and Organisation in UK Companies 1945–1987', DRC Discussion Paper No.50, SPRU, University of Sussex.

Perez, C. (1983), 'Structural Change and the Assimilation of New Technologies in the Social System', *Futures*, **15**, (5), pp. 357–75.

Perez, C. (1985), 'Micro-electronics, Long Waves and World Structural Change', *World Development*, **13**, (3), pp. 441–63.

Sahal, D. (1985), 'Technological Guideposts and Innovation Avenues', *Research Policy*, **14**, (2), pp. 61–82.

Schmookler, J. (1966), *Invention and Economic Growth*, Cambridge, Mass.: Harvard University Press.

Schumpeter, J. (1939), *Business Cycles: a Theoretical, Historical and Statistical Analysis of the Capitalist Process*, 2 vols, New York: McGraw-Hill.

Technology in Development Policy

Economists concerned with economic development are acutely aware that the direction and pace of technological change affect the rate of economic growth, productivity trends, interaction among economic sectors, international trade patterns, income distribution, employment levels and skill profiles of the labour force. Nevertheless, economists with neoclassical leanings see a very limited role for policy measures designed to directly influence technology. While many recognize the existence of market failures that lead to sub-optimal generation or use of technology, for example, externalities, risk aversion, price rigidities, information asymmetries, indivisibilities and public goods, their primary focus is on perfecting the market mechanism. Furthermore, technology is often slighted while attention is concentrated on savings and investment as the engines of economic expansion.

In contrast, no group of social scientists is more devoted than institutional economists to explaining the origins of technological advance and delineating its socioeconomic consequences. For them the repercussions of technological dynamics go far beyond the purely economic ones mentioned above; technology alters socioeconomic patterns, distribution of political power and cultural values. Other characteristics further differentiate institutionalism from neoclassical economics. Institutionalists view technology as a key element – some would say the central element – in the process of socioeconomic development and, partly owing to the importance accorded technology, technological change is routinely included as an endogenous variable within their analytical framework. They focus on the constant interaction and flux of social and technical systems rather than concentrating on equilibria or teleologically specified targets. A multidisciplinary, holistic approach to problem solving is the norm for institutionalists, and they are convinced that solving problems with a technological dimension requires conscious valuational judgements. Institutionalists consistently recommend policy measures that either augment or reshape market forces.

While it is true that institutionalists share concerns with orthodox economists about market failures, rather than being rare anomalies they are considered obvious, regular and frequent outcomes of a market-driven economy.

The solution lies not in attacking individual market failures on an ad hoc basis, but through a concerted planning effort, one which includes scientific and technological activities, featuring indicative goals, priorities and procedures. In this regard much admiration has been expressed for the way Japan has augmented and guided her private sector and, although it was never implemented, Mexico's 1976 indicative plan on science and technology is considered a model for developing countries.

In reviewing and evaluating alternative goals and priorities, conventional assessment techniques can, at best, tell only part of the story. Intergenerational consequences of employing some technologies – the shrinking and/or thinning of the earth's ozone layer or the accumulation of dangerous nuclear wastes being prime examples – render current discount rates suspect. Moreover, some technologies go beyond economics, narrowly defined – cost–benefit analysis is an inadequate guide as to who should receive a kidney transplant or whether, at some future date, it will be socially desirable to clone oneself or a close friend. For these and other reasons, instrumental valuational decisions must be made regarding whether and how to employ specific technologies.

Substituting pecuniary norms for instrumental values contributes to an unenthusiastic pursuit of ecologically sound technologies, a slighting of preventive medical technologies, inadequate public support for education and inequitable distribution of the fruits of technological progress. As the military–industrial complex has illustrated, the intensity and trajectory of scientific and technological effort is subject to encapsulization by controlling institutions. In these cases, vested interests and power bestowed by prevailing institutions discourage the discussion of alternative avenues for enhancing national security and attaining other socioeconomic goals.

Institutionalists are fully cognizant that *non*-market failures can lead to misuse of technology and/or inadequate technological advance. A considerable amount of effort is directed to analysing science and technology policies that have been implemented in national settings with different material and human resource bases, technological preconditions, economic systems and sociopolitical institutions.

Developing countries confront additional problems. Beginning in the 1950s, the dominant technology strategy of third world countries centred on acquiring technology from the more advanced industrial nations. Although most developing nations remained anxious to obtain new production techniques from abroad, they complained about monopoly elements in the markets for technology and about a poor fit between imported technologies and their factor endowments, market sizes and social conditions. As a result, in the late 1960s and early 1970s, many larger developing countries established regulations designed to reduce their disadvantages in the technology market and steer acquisitions to technologies more compatible with national needs. During the same period, many of these countries established national science and technology councils. In general, institutional economists were sympathetic to these moves and they also joined other development economists in recommending that third world countries strengthen their bargaining position with multinational enterprises, the suppliers of most technology being imported, by cultivating other sources (small and medium-sized firms, Eastern European countries, and other developing countries), accumulating skills in bargaining, and insisting that domestic personnel be placed in key positions in local multinational affiliates.

Beginning in the 1980s, there has been a marked change in emphasis by the third world. There is now a keen interest in accumulating internal technological capacity, a goal which embraces technology transfer, but one which includes other important ingredients. Illustratively, institutionalists and other heterodox economists are convinced that, for a variety of reasons, the domestic production of capital goods is exceptionally potent in generating and disseminating technical learning. Thus there may well be a case for protecting or otherwise supporting this sector as a means of fostering indigenous technological mastery.

At least four specific difficulties need to be ameliorated before widespread benefits will flow from internal R&D in the South (James, 1989). All too frequently, research institutions suffer from poor maintenance and irrational acquisition of equipment, from top scientists performing routine tasks owing to the shortage of technicians to career paths biased towards scientists moving into administrative positions. A second problem lies with R&D project selection in developing countries. It is widely held that there is such a proliferation of projects that few are able to muster a critical minimum of human and other resources necessary for a high probability of success. An excessive amount of developing nations' R&D budget tends to be spent on pure or basic projects *vis-à-vis* applied investigations. Furthermore, international R&D vogues exert a powerful influence on project selection, leading to the neglect of undertakings contributing to local development. The dearth of linkages between R&D, on the one hand, and supporting institutions, on the other, constitutes a third shortcoming. In the majority of developing countries, R&D institutes are poorly integrated with universities, technical consultants, financial institutions, relevant governmental ministries and, above all, the productive sector. The fourth impediment is the most elusive: even in some relatively advanced developing countries there is evidence that the potential benefits from science and technology are insufficiently appreciated, not only by the masses, but also in the political and economic arenas. In short, there is a lack of 'socialization' regarding science and technology. By identifying the most recalcitrant attitudes and suggesting the most promising 'pressure points' for instilling a realistic view of technical change and its consequences, institutional economics could provide some potent avenues for overcoming this condition.

The foregoing comments should not be misunderstood. Top-notch scientific and technological investigation and application is being done in the South. The problem is that it is not pervasive and commonly not cost-effective. Solutions lie in restructuring incentives in R&D institutes, altering institutions affecting project choice and encouraging a more positive attitude about science and technology through education and public awareness campaigns.

In addition to institutionalists, there is another group of evolutionary economists, often referred to as neo-Schumpeterians. Some of their key concepts, such as 'technological trajectories' and 'technoeconomic paradigms', correctly imply that they, like institutionalists, treat technological change as an important endogenous variable. Although still using orthodox analytical tools and dependent on conventional methodology in gauging costs and benefits, neo-Schumpeterian economists, by using an interdisciplinary approach, assumptions with empirical foundations and more imaginative ways of dealing with the dynamic aspects of technology, have begun to affect the direction and character of inquiry on technology policy. As a group they have led the way in investigating the socioeconomic impacts of emerging technologies that have far-flung applications, for example in modern biotechnology, microelectronics and new materials. Several neo-Schumpeterian economists have been instrumental in reviving interest in technology-driven, long-term economic cycles. Some are investigating the interaction between technological change and the behavioural facets of business firms, industrial organization and public policy. All recognize, as do institutionalists, the poverty of treating economic adjustment in terms of successive states of equilibrium since, through time, important elements of the whole economic environment are continuously altered.

Neo-Schumpeterians have been far more active in questioning orthodox theories of international trade than have the institutionalists. They eschew the neoclassical treatment of technology as discrete bits of knowledge that, once available, is freely transferable and they dispute the notion that the appropriate choice of technique rests primarily on relative factor prices. Neo-Schumpeterians insist that much technology cannot be easily codified and therefore is only partly appropriable through technology transfer. The cumulative process of technological advance is evolutionary in the sense that 'history counts' – the pace, general direction and specific branching of technological change is rooted in the ways innovative search processes are conducted, the intensity of linkages with various knowledge bases, the nature of supporting or inhibiting institutions and the degree to which gains from innovation can be appropriated. The composite situation will differ among firms and among nations, a circumstance that goes a long way to explaining persistent intra-industry and national technology gaps.

Using this foundation, one group of neo-Schumpeterians (Dosi *et al.*, 1990; Soete, 1990) have been developing the thesis that the process of evolutionary innovation gives rise to technologies that are unequivocally superior, regardless of relative factor prices. This leads them to contend that the volume and pattern of world trade depend on Ricardian comparative advantage *and absolute differences* in technology-determined competitiveness. To a large extent, the latter influence predominates. This suggests that, for most nations, free trade is a very inefficient vehicle for fostering national technological capacity. Most institutionalists look favourably on a strategic trade policy, supporting a portfolio of selected industries that have the potential for (a) attaining a dynamic comparative advantage through intra-industry technological improvements and (b) generating beneficial externalities in the form of technical learning that radiates to other segments of the economy. The neo-Schumpeterian position embraces a strategic trade policy, but goes much further in recommending improved economic incentives, educational reform and public support for basic R&D. They make a convincing case that exclusive reliance on comparative advantage resting on relative factor endowments merely perpetuates the prevailing 'pecking order' of technology gaps that one observes in contemporary global commerce.

It is clear that neo-Schumpeterians share with institutionalists a favourable view of active public policy designed to encourage technological advance. Although their efforts have focused primarily on mature industrial countries, one might expect that they will be increasingly enticed by the problems surrounding third world technology policy. In addition we might hope that the future holds a fruitful cross-fertilization between the institutional and neo-Schumpeterian strains of evolutionary economics.

DILMUS D. JAMES

See also:

Comparative Economic Systems; Cost–Benefit Analysis; Development Policy; Development Theory; Environmental Policy; Hirschman, Albert O.; Innovation, National Systems of; Instrumental Value Theory; International Economic Policy; Kapp, K. William; Long Waves; Myrdal, Gunnar; Planning, National Economic; Power; Schumpeter, Joseph Alois; Technical Change and Technological Regimes; Technology, Theory of.

Bibliography

Dietz, J.L. (1990), 'Technological Autonomy, Linkages and Development', in J.L. Dietz and D.D. James (eds), *Progress Toward Development in Latin America: From Prebisch to Technological Autonomy*, Boulder, Colo.: Lynne Rienner.
Dosi, G., C. Freeman, G. Silverberg and L. Soete (eds) (1988), *Technical Change and Economic Theory*, London and New York: Pinter.

Dosi, G., K. Pavitt and L. Soete (1990), *The Economics of Technical Change and International Trade*, New York: New York University Press.
James, D.D. (1989), 'Importation and Local Generation of Technology by the Third World: An Institutionalist Perspective', in T.R. DeGregori (ed.), *The Development Challenge: Theory Practice and Prospects*, Boston, Mass.: Kluwer-Nijhoff.
Lower, M.D. (1987), 'The Concept of Technology Within the Institutionalist Perspective', *Journal of Economic Issues*, **XXI**, (3), September, pp. 1147–76.
Soete, L. (1990), 'Technical Change Theory and International Trade Competition', in L. de la Mothe and L.M. Ducharme (eds), *Science, Technology and Free Trade*, London: Pinter.

Technology, Theory of

Technology has been central to evolutionary economic thinking from Thorstein Veblen onward. Inherent in the very concept of evolutionary economics is change. Technology has been understood to be the dynamic force in economic, societal and cultural transformation. A critical dimension of the institutional theory of technology was derived by Clarence E. Ayres from John Dewey's instrumental value theory. Tools or technology are instrumental in human problem solving. The success of an idea or its embodiment in technology is the degree to which it solves a problem. Problem solving involves the value-laden activity of problem definition. Without a theory of value, one cannot distinguish tools and technology from a trivial contraption. With a theory of value, one can speak about technological progress and use the concept to lay the foundation for a theory of economic development. As Dewey and Ayres repeatedly argued, the truth and its working out are two aspects of the same process. Technology is first and foremost ideas.

The term 'evolutionary' is appropriately used in economics to describe the development of technology. The implicit analogy to biological evolution is apt and historically justified. Our ancestors were using tools long before they were biologically human. Humans developed in conjunction with technology in a larger framework that we call culture. Technology and culture have often been seen as simply an extension of human capability. The anthropologist Clifford Geertz counters that, 'rather than culture acting only to supplement, develop, and extend organically based capacities genetically prior to it, it would seem to be an ingredient to these capacities themselves' (Geertz, 1973, p. 68). Geertz goes on to indicate how meaningless it is to conceive of a 'cultureless human' for our brain, 'having arisen within the framework of human culture, would not be viable outside it' (Geertz, 1973, p. 68).

Biologically, we are a tropical primate restricted to a narrow band of habitat subject to extinction as a result of climatic change. With technology, we adapted the environment to our needs rather than adapting through biological evolution to the imperatives of the environment. Technology is a dynamic cumulative process. It is from the cumulative body of knowledge which we have been using to transform the world that we derive the building blocks for new technological knowledge. The more technology/knowledge, the greater the possibilities for combinations and for new technologies. The process is not deterministic but it is probabilistic in that, in aggregate, technology is likely to accelerate through time. With the ever-increasing body of technological ideas has emerged knowledge of how the process itself works.

The institutional/instrumentalist theorizing on technology has always stressed that it is a continuing problem-solving process. It is neither teleological nor utopian. Problem solving treats ends-in-view rather than an 'ultimate' end. Technology is both a problem-solving and a problem-creating process. As Veblen aptly notes, invention is the mother of necessity, in that we adapt our lives and number to it. John Dewey saw human problems, not as a source of despair, but as an opportunity to create. The opening thesis of Dewey's *The Quest for Certainty* (1929) concerns the difference between responding to adversity by seeking to propitiate supranatural powers through a sheltering belief system or by fashioning the means to overcome adversity and in so doing generate the ideas and technology that enable us to create the arts and civilization. All the vital areas of human endeavour are transformed by technological change and the creative potential it engenders.

C.E. Ayres often explored the dual implications of the phrase, 'the power of ideas'. Ideas/technology have power because they are right and therefore convey problem-solving power to their users. Ideas/technology can also give power in an institutional context, where the power of ideas and symbols can be appropriated by individuals and groups for their personal benefit and often detrimentally to the community. Similarly, an organization can be an effective means to integrate people to perform a technological problem-solving task. J.K. Galbraith and Seymour Melman, along with Ayres, have argued that an organization can be a mechanism by which technology and the choice of technology can be controlled to benefit those who hold power. This is a functional analysis, since it is the same organization that utilizes the technology that is also used to extract a disproportional share of the usufruct that is produced. This structure is both an institution and an organization in the operational sense of the latter term. A particular organization may be more or less effective in the use of a technology or more effective than other organizations. However, the institutional component of an institution/organization will increasingly retard the use of a technology and direct it to goals other than human betterment, and delay the introduction of more effective technologies.

This conception of technology is theory, in the complete operational scientific sense of that term. The theory makes a difference both in understanding the world and in using that understanding to formulate policies to deal with it. In some areas, institutional theories of technologies mapped out intellectual terrain decades before those of mainstream economics. It came as no surprise to institutionalists in the 1950s and 1960s that capital theory explained only a small portion of measured past economic growth. The emergence of 'human capital' theory after 1960 came more than half a century after Veblen had cogently argued that a population's accumulated knowledge was the most important capital of any community, far greater than its material embodiment in physical capital. To most other economists, technology has remained a 'black box' into which no further inquiry was carried out or deemed necessary. Institutionalists can rightly claim to have long ago opened the black box and gained critical insight from it.

The theory of technology not only analyses the dynamic forces of technological development and diffusion but also the forces that retard those processes. Immediately after World War II, the consensus was that it would take decades for Europe to recover from the devastation of war. In fact, it took but a few precious years, a phenomenon understandable from Veblen's much earlier insight on the primacy of intellectual capital. The importance of technology transfer in the processes of third world development took non-institutional economists decades to comprehend. The most startling economic phenomenon in our time has been the rise of a number of Asian countries to become economic and technological powerhouses. The technologies that the countries of Asia are using are overwhelmingly technologies that were developed in the United States or Europe. Those who have succeeded with a technology are in possession of the knowledge and experience to further advance that technology, but they have also developed the institutions that sanctify existing practice and the success that argues against change.

Institutionalists have long argued that technological leadership passes from one region to another because of the development of institutions which resist innovation. Thus the larger theory of technology incorporating institutional resistance provides a framework for analysing the forces that led to the recent failure of the United States to capitalize on its own inventions and for examining the success of Japan and other countries in using these technologies to further their own development. This transformation of the last decades follows closely the overall historical pattern of technological evolution and diffusion as described in institutional theory.

The sustainability of human life on earth has to be the most vital issue of our time. Even if catastrophist rhetoric is excessive, there are still major problems of pollution, ozone depletion, global warming and feeding the world's population. And it is on this question of sustainability and survival that the theory of technology is most germane. In the 1970s, there was considerable concern that the world was exhausting its supply of 'natural' resources. This concern was not new. What was different about the 1970s resource exhaustion prophecies was that they were presumably the result of scientific analysis using the latest in theories (systems dynamics) and computer technologies. The resource exhaustion forecasts found a receptive audience that had been conditioned by close to a decade of the most dire predictions of population growth and global famine. The famed Club of Rome study (1972) forecasting resource exhaustion, followed by the 'energy crisis', sealed the verdict for many that the world was running on empty. Empirical studies by mainstream economists and geologists both before and after the *Limits to Growth* report consistently showed that resources were becoming more available and their real price was falling, even though our use of them had been growing rapidly. Mainstream economists argued against resource exhaustion with explanations about resource substitutions and greater efficiency. Neither thesis is capable of explaining a general decline in the real price. If resources are in fact fixed and finite, substitution and greater efficiency can only delay resource exhaustion, not prevent it.

The institutional theory of technology allows for a consistency between observed fact and theory. Resources are not 'natural', they are a quality of the stuff of the universe that we impart by our ability to use them. Technology is what allows us to impart this resource character to the stuff of our existence. As Wesley C. Mitchell (1941) puts it: 'Incomparably greatest among human resources is knowledge. It is greatest because it is the mother of other resources. ... Not only is knowledge the greatest of resources, it is the resource that we have counted upon to grow richer with every decade.' There is a difference between using resources and using them up. There is nothing in the institutional theory of technology that would warrant being profligate with resources or taking a laissez-faire approach. We create resources by using the ones that we have in a process that involves furthering technological and scientific development. The theory of technology has implications for science and technology policy as well as for economic policy. The theory also clearly mandates an overall educational policy for the creation of what the mainstream has come to call human capital.

What the critics of technology fail to understand is that we are inherently technological beings. We are the only species dependent upon non-renewable resources. Technology continually expands our range of choice but denies us the choice of not choosing or reverting back to some non-existent pre-technology utopia. The second law of thermodynamics guarantees that conservation and recycling can never be complete. There is one fundamental pathway to sustainability and that is through sustainability of the technological process of continued resource creation. Within this framework, there are many possible policy options and policy debates. The institutionalist theory of technology does not shut out inquiry but grounds it in the realities of human life and technological processes.

Modern technology has undoubtedly brought us problems. That, as we have noted, is part of the process. Technologies (for example, public health and food production) that facilitated population growth created new 'necessities' that cannot be ignored, including environmental problems. There are no utopian problem-free solutions, not even those (or we should say particularly those) offered by critics of technology. The issue is not whether we have problems but how we address them. Properly understood, we need more technology, not less, to solve the technological problems of our time.

Just as the theory posits a technology that is dynamic, the institutionalist theory of technology itself has been one of continuing change and development. Though the institutional theory of technology may not be in the mainstream, its origins are. Adam Smith, in the *Wealth of Nations*, embodied his economic theory in a rich fabric of institutional and technological history. His perspective on technological change, particularly on the issue of specialization and the division of labour, was a vital part of his inquiry which, unfortunately, was abandoned by many of his successors.

Almost alone among the major nineteenth-century theorists, Karl Marx recognized the centrality of technology in historical change and in the formation and evolution of social structures and social relations. Volumes have been written and to some extent there has been debate about whether Marx had an implicit or explicit theory of technological change embedded in his massive historical narrative. What is clearly unchallengeable is that his analysis is fundamentally evolutionary and that his discourse on technology is capable of interpretation or reinterpretation in terms of more modern understanding.

Of major twentieth-century theorists, Joseph A. Schumpeter stands alongside Veblen in emphasizing the technology in economic change. The differences between the institutionalists and the Schumpeterians have been profound and have seemed unbridgeable. In recent years, there has been a convergence in the two perspectives. Both see technology as being cumulative and agree that technologically induced change and not equilibrium is the normal condition of the economy. Two recent edited volumes, *Technical Change and Economic Theory* (1988) and *Evolving Technology and Market Structure* (1990), provide empirical and theoretical studies on technology in a Schumpeterian tradition and lay the foundation for a comprehensive evolutionary theory of technology, particularly as it applies to the firm in an advanced economy.

What we have presented here is the broad outlines of a theory still vigorously evolving. Its fundamental tenets have shown extraordinary predictive powers and continue to provide the best operational framework for formulating policies to meet the needs of our time. The theory provides an intelligent middle ground between the anti-technological catastrophists, who see modern technology leading rapidly and ineluctably to planetary destruction, and their laissez-faire opposite numbers who deny any problems that cannot be solved by markets if they are free from governmental interference. In the extreme view, the institutional theory of technology seems technophilic to the catastrophists and interventionist to the laissez-faire enthusiasts. Not only is the understanding of the basic processes of technology central to institutional economics, but also the theory of technology is necessary for comprehending and addressing the major economic issues of our time.

THOMAS R. DEGREGORI AND DEBORAH A. SHEPHERD

See also:

Ayres, Clarence E.; Biology and Economics; Capital Theory; Culture; Development Policy; Development Theory; Dewey, John; Growth, Limits to; Innovation, National Systems of; Marx, Karl; Schumpeter, Joseph Alois; Technical Change and Technological Regimes; Technology in Development Policy; Veblen, Thorstein; Veblenian Dichotomy and Its Critics.

Bibliography

Ayres, C.E. (1944), *The Theory of Economic Progress: A Study of the Fundamentals of Economic Development and Cultural Change*, Chapel Hill: University of North Carolina Press.

Basalla, George (1989), *The Evolution of Technology*, Cambridge: Cambridge University Press.

Dewey, John (1929), *The Quest for Certainty*, New York: Minton, Balch & Co.

Dewey, John (1939), *Theory of Valuation*, Chicago: University of Chicago Press.

Dosi, Giovanni, Christopher Freeman, Richard Nelson, Gerald Silverberg and Luc Soete (eds) (1988), *Technical Change and Economic Theory*, London and New York: Pinter.

Geertz, Clifford (1973), *The Interpretation of Culture: Selected Essays*, New York: Basic Books.

Heertje, Arnold and Mark Perlman (eds) (1990), *Evolving Technology and Market Structure: Studies in Schumpeterian Economics*, Ann Arbor: The University of Michigan Press.

Meadows, D.H., D.L. Meadows, J. Randers and W. Behrens (1972), *The Limits To Growth: A Report for the Club of Rome's Project on the Predicament of Mankind*, New York: Universe Books and London: Pan Books.

Mitchell, Wesley C. (1941), 'Conservation, Liberty, and Economics', *The Foundations of Conservation Education*, New York: National Wildlife Federation.

Mokyr, J. (1990), *The Lever of Riches: Technological Creativity and Economic Progress*, Oxford: Oxford University Press.

Veblen, Thorstein (1914), *The Instinct of Workmanship*, New York: B.W. Huebsch.

Veblen, Thorstein (1915), *Imperial Germany and the Industrial Revolution*, New York: Macmillan.

Veblen, Thorstein (1919), *The Place of Science in Modern Civilisation and Other Essays*, New York: B.W. Huebsch.

Zimmermann, Erich W. (1933), *World Resources and Industries*, New York: Harper and Brothers.

Time

We have all experienced time, but attempts to conceptualize it precisely face enormous and frequently confounding tasks. When we attempt to introduce time into economic models we enter a domain requiring subtle intellectual navigation and careful handling of ideas. Nonetheless, the journey must be made.

Static economic analysis abstracts from time altogether, thereby leaching much complexity from its purview and inadequately addressing many questions of human and social behaviour. Essentially lacking any concept of time, static economics necessarily offers nothing to elucidate concerns for evolution of systems and institutions, and the growth, development and decay of social patterns, and cannot incorporate a phenomenon's historical context into its analysis. Anything to do with change escapes it.

The most familiar device by which time enters economic models comes from mechanics. In this *logical-time* construction, a real variable denotes an event's date, and duration between events is identified as the difference between the numbers naming their dates. Modelling time as a real-valued variable imputes to it the mathematical structure of a set of points on the real line. Time's passage thus appears in the model as motion in space. The experience of duration and change is intellectually reduced to geometrical displacement. Such a modelling strategy's chief advantage lies in gaining access to the mathematics of the mechanics of physical motion. Introduced to physics by Newton, this programme conceives of time as simply an additional dimension, and articulates it in a way conceptually coherent and logically consistent with the other variables. In particular, time becomes just another variable on which differential and integral calculus can be used. For economics, this extends the theory of optimization to dynamics, and sustains the identification of extrema with optima in time: the marginal conditions for optimal choice through time exactly mimic those of other variables, since all are, mathematically, associated with the geometry of dimensions in real spaces.

Logical-time modelling can be further decomposed into 'continuous' and 'discrete' time. In continuous time the index set of dates has the same cardinality as the continuum. That is, there are as many instants in time as there are real numbers. Alternatively, in 'discrete' time, the set of possible dates has the same cardinality as that of the integers. Discrete-time modelling allows identification of the next and previous 'periods', and requires that equations of motion be phrased as difference rather than differential equations. Since both discrete and continuous time rely, essentially, on the dimensional properties of points on a line, each is a variant of 'logical-time' modelling.

Formally, a model in continuous logical time might consist of an n-dimensional vector of real 'state' variables and t, the real-valued variable identifying 'time'. Thus the system's 'motion' through time could be specified by a set of n differential equations of the form $\partial x_i / \partial t = f_i(x,t)$, where $i = i,$ ..., n. Modelling time as merely an additional spacial dimension introduces a conceptual conundrum, however. Since any point replicating the current moment lies on a line, motion can be in either of two directions: forward or backward. Geometrically, either direction is symmetrical around 'now' with respect to the other. Nothing inherent in this conceptualization requires time to flow 'forward'. As a matter of convention, we associate larger real numbers with later dates, but the model's mathematical structure allows time to go either way. Nothing implicit in this image of time distinguishes past from future. Either direction will, and can, do. The significance of this intertemporal symmetry is fully appreciated only in a steady state, in which the current state of the system exactly reproduces itself with the passing of each moment. Past and future are profoundly indistinguishable, for there is no true motion at all. Indeed, steady states lose the capacity to reflect historical context, for in them nothing changes, so there is no historical context to consider. Past, present and future become conceptually conflated and time effectively vanishes.

This indeterminacy of time's arrow, and the disappearance of timing and history at a logical-time steady state are not consistent with the everyday experience of time. An alternative image informs economics cast in *historical time*. Concerns over the human experience and epistemics of time inform economic thought cast in terms of historical rather than logical time. The most fundamental insight guiding this analysis is that we all live in the present, what Shackle (1974) has called the 'moment-in-being'. We always exist now, but in that being we remember the past and imagine the future. Thus our understanding of time, and especially of behaviour in time, must accommodate an understanding of human epistemology.

We have perceived and recalled events in the past, but regarding the future we have no *evidence*, and no knowledge. We may have confidence and faith, but regarding what will be we must first invoke imagination. The future is profoundly uncertain, and although our imaginings of it are powerfully coloured by our memories and experiences of the past, regarding the future we truly do not, indeed, cannot know. Thus the means by which we apprehend the future is epistemically distinct from our cognitive and sensory attachments to the past. This basic asymmetry in human psychology permeates our experience of time and of time's passage, for it is through witnessing what had previously only been an imagined possibility that we discern time's flight at all. This means, however, that each instant is uniquely endowed with recollections of the past and with dreams of the future. No other can be exactly like it. Each day is uniquely embedded in the web of history, and our psychological, epistemic and volitional states can never be historically reproduced. Once time has flown, we can never return to what we had been. Epistemically, each new instant necessarily proclaims us as something somehow new. Were we to remain exactly the same, for us time would cease.

These same concerns, moreover, inform our understanding of cause and effect, and thus of choice and motivation as well. They make the future into an unknowable opportunity. We expect and hope for the future, and plan and choose strategies to affect it. On the other hand, in recognizing an event as past we also recognize it as past changing. Therefore time not only introduces an epistemic asymmetry around the present, but it also generates a sense of causal asymmetry around the present as well. We can 'cause' things to happen in the future through motivated decisions and current actions. Regarding past events, however, we may ponder what we might have done, but cannot now sanely decide what we will do yesterday. Similarly, we can never make exactly the same decision again, for the very act of choosing thrusts us forward in time, and forever destroys the historical context of the decision. Strictly speaking, opportunity never does knock twice.

These considerations yield three criteria that historical-time analysis must satisfy. First, since each moment is uniquely embedded in history, the set of expectations imaginable to an agent at any moment must also be unique. Subsequent dates must be associated with different memories, and thus must provoke expectations only over the (now relatively truncated) remaining future. Thus the state of any agent's expectations cannot be an historically steady state.

Second, since decisions are made today and address uncertain events in an unknowable future, the consequences of any choice must be strictly temporally after that choice. Moreover, choice must therefore be modelled as logically antecedent to knowledge of the outcomes of selected strategies. We must recognize that people may be surprised by the outcomes of their own acts, and that they cannot coordinate their behaviour into the tidily equilibrated states of competitive equilibrium unless they can somehow transcend time itself. That is, time must authentically stop for the Walrasian auctioneer to get the job done.

Third, historical-time models must be capable of disequilibrium. The uncoordinated as well as the compatibly equilibrated states must be representable within them. That is, they must not be constrained only to equilibria in which *ex post* outcomes are indistinguishable from *ex ante* attempted actions.

We can now understand how historical-time thinking compares with logical-time thinking about the economy. Since logical-time analysis identifies time with a spacial dimension, no essential qualities distinguish different points. Except for placement and name they could all be identical. Thus there can be steady states and, more importantly, there need be no temporal separation of cause and effect. Astonishingly, this is what permits the laxness in time by which equilibration might occur, for the back-and-forth movement through time required so that the auctioneer can get it 'right' is perfectly permissible when time is conceived as space through which motion is reversible. The flow of historical time, on the other hand, is both epistemically and causally unidirectional. Events are uniquely embedded in time, and each moment supports its own special future of unknowable but imagined possibilities. Thus, since people act under true uncertainty and without knowledge, they may make mistakes. In their blundering, moreover, there can be no assurance that different agents are pursuing mutually consistent activities or that equilibrium is achieved. In addition, agents may react with surprise to the consequences of their own actions, and their surprised reactions may provoke further surprised responses elsewhere in the economy. Thus the system may not travel smoothly from moment to moment in serene equilibrium, but may lurch to and from surprising disequilibrium to surprising disequilibrium. The economy's very texture may grow complex and its institutional fabric constantly change and evolve, becoming what Shackle calls 'kaleidics'. At the microeconomic level, individuals adapt to surprising events, and at the macroeconomic level the system may grow or decline. Consequently, the recognition of historical time's significance mandates the study of disequilibrated adaptation to surprising outcomes. Accordingly, to apprehend how the economy evolves through time, economists must liberate their thinking from the constricted image that is logical-time equilibrium.

In addition to Shackle (1974), a rich discussion of historical-time modelling is contained in Vickers (1987). Bausor (1982–3) provides a general model of an economy in historical time. Hirsch and Smale (1974) is an elegant and sophisticated presentation of the mathematics underlying logical-time dynamics.

RANDALL BAUSOR

See also:

Biology and Economics; Chaos Theory and Economics; Cumulative Causation; Entropy and Economics; Georgescu-Roegen, Nicholas; Keynes, John Maynard; Long Waves; Shackle, George Lennox Sharman; Uncertainty.

Bibliography

Bausor, Randall (1982–3), 'Time and the Structure of Economic Analysis', *Journal of Post Keynesian Economics*, **5**, (2), Winter, pp. 163–79.
Hirsch, Morris W. and Stephen Smale (1974), *Differential Equations, Dynamical Systems, and Linear Algebra*, New York: Academic Press.

Shackle, G.L.S. (1974), *Keynesian Kaleidics, the Evolution of a General Political Economy*, Edinburgh: Edinburgh University Press.
Vickers, Douglas (1987), *Money Capital in the Theory of the Firm*, Cambridge: Cambridge University Press.

Transaction

The concept of a 'transaction', as distinct from an 'exchange', was introduced into economics by John R. Commons. Commons understood scarcity to be an insurmountable condition of human existence. He also understood human beings to be mainly self-interested creatures, that is, generally to desire more for themselves rather than less. These presumptions led him to conclude that conflict of interest due to scarcity is a fundamental problem of social life. For in any context where division of labour obtains, an individual who seeks more for himself can achieve this end only by gaining control over the use of objects and faculties possessed by another who would rather not surrender such control. According to Commons, the nineteenth-century economists, by concentrating single-mindedly on exchange, had failed to distinguish between the legal transfer of the rights to a thing and its physical transfer. This had led them to a faulty understanding, as the crucial element of economic life, Commons averred, is not physical but *legal* control.

It is in the transaction that legal control over a needed or desired thing is gained and the conflict of interest between individuals who are at the same time dependent on each other is resolved in such fashion that the social need for order is obtained. Hence transactions are 'the strategic relation[s] in economic activity', for without them there could be no producing, consuming, buying, selling, investing, speculating and so on. Commons accordingly made ownership – whose essence is the legal right to withhold from another what he needs or wants – 'the foundation of institutional economics' and deemed the transaction 'a unit of transfer of legal control' and 'the place where the wills of men meet', to be the 'smallest unit of institutional economics'. That is, Commons declared the transaction to be the elemental constituent of economic activity and hence the 'ultimate unit of economic investigation'.

Transactions and the character of economic activity

Rather than starting with the individual, Commons began with the insight that human provisioning (production and distribution), based as it is on division of labour, almost always takes place within *groups* 'consisting of a succession of individuals which enter, cooperate, and disappear while the [group] itself goes on indefinitely' – that is, within the ambit of 'going concerns'. The manor, the kibbutz and the corporation are examples of such concerns, as, at a higher level, is the nation. In order to keep the peace, the first requirement of continuity, a going concern must have an 'authoritative figure' who himself, or through his designated representative(s), resolves disputes arising out of conflict of interest by selecting which, from competing customs or practices, provides that 'good' rule of action to be followed in all future transactions within the concern embodying the same potential conflict. These working rules specify, sometimes in general and sometimes in specific terms, what individuals can, may or must do, or not do, in their transactions with one another. It is the expected trend in the decision of future disputes which 'brings the individual into line with the rule'. In other words, by placing limits on conduct the working rules reduce individual wills, whatever their inclinations, to a uniformity of action. Moreover, it is the presumption that adopted working rules will be enforced in the future which enables potential participants in a transaction to be secure in their expectations as to the future performance of others. Without this security of expectations, transaction could not be concluded and forward-looking cooperative activity simply could not occur. In short, the working rule is the source of order (correlated behaviour) in economic life. Or put slightly differently, since the group *must* control the behaviour of individuals if the concern is to keep going, the operative principle of economic life is 'collective action in control of individual action'.

From Commons's standpoint, then, authoritative resolution of disputes, or, alternatively, authoritative adjustment of working rules, constitutes the true 'balancing wheel' or 'regulator' of economic life. Commons understood the 'market mechanism', which economists so often attribute to 'natural law' or 'human nature', to have been created through this process. That is, Commons understood economic 'competition', as it proceeds in any nation, to be *entirely* a socially constructed process volitionally crafted slowly, over many centuries, by means of authoritative selection of 'good' customs. As far as the United States is concerned, first British common law judges and then, after independence was attained, Supreme Court justices gradually fashioned the character of 'competition' or, alternatively, the 'market mechanism', *pari passu* as they built a 'business law' to regulate transactions. For, in determining, in the context of the consecutive specific disputes brought before them, what in fact are a transactor's *rights*, the judges defined what individuals *can* do in their transactions, with the positive assistance of the state if necessary; by specifying in the same disputes what in fact are the correlative *duties* of other transactors, they defined what individuals *must* and *must not* do, subject to compulsion by the state if necessary; by specifying what is not a duty, that is, by defining what individuals may do without interference from the state, *protected* by the state also keeping other people from interfering if necessary, they created *liberties*; and by simultaneously determining what is therefore not a right, they defined when an individual cannot expect the assistance of the state, that is, they created the correlative *exposures*. It was through this process, Commons emphasized, that property rights were established as an authorized domain for the exercise of free choice in determining the terms of transactions – in a word, competition – was created.

As noted, Commons maintained that the market mechanism is in actuality patterned behaviour conforming to the *instituted* set of working rules, not a natural mechanism rooted in urges or generic 'propensities' implanted in man by God or nature, as implicit in the 'invisible hand' metaphor. Moreover, judging that 'collective action in control of individual action' is the fundamental principle of market activity, he concluded that transactions can neither be understood nor evaluated in individualistic terms. This being the case, he averred, the operation of an economy is properly assessed not in terms of abstract universal and individualistic constructs such as 'allocative efficiency' but only in terms of, first, whether or not the purposes of those consecutively empowered to decide disputes are actually 'good' ones and, second, if it is so determined, how well actual transactions effectuate those purposes. Based on his own review of court decisions, Commons's conclusion was that the purposes guiding the adoption of the rules currently controlling transactions in the United States are indeed 'good' ones, namely, to ensure equal access to opportunities (to enter into a transaction), fair competition and equality of bargaining power, as constrained by the necessity of ensuring due process of law in the taking of 'property'. Throughout his long career, Commons attempted to determine how the working rules controlling 'strategic transactions' could be altered so as to more completely effectuate the already implanted purposes in a manner consistent with the constitutional requirement of due process. That is, in his own words, he 'was trying to make capitalism good'.

Types of transactions
According to Commons there are three general types of transactions which in the ebb and flow of economic life are substantively inseparable but nonetheless distinguishable by their function and the status of participants. Commons dubbed them the bargaining, the managerial and the rationing transaction. In the *bargaining transaction*, ownership of property is transferred and commitments for future actions (performances) are entered into at terms mutually agreed to by legal, although not always economic, equals authorized to use both persuasion and economic coercion (power) in their negotiations. However, forbearance in the exercise of one's power may be compulsory, for negotiated terms must not violate limits on the degree of power in acting prescribed by established rights and correlative duties (as would be

the case, for example, by agreeing to a wage rate below the statutory minimum) and must not be arrived at through the use of unauthorized inducements (bribes, for example). It is through bargaining transactions that individuals in a market system are provided with inducements to produce and deliver wealth. Bargaining transactions grow out of a relation between four persons, the two who provide the prospective seller with his two best options and the two who provide the prospective buyer with his two best options, since it is the options actually available to a potential transactor that establish the range within which bargaining can take place. Since only the state can transfer ownership and enforce contracts (agreed upon performances), it is in reality always a silent fifth participant in all bargaining transactions.

Wealth is actually produced and delivered by means of *managerial transactions*. These transactions involve the relationship of command and obedience between a legal superior and inferior (such as a foreman and a worker or a sheriff and a citizen). The superior gives an order relating to the acquisition, alienation or the use of a thing or faculty, and the inferior must obey. The superior, of course, is enjoined to issue commands that do not violate established working rules. As noted, a key function of the bargaining transaction is to provide individuals with an inducement for participating in the production of wealth. Put somewhat differently, bargaining transactions prefigure how the 'burdens and benefits of collective wealth production' are actually shared. But *rationing transactions*, 'the negotiations of reaching an agreement among several participants who have the authority to apportion the benefits and burdens to members of a joint enterprise', also give shape to the actual distribution of real income (wealth). Under the name of policy, these 'authoritative apportionings' also involve the command and obedience relationship of a legal superior and a legal inferior, as in the case of the state establishing a budget and decreeing a tax or a board of directors establishing a wage or dividend policy.

In Commons's mind these three 'units of activity' exhaust all the activities of the 'science of economics'. As he summarized it himself: 'Bargaining transactions *transfer ownership* of wealth by voluntary agreement between legal equals. Managerial transactions *create wealth* by commands of legal superiors. Rationing transactions apportion the burdens and benefits of wealth creation by the *dictation* of legal superiors.' Of the three, rationing transactions would appear to be the most strategic, since they place limits on the potential content of bargaining and managerial transactions. All, however, must conform to the decisions rendered by the courts. And, given the role of purpose in determining those decisions, we find reflected in all transactions a correlation of ethics (the guide to purpose), law and economics.

Transaction cost analysis

Since the concept of a transaction is an integral part of Commons's framework, it is not easy – indeed, it is probably impossible – to detach it, with its manifold facets, from the larger scheme (herein only partially summarized) without altering its substance and obscuring its significance. Thus it is not surprising that the concept of a transaction has never been incorporated as a 'unit of economic investigation' into the Veblen–Ayres–Foster 'instrumental value' paradigm. The transaction *has* become central to the 'new institutional economics' via 'transaction cost analysis', which attempts to show how the single-minded drive for cost minimization (profit maximization) induces the firm to negotiate property transfers which allow it to reduce transactions costs by converting bargaining transactions with others into managerial and rationing transactions under its own control; hence the division of tasks (transactions) between 'hierarchy' and 'the market'. But in this usage the concept has been transplanted into a framework moored in different conceptions of the mind and human behaviour and also disassociated from the criteria of evaluation provided by the fundamental purposes Commons discerned to have actually given direction to the centuries-long construction of business law (broadly conceived). Indeed, in its most noxious form, the new institutional economics purports to reveal that the 'invisible hand' of transaction cost minimization has guided the actual evolution of property rights and urges that further social alteration of still imperfectly defined property rights *should* be undertaken only in furtherance of that 'natural' tendency. From this perspective, obviously, Commons's own desideratum of equal participation by all affected parties in the processes through which the going concern's working rules are adjusted to new conditions is revealed to be aberrant and against the public interest. Had he lived longer, Commons, the self-avowed 'partner' of the wage-earning class, would no doubt have been greatly saddened by the irony of his principal contribution to economic analysis, the concept of a transaction, being transmuted into an intellectual 'tool' helping to make the case of zealots championing a cause antithetical to his own.

YNGVE RAMSTAD

See also:

Ayres, Clarence E.; Commons, John R.; Institutional Economics, Wisconsin School of; Institutionalism, 'Old' and 'New'; Instrumental Value Theory; Interest Groups; Labour Markets; Law and Economics; Market, Institutionalist View of the; Property; Public Policy: Contributions of American Institutionalism; Veblen, Thorstein; Williamson, Oliver E.

Bibliography

Commons, J.R. (1924), *Legal Foundations of Capitalism*, New York: Macmillan, esp. ch.IV.
Commons, J.R. (1934), *Institutional Economics: Its Place in Political Economy*, New York: Macmillan, esp. pp. 52–93.

Parsons, K.H. (1942), 'John R. Commons' Point of View', *The Journal of Land and Public Utility Economics*, **18**; reprinted 1950 as Appendix iii in John R. Commons, *The Economics of Collective Action*, New York: Macmillan.

Ramstad, Y. (1990), 'The Institutionalism of John R. Commons: Theoretical Foundations of a Volitional Economics', in *Research in the History of Economic Thought and Methodology*, Vol. 8, ed. W.J. Samuels, Greenwich, Conn.: JAI Press.

Trebing, Harry M.

Harry M. Trebing was born on 14 September 1927 in Baltimore, Maryland. In his distinguished career as teacher, scholar and practitioner of public utility economics, Harry M. Trebing applies and extends institutionalist principles to issues of industrial evolution and structure and the social control of business. His work combines theory and practice, each tempering and enriching the other. His activity in both the lecture halls and the trenches of regulation, his association both with its scholars and its foot soldiers, along with his unwavering institutional perspective, contribute to the grounding of his analytic work in the facts of contemporary industrial organization. His analysis is further illuminated and given added dimension by the exhaustive historical memory he puts to its service.

Trebing received his PhD at the University of Wisconsin after completing earlier degrees at the University of Maryland. At each institution he studied with some of the luminaries of institutional economics. Among his major professors were Martin G. Glaeser at Wisconsin and Eli W. Clemens at Maryland, each a significant contributor to the institutional expression of public utility economics. Additional major influences were such distinguished institutionalists as Allan Gruchy at Maryland and Edwin Witte and Selig Perlman at Wisconsin.

Prior to his lengthy affiliation with Michigan State University, Trebing held faculty positions at the Universities of Nebraska and Indiana. He also held appointments at the US Postal Rate Commission as chief economist and, at the Federal Communications Commission, successively as supervisory industrial economist and as chief of the economics studies division. Over the years he has been pressed into frequent service to work with governmental task forces, committees and advisory panels.

At Michigan State University, Trebing served, until his retirement in 1991, as Professor of Economics and Director of the Institute of Public Utilities. In the latter capacity he administered numerous conferences and seminars and edited quantities of session proceedings and other work in public utility economics. He organized and lectured in a variety of educational programmes, including the annual training sessions of the National Association of Regulatory Utility Commissioners for regulatory commissioners and staffs. The variety of viewpoints invited resulted in seminars, symposiums and published proceedings that were unique forums for debate, running the gamut of regulatory viewpoints and themes. Trebing is mentor and guide both for his fledgling university students in public utility economics and for the seasoned professionals from all walks of regulation who participated in these forums.

Trebing's professional involvement covers a period of time when the neoclassical voice, always dominant within the discipline, threatened to drown out all others. In no area was this as evident as in the subspeciality of public utility and regulatory economics. Courses in the subfield became little more than applications of price theory. Scholarly books and articles increasingly were devoted to broadening the applicability of competitive principles to the regulated sector and demonstrating the ineffectiveness and sheer mischievousness of regulation. Trebing's work is a counterforce articulating a public interest theory of regulation. He is not an apologist for regulation. His work contains sharp criticism of regulatory performance: its failure to fulfil its express purposes, the paths left unexplored. His criticisms include the acceptance by regulation of a judicial role and passive review function as opposed to the use of a forward-looking, planning model. He criticizes regulation also for its failure to seize opportunities to improve industry performance and to identify and break down barriers in potentially competitive markets such as wholesale gas and bulk power (Trebing, 1974, pp. 41–65). His work also contains specific suggestions for regulatory reform, such as the adoption of a Glaeser-TVA cost allocation model to ensure that burdens and benefits are appropriately shared among customer classes in enterprises with high proportions of joint costs (Trebing, 1989a, pp. 121–2).

Trebing apprehends also, however, the hazards attendant upon the current expansive deregulatory approach. He examines the neoclassical regulatory model, including the Chicago School variant, and contrasts this with an institutional, public interest paradigm (for example, Trebing, 1976, pp. 97–126; 1987, pp. 1716–22). For, notwithstanding past regulatory missteps and inadequacies, Trebing perceives that specific characteristics of complex industrial societies make it imperative that they develop tools of intermediation, including economic regulation, to facilitate efficient and equitable social provisioning (Trebing, 1989b, pp. 393–411). Thus, while he recognizes that regulatory performance has often been ineffectual, he notes also: 'Yet market power persists and the control of such power remains a principal task of regulation' (Trebing, 1984, p. 246).

Appreciation of the distinction between institutional and orthodox approaches to regulation requires that concepts of market failure be distinguished. The mainstream perceives market failure almost exclusively as a function of the existence of economies of scale, defined as natural monopoly, and perceived as an uncommon, and frequently a temporary, phenomenon.

Trebing, in contrast, attributes market failure and the persistence of market power to the presence of specific inherent, prevalent characteristics of modern industry. He discerns a market that ranges over the structural spectrum and that is often hospitable to the development and exercise of oligopolistic power. He notes such additional factors as high threshold levels of investment, the presence of monopoly focal points, the existence of externalities and a high incidence of interdependence that makes joint planning a requirement of effective operation, as setting modern economies apart from the textbook ideal, and even from that of workable competition (Trebing, 1974b, pp. 224–5). Under such circumstances there is substantial potential for the emergence of such inefficiencies and inequities as facility duplication and overcapacity, rate wars and bankruptcies, mergers and increased concentration, and exploitative, discriminatory and limit entry pricing.

Trebing examines, for each of the regulated industries, the effects of current deregulatory measures upon market structure and explores the interaction between market structure and price. In telecommunications, for example, current policies of deregulation erode profit and earning restraints. Absent such restraints, the prevailing pattern of concentration permits the exercise of discretion when it comes to pricing; the use of strategic pricing in itself enhances economic strength. To illustrate, industries serving in both captive and competitive markets segment markets and differentiate prices according to relative demand elasticities. Economic power on the supply side of the market is synchronized with power on the demand side. High-volume customers are heavily concentrated. They are also the group most likely to possess competitive options. This group of customers is able to use its bargaining strength to achieve price concessions. Low-usage, captive, demand-inelastic customers, who lack competitive options, absorb the revenue slack. The earnings flow from the large body of captive consumers, in turn, provides for low- or no-cost entry into diversified activities, and for a pricing advantage *vis-à-vis* competitors.

Trebing also explores current popular policy adaptations of the deregulatory model, such as the substitution of price cap and incentive regulation schemes for traditional rate of return regulation. It is his contention that such relaxation of profit and earning control combines with the lifting of prohibitions against diversification and lax standards of cost allocation to produce a maximum ability to shift risk forward to captive consumers and to engage in cross-subsidization and limit entry pricing in ancillary and unrelated diversified endeavours. At the same time, implementation of the holding company structure removes public utilities ever further from regulatory control (Trebing, 1989a, pp. 112–20).

The question addressed is that of whether abusive practices can be prevented in partially deregulated imperfect markets. Trebing holds no brief for the many variants of the orthodox approach that move monopoly and oligopoly markets inexorably and automatically in competitive directions by the use of simple *deus ex machina* ranging from technological advance to the removal of legal entry barriers (for example, Trebing, 1989a, pp. 102–6; 1976, pp. 100–109). The consequences of recent policy implementations for the body of captive customers most vulnerable to exploitative practices is a major concern. Of equal importance, however, are considerations of the efficacious functioning of the economic system. Trebing perceives the current ethic of deregulation and resultant policy as allowing free latitude for the exercise of private, unrestrained power that is conducive neither to efficiency nor to equity.

Trebing has received many honours and awards from his academic and regulatory peers. For example, the National Association of Regulatory Utility Commissioners and the National Association of State Utility Consumer Advocates have recognized his many contributions. In 1972, he was elected chairman of the Transportation and Public Utilities Group of the American Economic Association, receiving its most distinguished member award in 1983. He was elected President of the Association for Evolutionary Economics (AFEE) in 1973. In 1983, AFEE awarded him its highest honour, the Veblen–Commons Award.

EDYTHE S. MILLER

See also:

Commons, John R.; Gruchy, Allan Garfield; Industrial Structure and Power; Law and Economics; Power; Public Policy: Contributions of American Institutionalism; Public Sector, Role of the; Regulation, Theory of Economic; Witte, Edwin Emil.

Bibliography

Trebing, Harry M. (1974a), 'A Critique of Regulatory Accommodation to Change', in William G. Shepherd and Thomas G. Geis (eds), *Regulation in Further Perspective*, pp. 41–65, Cambridge, Mass.: Ballinger Publishing Co.

Trebing, Harry M. (1974b), 'Realism and Relevance in Public Utility Regulation', *Journal of Economic Issues*, **VIII**, June, pp. 209–33.

Trebing, Harry M. (1976), 'The Chicago School versus Public Utility Regulation', *Journal of Economic Issues*, **X**, March, pp. 97–126.

Trebing, Harry M. (1984), 'Public Utility Regulation: A Case Study in the Debate over Effectiveness of Economic Regulation', *Journal of Economic Issues*, **XVIII**, March, pp. 223–50.

Trebing, Harry M. (1987), 'Regulation of Industry: An Institutionalist Approach', *Journal of Economic Issues*, **XXI**, December, pp. 1707–37.

Trebing, Harry M. (1989a), 'Telecommunications Regulation – The Continuing Dilemma', in Kenneth Nowotny, David B. Smith and Harry M. Trebing (eds), *Public Utility Regulation*, pp. 93–136, Boston, Dordrecht, London: Kluwer Academic Publishers.

Trebing, Harry M. (1989b), 'Restoring Purposeful Goverment: The Galbraithian Contribution', *Journal of Economic Issues*, **XXIII**, June, pp. 393–411.

Trust

The phenomenon of trust underlies, to varying degrees, most economic transactions and cooperation. Surprisingly, it has received little attention from economists, including evolutionary and institutional ones. Other social scientists also have rarely accorded it any theoretical importance. However, this is changing in the fields of sociology (for example, Meeker, 1983; Eisenstadt and Roniger, 1984; Lewis and Weigert, 1985) and business administration (for example, Husted, 1989).

The following account treats trust only with regard to economic life, disregarding its important roles in the political order and personal life. It is divided into six sections. First, an attempt is made to define trust and distinguish it from other virtues, as well as from confidence and hope. The second section indicates the importance of trust in any cooperative effort, and more so in cooperative efforts undertaken in capitalist societies characterized by formal contracts. Third, a way is suggested to monitor the state of trust in a society, that is, through changes in what is called 'organization cost', which is distinct from transaction cost. Fourth, two different neoclassical treatments of the phenomenon are exposed. Fifth, the shortcomings of the neoclassical treatments are identified. In the last sixth section, it is argued that what is basically lacking in the neoclassical approach is a theory of self. A proper theory of self has implications in regard to the phenomena of honour and respect. These phenomena cannot be reduced to the level of personal tastes for goods like clothes and food.

What is trust?
Trust amounts to the expectation that the other party, even if circumstances change, would stick to an agreement. Such a commitment, which might engender a lower pecuniary gain, arises more from the senses of duty and honour than from other virtues such as altruism, beneficence and justice. Furthermore, trust should be distinguished from confidence, on the one hand, and (for the lack of a better word) hope, on the other. Trust has to do with intention or motivation, whereas confidence concerns ability or competence; and hope to do with chance or fortune. For example, one may trust that firm X will honour its commitment and deliver the raw material even if its market price rises, whereas one may not have the confidence in the ability of firm X to produce the raw material on schedule; and one may have great hope that no war or earthquake will obstruct the delivery.

Subtle differences exist among these three types of expectations, which orthodox theory fails to highlight. Trust and confidence are distinguished on the ground of intentionality. While one may have confidence in the market, one cannot trust or distrust it because it lacks motives. In contrast, hope is set apart from trust and confidence on the ground of chance. While high hopes and prayer for the weather to improve or for the machine to work do not generate a better weather or a better machine (at least as far as experimental evidence has shown), confidence in the economy or trust among partners engenders a series of decisions which might affect the actual performance.

To put the difference differently, while one could formulate a probability expectation of future weather or the lifespan of a machine, it is more problematic with regard to events contingent on trust and confidence. Such events are shrouded in uncertainty (not unlike Heisenberg's uncertainty principle) because they are, unlike the weather, the product of specific expectations. Trust, confidence and hope overlap for the simple reason that they become more prominent with greater division of labour (see Fox, 1974). In a Robinson Crusoe economy one could conceive trust (trust in one's motives), confidence (self-confidence), and hope (in relation to fertility of land). While hope is characteristic of many transactions, such as hoping that the purchased goods would meet one's eccentric taste, it is not intrinsic to division of labour like the cases with confidence and trust.

Division of labour calls for confidence in a different way from its need for trust. Confidence on the part of economic agents is called for in order to facilitate the functioning of the organization of labour. Any organization is characterized by a certain degree of complexity or abstractness; that is, skills of agents are not comprehensive but rather specialized in specific jobs. There has to be confidence in the specializations or abilities, for example, of the home builder and the motor car manufacturer before consumers buy their products. In contrast, trust is needed to ensure that, given the specialization of ability, the other agent will carry out what has been agreed upon, irrespective of new circumstances or unexpected outcomes.

Importance of trust

Ironically, capitalist society, which has been celebrated and criticized for unleashing the forces of self-interest, needs trust the most, for two reasons. First, as economic exchange becomes less intermingled with kinship and more based on formal contractual relationship (see Eisenstadt and Roniger, 1984), the monitoring conducted by the kin members and the threat of ostracism almost vanish. Second, the modern judicial system, which replaces the threat system of ostracism and shunning, cannot practically monitor the extensive growth of contractual agreements – even the explicit ones.

The history of the emergence of capitalism in Europe shows that trust was generated by grass-root religious revivals, such as the Reformation, and also by dictates of political authority. These dictates, associated with benevolent dictators such as Peter the Great and Frederick the Great, imposed meritocracy and standardized the rules of conduct. Either the spontaneous or the constructivist pathway to the generation of trust has worked in many cases because trust is not a scarce commodity. Nor is it a free commodity in the textbook sense. The quantity of trust, if it could be measured by the proxy suggested below, increases as people use it – very much like the oil in the Biblical story of the widow's cruse. There is something about the integrity of the human character or self that tends to make us feel morally obliged to act trustworthily when others behave so towards us. Therefore, once the drive for greater trust is put in motion, it generates the conditions for the continuity and growth of further trust. The same self-propelling process also works in the opposite direction, when trust starts to erode in society.

The historical generation of trust through grass-root movements or from above has amounted to the painful and revolutionary replacement – which was by no means uniformly successful – of kinship-based cooperation by juridically based cooperation. Karl Marx has referred to this great transformation as the switch from subjective dependency to objective dependency. The German sociologist Ferdinand Tönnies has identified it as the emphasis of *Gesellschaft* (commercial company or society), at the expense of *Gemeinschaft* (community). An established profusion of juridically based cooperation and trust is essential for the maturation of the credit system. Such an objective trust relationship is also essential for the extension of division of labour, the delegation of responsibility and the separation of management and ownership in the modern corporation. Not all these developments can be accommodated within even the most sophisticated kinship-based society. It is needless to mention the importance of a highly objective credit system and division of labour for the development of capitalism. Thus capitalist development and even the continuity of capitalist institutions are, at least partially, premised on the well-being of trust in society.

Edward Lorenz (in Gambetta, 1988) shows the importance of trust in an advanced capitalist economy such as France. He argues that subcontracting among 'lock-in' firms in modern France is based on informal networks of trust, for which formal contracts cannot substitute. In contrast, Keith Hart (in Gambetta, 1988) thinks that less developed countries like Ghana have the greatest need for trust because their disintegrated, kinship-based organizations of traditional obligations have not been fully replaced by formal contracts. In any case, no one disputes the ubiquity of and need for trust in advanced countries. All the contributors to Gambetta (1988) agree that the lack of trust engenders economic underdevelopment and stagnation, as the particular history of the Mafia in Southern Italy testifies. The contraction of trust in any society entails a rise in the cost of running a business, as the recent explosion of litigation in the USA shows. The output lost as a result of distrust, which includes shirking and cheating, is wasteful since it lowers the profit rate and maybe investment as well.

Organization cost and trust

The reverse side of shirking and cheating is the cost incurred in order to minimize such activities. Such minimization effort takes two forms: one is supervision cost and the other is the cost of undertaking trust-building measures. The cost of distrust and the cost to minimize it add up to what may be dubbed 'organization cost'. It may be suggested that organization cost could act as a proxy for measuring the quantity or the state of trust in an undertaking. From the operational standpoint, however, one can at best measure the *change*, and not absolute level, of organization cost.

An economic actor, exchanging products via the market, usually has to assume some organization cost. The actor cannot take for granted the course of action of others which affect the outcome of his or her decision. This is especially the case if the agent is in a 'lock-in' arrangement with others. It is contended, without discussion here, that, if organization cost which arises from market contracts becomes higher relative to organization cost within the firm, there will be an incentive for the agent to acquire and integrate the pertinent businesses.

The concept of organization cost proposed here is different in one important regard from transaction cost associated with the works of Ronald Coase and Oliver Williamson. The transaction cost approach is aimed at providing an *exhaustive* explanation of the nature of the firm. However, transaction cost involves only the cost of entering contracts characterized by explicit or complete information (which could be probabilistic) over well defined outcomes. In contrast, organization cost is incurred when one enters contracts distinguished by implicit or incomplete information over outcomes. (Such incomplete contracts have been discussed among others, by, Oliver Hart, for example, 1988.) Organization cost is expended when contracts are incomplete in order to maintain a milieu of congeniality. When outcomes, even in probabilistic terms, are indeterminate and ambiguous, mutual trust is necessary in order to ensure the continuation of cooperative efforts. If rewards of the efforts are uncertain, an agent will not cooperate unless he or she trusts that the rest will honour, irrespective of the reward and its magnitude, the principle of fairness.

Besides the reduction of the transformation or production cost, it is submitted, without space to argue the point here, that the firm is primarily formed in order to reduce organization cost, and only secondarily to contain transaction cost. However, the integration of activities within the firm does not guarantee a steady level of organization cost; non-cooperative behaviour could take place within the firm and management still has to incur certain costs in order to nurture trust among employees, and may have to undertake monitoring. As already stated, the integration of activities within the firm is premised on the relatively lower organization costs inside the firm than organization costs involved in inter-firm exchanges. As already asserted, the integration of activities within the firm takes advantage of relatively lower organization costs. However, there is no guarantee that such costs would not absolutely and relatively rise with the increase of distrust within the firm. That is, integration of activities within the firm does not guarantee that distrust, and its familiar Prisoner's Dilemma outcomes, could be contained at a steady level.

One of the goals of the firm, in its intra- and inter-firm exchanges, is to lower distrust or at least keep it at a steady level in order to avoid Prisoner's Dilemma outcomes. Within the game-theoretic approach of the Prisoner's Dilemma, if economic cooperation is organized according to complete trust, the outcome will be the best in terms of all possible returns for both players – precisely because they have not chosen the dominant strategies recommended by myopic self-interest. Thus, ironically, trustful relations generate the best outcome because agents are *not* maximizing their utility functions.

Neoclassical view of trust
The irony that sub-optimal behaviour could ensure the best outcome is an anomaly for the neoclassical paradigm. However, this anomaly could be resolved, with some auxiliary qualifications, without sacrificing the neoclassical axiom of maximizing behaviour. Speaking broadly, the solution offered by neoclassical economics comes in two flavours. The first, identified most closely with the work of Gary Becker, is to equate trust with altruism and treat it, like altruism, as another taste in the preference ordering which is subject to maximization. This assumes that individuals are motivated by a unidimensional utility function. That is, trust is a fungible good which could be traded, along a continuous curve, with other goods in order to maximize an agent's utility function. As put by Michael Ghiselin, 'scratch an altruist, and watch a hypocrite bleed'. Gary Becker was quick to appeal to the newly emerging school of sociobiology and its hypothesis of 'inclusive fitness'. This school offered a solution to a similar anomaly within the neo-Darwinian paradigm, that is, altruistic behaviour exhibited by insects and other animals.

The second way in which neoclassical economics explains away trust is by treating it as a commodity which is not subject to maximization as in Becker's case. For example, according to Partha Dasgupta (in Gambetta, 1988), one sells trustworthiness because competitive market forces penalize the dishonest. That is, deceitful agents, who try to maximize utility with each act, will sooner or later find fewer people willing to conduct economic transactions with them. Robert Frank (1987) stated the same proposition in terms borrowed from the Darwinian theory of evolution: the market would not have selected trust if it was not useful. Therefore, in regard to long-term interest, people will behave trustworthily, that is, according to sub-optimal rules. Likewise, according to Nicholas Rowe (1989), such rules, which forsake optimizing outcome with each act, will make sense within the neo-classical assumption of rationality (optimizing behaviour) once it is under-stood that agents are involved in a series of acts. That is, an agent will obey rules of trust out of consideration for non-myopic self-interest.

Shortcomings of the neoclassical view

There is a problem with Gary Becker's approach which places trust on the same continuum as all other tastes. Individuals tend to help each other, even when they hardly know each other – as with helping earthquake victims in Iran – and hence, in most cases, cannot be part of each other's utility function. Individuals seem to derive from acting trustworthily a satisfaction which cannot be reduced to the pleasure derived, say, from eating ice-cream. The satisfaction of acting trustworthily arises from adhering to one's prior commitment and the pursuit of virtue, which Adam Smith recognized in *The Theory of Moral Sentiments* (see Khalil, 1990).

The treatment of trust as a commodity or set of rules is similar to Becker's view of trust as a taste in the utility function. Both approaches attempt to explain ethical rules without abandoning the individualist mode of concep-tion, that is, the reduction of a macro phenomena to the characteristics of the agents. Likewise, Robert Axelrod argues that the rise of cooperation among egoists in repeated games is the result of tit-for-tat strategy or fear of re-prisal. It is true that trustworthy behaviour and ethically constrained actions could be explained by ulterior motives such as the concern over reputation or reprisals, but it is doubted whether such an explanation exhausts all empirical phenomena. Individuals may not go against certain principles even when no pertinent people are watching or reprisals are threatened. A person who follows certain principles may not indulge in cunning when conducting one-time transactions in foreign lands, or may, for example, leave the usual tip in a restaurant which he or she does not expect to visit again.

Self and trust

Thus acts such as leaving tips, behaving with self-respect in faraway places, and helping anonymous others (as when refereeing papers!) cannot be ex-plained within the neoclassical approach, even as reinterpreted by Becker and Rowe. In contrast, such acts and many more common ones could be easily explained within the view that people like to maintain a good self-image. Such self-image cannot be reduced to the ordinary tastes for products and to pecuniary calculations. As has been explained elsewhere (Khalil, 1990), Adam Smith objected to this Hobbesian thesis that ethical principles arise from self-serving motives (Smith, 1976, p. 317). (Incidentally, Smith also objected to the theses that moral conduct arises from soft humanity or rational calculation of the public interest (Smith, 1976, p. 137).) Smith asks, 'what is it which prompts the generous, upon all occasions, and the mean upon many, to sacrifice their own interests to the greater interests of others?' What urges sacrifice is 'conscience, the inhabitant of the breast', or the spectator within (Smith, 1976, p. 137).

The spectator within provides a sense of integrity or self that is predicated on commitments to some courses of action. The view of trust as intrinsic to the human character is not invalidated by the existence of legally binding contracts and prisons in modern culture, as observed by Bernard Barber (1983), or binding customs and social ostracism in other cultures. The fact that such external constraints are accepted, and hence regarded as legitimate, by most members in a given society, for at least a steady period of time, indicates that the constraints may be indeed denotative of deep, internal commitments, which are integral to what defines the self.

The problem with the neoclassical theory of choice, as has been pointed out by evolutionary and institutional economists, is the treatment of choice as unrelated to the integrity of the self. It has been recognized, even by somewhat mainstream economists such as Robert Frank and Thomas Schelling, that trustworthy behaviour cannot, at least on some occasions, be explained as the result of far-sighted pecuniary calculations. One acts or is supposed to act trustworthily because this is part of one's sense of self, without which the person would be lacking in integrity and self-respect.

ELIAS L. KHALIL

See also:

Cooperation, The Evolution of; Culture; Determinism and Free Will; Firm, Theory of the; Habits; Human Nature, Theory of; Institutions; Neoclassical Microeconomic Theory, Critique of; Rationality and Maximization; Rules; Smith, Adam; Spontaneous Order; Uncertainty.

Bibliography

Barber, Bernard (1983), *The Logic and Limits of Trust*, New Brunswick, NJ: Rutgers University Press.

Eisenstadt, S.N. and Louis Roniger (1984), *Patrons, Clients and Friends: Interpersonal Relations and the Structure of Trust in Society*, Cambridge: Cambridge University Press.

Fox, Alan (1974), *Beyond Contract: Work, Power and Trust Relations*, London: Faber.

Frank, Robert H. (1987), 'If *Homo Economicus* Could Choose His Own Utility Function, Would He Want One With a Conscience?', *The American Economic Review*, **77**, (4), September, pp. 593–604.

Gambetta, Diego (ed.) (1988), *Trust: Making and Breaking Cooperative Relations*, Oxford and New York: Basil Blackwell.

Hart, Oliver (1988), 'Incomplete Contracts and the Theory of the Firm', *Journal of Law, Economics and Organization*, **4**, (1), pp. 119–39.

Husted, Bryan W. (1989), 'Trust in Business Relations: Directions for Empirical Research', *Business & Professional Ethics Journal*, **8**, (2), Summer, pp. 23–40.

Khalil, Elias L. (1990), 'Beyond Self-Interest and Altruism: A Reconstruction of Adam Smith's Theory of Human Conduct', *Economics and Philosophy*, **6**, (2), October, pp. 255–73.

Lewis, David J. and Andrew J. Weigert (1985), 'Social Atomism, Holism, and Trust', *The Sociological Quarterly*, **26**, (4), Winter, pp. 455–71.

Meeker, Barbara F. (1983), 'Cooperative Orientation, Trust, and Reciprocity', *Human Relations*, **37**, (3), pp. 225–43.

Rowe, Nicholas (1989), *Rules and Institutions*, Ann Arbor: The University of Michigan Press.

Smith, Adam (1976), *The Theory of Moral Sentiments*, ed. D.D. Raphael and A.L. Macfie, Oxford: Clarendon.

Ullmann-Margalit, Edna

Following the famous distinction made by Carl Menger, there are basically two views of institutions. In the first, which we shall call the rules view, social or economic institutions are seen as sets of rules that constrain individual behaviour and define social outcomes that result from individual action. This view is most closely associated with the work of scholars belonging to what we shall call the *design and implementation school*. In this school, mostly associated with the names of economists working in the area of mechanism design and implementation (Maskin, Hurwicz, Moulin, Groves, Ledyard and so on), the emphasis is on institutional engineering and the conscious creation of institutional forms. Game theory plays a major role in the analysis of these institutions because designing an institution is equivalent to designing a game of 'game form' for social agents to play. The question is, what is the best game (or institution) to have people play so as to satisfy some exogenously given objective function?

The other view of social institutions, which I shall call the behavioural view, is present in the work of Edna Ullmann-Margalit, Senior Lecturer in Philosophy at Hebrew University, Jerusalem, who looks at social institutions or norms, not as predesigned rules, but rather as unplanned and unintended regularities of social behaviour that emerge organically (to use Menger's term). We can call this school the *organic school*. Institutions here are the outcomes of human action that no one individual intended. The object of analysis is not the rules of social conduct, but rather the conventions or norms of social behaviour that evolve as social agents repeatedly face the same types of social problems. The rules are not as important as the regularities of behaviour established given certain situations describable by rules of simple games.

Edna Ullmann-Margalit's *The Emergence of Norms* (1977) must be considered one of the major modern foundations upon which the organic school of social institutions was built. The book takes a rational reconstructionist approach to the creation of social norms defined as a 'prescribed guide for conduct or action which is generally complied with by the members of a society'. These norms help to fill the gaps left either by the multiplicity of equilibria (coordination norms), the inefficiency of equilibria (Prisoner's Dilemma norms), or the unfairness of equilibria (norms of partiality) in the types of games that led to their creation. More specifically, Ullmann-Margalit isolates three primary situations, all of which lead to the creation of a norm of behaviour. The first is the Prisoner's Dilemma situation where, if left alone, rationality would dictate an inefficient outcome for social agents. Cooperative norms emerge here to help society break this unsatisfactory situation. Coordination norms emerge because a strategic situation defines many different equilibria, all of which could guide the actions of social agents. Here people need some prescribed guide of conduct which will allow them to pick out one of these equilibria for adherence. Finally, norms of partiality emerge to help favoured social agents maintain their favoured position in the game played by society. For norms of partiality, the analysis starts out by fixing historically some status quo position and then investigating its stability. Norms of partiality emerge to help stabilize inequitable and unstable equilibria.

In addition to playing a seminal role in this organic school, Ullmann-Margalit's work (1978, 1990), to mention just a part, makes her a paradoxical figure in the literature. The reason for this paradox is ideology. While most members of the organic school (Hayek in particular) are ideologically conservative and view unintended and unplanned social norms and institutions as unimpeachable and beyond the scope of intervention, Ullmann-Margalit does not see intervention as inconsistent with concerns for organically created social institutions. The paradox is resolved in her papers on 'invisible-hand' explanations (1978). In that paper she explains that there has been a confusion in the literature in its interpretation of the meaning of 'invisible-hand explanations'. To the more conservative followers of the organic school, invisible-hand explanations take on a functional–evolutionary form in which what exists has evolved over time to solve problems efficiently and hence should not be tampered with. Ullmann-Margalit sees her work more in what she calls the aggregate mould of analysis in which one looks for explanations of the way institutions or norms emerged from the unplanned actions of individuals. While the aggregate model investigates the question of the emergence of norms, it says nothing about the desirability of their continued existence. This is the area of the functional–evolutionary school, with its biological analogies.

While much work has been done on the emergence and function of norms and institutions, relatively little has been done on the way norms or institutions change or are revised. Ullmann-Margalit (1990) makes a distinction between norm change, which is an unplanned fact of dynamic social life, and norm revision, which is a conscious act by members of society to alter the way they do things. While Prisoner's Dilemma norms of cooperation may disintegrate over time and hence crumble or change in an unplanned manner, coordination norms are more likely to need concerted social action, since they involve huge costs if disequilibrium states occur. For example, switching people from driving on the left to driving on the right side of the road is unlikely to occur through norm change but must be directed from above through a process of norm revision (as was done in Sweden years ago).

In the process of discussing the change and revision of norms, Ullmann-Margalit makes a distinction between *presumptive* and *conclusive* norms. A norm is presumptive if it is supplemented by an additional rule specifying what the person should do when the conditions of the norm are ambiguous. For example, as she states, in law a person is innocent until proved guilty. The presumption is that the burden of proof is on the state and, if no guilt *beyond a shadow of doubt* can be established, the ambiguity created by doubt leads to the default presumption of innocence. Conclusive norms either admit no uncertainty or else they are silent about it. Presumptive norms are many times the objects of norm revision. The need for revision comes about because, as Ullmann-Margalit states, first, with the passage of time the social agents may be in the possession of new information; second, a change in technology may open up new strategic possibilities to the agents; and finally, the preferences of the agents may change over time.

Ullmann-Margalit's discussion of norm revision again brings her into the ideological realm. When one talks about norm revision or consciously planned norm alteration, one is forced to examine one's view of the way social institutions are created. Again the conservative refrain is to let norms change but resist their revision, while the enlightenment attitude is to espouse norm revision in the name of reason and progress.

In conclusion, we may say that Edna Ullmann-Margalit's work provides a perfect example of the fact that, no matter how hard we as economists have tried to make economics a science, the link between philosophical inquiry and economic studies is as useful today as it was when Mill, Smith and Hume combined the two as a natural union of intellectual interests. Ullmann-Margalit's work, along with that of David Lewis (1969), has enlarged the scope of economic inquiry to include not only market institutions with prices as informational signals, but other, non-market institutions supplemented by norm and conventional information structures. Her impact is significant and destined to grow.

ANDREW R. SCHOTTER

See also:

Atomism and Organicism; Cartesianism in Economics; Cognition, Cultural and Institutional Influences on; Cooperation, The Evolution of; Culture; Determinism and Free Will; Habits; Hayek, Friedrich A.; Institutionalism, 'Old' and 'New'; Institutions; Money, Evolution of; Part–Whole Relationships; Power; Prigogine, Ilya; Rules; Schotter, Andrew; Spontaneous Order; Transaction.

Bibliography

Lewis, David (1969), *Convention: A Philosophical Study*, Cambridge, Mass.: Harvard University Press.
Ullmann-Margalit, Edna (1977), *The Emergence of Norms*, Oxford: Oxford University Press.
Ullmann-Margalit, Edna (1978), 'Invisible Hand Explanations', *Synthese*, **39**, pp. 282–6.
Ullmann-Margalit, Edna (1990), *Ethics*, **100**, Chicago: University of Chicago Press.

Uncertainty

Conceptions of uncertainty are central to economic theorizing. However, the term is often employed in very different ways in the various contributions of subjectivists, Keynesians, neoclassicists, institutionalists, Austrians and so on, and this inevitably gives rise to a degree of confusion and incoherent cross-talk. A particular consequence is that competing conclusions can be found to the effect that the prevalence of uncertainty is 'analytically innocuous', 'indiscriminately destructive', the 'very source of predictable behaviour' and so on.

One relatively persistent feature of the economics literature, however, is that notions of uncertainty tend to be associated with, or defined against, specific conceptions of probability (Lawson, 1988; de Carvalho, 1988; Rotheim, 1988). As an aid to categorizing interpretations of the notion of uncertainty, then, it is relevant to enquire first of all whether the various conceptions of probability can be delineated. This, in fact, can be achieved quite straightforwardly. For, if the recent realist literature is correct to warn against supposing that questions bearing upon the object of knowledge can always be rephrased as questions about knowledge (of the object), it is pertinent to ask at the outset whether, in any specific account, probability is conceived of as an object, or as a form, of knowledge. Through addressing this question, it will be seen, significant strands in probabilistic thinking in economics – and in turn conceptions of uncertainty – can be systematically differentiated.

An important first indicator of the nature of any conception of probability is the sort of language used. Specifically, some economists write of probabilities as something to be *discovered*, *learned* about, and *known*: others avoid such terminology and write instead of probabilities as something which agents *possess*, or *attach* to particular propositions, and so on. It is the former group, typically, that envisage probability as an object of knowledge, the latter that interpret it as a form or aspect of knowledge.

The subjectivist theory

Within the latter group are the subjectivists, including Savage, Ramsey, de Finetti and Friedman. For subjectivists, probability is the degree of belief attached to a given proposition or event by an actual individual at some specific point in time. It is not an object of the individual's knowledge. As Lucas (in conversation with Klamer, 1984) observes of Milton Friedman: 'He's very influenced by Savage and by his Bayesian way of thinking about probabilities. So when I talk about people "knowing" a probability, he just can't reach that language' (p. 40). In addition, the subjectivist denies the possibility that knowledge can be objective in any sense. Personal probabilities about any proposition or event cannot meaningfully be said to be right or wrong or rational and so on: there is only individual belief. As Weatherford (1982, p. 226) notes, the 'subjectivist ... recognizes that his opinion is the final authority, and is free to consider or ignore any data about any classes whatsoever. There is no *correct* reference class since there is no correct probability. This is so even for those highly uniform occurrences which objectivists call "repetitive events".'

In short, while subjectivists tend to agree with de Finetti (1985) 'that probability does not exist in the world of hard fact but only in the realm of human reasoning' (p. 351), they also suppose, with Savage (1962, p. 14), that any idea of objectiveness in knowledge should be rejected as not 'valid, fruitful or practical'.

Keynes's theory of probability

An alternative conception of probability is elaborated by Keynes in his *A Treatise on Probability* (1973a). Here Keynes introduces the *probability relation* whereby he is concerned 'to emphasize the existence of a *logical relation between two sets of propositions* in cases where it is not possible to argue demonstratively from one to the other' (p. 9). Any conclusion, a, is related to a given set of premises or background knowledge, h, via a probability relation denoted a/h. In this view, then, probability is relational. Just as no place is intrinsically distant, so no proposition is intrinsically probable: a proposition has a certain probability relative to given evidence or background knowledge. If new evidence, h_1, is obtained, it does not throw increased light upon the previous probability. Rather, it gives rise to a new probability relation a/hh_1.

In this framework, clearly, probability is again not something that can be learned about as new information is acquired. However, it is a form of objective belief. Although probability is not a property of the actual material world but a feature of the way we think about the world, the degree of belief that, rationally and (typically) actually, is held given the evidence available is fixed, and in that sense is objective (see Lawson, 1985a, 1985b).

The difference between Keynes's theory and the subjectivist view, clearly, is that, although both accept that probability exists only on the level of knowledge or opinion, Keynes, unlike subjectivists, believes that probability is objectively determined. Before turning to the associated conceptions of uncertainty it is instructive to consider first some further prominent contributions which, in contrast to those just considered, allow that probabilities *do* exist in external material reality and thereby are potential objects of knowledge.

The rational expectations theory

A viewpoint which supposes that external reality is representable as of a joint probability distribution is that associated with the rational expectations hypothesis. According to this, agent knowledge takes the form of a subjective probability distribution while underlying reality, which is being learned about and predicted, can be described and should be understood as an objective or 'true' probability distribution. Thus, in the words of Lucas (1981, p. 223), 'John Muth (1961) ... [proceeded] ... by identifying agents' subjective probabilities with observed frequencies of the events to be forecast, or with "true" probabilities, calling the assumed coincidence of subjective and "true" probabilities *rational expectations*.' For the rational expectationist, then, and in contrast to the subjectivist and Keynes, "true" probabilities are properties of events that actually take place in the world, and we are conceived of as objects of knowledge, as phenomena that can be known (or unknown).

Knight's view of probability

A final prominent account of probability to be considered explicitly is that provided by Frank Knight (1921). Knight acknowledges the fact of probability judgements but also accepts the conception of probability as a feature of external reality, as an object of knowledge – due to real indeterminacy in the cosmos itself (p. 220) – which is referred to as *real* (p. 219), *actual* (p. 215) or *true* (p. 235) probability. He is explicitly sceptical of any view that attributes probability to the fact of mere ignorance (p. 221).

Knight in fact distinguishes three types of probability situations. In the first two, probability *judgements* are referred to as *a priori* probability and statistical probability, respectively. In both situations, probability judgements can, in principle, correspond in some way to underlying true probabilities: 'In the former the "chances" can be computed on general principles, while in the latter they can only be determined empirically' (p. 224). And in both these examples it is real indeterminacy that underlies the defining characteristics. Thus, when considering *a priori* probability, Knight stresses the 'absolutely homogeneous classification of instances completely identical except for really indeterminate factors' (p. 224); and when referring to statistical probability, he emphasizes that 'any high degree of confidence that the proportions found in the past will hold in the future is still based on an *a priori* judgement of indeterminateness' (p. 225). In the third type of probability situation the relevant 'judgement' that is formed is referred to as an estimate. Typically, the situation is one in which the event in question is considered to be irredeemably unique. Nevertheless, Knight believes that in such a situation we may still form an opinion and that, if so, 'we do estimate the value or validity or dependability of our opinions and estimates, and such an estimate has the same *form* as a probability judgement' (p. 231).

Certainly, this (second-order) estimate of the validity of some (first-order) estimate (of some relatively unique outcome) is seen as being significantly different from the two types of probability judgements mentioned above: in the cases of *a priori* and statistical probability judgements, there are objective or true probabilities to be determined (p. 230), while in the third case, of an estimate of an estimate, the 'conception of an objectively measurable probability or chance is simply inapplicable' (p. 231). Nevertheless, Knight persists in referring to this estimate as a probability judgement, if only because 'there is little hope of breaking away from well-established linguistic usage' (p. 231).

In sum, a distinction drawn between probability interpreted as a property of underlying material reality and probability interpreted merely as a feature, or form, of knowledge is seen to be one of consequence when attempting to compare and delineate various accounts that are currently prominent in economic analysis. So far, however, no reference has been made to the notion of uncertainty. What, then, is the connection? Consider first those accounts wherein probability is interpreted as a form of knowledge only. A point to note here is that, while for many subjectivists numerical probabilities can be assigned to more or less any event or proposition imaginable, for Keynes, in contrast, a numerically determinate probability is relatively uncommon. Yet both seem to take it for granted that uncertainty is a pervasive fact of life. So what is the relationship between probability and uncertainty in these accounts? In fact, the distinction just made concerning the pervasiveness or otherwise of numerically determinate probabilities effectively underlies the respective interpretations of uncertainty. Specifically, for subjectivists, uncertainty corresponds to a situation of probabilistic knowledge; for Keynes, uncertainty is associated with a situation wherein numerically determinate probabilities are *not* to be had. It will be seen below that

Table 1 Probability and uncertainty

	Probability is a property of knowledge of belief	Probability is also an object of knowledge as a property of external material reality
Uncertainty corresponds to a situation of numerically measurable probability	Subjectivists (e.g. Savage, Friedman)	Proponents of the rational expectations view (e.g. Muth, Lucas)
Uncertainty corresponds to a situation of numerically immeasurable probability	Keynes	Knight

this distinction between measurable and immeasurable probabilities also underlies the different conceptions of uncertainty associated with accounts in which probability is also an aspect of material reality. In short, the various accounts of probability and uncertainty that are currently prominent within economics can be classified schematically as in Table 1.

Let me briefly consider some substantiation for the suggested categorization of different interpretations of the notion of uncertainty.

Subjectivist uncertainty
The interpretation of uncertainty that has been associated above with the subjectivist school seems uncontroversial. As Hey (1983) asserts, subjective expected utility theory, which is intrinsically bound up with subjective probability theory, is the very 'foundation stone of the Economics of Uncertainty' (p. 130). In addition, Diamond and Rothschild (1978) provide a collection of 30 papers in a volume entitled *Uncertainty in Economics*, all of which associate uncertainty with the Ramsey/Savage subjectivist view of probability. And in their expository survey of the 'analytics of uncertainty and information' this view of uncertainty is also held by Hirshleifer and Riley (1979).

One possible qualification here concerns the observation made above that subjectivists tend to assume that agents can and do attach probabilities to *any* proposition state of affairs or event. As Weatherford (1982, p. 222) notes, 'Generally, subjectivists have tended to act as if each of us has an opinion about everything, because there are always some odds at which we will make bets on some contingent proposition or event' (and thus reveal a supposed probability concerning this proposition or event). However, a point to note is that, following contributions by Savage (1954) and Arrow (1964), subjectivists often refrain from assigning probabilities to general economic variables, but attach them, instead, to presumed different and mutually exclusive 'states of the world', any one of which may occur. Even so, the situation is still characterized as one of uncertainty. Uncertainty and probabilistic knowledge for the subjectivist go hand in hand and, although various contributions differ markedly in the way they are set up (for example, Arrow and Debreu introduce preferences as primitive concepts, whereas for Savage they are represented in terms of a probability measure over states and a utility measure over consequences) such differences do not disturb this general conclusion.

Keynesian uncertainty
Keynes's account, in contrast, associates uncertainty not with probabilistic knowledge but with the *absence* of probabilistic knowledge. Uncertainty corresponds (if among other things – see Runde, 1990, 1991) to a situation

in which probabilities are *not* numerically determinate, or even comparable, in terms of more or less, with other probability relations (see Lawson, 1985a). Thus Keynes indicates that by 'uncertain knowledge' he does not mean

> merely to distinguish what is known for certain from what is only probable. The game of roulette is not subject, in this sense, to uncertainty; nor is the prospect of a Victory bond being drawn. Or, again the expectation of life is only slightly uncertain. Even the weather is only moderately uncertain. The sense in which I am using the term is that in which the prospect of a European war is uncertain, or the price of copper and the rate of interest twenty years hence, or the obsolescence of a new invention, or the position of private wealth owners in the social system in 1970. About these matters there is no scientific basis on which to form any calculable probability whatever. We simply do not know. (Keynes, 1973b)

Clearly, Keynes's notion of uncertainty corresponding to an absence of numerically measurable probabilistic knowledge is significantly different from that associated with the subjectivist school whereby, ultimately, a situation of uncertainty and of probabilistic knowledge tends always to mean one and the same thing. This distinction, moreover, can be shown to be equally significant for differentiating between those accounts in which probability is interpreted as also being a property of material reality.

Uncertainty and rational expectations

It is not unusual for proponents of the rational expectations hypothesis to introduce a probabilistic set-up in which the distributional parameters are unknown and to characterize this as a situation of uncertainty. Even Lucas – who is more circumspect than most about using the term 'uncertainty' in this way – on occasion follows suit. For example, in a paper entitled 'Investment Under Uncertainty', Lucas and Prescott (1971) characterize a situation of 'demand uncertainty' as 'stochastic demand' whereby 'product demand shifts randomly each period' (p. 65). The forecasting of demand, which, in their set-up, amounts to forecasting output prices, is, of course, possible; this merely represents the application of the rational expectations hypothesis. For rational expectations proponents, then, uncertainty corresponds to a situation of numerically determinate probabilistic knowledge.

Knight's uncertainty

Knight, like the rational expectationists, recognizes the existence of external probabilities but, unlike the latter, restricts the notion of uncertainty to situations in which the probabilities are unknown. Initially, Knight writes (1921, pp. 19, 20) of measurable versus unmeasurable uncertainty where the former corresponds to situations in which the *a priori* and *statistical* probability judgement are in principle possible and where the latter, unmeasurable, uncertainty corresponds to a situation in which the third type of probability judgement – an estimate of an estimate – can be formed. However, because Knight is of the view that the two situations are so radically different, he insists that the former is not really one of uncertainty at all and is best referred to as one of risk: 'It will appear that a *measurable* uncertainty, or "risk" proper, as we shall use the term, is so far different from an *unmeasurable* one that it is not in effect an uncertainty at all. We shall accordingly restrict the term "uncertainty" to cases of the non-quantitative type' (p. 20).

Uncertainty, then, corresponds to a situation wherein no real, true or objectively measurable probability is possible, wherein the 'conception of an objectively measurable probability or chance is simply inapplicable' (p. 231). Thus Knight's position has been characterized as in Table 1. This diagrammatic representation might have to be slightly qualified, however, *if,* in a situation where the relevant event is unique and a mere estimate is obtained, it were to be insisted that this situation can be characterized as one in which a *measurable* probability is possible, albeit a non-objective one. As noted above, Knight does refer to the estimated value of any estimate formed in a situation of uncertainty as a 'probability judgement', but does so mainly to conform to linguistic convention. As such, he insists upon stressing the differences of this estimate from other forms of probability judgement. In consequence, the representation in Table 1 seems to be the most appropriate interpretation of Knight's position to retain.

In conclusion, in the light of the categorization of Table 1, it is not surprising that mutually inconsistent claims abound concerning the nature and consequences of uncertainty. Specifically, it is not surprising that analyses which accept the interpretations of uncertainty as associated with the accounts of the subjectivist or the rational expectations proponents tend to view the notion as less debilitating than do other studies.

TONY LAWSON

See also:

Information Theory in Economics; Keynes, John Maynard; Neoclassical Microeconomic Theory, Critique of; Realism, Philosophical; Shackle, George Lennox Sharman.

Bibliography

Arrow, K. (1953), 'Le Rôle des valeurs pour la répartition la meilleure des risques', *Econométrie*, pp. 41–8, Paris: CNRS; translated 1964, as 'The Role of Securities in the Optimal Allocation of Risk-Bearing', *Review of Economics Studies*, **31**, pp. 91–6.

Carvalho, F.J.C. de (1988), 'Keynes on Probability, Uncertainty and Decision-making', *Journal of Post Keynesian Economics*, **11**, (1), Fall.

Carvalho, F.J.C. de *et al.* (1988), 'Symposium: Probability and Uncertainty', *Journal of Post Keynesian Economics*, **11**, (1), Fall.

Diamond, P. and M. Rothschild (eds) (1978), *Uncertainty in Economics*, New York: Academic Press.

Finetti, B. de (1985), 'Cambridge Probability Theorists', *The Manchester School*, **53**, pp. 348–63.

Hey, J.D. (1983), 'Whither Uncertainty?' *Economic Journal* (Conference Papers), pp. 130–39.

Hirshleifer, J. and J.G. Riley (1979), 'The Analysis of Uncertainty and Information – An Expository Survey', *Journal of Economic Literature*, **17**, pp. 1375–1421.

Keynes, J.M. (1973a), *A Treatise on Probability. Collected Writings of John Maynard Keynes, Vol. 8*, London: Macmillan.

Keynes, J.M. (1973b), *The General Theory and After, Part II: Defence and Development. Collected Writings of John Maynard Keynes, Vol. 4*, London; Macmillan.

Klamer, A. (ed.) (1984), *The New Classical Macroeconomics: Conversations with New Classical Economists and Their Opponents*, Brighton: Wheatsheaf.

Knight, F. (1921), *Risk, Uncertainty and Profit*, Boston and New York: Houghton; Cambridge: Riverside Press.

Lawson, T. (1985a), 'Uncertainty and Economic Analysis', *Economic Journal*, p. 95.

Lawson, T. (1985b), 'Keynes, Prediction and Econometrics', in T. Lawson and H. Pesaran (eds).

Lawson, T. (1988), 'Probability and Uncertainty in Economic Analysis', *Journal of Post Keynesian Economics*, **11**, (1), Fall, pp. 38–65.

Lawson, T. and H. Pesaran (eds) (1985), *Keynes' Economics: Methodological Issues*, London and Sydney: Croom Helm.

Lucas, R.E. (1981), *Studies in Business Cycle Theory*, Cambridge, Mass.: MIT Press.

Lucas, R.E. and E.C. Prescott (1971), 'Investment Under Uncertainty', *Econometrica*, **39**, (5), pp. 659–81.

Muth, J.F. (1961), 'Rational Expectations and the Theory of Price Movements', *Econometrica*, **29**, pp. 315–35.

Rotheim, R.J. (1988), 'Keynes and the Language of Probability and Uncertainty', *Journal of Post Keynesian Economics*, **11**, (1), Fall, pp. 82–99

Runde, J. (1990), 'Keynesian Uncertainty and the Weight of Arguments', *Economics and Philosophy*, **6**, pp. 275–92.

Runde, J. (1991), 'Keynesian Uncertainty and the Instability of Beliefs', *Review of Political Economy*, **3**, (2), pp. 125, 145.

Savage, L.J. (1954), *The Foundations of Statistics*, New York: Dover Publications.

Savage, L.J. (1962), *The Foundations of Statistical Inference*, London: Methuen.

Weatherford, R. (1982), *Philosophical Foundations of Probability Theory*, London: Routledge & Kegan Paul.

Unemployment

Neoclassical theory assumes that the level of employment (and hence the amount of unemployment given the available labour supply) is determined in the labour market in the same way that the output of peanuts is determined in the market for peanuts. Profit-maximizing competitive firms will employ labour up to the point where its marginal product is equal to the real wage. Diminishing returns in the short period imply that each firm's marginal product of labour curve is downward-sloping (and its marginal cost curve upward-sloping) as extra labour is employed with a fixed amount of plant and equipment. The whole economy is then analysed as if it were one giant firm with an aggregate production function and downward-sloping aggregate marginal product of labour curve – the economy's supposed 'demand curve' for labour. As the real wage (the price of labour) falls, the demand for labour rises. Utility-maximizing households supply labour until the marginal disutility of work is equal to the real wage. Aggregating over all households, the supply of labour to the economy is assumed to increase as the real wage rises.

Given these aggregate demand and supply curves, the real wage is assumed to adjust until the equilibrium level of employment – the natural rate of unemployment in Friedman's (1968) terminology – is attained. All unemployment in equilibrium is voluntary, in the sense that workers in aggregate are on the labour supply curve, and consists of the inevitable frictional unemployment (as labour moves between firms in search of better conditions) and structural unemployment (as the changing output mix of the economy requires labour to be reallocated across industries). There can be additional, involuntary unemployment, above the natural rate, with labour off the supply curve, but such unemployment is a temporary, disequilibrium phenomenon arising from market imperfections, whether structural or informational. Thus trade unions can cause unemployment by preventing the real wage from falling to the market-clearing level. There can be cyclical variations in unemployment around the natural rate caused by unexpected demand shocks (usually assumed to be of monetary origin) but the rate of interest is assumed to equilibrate savings and investment at the level of output consistent with the natural rate of unemployment, so that Say's Law holds and the economy self-adjusts to full employment. The general Panglossian picture is of a smoothly self-equilibrating market mechanism with substitution effects, resulting from relative price chances, dominating income effects. Households continually substitute between present goods and between present goods and future goods (savings) and firms continually substitute between capital and labour, so that all income is spent and all factors fully utilized as the economy enjoys steady growth at the natural rate of unemployment. The Clower–Leijonhufvud interpretation of *The General Theory* as the economics of disequilibrium does not change the picture significantly: they accept the overall validity of the above system, but stress that the income effects of disturbances may initially dominate price-substitution effects so that the return to equilibrium may take a considerable time.

Institutionalism and radical political economy completely reject the above 'imperfectionist' approach to explaining unemployment in a developed, capitalist market system. Unemployment, over and above the irreducible minimum of frictional and structural unemployment, is endemic in a dynamic monetary production economy and is the result of a chronic lack of aggregate effective demand. Left to itself, the economy grows irregularly through time, as demand grows irregularly, reaching full employment (a situation of zero involuntary, demand-deficient unemployment) only temporarily at the peak of strong booms. For most of the time there is likely to be an excess supply of labour (involuntary unemployment) and firms are likely to be operating below capacity. Keynes explained how this comes about in *The General Theory* (1936), which was his attempt to break away completely from the orthodox neoclassical theory, described above, which has no relevance to real-world economies because there is no room in it for *time, change, uncertainty* and *money*. Keynes's central message is that, to understand the forces which determine changes in the scale of output and employment as a whole, it is first necessary to understand that the real world we inhabit is a dynamic *monetary production* economy – what Keynes (1979) called a 'money-wage or entrepreneur economy' to distinguish it from what he called a 'real-wage or co-operative economy' in which Say's Law always holds true – moving irreversibly through calendar (historic) time from an unchangeable past to a necessarily uncertain future; uncertain because it has yet to be created and is certain to be different! The decisions of firms regarding the level of employment they will offer and the amount of investment they will undertake are guided by their (uncertain) *expectations of demand* in the near or more distant future. Firms are demand-constrained *not* resource-constrained, as orthodox theory assumes. In Keynes's model, short-period equilibrium is a very different concept from the neoclassical general equilibrium attained by flexible prices rapidly adjusting to clear all markets, including the factor markets. In Keynes, equilibrium simply means that, in aggregate, firms have guessed correctly what the level of output for the period should be; they have produced and sold just the amounts of consumer goods and services and capital goods which they expected to sell. If the state of short-term expectations governing the *supplies* of all goods (both current and capital) and the state of long-term expectations governing the *demand* for capital goods remain unchanged, employment will remain unchanged. This is a very limited concept of equilibrium. It is at most a 'quasi', temporary equilibrium, which will change as expectations change and which contains the seeds of its own destruction as net investment (necessary to maintain aggregate demand) adjusts the capital stock to the level appropriate to the equilibrium level of output and, therefore, ceases. There is no suggestion that all markets should clear; firms in the aggregate are in temporary equilibrium because aggregate supply is equal to aggregate demand on the goods market, and this has come about because output and employment have adjusted through the multiplier process until planned investment equals planned saving. Investment calls the tune and, given the psychology of the public as expressed in the consumption function, determines output, employment *and* saving. The labour market – the nucleus of the neoclassical theory of employment – determines neither employment nor the real wage in Keynes's system.

The fact that we live in a *monetary* production economy moving irreversibly through time towards an *unknowable* future explains why investment, the *causa causans* (Keynes, 1937), is subject to severe fluctuations and, on average, insufficient to ensure full employment. Production processes take time and hence the decision to organize production must occur earlier in time than the outcome. In an uncertain environment, the outcome is more or less unpredictable and fallible humans therefore evolve an institutional framework to reduce uncertainty as much as possible, in particular a system of fixed forward money contracts. Such fixed money contracts (the money wage contract is the most common) are an essential adjunct of organizing time-consuming production processes (Davidson, 1981). Thus the prices of newly-produced goods are anchored to labour costs and fixed over the contract period. It follows that the labour market's function in Keynes's system is to determine the structure and general level of *money* wages through the institutions of collective bargaining. It therefore plays a crucial role in the determination of labour costs, prices and inflation but *not* employment. A monetary production economy could not function without the degree of price stability provided by a system of forward contracting: the value of money must be reasonably stable if money is to fulfil its key roles of a medium of exchange and hence a liquid store of value – *a refuge from uncertainty* and a means of carrying *uncommitted* purchasing power through time.

When deciding whether to undertake the formidable risks of embarking on real investment projects where the return is highly uncertain, entrepreneurs may often be tempted to postpone such difficult decisions and keep their funds relatively liquid; they will prefer financial (portfolio) investment or investment in *existing* real assets to investment in newly-produced capital goods. Liquidity will triumph over enterprise and unemployment will ensue (Shackle, 1983). Moreover, the preference for liquidity over enterprise is likely to result in long-run demand deficiency, as Harrod (1939) envisaged. Harrod believed the normal lot of an advanced capitalist economy would be for its warranted growth rate (dependent on the propensity to save) to exceed its natural growth rate (dependent on technical progress and the consequent investment opportunities) resulting in chronic demand deficiency and unemployment. (On the other hand, in the case of underdeveloped countries, the natural rate would exceed the warranted rate, causing a different kind of unemployment, that which results from a shortage of capital equipment for labour to operate.) Worse still, not only is the propensity to save of a rich country likely to exceed its propensity to invest, it is extremely unlikely that all potentially profitable investment projects will be implemented, for technical progress, the essential engine of growth, is also one of the fundamental sources of *change* and therefore of *uncertainty*. Technical progress changes the whole structure of the economy, leading to new products and new processes which entrepreneurs, pursuing greater profits, must endeavour to seek out and invest in before their competitors. Technical progress will result in labour productivity increasing at different rates in different lines of production. Hence relative costs and the price structure will change. More importantly, the structure of demand will change. Demand determines output and the actual output of each product will follow its own non-steady time path. New products and modifications of old ones will be introduced. No wonder that Keynes, when considering the long-term expectations governing the investment intentions of entrepreneurs, emphasized the importance of 'animal spirits' and 'spontaneous optimism' in the face of the 'dark forces of time and ignorance' and the likelihood that investment would be inadequate and subject to fluctuations with consequent cyclical and secular unemployment.

Since the economic system is not a self-equilibrating mechanism but an irregularly unfolding cumulative process, there are obvious implications for economic policy. We do not have sufficient knowledge to 'fine-tune' the economy, but we should be able to limit deviations from a high employment growth path by a judicious combination of fiscal and monetary demand management policies. The only way to combine a high employment policy with low inflation is to set up permanent institutions to monitor and control the behaviour of the general level of money wages and prices. There will be considerable scope for the government to undertake (or assist the private sector to undertake) long-term investment in the infrastructure and high-risk projects. Above all, there must be substantial government investment in human capital – expenditure on health, education and training to improve the quality of labour, the ultimate factor of production and source of wealth. This will be particularly necessary for an open economy to maintain its competitiveness; otherwise growth will be constrained and unemployment result from an inability to export enough to finance the import requirements of high employment growth.

JOHN F. BROTHWELL

See also:
Cumulative Causation; Keynes, John Maynard; Labour Markets; Macroeconomic Policy; Macroeconomic Theory; Monetary Theory; Planning, Theory of; Uncertainty.

Bibliography
Davidson, P. (1978), *Money and the Real World*, 2nd edn, London: Macmillan.
Davidson, P. (1981), 'Post Keynesian economics: solving the crisis in economic theory', in D. Bell and I. Kristol (eds), *The Crisis in Economic Theory*, pp. 151–73, New York: Basic Books.
Friedman, M. (1968), 'The role of monetary policy', *American Economic Review*, **58**, March, pp. 1–17.
Harrod, R.F. (1939), 'An essay in dynamic theory', *Economic Journal*, **49**, pp. 14–33.

Keynes, J.M. (1936), *The General Theory of Employment, Interest and Money*, London: Macmillan.

Keynes, J.M. (1937), 'The general theory of employment', *Quarterly Journal of Economics*, **51**, pp. 209–23.

Keynes, J.M. (1979), 'The Distinction between a Co-operative Economy and an Entrepreneur Economy' in D. Moggridge (ed.), *The General Theory and After: a Supplement*, Vol. XXIX of *The Collected Writings of John Maynard Keynes*, pp. 76–83. London: Macmillan.

Sawyer, M.C. (1989), *The Challenge of Radical Political Economy*, Hemel Hempstead: Harvester Wheatsheaf.

Shackle, G.L.S. (1967), *The Years of High Theory*, Cambridge: Cambridge University Press.

Shackle, G.L.S. (1983), 'Levels of Simplicity in Keynes's Theory of Money and Employment', *The South African Journal of Economics*, **51**, (3), September, pp. 357–67.

Weintraub, S. (1978), *Capitalism's Inflation and Unemployment Crisis*, Reading, Mass.: Addison-Wesley.

Veblen, Thorstein

Thorstein Veblen (1857–1929) is widely credited with originating what Walton Hamilton in 1919 dubbed the 'institutional' approach to economic analysis. A trenchant critic of business civilization and the 'orthodox' economics through which its operation was apprehended, Veblen crafted an alternative 'evolutionary' standpoint exhibiting almost no point of contact with received doctrine. In truth, Veblen was probably the most radical thinker in the history of economics.

Overview

Veblen was the son of Norwegian immigrants who settled while he was still a young boy in south-eastern Minnesota, a farming region populated mostly by other 'Norskies'. Raised almost entirely within the insulated immigrant community, Veblen absorbed its 'old country' ethos and throughout his life remained a lone figure with the perspective on American life of a dispassionate alien. Despite having received little formal instruction and knowing little English, Veblen was enrolled in 1874 by his father at Carleton College, a small Congregationalist institution in Minnesota, where he spent three years in preparatory schooling, followed by another three to obtain his degree. While at Carleton, Veblen showed an interest in philology, natural history (biology), philosophy and economics, the latter of which he studied under the tutelage of John Bates Clark, a strong believer in the marginalist conceptions then being developed to replace classical value theory.

After leaving Carleton, Veblen enrolled at Johns Hopkins to pursue a doctorate in philosophy. Failing to obtain a fellowship, he decided after one year to move on to Yale, from which he obtained his PhD in 1884. While at Yale, Veblen took courses from William Graham Sumner, the American proselytizer of Herbert Spencer's evolutionary theories. Despite his distaste for its apologetic animus, many of Veblen's most important ideas have their roots in Spencer's analysis. Unable to obtain a teaching post, Veblen spent the next seven years unemployed. He passed the time by reading whatever he found of interest. It was during this period that his unique perspective gradually took form. Eventually, Veblen decided he should undertake new graduate studies in order to 'credentialize' himself in a new field. Deciding on political economy, he enrolled in 1891 at Cornell and quickly made a favourable impression on J. Laurence Laughlin, who the next year took Veblen with him when called to organize an economics department at the newly established University of Chicago. Once at Chicago, Veblen was appointed an instructor and soon also became the managing editor of the new *Journal of Political Economy*. Preoccupied with his duties, Veblen never completed his degree in political economy.

Beginning in 1898, Veblen wrote a remarkable series of articles, the majority of which are reprinted in *The Place of Science in Modern Civilisation* (1919) and *Essays in Our Changing Order* (1934), delineating the inadequacies of received economic doctrines and methodological practices. But he did not limit himself to criticism; Veblen simultaneously proceeded to indicate the character of a scientifically adequate 'evolutionary' standpoint in two books, *The Theory of the Leisure Class* (1899), directed to the task of developing a theory of consumption rooted in a cultural interpretation of personality, and *The Theory of Business Enterprise* (1904), directed to the related task of developing a theory of the modern economy in which giant corporations, trusts and high finance take centre stage. Even though the former was an important work in social theory, its seeming mockery of leisure class practices attracted a wide readership and made Veblen something of a celebrity. Veblen revealed in these theoretical treatises an astounding knack for crafting just the right phrase; indeed, in the judgement of Max Lerner, who wrote in 1948 what is still the best brief overview of Veblen's work as a whole, 'at his best ... [Veblen possessed a style that] must rank with the great expository and polemical styles of the English language'.

With the publication in 1914 of what he considered to be his most important book, *The Instinct of Workmanship and the State of the Industrial Arts*, Veblen had laid the foundation for a completely different type of economic analysis from that reflected in the mainstream tradition, yet, despite his remarkable intellect and national prominence, Veblen's career was far from being a happy one. He had attained only the rank of assistant professor before he was forced to leave Chicago in 1906 owing to conflict with the university's president over the propriety of his personal affairs. Veblen next took a position at Stanford University, but similar problems resulted in his moving on, after only three years, to the University of Missouri. Significantly, at this point in his career Veblen's focus seemed to change somewhat, and subsequent to the publication of *The Instinct of Workmanship* his inquiries were directed less to issues of economic theory and more to issues of social organization. Critics have complained that these 'later' works were also marred by extensive and tiresome repetition.

While at Missouri, Veblen completed *Imperial Germany and the Industrial Revolution* (1915), a prescient exploration of the cultural incidence of the machine process as it would reveal itself in Germany; *An Inquiry Into the Nature of Peace and Terms of Its Perpetuation* (1917), an argument that lasting peace and maintenance of the system of business enterprise are mutually incompatible; and *The Higher Learning in America* (1918), a devastating critique of business control of higher education. Out of a misguided belief that he could contribute to planning for peace after the conclusion of World War I, Veblen left academia in 1918 to take a minor post as a special investigator for the Food Administration; in fact, his ideas were far too radical to muster any support. After the war, Veblen assumed the coeditorship of *The Dial*, a liberal periodical, but his literary style was unsuited to a popular journal, and his tenure lasted little more than a year. Two series of articles written for *The Dial* readership were reissued as books. In the first, *The Vested Interests and the State of the Industrial Arts* (1919), Veblen did little more than provide a popularized version of his earlier works, but in the second, *The Engineers and the Price System* (1921), he advanced the novel view that engineers, not workers, would spearhead the 'revolution' through which modern industry would at last be put to the effective service of man.

In 1919, Veblen moved on again, this time to join his former student, Wesley C. Mitchell, on the faculty of the New School for Social Research, then being formed. Veblen had always been a poor teacher, however, and after 1922 his failure to maintain large enrolments placed his status in jeopardy. Despite growing interest in his work and another book, *Absentee Ownership and Business Enterprise in Recent Time* (1923), a final attempt to spell out how the business system actually functions, Veblen was unable to obtain another academic appointment and his situation remained tenuous until he retired to his California cabin in 1927. Veblen died on 3 August 1929.

Economics as an evolutionary science

It was Veblen's determination that, rather than being a body of scientific propositions, the received doctrines of economics were in actuality a system of apologetics for vested interests (property owners). He also considered economics to be 'premodern', in that it was based on natural law preconceptions and had not adopted a Darwinian stance towards its subject matter. That is, it embodied an animistic mode of apprehension ('sufficient reason') and an outdated psychology (hedonism), and limited itself to the 'taxonomic' task of distinguishing how 'disturbing factors' influence the 'normal', meliorative propensity in events. In order to achieve the status of an up-to-date science, Veblen insisted, economics had to adopt a standpoint from which its phenomena can be understood in evolutionary terms. In consonance with his own mandate, Veblen embraced an activist instinct psychology through which behaviour was understood in terms of basic drives and propensities given form by 'institutions', that is, 'habits of thought common to the generality of man'. The origins, development and contemporary character of the institutions giving form to the basic drives and propensities were accordingly deemed by Veblen to be the proper subject matter of an *evolutionary*, that is, truly scientific, economics. An evolutionary *theory*, he further declared, must be capable of explaining in non-teleological terms the *process* of cumulative change through which those institutions evolve.

The theoretical standpoint

Veblen's work is far too broad-ranging to summarize adequately in a brief overview. Nevertheless, the core of his standpoint can be indicated. Central to Veblen's perspective is the view, one putatively extracted from the anthropological literature, that human beings are by nature endowed with antagonistic drives and propensities. On the positive side, in Veblen's view, are the 'instincts' of parental bent, idle curiosity and workmanship, which together impel individuals to labour industriously, creatively and peaceably as they participate in the inescapable societal task of provisioning the community; these primal urges conduce to the betterment of the human condition, viewed impersonally. On the negative side are the predatory 'instinct' and the propensity for emulation, that is, the desire to create invidious distinctions by outdoing others, principally by emulating those of higher social status; these urges, viewed impersonally, conduce to the impairment of human welfare.

Under the impetus of the first set of 'instincts' and propensities, Veblen argued, humans naturally strive to develop more effective methods of meeting their generic needs (food, shelter, health and so on). That is, evolving technology is rooted in 'human nature' and, indeed, is the main driving force in human history. Often the new practices through which technological innovations might be implemented produce challenges to established practices and vested interests. The question of whether or how to implement new technology, that is, whether and how to alter established practices, is governed by antithetical criteria of judgement rooted in the two antagonistic sets of 'instincts' and propensities. The first set gives rise to a criterion which is technological in nature: is a new practice more *serviceable* that the present one; that is, does it allow members of the community to satisfy a generic need more effectively or with less effort? The second set induces individuals to apply a criterion of judgement which is 'ceremonial' in nature: is a new practice consistent with the maintenance of an established invidious distinction? The degree to which the welfare-enhancing potential of evolving technology is fully realized will depend upon the specific manner in which these adverse standards of judgement exert their influence upon the decision-making process.

Intertwined in Veblen's various writings are, first, his attempt to pinpoint the principal institutions – or their objectification, customary practices – through which production and consumption are patterned in the modern machine-based stage of society; second, his attempt to trace the manner in which these institutions have evolved out of earlier practices and hence to determine in which of the two contradictory criteria of judgement each is therefore rooted; and third, his attempt to ascertain where the continuing process of institutional evolution is headed. It was Veblen's determination that both the consumption and the production activities of modern-day

America are patterned principally by *disserviceable* institutions and hence that modern-day economic life is largely an exercise in waste and futility. Indeed, he argued that business practices rooted in the predatory instinct allowed functionless absentee owners to capture their pecuniary returns only by sabotaging the industrial process itself. In short, Veblen perceived an industrial civilization in which 'imbecile institutions', those rooted in invidious distinctions, prevail and in which the welfare-enhancing potential of machine techniques is therefore mostly squandered. However, since he perceived the mental discipline of the common man as increasingly wrought out under the guidance of science and its product, the machine process, Veblen envisioned that serviceability would gradually come to displace ceremonial adequacy as the dominant criterion of judgement. Thus he remained cautiously optimistic that the full welfare-enhancing potential of modern technology would in fact eventually be realized.

Enduring influence
To a profession acclimatized to mathematics, econometrics and methodological debates rooted in issues related to the practice of physics, Veblen's writings will no doubt appear quaint. Worse, they may be dismissed as 'sociology'. Yet the present-day reader who remains open-minded will find that Veblen's discussion of epistemological and methodological issues has lost none of its relevance and that his dichotomy provides insight into a host of contemporary issues. Even though the underlying instinct psychology has been discarded, and in some cases reservations are expressed about the utility of his technological value scheme as a normative guide, Veblen's instrumental–ceremonial dichotomy lies at the heart of the research programme pursued by many, if not the majority, of present-day American institutional economists.

YNGVE RAMSTAD

See also:
Ayres, Clarence E.; Capital Theory; Cumulative Causation; Evolution, Theories of Economic; Foster, J. Fagg; Hamilton, Walton Hale; Institutions; Instrumental Value Theory; Social Change, Theory of; Technology, Theory of; Veblenian Dichotomy and Its Critics.

Bibliography
Bush, P.D. (1987), 'The Theory of Institutional Change', *Journal of Economic Issues*, **XXI**, (3), pp. 1075–1116.
Dorfman, J. (1972), *Thorstein Veblen and His America*, New York: Augustus M. Kelley.
Dowd, D.F. (ed.) (1958), *Thorstein Veblen: A Critical Reappraisal*, Ithaca, NY: Cornell University Press.
Veblen, T. (1899), *The Theory of the Leisure Class*; republished, 1934, by New York: Modern Library.
Veblen, T. (1904), *The Theory of Business Enterprise*, New York: Charles Scribners.

Veblen, T. (1914), *The Instinct of Workmanship and the State of the Industrial Arts*, reprinted 1990 with introductory essay by Murray G. Murphey, New Brunswick: Transaction Publishers.
Veblen, T. (1919), *The Place of Science in Modern Civilisation*, reprinted 1990 with introductory essay by W.J. Samuels, New Brunswick: Transaction Books.
Veblen, T. (1948), *The Portable Veblen*, ed. M. Lerner, with introductory essay, New York: Viking Press.

Veblenian Dichotomy and Its Critics

The Veblenian dichotomy is a central analytic tool in the Veblen–Ayres tradition of institutionalism. It developed from a distinction made repeatedly in the work of Veblen between behaviour legitimized by habits of thought and behaviour legitimized by matter-of-fact knowledge. The concept of the Veblenian dichotomy has evolved in both its use and analytic character.

In Veblen's work the dichotomy is a categorical tendency. Veblen uses habits of thought and matter-of-fact knowledge as characteristics of actual behaviours occurring in the social situation he is analysing. In *The Theory of Business Enterprise* (1904), Veblen distinguishes business (making money), which is characterized by habits of thought, from industry (making goods), which is characterized by matter-of-fact knowledge. Similarly, in *The Theory of the Leisure Class* (1899), conspicuous consumption, the consumption of goods for honorific display, supported and encouraged through habits of thought underpinning the status system, is distinguished from serviceable consumption which results from matter-of-fact valuations of human needs. One particular manifestation of Veblen's categorization schema has subsequently been adopted as archetypal; that is, the contrast between institutions and technology. Veblen sees institutions as settled patterns of behaviour repeated habitually and using the past or tradition for their warrant. Technology is behaviour governed by matter-of-fact knowledge, meaning mechanical cause and effect of the kind Veblen identified with the machine-based technology of his day. In the particular behaviour analysed by Veblen, technology – meaning behaviour warranted by matter-of-fact knowledge – was the source of change and institutional behaviour was past-binding and resistant to change or progress. Neither the ontological nor the analytic status of these concepts is expressly discussed by Veblen; consequently, usage by his followers has varied considerably.

C.E. Ayres's formulation of the Veblenian dichotomy somewhat clarified its analytic status. Ayres argued that social behaviour had both ceremonial and technological aspects, though notably he refers to the behaviour, rather than the aspects, as being ceremonial or technological. Through Ayres's combination of Veblen's economic analysis with Dewey's instrumentalism two major changes occur: technology (now referred to as the technological process or instrumental behaviour) and matter-of-fact knowledge become linked with Dewey's instrumental valuation, and institution (often previously confused with social structure by many institutionalists) is identified with ceremonial aspects of behaviour and is similarly connected with traditional forms of social valuation. Thus human social behaviour could be analysed by inquiring into the warrant for a particular aspect of behaviour.

In Veblen, institutions and technology were categories into which behaviour or aspects of behaviour might fit. With Ayres, these categories become aspects of all behaviour that the analyst seeks to reveal. It is only the careful treatment of all behaviour as cultural processes that keeps these categories from being reified into a dualism (we shall return to this issue later). Like Veblen, Ayres sees technological aspects of behaviour as causing change and ceremonial aspects of behaviour as inhibitive of change. At times, Ayres seems to be close to adopting a version of technological determinism that borders on establishing an identity between technological development and social progress.

J. Fagg Foster addressed the potential consequences of the reification of these categories by redefining the concept of an institution so that it had both ceremonial aspects and instrumental aspects, thus breaking the long association of the term 'institution' with ceremony. By treating all behaviour as part of a cultural process and the categories of the dichotomy as constituent elements – simultaneously present in all behaviour (at least potentially) – to be teased out by the analyst, Foster reasserted the categorical tendency of Veblen and diminished the likelihood of employing the dichotomy as a dualistic, reified, taxonomic set of universal categories (a tendency that would have been anathema to Veblen). Foster's students, notably Marc Tool and Paul Bush, have strengthened the tie between the dichotomy and social valuation processes. Foster's conceptualization of the dichotomy has led to a more explicit consideration of the dominance of either ceremonial or instrumental aspects of particular behaviour and the impact of that dominance on both that behaviour and on cultural processes more generally.

Throughout this evolution the ontological status of the relevant terms of the dichotomy ebb and flow between two polar interpretations (often within the work of single individuals) from descriptive categories to reified universal aspects of human behaviour, though rarely are the polar extremes explicitly adopted. This ambiguity has led to considerable reflection, reformulation and criticism of both the Veblenian dichotomy and its constituent terms. The Veblenian dichotomy has been the subject of critical methodological scrutiny both internally and externally. The internal criticisms are of three main types: first, that the terms 'ceremonial' and 'instrumental' and the relationship between the two categories are poorly or inconsistently defined; second, that the treatment of the Veblenian dichotomy, most particularly in the Ayresian framework, has changed from a categorization schema to an elemental human strategy; and third, that the Veblenian dichotomy has itself been construed dualistically by some institutionalists.

The first criticism, described by Warren Samuels, notes that there has been little consistent usage of the terms or the relationship between the terms among professed institutionalists (Samuels also reviews other internal criticisms). William Waller traced the evolution (and variety of usage) of the dichotomy from Veblen to Foster, concluding that the direction of that evolution seemed to be in making subtler distinctions about the interaction of the two categorical tendencies within social processes. The second criticism of the dichotomy is really an extension of Anne Mayhew's concern that the concept of culture and instrumental valuation, both defining aspects of institutional analysis in the Veblen–Ayres tradition, are in fundamental conflict. Mayhew argues that instrumental valuation (associated by many institutionalists with technological or instrumental aspects of behaviour) is an elemental human strategy, meaning a pan-cultural standard of value and universal strategy for progress. She notes that acceptance of an elemental human strategy is incompatible with the concept of culture. The third criticism is related to the second. It has been argued by James Swaney that in the work of some institutionalists the categories constituting the Veblenian dichotomy have become reified. The dichotomy has become just another dualistic construction. Swaney argues that for some institutionalists the categories are no longer descriptions applied to actual social processes and evaluated for their closeness of fit, and then reevaluated subsequent to the analysis. He describes this problem as one that occurs when behaviour that in the opinion of the analyst is thought to contribute to progress (which is good) is identified as instrumental and behaviour that inhibits progress (which is bad) is identified as ceremonial. In this usage the terms of the dichotomy are reified – they construct two mutually exclusive categories that, when taken together, are universally inclusive and distinguish between the good and the bad, thus separating them from social processes and rendering them static. If 'instrumental' only signifies the analyst's notion of good (or progress), then the elemental human strategy identified by Mayhew emerges and along with it an unseemly ethnocentrism.

These internal criticisms suggest that the Veblenian dichotomy is likely to evolve further within institutionalism. The direction is already somewhat apparent. From Veblen to Foster the general direction has been, first, to analyse more finely social processes and behaviour, then to analyse *aspects* of social processes and behaviour, applying ceremonial and instrumental (or technological) as descriptive and evaluative categories. But, as the analysis of particular social processes becomes more focused, specific and detailed, these categories require further refinement. It is likely that many institutionalists will begin with the categories of ceremonial and instrumental (or technological) aspects of behaviour, but will develop more refined categories, or categories specific to the social process or processes that they are investigating, very much in the tradition of Veblen's work.

The content of the *external* criticisms of the Veblenian dichotomy are less interesting, since most are based on a rather profound misconception of what the dichotomy means. This misconception is based on interpreting the dichotomy from an epistemological perspective within which the dichotomy is either meaningless or profoundly misleading. Simply put, most criticisms by orthodox economists of the Veblenian dichotomy emanate from an epistemological position that accepts dualistic separations generally and, of particular relevance to their criticisms, the dualistic separation between individuals and society. The orthodox critics usually employ methodological individualism and assume that institutionalists simply adopt the social side of the individual/social dualistic framework the critics are familiar and comfortable with, thus assuming that institutionalists uniformly adopt a form of methodological collectivism which precludes individual behaviour. It is the rejection of Cartesian dualism (in all of its manifestations) that informs and differentiates institutionalism's epistemology from the pseudo-positivism of orthodoxy. Consequently, embracing either side of this or other dualisms is treated as equally fallacious by institutionalists. This recognition and rejection of the dualistic relationship between individuals and society is an important area of convergence among 'old' and many of the 'new' institutionalists.

The critics who make their arguments from the above described perspective (or variants of it) are generally making arguments that are quite telling from their epistemological perspective and utterly irrelevant from the perspective of the institutionalists. The tendency to construct social understanding around dualistic concepts is an old one in the Western intellectual tradition and is carried in the structure of our language in such a way as to make it difficult to communicate without resort to one form of dualism or another. This problem is compounded by the fact that institutionalists often inadvertently use the same dualistic constructs when presenting their arguments, thereby contributing to the muddle. The result of this characteristic in the structure of our language is that there are very few fruitful conversations between orthodox and institutional economists.

Another related type of external criticism resides in understanding the dichotomy in a static sense, rather than as a descriptive framework for analysing cultural processes. The usual form of this criticism is to argue that institutionalists reject the possibility of meaningful and purposeful individual action. The two elements of the dichotomy (usually institutions and technology) are understood in the sense they are used in common speech:

institutions are treated as synonymous with social structure and technology is treated as tools and tool behaviour. Then it is argued that institutionalists believe that tool behaviour is inherently progressive and reproduces independent of any individual action or motivation. Further, institutions are inherently conservative and past-binding, thereby creating a cultural lag. Thus technology leads the way, institutions slow the progress and all individual behaviour is conditioned and controlled by the institutions. David Seckler, in his analysis of Ayres's formulation of the dichotomy, has argued that, while institutionalists claim this is not what Ayres meant, he, Seckler, notes that it is what he said. From this Seckler concludes that institutional analysis in the Ayresian tradition is naively technologically deterministic and neglects the role of the individual in social analysis. Seckler's critique and reading of Ayres illustrates the point made earlier: the tendency built into the structure of the language to communicate in terms which evoke dualistic understandings of social analysis.

External critics of the Veblenian dichotomy tend to understand the dichotomy in non-processual dualistic terms. This makes it difficult for institutionalists to respond intelligibly to their concerns. Moreover, a significant amount of the institutionalist discourse on the Veblenian dichotomy will support both a processual, non-dualistic and a static, dualistic reading. Thus miscommunication, with all participants literally and epistemologically talking past one another, is the dominant characteristic of the discourse between those offering external criticism of the Veblenian dichotomy and institutionalists.

WILLIAM WALLER

See also:
Ayres, Clarence E.; Cartesianism in Economics; Culture; Foster, J. Fagg; Habits; Institutions; Methodological Individualism; Social Change, Theory of; Technology, Theory of; Veblen, Thorstein.

Bibliography
Langlois, Richard (1989), 'What was wrong with the old institutional economics (and what is still wrong with the new)?' *Review of Political Economy*, **1**, (3), pp. 270–98.
Mayhew, Anne (1987), 'Culture: Core Concept Under Attack', *Journal of Economic Issues*, **XXI**, (2), pp. 587–603.
Samuels, Warren (1977), 'Technology vis-a-vis Institutions in the JEI', *Journal of Economic Issues*, **XI**, (4), pp. 871–95.
Seckler, David (1975), *Thorstein Veblen and the Institutionalists*, Boulder, Colo.: Colorado Associated University Press.
Swaney, James (1989), 'Our Obsolete Technology Mentality', *Journal of Economic Issues*, **XXIII**, (2), pp. 569–78.
Waller, William (1982), 'The Evolution of the Veblenian Dichotomy', *Journal of Economic Issues*, **XVI**, (3), pp. 757–71.
Waller, William (1989), 'Criticism of Institutionalism, Methodology and Value Theory: A Comment on Langlois', *Journal of Economic Issues*, **XXIII**, (3), pp. 873–9.

Welfare Economic Theory

Because the subject-matter of economics is so diverse, there are many criteria by which the notion of 'welfare' may be considered. One criterion involves the question of whether welfare is automatically enhanced when more rather than less goods are produced. Although there is a tendency within economics to emphasize more goods rather then fewer, it is widely recognized that any such judgement is rendered complicated and problematic in the face of such further considerations as (a) non-renewable resources, (b) trade-offs between consumption and leisure, (c) environmental degradation, (d) the coherence of felicific calculations, and (e) unequal distributions of income and wealth both within and between countries.

Mainstream neoclassical welfare economics has been bifurcated when it comes to questions of welfare but is nonetheless driven by the combination of the logic of constrained maximization and the desire for determinate optimal equilibrium solutions. The bifurcation has taken the form of conflict between Pigovian and Paretian welfare economics. Pigovian welfare economics addresses both production and distribution. In both respects it contemplates a broadly reformist activist agenda for government. With regard to production, the Pigovian approach assumes that the optimal (welfare-maximizing) allocation of resources (and thereby structure of production across goods) is achieved when marginal private cost equals marginal social cost, so that all cost is borne by those who generate or benefit from them, and when marginal private benefit equals marginal social benefit, so that all benefit accrues to those who generate them. In the event of an inequality, there is either under- or overproduction of the good in question, the former when producers fail to receive the full benefits they create, the latter when producers are able to shift costs to others. This is the classic Pigovian externality situation, with the implied role for government of ensuring that costs and benefits somehow accrue to those who create them.

With regard to distribution, the Pigovian approach assumes that welfare is maximized when the marginal utilities of the final pound of income is equal across individuals. This requires a number of assumptions, including (a) that individuals' marginal utilities of income can be both measured and compared, or else that some reasonable assumption can be made with regard to the capacity of individuals *qua* individuals to derive utility from income; (b) that either there is no disincentive effect consequent to redistribution or that disincentive effect is considered minor relative to the gains from redistribution; and (c) that either individuals are assumed to be roughly equal or identical in their capacity to derive utility, so that the resultant distribution of income will be roughly equal, or that individuals are assumed to be unequal in their capacity to derive utility, so that the resultant distribution of income will be unequal, perhaps even more so than the existing distribution.

In contrast, Paretian welfare economics is concerned only with exchange of already produced goods, and contemplates a limited agenda for government. The Paretian criterion is that welfare is unequivocally maximized when all gains from trade are exhausted, given an initial distribution of goods or entitlements (property rights); which is to say that, when trade ceases, no party can gain without a putative loss being incurred by another party. The only relevant domain is exchange, and the role of government is solely to define and protect property rights, thereby enabling exchange. The Paretian approach, as amplified by the Coase theorem, maintains that, in a world of fully defined rights and fully developed markets, including markets for externalities, there would be no further need for government corrective action and, especially in the case of zero transaction costs (so that no allocative differences result between varied transaction cost systems), the consequential allocation of resources will be independent of the initial distribution of rights. Any resulting externality, in this view, would be trivial, no eliciting further trades.

Both the Pigovian and the Paretian approaches have serious limitations, even in addition to the assumptions which each makes. The Pigovian approach, for example, both neglects the reciprocal nature of externalities, so that a putative externality solution necessarily imposes an opposite externality, and opens up an extensive and perhaps unmanageable potential agenda for government decision making and corrective action. The Paretian approach can yield unique results only if one ignores questions of the initial and the consequential distributions of income and wealth, and the reality of varied non-zero transaction cost systems, among other considerations.

Both the Pigovian and Paretian approaches to welfare economics make implicit assumptions as to whose interests are to count. This is evident, for example, in cost–benefit analysis, a set of tools for dealing with constrained-maximization decision making in a utilitarian manner, through assumptions which determine, *inter alia*, first, whose benefits and whose costs will count and, second, the specific magnitude of those benefits and costs. The role of implicit assumptions is also evident in the use of an assumed social welfare function. The usual model involves the identification of certain goods as values on the axes and the assumption of both a production possibility function and a social welfare function. In so far as these identifications and assumptions are made by the analyst, the preferences and perceptions of the analyst are substituted for those of actual economic actors and the operation of the processes actually at work in the economy is foreclosed. In the actual economy, four interconnected processes are at work: that determining which values are to be on the axes, that is, the agenda options open to choice; that

determining the production possibility curve, which includes both technological and power factors; and those determining the actual (rather than the
assumed or hypothetical) social welfare function, specifically the processes
determining individual preferences for the goods on the axes; and the power
structure by which the preferences of different individuals are to be weighted.

While a Pigovian concern with externalities, for example, environmental
pollution and degradation, is widespread among economists, it is testimony
to both the increasingly narrow domain of neoclassical economics and the
strength of Chicago School economics that Paretian welfare economics is
perhaps equally prominent and, in some areas, such as law and economics,
Chicago-style is predominant. Both the scope of what constitutes welfare
and the mode of its achievement are thereby contemplated largely in terms
only of exchange. In this light, it is particularly ironic that Paretians claim
that their analysis makes minimal normative assumptions. In practice, these
assumptions tend to result in a minimization of government corrective action
of any kind, thereby reinforcing, often only selectively, the status quo.

The institutionalist or evolutionary approach to welfare manifests the
same differences from mainstream neoclassical economics as it does in other
areas. Whereas the neoclassical approaches tend both to seek determinate
optimal equilibrium allocative (and, in the case of the Pigovian, distributive)
solutions and to show how markets, when properly functioning, provide
such results, the institutionalists insist that the vision of unique welfare-
maximizing results is both illusory and unduly constraining. They argue that
analysis can fruitfully be conducted of the factors, forces and processes
actually at work in the economy which govern, for example, how markets,
preferences and power structure are formed and reformed. Institutionalists
emphasize, with Thorstein Veblen, the larger life process which encompasses but goes beyond markets, and, with John R. Commons, the welfare-
determining role of the working rules of law, custom and morals. Institutionalists also emphasize the fundamental welfare-determining roles of government, roles which the Pigovian would direct and the Paretian either deny or
restrict. Finally, institutionalists emphasize the importance of technology
(industrialization) and institutions in determining the realization and distribution of welfare; and among the institutions which institutionalists emphasize is government, or the legal–economic nexus.

Contrary to the tendency of neoclassical welfare economics to affirm
unique solutions to problems of policy, institutionalists take seriously the
Arrow impossibility theorem (that it is impossible to find a decision rule
which satisfies all the desired criteria of democratic decision making) with
regard to what can be said by technical experts concerning politics and
policy solutions. Institutionalists therefore emphasize the role of politics in
working out policy solutions. Following Commons, they understand the

modern liberal state to comprise a process of bargaining between interested groups, a collective bargaining state. Institutionalists, therefore, emphasize that distribution is, willy-nilly, important in welfare economic considerations. Efficient results are a function of the starting place with regard to the identification and assignment of rights and the determination of the rules governing access to and use of power. *Some* assumption as to distribution must be and indeed is made in all policy analysis.

Whatever conflicts may be deemed to exist between efficiency and equity, fundamentally each efficient result is efficient precisely because some initial distribution and so on is taken to be equitable. Institutionalists find that, while there are neoclassicists interested in furthering the pluralization (wide diffusion) of power, the fundamental logic of neoclassical analysis as conventionally practised tends to assume as proper the existing distributions of income and wealth, so that policy implications tend to give effect to and reinforce those distributions. Institutionalists tend to favour a wider diffusion of power in society, notably the restructuring of society in favour of the working masses rather than the socially and economically privileged (including large corporations). But they make these normative assumptions about helping certain groups without any pretence that doing so would produce the best of all possible worlds or on the basis of economic science alone. They believe that some such assumption as to desirable power structure is inevitable, and they desire to make explicit problems of inequality in an effort to promote effective change in favour of freedom and individualism for all, not only for those already favoured. In their normative work, institutionalists tend to be in favour of pluralism. In their positive work, they stress the importance of the total welfare-economic process in society, plus the inexorable operative role of normative assumptions as to whose interests are to count. Institutionalist analyses therefore encompass both freedom and control, both continuity and change, both hierarchy and equality, and both deliberative and non-deliberative social control and decision making. For all its distinctive explicit normative emphasis on pluralism, however, institutionalism both positively and normatively has a place for contradictory forces and their continuing resolutions.

With regard to the positive analysis of welfare, institutionalists stress that the level and the distribution of welfare are a function of technology and institutions, the latter including the state. Technology consists of certain technological regimes, which have pervasive impacts on the conditions and conduct of ordinary lives, so that technology affects welfare in ways beyond its impact on the number and types of goods produced. Institutions influence which technological alternative, out of an existing array, is chosen, having earlier influenced the formation of technology through support given to one or another technological regime, in part through government policy. Institutionalists therefore insist on the importance of such interdependencies as the following: distribution is a function of institutions, and institutions are a function of distribution; the working rules of law and morals are a function of the distributions of income and wealth, and the distributions of income and wealth are a function of the working rules of law and morals; always in interaction with a continuing technological opportunity set.

As a matter of both positive and normative welfare economics, institutionalists insist on the necessity to think about what is a good institution. Institutions evolve through various combinations of deliberative and non-deliberative forces, and through various interactions between power, knowledge and psychology. At every point a contest exists as to whose interests are to count in the operation and reformulation of the institution in question. Rather than the neoclassical emphasis on the conditions of a stable, determinate optimal equilibrium solution to a problem, the institutionalist emphasizes the working out of solutions through the interactive processes, noted above, governing the values on the public decision-making agenda, the technological production possibility function, individual preferences and the structure of power. That the institutionalists affirm, that is, make explicit, some values, such as those given voice in the instrumental value principle, is due to their recognition of the inevitability of values in welfare economics and of the status quo-reinforcing nature of Pareto optimality, which largely affirms only gains from trade on the basis of given distributions.

WARREN J. SAMUELS

See also:

Commons, John R.; Cost–Benefit Analysis; Environmental Theory; Evolution and Optimality; Growth, Limits to; Hale, Robert Lee; Institutional Theory of Economic Policy; Institutionalism, 'Old' and 'New'; Institutions; Instrumental Value Theory; Law and Economics; Neoclassical Microeconomic Theory, Critique of; Power; Property; Public Choice; Public Sector, Role of the; Regulation, Theory of Economic; Technical Change and Technological Regimes; Technology in Development Policy; Technology, Theory of; Witte, Edwin Emil.

Bibliography

Bromley, Dan W. (1989), *Economic Interests and Institutions: The Conceptual Foundations of Public Policy*, New York: Blackwell.
Dragun, Andrew K. (1983), 'Externalities, Property Rights, and Power', *Journal of Economic Issues*, **XVII**, September, pp. 667–80.
Heilbroner, Robert L. (1970), 'On the Possibility of a Political Economics', *Journal of Economic Issues*, **IV**, December, pp. 1–22.
Hodgson, Geoffrey M. (1988), *Economics and Institutions*, Philadelphia: University of Pennsylvania Press.
Samuels, Warren J. (1972), 'Welfare Economics, Power, and Property', in G. Wunderlich and W.L. Gibson, Jr. (eds), *Perspectives of Property*, University Park: Institute for Research on Land and Water Resources, Pennsylvania State University, pp. 61–148; reprinted 1981 in Warren J. Samuels and A. Allan Schmid (eds), *Law and Economics: An Institutionalist Perspective*, Boston, Mass.: Martinus Nijhoff; and 1992 in Warren J. Samuels, *Essays on the Economic Role of Government*, vol. 1, London: Macmillan.

Samuels, Warren J. (1974), *Pareto on Policy*, New York: Elsevier.
Schmid, A. Allan (1987), *Property, Power and Public Choice*, 2nd edn, New York: Praeger.

Williamson, Oliver E.

Oliver E. Williamson (born 1932) is former professor of economics at Yale University and now Professor of Business, Economics and Law at the University of California at Berkeley. He is best known for his transaction cost analysis and is a leading 'new institutionalist'. The growing influence of Williamson and the new institutionalism may represent an extension of institutionalism into the neoclassical mainstream of economics. Perhaps neoclassicism won the first battle over historicism, only to lose the war years later. But probably not, for only selectively realistic historical analysis is entering the mainstream by way of the new institutionalism. What Williamson's work represents is a hybrid institutionalism, not the pure strain.

Williamson adopts the transaction as his unit of analysis, citing old institutionalist John R. Commons as his predecessor. However, Williamson does not use Commons's principles of scarcity, efficiency, futurity, sovereignty and working rules. Instead, he derives his transaction cost perspective primarily from R.H. Coase's analysis of the firm. Williamson also uses Herbert Simon's work on satisficing as a starting-point. He then goes on to develop his own concepts of bounded rationality, opportunism and asset specificity. What emerges from Williamson's conceptualization is a hybrid unit of microeconomic analysis. Starting with Commons, but then pulling away from him, Williamson does not analyse transactions in their broader context of the working rules distilled from the collective actions of going concerns, but looks at the way individual choice in transacting is affected by certain assumptions and how those assumptions can lead to a fundamental transformation in individual relations. So Williamson's transaction cost analysis is not the economics of collective action that Commons groped for, but the microeconomics of individual choice in a world limited by the assumption of bounded rationality and influenced by the assumptions of opportunism and asset specificity.

With bounded rationality, Williamson assumes that people intend to be rational but are limited or bounded by their own inability to know or calculate all the potential risks and uncertainties they may encounter in a contract. It will help to locate Williamson's assumption of bounded rationality on a spectrum of gender-neutral, theoretical constructs. On one end of the spectrum is the ultra-rationality of 'economic man' (the utility-maximizing, neoclassical construct). On the other end of the spectrum is the cultural rationality of 'institutional man' (the culture-learning, institutional construct).

Bounded rationality is a hybrid of the two. Economic man's knowing and calculating abilities are unlimited and his wants are self-determined. He is all-knowing and independent. Hybrid man's knowing and calculating abilities are limited but his wants are still self-determined. He is not all-knowing but he is independent. Institutional man's knowing and calculating abilities are not only limited but his wants are learned from his culture. He is neither all-knowing nor strictly independent. Williamson traces his hybrid man to Herbert A. Simon's work on bounded rationality, but, whereas Simon argues that bounded rationality leads to satisficing rather than maximizing behaviour, Williamson argues that bounded rationality leads to economizing on transaction costs. However, this makes Williamson's cost-minimizing approach incompatible with Simon's bounded rationality approach. In particular, the computational limitations central to bounded rationality rule out the calculations required by Williamson's cost-minimizing.

Williamson explains that transaction costs become significant with the addition of another assumption, that of opportunism. Again, placing Williamson's assumption on a theoretical spectrum will be helpful. On one end of the spectrum, economic man pursues his self-interest, but with neither guile (deceit) nor coercion (power). On the other end of the spectrum, institutional man pursues his self-interest (as he learns to understand it) with both guile and coercion. Williamson's hybrid man pursues his self-interest with guile but without coercion. Williamson's opportunistic man is self-interested enough to resort to deceit but not powerful enough to resort to coercion. Opportunism involves the withholding or distortion of information from others to benefit oneself, but not the coercion of others. Opportunism makes the ultimate outcome of market transactions risky and uncertain, giving rise to significant transaction costs.

Add asset specificity to opportunism and, Williamson explains, economizing on transaction costs leads to a fundamental transformation in economic relations, which occurs when a market relation between independent buyer and seller is transformed into a hierarchical relation between corporate headquarters and an owned subsidiary. Asset specificity arises when investments must be made by either party to a transaction, in order to support the specific transaction. For example, if a supplier must invest in specific assets to meet the needs of a customer, asset specificity arises. With growing asset specificity, it becomes cheaper for the buyer and seller to merge than to incur the rising transaction costs that their mutual dependence will generate. Their mutual dependence calls for a governance structure to coordinate their activities.

Here is where Williamson makes a very significant contribution to microeconomic theory. He conceptualizes the firm as a governance structure, a kind of state within a state, a private ordering of individual priorities into collective ones. The firm, Williamson explains, is far more than a mere production function. The hierarchy of the firm is a substitute for the costly transactions of the market. Economizing on transaction costs involves a choice between hierarchy and market. Choosing the market means relying on the ordering of the centralized, formal state. Choosing the hierarchical firm means relying on the ordering of the decentralized, private firm. The private ordering of the firm, Williamson argues, is usually preferable to the public ordering of the state. Although Williamson prefers the ordering of the firm's hierarchy over the ordering of the state's market, in doing so he clearly recognizes that the market is not a natural or autonomous phenomenon. Instead, it is seen as an artificial institution, created and maintained by the sovereignty of the state itself.

Williamson's transaction cost analysis is a part of the new institutionalism and is an advance upon unrealistic neoclassicism. But it is a hybrid institutionalism. His realism is selective. The bounded rationality of his hybrid man is more realistic than economic man, but Williamson still fails to incorporate cultural learning into his model; the opportunism of his hybrid man is also more realistic than economic man, but Williamson also fails to incorporate the power to coerce into his model. Nonetheless, his conceptualization of the firm as a governance structure is a major advance towards a realistic theory of the firm.

WILLIAM M. DUGGER

See also:

Commons, John R.; Firm, Theory of the; Information Theory in Economics; Institutionalism, 'Old' and 'New'; Law and Economics; Methodological Individualism; Rules; Simon, Herbert Alexander; Transaction.

Bibliography

Williamson, Oliver, E. (1975), *Markets and Hierarchies*, New York: The Free Press.
Williamson, Oliver E. (1981), 'The Modern Corporation: Origins, Evolution, Attributes', *Journal of Economic Literature*, **19**, December, pp. 1537–68.
Williamson, Oliver E. (1985), *The Economic Institutions of Capitalism*, New York: The Free Press.
Williamson, Oliver E. (ed.) (1990), *Organization Theory*, New York: Oxford University Press.

Winter, Sidney G., Jr.

Sidney G. Winter Jr. was born in Iowa City, USA in 1935. He is known both for his independent application of evolutionary theory to economic phenomena such as the firm, and for his book on economic evolution written jointly with Richard Nelson. Winter's first major work is a critique of Milton Friedman's famous defence of the orthodox assumption that agents maximize their utility or returns. Friedman (1953, p. 22) argues that it does not matter what the 'immediate determinant of business behavior' is. 'Whenever this determinant happens to lead to behavior consistent with rational and informed maximization of returns, the business will prosper and acquire resources with which to expand; whenever it does not, the business will tend to lose resources and can be kept in existence only by the addition of resources from outside.' Friedman thus sees a process of 'natural selection' in which the firms that are acting as if they maximize are the ones that survive. This, in Friedman's view, validates the maximization hypothesis.

Winter (1964) sees several difficulties and ambiguities in Friedman's argument. His major line of attack is to point out that for selection to work there must be some sustaining feature that ensures that the maximizers or near-maximizers that are 'selected' through competition will continue for some time in that mode of behaviour. For instance, if firm behaviour is random, then there is no reason to assume that a firm that happens to be maximizing will continue to do so in the next period. Further, such randomness could mean that a firm on the brink of bankruptcy at one instant could by chance be a good profit maximizer in the next. Finally, even if 'habitual reaction' is the actual determinant of firm behaviour, the selection of maximizers is not guaranteed.

For natural selection to work there must be heritable variation in fitness. The heritable element is missing from Friedman's account. For selection to work consistently in favour of some characteristics rather than others, behaviour cannot be purely accidental. There has to be some equivalent to the genetic constitution or genotype, such as the structural characteristics, routines or culture of the firm, which fixes, determines, moulds or constrains the phenotype in some way. Winter points out that to presume that maximization emerges from an evolutionary process means that the organizational forms, habits or routines giving rise to such behaviour are being selected through their superior capacity for survival. What is required is a degree of inertia in such routines to restrict change so that selection can operate effectively. Although they are not nearly as permanent as the gene, organizations nurture routines and patterns of thought and action which have self-reinforcing and durable qualities.

Richard Nelson and Sidney Winter (1982) develop the idea that routines act as the economic analogue of the gene in biology, although this notion has earlier origins in the work of Thorstein Veblen. Routines in the firm have a relatively durable quality through time. They may help to retain skills and other forms of knowledge, and to some extent they have the capacity to replicate through imitation, personal mobility, takeovers and so on. Further, routines can change through managerial or other action when the firm's profits are below a satisfactory level. In sum: 'The assumption that firms have decision rules, and retain or replace them according to the satisficing principle, provides both genetic stability and an endogenous mutation mechanism' (Winter, 1971, p. 247).

However, in identifying an economic analogue to the mechanism of heredity provided by the gene in biology, Nelson and Winter argue that such an evolutionary process does not always result in a preponderence of profit-maximizing firms. As Winter (1964, p. 240) puts it:

> If the habitual reactions of some firms at a particular time are consistent with profit maximization, and if as a consequence these firms expand relative to other firms in the economy, this very fact will tend to alter the market price environment facing all firms. It is not clear why, in this altered environment, the same firms should continue to have the good fortune to be closer to maximizing behavior than their competitors ... the environment is changed by the dynamic process itself.

Here Winter has exposed a central problem with Friedman's argument which can be illuminated by use of evolutionary concepts from modern biology. Indeed, Winter's suggestion that the 'environment is changed by the dynamic process itself' has its analogue in feedback effects between organisms and their environment, the full biological significance of which has been recognized in recent years.

In addition, an important point is that the question of the characteristics of new entrants to the industry has to be considered. In Winter (1964, p. 242) there is a brief suggestion that problems may arise if selection is thwarted by a 'disruptive entry of non-maximizers'. Winter also goes on to consider the question of returns to scale. He argues that in the cases of decreasing and increasing returns the evolutionary selection of maximizers is likely to be thwarted. In a subsequent article, Winter (1971) develops some of the arguments of his earlier paper. In particular, he enhances key links with the works of Herbert Simon and Joseph Schumpeter which are sustained in his later joint work with Nelson. One feature of the Winter (1971) and Nelson and Winter (1982) works is that, despite their dynamic and evolutionary qualities, they are attempts to show that the Nelson–Winter type of theory subsumes neoclassical analysis as a special case. Thus they try to reproduce neoclassical equilibria or production functions by tuning their parameter values, but on the basis of a broader theory which allegedly has greater 'behavioural realism'. Consequently, their work has occupied an uncomfortable no-man's-land between neoclassical theorists who do not care about realism, on the one hand, and institutionalists and allies who reject neoclassical assumptions, on the other. However, Winter's continuing willingness to expose the limitations of orthodox economics is evidenced in a later critique of neoclassical rationality (Winter, 1986).

Winter's work is important not only for its penetrating critique of Friedman, but also for its pioneering development of evolutionary theory, involving detailed analysis and simulation of selection mechanisms. Not only are there links with Schumpeter and Simon, but also with Veblen and the institutionalist tradition. His work does not exhibit formalism for its own sake, but is a genuine attempt to rebuild economics as an operational and empirically enriched science.

GEOFFREY M. HODGSON

See also:

Evolution and Optimality; Evolution, Theories of Economic; Firm, Theory of the; Institutions; Natural Selection, Economic Evolution and; Nelson, Richard R.; Routines; Rules; Schumpeter, Joseph Alois; Simon, Herbert Alexander; Veblen, Thorstein.

Bibliography

Friedman, M. (1953), 'The Methodology of Positive Economics', in M. Friedman, *Essays in Positive Economics*, Chicago: University of Chicago Press; reprinted 1984 in B.J. Caldwell (ed.), *Appraisal and Criticism In Economics: A Book of Readings*, Boston, Mass.: Allen & Unwin.
Hodgson, G.M. (forthcoming), 'Optimisation and Evolution. Winter's Critique of Friedman Revisited', *Cambridge Journal of Economics*, forthcoming.
Nelson, R.R. and S.G. Winter (1982), *An Evolutionary Theory of Economic Change*, Cambridge Mass.: Harvard University Press.
Winter, Jr., S.G. (1964), 'Economic "Natural Selection" and the Theory of the Firm', *Yale Economic Essays*, **4**, (1), pp. 225–72.
Winter, Jr., S.G. (1971), 'Satisfying, Selection and the Innovating Remnant', *Quarterly Journal of Economics*, **85**, (2), May, pp. 237–61.
Winter, Jr., S.G. (1975), 'Optimization and Evolution in the Theory of the Firm', in R.H. Day and T. Groves (eds), *Adaptive Economic Models*, pp. 73–118, New York: Academic Press.
Winter, Jr., S.G. (1986), 'Comments on Arrow and Lucas', *Journal of Business*, **59**, (4.2), pp. S427–34; reprinted 1987 in R.M. Hogarth and M.W. Reder (eds), *Rational Choice: The Contrast Between Economics and Psychology*, Chicago, University of Chicago Press; and 1990 in C. Freeman (ed.), *The Economics of Innovation*, Aldershot: Edward Elgar.

Witte, Edwin Emil

Edwin Emil Witte (1887–1960) had a distinguished career as professor of economics at the University of Wisconsin, 1933–57, specializing in labour economics and social legislation. Earlier (1922–33) he had been Chief of the Legislative Reference Service of the State of Wisconsin. He was Executive Director of the Committee on Social Security (1934–5), in which capacity he drafted the Social Security Act of 1935, thereby becoming to many the Father of Social Security, having earlier been involved in drafting the Norris–LaQuardia Act of 1932, the first major modern piece of US labour relations legislation; and chairman of the Detroit War Labor Board, 1942–5. He served as a labour mediator on numerous occasions, several times on nationally important cases. Witte was president of the American Economic Association in 1957, having been the first president of the Industrial Relations Research Association in 1948.

He was a student and disciple of John R. Commons, under whom he wrote his dissertation on restrictive labour injunctions (1927) and of whose school of institutional economics he was both a practitioner and an interpreter, especially with regard to social reform and as a theorist on the economic role of government. Both Commons and Witte were part of the Wisconsin Progressivism of Charles McCarthy and Robert M. La Follette. Witte's *The Government in Labor Disputes* (1932), a sequel to his dissertation, presented the case, with supporting materials, for a more even-handed treatment of labour unions in trade disputes, rejecting the often *ex parte* issuance of injunctions by courts siding with employers, in favour of a more procedurally neutral system.

Witte's work in the fields of labour and of social legislation, most notably social security and unemployment compensation, gave effect to certain beliefs and values. These centred on the idea of economic democracy, according to which all individuals, and all interests and groups in society, not only the already privileged ones, should have access to political processes and have their reasonable interests and expectations given legal protection. These beliefs and values included the ideas that labour unions were, in matters of collective bargaining over wages, hours and working conditions, important and legitimate institutions for the pursuit of the economic interests of workers; that the socioeconomic changes which so dramatically characterized industrial capitalism visited great economic insecurity upon workers and the poor; and that collective action, especially through government, was a distinctively American response to problems.

Witte gained a reputation as a cautious reformer, in which formulation either term could be emphasized. As stated by Wilbur J. Cohen (1960, p. 8), 'Witte saw himself as both a radical and a conservative; radical in espousing reforms and challenging the status quo; conservative in that these reforms, by moderating abuses, preserved the free-enterprise economic system, the federal–state political structure, and the democratic political process.' Typical, therefore, of the Wisconsin School of institutionalism, Witte favoured reform within the market system which strengthened it by democratizing it.

As an institutionalist, Witte believed that, while institutions normally change only slowly, they do change, and that they are and must be subject to deliberative critique as part of the process through which they are made to change. This includes, indeed inexorably requires, both a fundamentally activist economic role for government and a bringing to bear on problems of policy comprehensive multidisciplinary knowledge. His version of institutional economics, therefore, went beyond a critique of the dominant economic system and reigning economic doctrine, and emphasized the conduct of problem-solving research and activism.

Witte, like other institutionalists, did not believe that economic laws were either timeless and placeless or automatic and beyond human control. Economic laws gave effect to the institutions which operated through them. To understand economic structure, operation and performance, institutions must be studied. Moreover, institutions cannot be taken for granted, as they are man-made and changeable, and they change in part through the exercise of deliberative collective choice, most notably the state.

Witte thus stressed the historical and empirical fundamental importance of the economic role of government and of legal change of law as a mode of social reform and social change. The basic economic institutions which form and operate through the market are legal in character and subject to change. Government was a mode of mediating between various claimants to freedom and between continuity and change. In the American experience, in his view, government was an institution through which people sought to pursue and realize their individual and group goals (Witte emphasized that the American economy was much more an associational than an individualist system – and government was one such association). Witte therefore followed Commons in comprehending government in the United States as a 'collective bargaining state' in which conflicting claims were worked out; a view which itself was derivative of their belief in both the positive and the normative status of pluralism, the diffusion of economic and political power. Clearly, there is a mixture here of idealism and pragmatic realism.

WARREN J. SAMUELS

See also:
Commons, John R; Institutional Economics, Wisconsin School of.

Bibliography
Cohen, Wilbur J. (1960), 'Edwin E. Witte (1887–1960): Father of Social Security', *Industrial and Labor Relations Review*, **14**, October, pp. 7–9.
Samuels, Warren J. (1967), 'Edwin E. Witte's Concept of the Role of Government in the Economy', *Land Economics*, **43**, pp. 131–47.
Schlabach, Theron F. (1969), *Edwin E. Witte: Cautious Reformer*, Madison: State Historical Society of Wisconsin.
Witte, Edwin Emil (1954), 'Institutional Economics as Seen by An Institutional Economist', *Southern Economic Journal*, **21**, October, pp. 131–40.

Worker Participation

Worker participation generally makes us think first of Karl Marx and his treatment of alienated labour in *The Economic and Philosophic Manuscripts of 1844* (Marx, 1964). Marx argued that it is not the actual activity of labouring to eat and live that is alienating, but the activity of labouring to eat and live *in capitalism*. Since capitalists only buy the labour ability of workers if it helps them make profits and, once bought, this activity of labour is directed by the profit interests of capitalists, the wage workers become separated or alienated from control over their job activities. Their labour is alienated and they are denied effective worker participation in the basic conditions of their jobs and the productive process.

Worker participation is often referred to as worker self-management, industrial democracy or economic democracy. Marx viewed it as the resolution of alienated labour. In the 1844 *Manuscripts*, socialism for Marx is actually understood as the absence of alienated labour, and thus it implies democratic control of the work process by the collective, cooperative activity of the 'associated producers'. Although Marx's discussion of alienated labour in the 1844 *Manuscripts* was not published until 1932, worker participation on a democratic basis has always been a vital aspiration of the socialist movement in Europe and the United States, and at points it has been influential in the labour movement of these nations.

The role of worker participation in institutional economics is more complex. In some senses it is a richer role, even though, if we examine Veblen's views on worker participation, we find them to be sketchy at best. Certainly, Veblen believed in some form of worker participation (the 'soviet of technicians' notwithstanding) because this would enhance the 'instinct of workmanship' and contribute to more efficient production. Yet for him, the system of capitalism made workers as greedy and self-interested as business owners, and simply giving them control would only turn over production from one invidious, vested interest to another equally predatory interest.

The problem of Veblen was the pecuniary culture of capitalism itself. Therefore the solution would require a broader, more inclusive role for participation beyond that of 'worker'. Democratic participation in all spheres of life, including the construction of social values, is the solution one gleans from Veblen's work. This has been more the focus of institutionalism since Veblen, and this is a deeper and richer approach to participation than that of worker participation as we have inherited this concept from Marx. Veblen did believe that pecuniary culture distorted the instinct of workmanship, which had to do with the efficiency and the satisfaction a craftworker derived, by matter of habituation, from manual tasks in pre-capitalist societies. It gave work a dimension of individual fulfilment and gratification (Veblen, 1964, pp. 31–2). On the other hand, Marx tended to view work as *the* main avenue for the realization of life itself. Thus alienated labour meant alienated life. The human essence was fulfilled through labour, so democratic worker participation was the necessary and sufficient condition for self-realization.

Veblen was more pragmatic than Marx. Greater worker control and decision-making power was not so much necessary to free the instinct of workmanship or realize human essence, but necessary to produce more goods with less toil and better quality and serviceability. However, because capitalism was driven by pecuniary values, Veblen suggests that

> the instinct of workmanship is accordingly contaminated with ideals of self-aggrandizement and the canons of invidious emulation, so that even the serviceability of any given action or policy for the common good comes to be rated in terms of the pecuniary gain which such conduct will bring to its author. (Veblen, 1964, p. 217)

Veblen then says that 'innovation, the utilization of newly acquired technological insight, is greatly hindered by such institutional requirements that are enforced by other impulses than the sense of workmanship' (Veblen, 1964, pp. 41–2). Compared to Marx, Veblen was more concerned with the waste caused by the *capitalist system* bent on money making than with the exploitation of workers resulting from *capitalist control*. For example, 'it is the nature of things unavoidable that the management of industry by modern business methods should involve a large misdirection of effort and a very large waste of goods and services' (Veblen, 1927, p. 65).

Even though admitting that labour was alienated in capitalism, Veblen has less confidence in worker participation if workers, through habits of life and mind, had been corrupted by the predatory, invidious and pecuniary values of capitalist society (see Veblen, 1964, p. 307; 1927, p. 310). Just as capitalists practised industrial sabotage, predatory behaviour and the 'conscientious withdrawal of efficiency', so would workers with the aid and leadership of their unions (Veblen, 1954, pp. 4–8, 77). Of the American Federation of Labor, Veblen commented, 'it is, in effect, an organization for the strategic defeat of employers and rival organizations, by recourse to enforced unemployment and obstruction; not for the production of goods and services' (Veblen, 1954, pp. 88–9). He had even less faith in the Industrial Workers of the World, as this 'flotsam of industry is not organized to take over the highly technical duties involved in the administration of the industrial system' (Veblen, 1954, p. 90).

From a Veblenian perspective, market socialism in which there is worker participation (self-management) within a market-based economy will not remedy the problems of waste and inefficiency associated with the pecuniary culture of capitalism. Something like the Yugoslav model under Tito is then insufficient, because workers become collective capitalists and perpetuate the invidiousness of capitalism. Participation has to be broader if it is going to address these problems.

Particularly as a result of John Dewey's pragmatic and instrumental approach to democracy, institutional economics developed a perspective that worker participation is a necessary but not sufficient condition for social progress. With the continuing evolution of institutionalism since Veblen and Dewey, the concept of 'worker participation' has been implicitly qualified in two ways: (a) 'participation' effectively should mean 'democratic participation' on an equal basis in the basic conditions and values that affect one's life; and (b) democratic participation must apply to more than the role of worker, extending to the entire social process through which the cultural values that inform the system are determined.

For institutionalists the problems of capitalism are more numerous and fundamental than simply the alienation of labour remedied by worker participation. As Dewey stated, 'the idea of democracy is a wider and fuller idea than can be exemplified in the state even at its best. To be realized it must affect all modes of human association, the family, the school, industry, religion' (Dewey, 1954, p. 143). Equal participation in social decision making is in effect the very essence of democracy, and the spheres of 'social' decision making are many. So democracy, for institutionalists, must be applied as 'a way of life'. Dewey suggests that 'the keynote of democracy as a way of life may be expressed ... as the necessity for the participation of every mature human being in the formation of the values that regulate the living of men together; which is necessary from the standpoint of both the general social welfare and the full development of human beings as individuals' (Dewey, 1939, p. 400; see also Dewey, 1954, p. 147; Dugger, 1989, p. 163; Tool, 1979, p. 144; 1986, pp. 37–41).

As Veblen and Dewey suggested, the consideration of *worker* participation in institutional economics points directly to the need for a broader approach to *democratic* participation. They, as well as other institutionalists including Clarence Ayres, emphasized the notion that much of the inefficiency and dysfunctionality of a market economy results from its predatory and pecuniary value structure, rather than from the exploitative relationship between workers and capitalists. Ayres stated that 'democracy stands for the procedure by which alone all the other values can be achieved. It is the technique of self-government, and therefore of self-realization' (Ayres, 1961, p. 282). Additionally, 'unless democracy is more efficient than other systems in the long run when all the chips are down, it is not only doomed – it is a sad mistake and altogether bad' (Ayres, 1961, pp. 8–9).

Following Veblen, institutionalism has continued to emphasize the necessity for democratic participation in all public/social spheres including, but not limited to, the economy and *worker* participation. Institutionalists have emphasized that *worker* participation will improve economic performance, but the extent of the performance dividend is circumscribed by the institutional and cultural context in which increased worker participation occurs. The theoretical generalization one could draw from this is that worker participation will have greater performance benefits if it occurs within a fully democratized society rather than in capitalism. What does the empirical evidence suggest in this regard? Was Veblen correct? The literature and empirical evidence that connects increased worker participation with increased productivity and economic performance is vast as well as diverse. In general, it substantiates the institutionalist view that more democracy means more efficiency. Of course, there are many variables to consider, including the political climate, the state of the economy, the quality of the participation schemes and so on. For example, in a well documented study by Juan Espinoza and Andrew Zimbalist, the worker participation policies under Salvador Allende's Popular Unity government in Chile from 1970 to 1973 were very successful. Espinoza and Zimbalist did an econometric analysis of 35 participatory firms and found that for 29 of them productivity increased and, moreover, in 14 of the 29, productivity increased by more than 6 per cent per year (Espinoza and Zimbalist, 1981, p. 162). Higher participation, especially at the shopfloor level, was positively correlated with higher productivity.

With respect to worker participation schemes in the United States, many studies have been done and, although the findings are not conclusive, these studies support the institutionalist view as well. For example, E.S. Greenberg's study of worker-owned and self-managed plywood cooperatives in the Pacific Northwest indicated that worker incomes were 30 per cent higher than in comparable capitalist firms (Greenberg, 1980). Another recent econometric study of 98 US firms by Michael Conte supports the positive link between worker ownership and profit performance. He concludes that 'the greater is worker ownership as a *percent* of total ownership in the company, the greater is profit performance in relation to the industry average' (Conte, 1982, p. 234).

An econometric study of US firms during the 1980s used the new Columbia Business Unit data set and found that employee participation, profit sharing and Employee Stock Ownership Plans (ESOPs) have positive effects on productivity averaging 8.4 per cent (Mitchell, Lewin and Lawler, 1990). The authors conclude that, 'during the difficult transition period of the mid-1980s, firms that featured economic participation for employees seemed to make the adjustment from recession to recovery more easily' (Mitchell, Lewin and Lawler, 1990, p. 87). Additionally, Martin Weitzman and Douglas Kruse studied the effects of profit sharing within capitalist economies and concluded that such schemes increased productivity by an average of 7.4 per cent (Weitzman and Kruse, 1990, pp. 138–9).

David Levine and Laura D'Andrea Tyson have concluded one of the most thorough studies of all of the previously published work in this area. Previously published research spans the entire spectrum from Swedish motor car producers and primary Japanese firms to the worker cooperatives in

Mondragon, Spain and Hewlett-Packard in the USA. Some schemes, such as quality circles, are very cosmetic, while others involve shopfloor democratic decision making and worker ownership. An overwhelming majority of these studies, but by no means all, supported the argument that increased participation is linked to increased economic performance and productivity (Levine and D'Andrea Tyson, 1990, pp. 190–92). The authors also concluded that productivity effects are greater when participation is shopfloor-related, is substantive, involves worker rights and occurs in a supportive political/cultural environment.

Finally, and as institutionalists have suggested, democracy on the job is both reinforced by and reinforces democracy in other spheres. It is the totality of democratic decision making that counts, and through this the greatest economic benefits can be derived. A recent econometric study by Stephen Smith supports this. He surveyed 1400 employees in 55 US firms and found that 'increased decision-making participation within the firm is mutually reinforcing with participation in the political process of the community' (Smith, 1985, p. 123).

The critical issue is not one merely of worker participation, but that of identifying the institutional mechanisms and appropriate policy prescriptions in which the proper balance is found between worker, citizen, consumer, family and neighbourhood participation, to name a few. As Marc Tool has suggested, what is needed is a participatory type of democracy and thus 'an evolving, functional economy which places discretion over policy with those significantly affected by that policy', that is, 'a popularly controlled discretionary economy' (Tool, 1979, p. 141).

If full democratic participation in all social spheres is truly the best method of producing and reproducing life, it will be, as institutionalism suggests, because it is the most efficient means. The next century is likely to see a global, political–economic groping process and institutionalism will, it is hoped, play a role in influencing this towards a democratic participatory society in which worker participation is one of several codetermining areas of democratic decision making.

Doug Brown

See also:
Democracy, Economic; Dewey, John; Labour Markets; Leibenstein, Harvey; Marx, Karl; Planning, Theory of; Power; Trust; Veblen, Thorstein.

Bibliography
Ayres, Clarence (1961), *Toward A Reasonable Society: The Values of Industrial Civilization*, Austin, Texas: University of Texas Press.
Conte, Michael (1982), 'Participation and Performance in U.S. Labor-Managed Firms', in Derek Jones and Jan Svejnar (eds), *Participatory and Self-Managed Firms: Evaluating Economic Performance*, pp. 213–37, Lexington, Mass.: Lexington Books.

Dewey, John (1939), *Intelligence in the Modern World: John Dewey's Philosophy*, ed. Joseph Ratner, New York: Modern Library.

Dewey, John (1954), *The Public and Its Problems*, Chicago: Swallow Press; first published 1927.

Dugger, William (1989), *Corporate Hegemony*, Westport, Conn.: Greenwood Press.

Espinoza, Juan and Andrew Zimbalist (1981), *Economic Democracy: Workers' Participation in Chilean Industry 1970–1973*, New York: Academic Press.

Greenberg, E.S. (1980), 'Participation in Industrial Decision Making and Work Satisfaction: The Case of Producer Cooperatives', *Social Science Quarterly*, **60**, (4), March, pp. 551–69.

Levine, David and Laura D'Andrea Tyson (1990), 'Participation, Productivity, and the Firm's Environment', in Alan Blinder (ed.), *Paying For Productivity*, pp. 183–244, Washington, DC: The Brookings Institution.

Marx, Karl (1964), *Economic and Philosophic Manuscripts of 1844*, ed. Dirk Struik, New York: International Publishers.

Mitchell, Daniel, David Lewin and Edward Lawler (1990), 'Alternative Pay Systems, Firm Performance, and Productivity', in Alan Blinder (ed.), *Paying For Productivity*, pp. 15–94, Washington, DC: The Brookings Institution.

Smith, Stephen (1985), 'Political Behavior as an Economic Externality: Econometric Evidence on the Relationship Between Ownership and Decision Making Participation in U.S. Firms and Participation in Community Affairs', in Derek Jones and Jan Svejnar (eds), *Advances in the Economic Analysis of Participatory and Labor-Managed Firms*, pp. 123–36, Greenwich, Conn.: JAI Press.

Tool, Marc R. (1979), *The Discretionary Economy: A Normative Theory of Political Economy*, Santa Monica, CA: Goodyear.

Tool, Marc R. (1986), *Essays in Social Value Theory: A Neoinstitutionalist Contribution*, Armonk, NY: M.E. Sharpe.

Veblen, Thorstein (1927), *The Theory of Business Enterprise*, New York: Charles Scribner's Sons; first published 1904.

Veblen, Thorstein (1954), *The Engineers and the Price System*, New York: Viking; first published 1921.

Veblen, Thorstein (1964), *The Instinct of Workmanship and the State of the Industrial Arts*, New York: Norton; first published 1914.

Weitzman, Martin and Douglas Kruse (1990), 'Profit Sharing and Productivity', in Alan Blinder (ed.), *Paying For Productivity*, pp. 95–141, Washington, DC: The Brookings Institution.